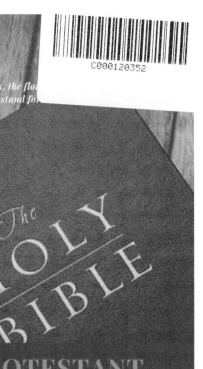

"The grass withers, the flo...
of our God will stand for...

WHY PROTESTANT
BIBLES ARE SMALLER

A DEFENSE OF THE PROTESTANT
OLD TESTAMENT CANON

STEVE CHRISTIE

WHY PROTESTANT BIBLES ARE SMALLER

A Defense of the Protestant Old Testament Canon

Steve Christie

BookMark Press

Cambridge, Ohio

WHY PROTESTANT BIBLES ARE SMALLER: A Defense of the Protestant Old Testament Canon by Steve Christie

ISBN-13: 9781097216994

ISBN-10: 1-0972-1699-3

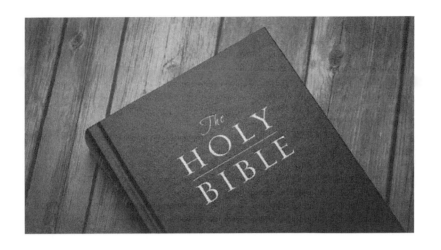

Endorsements

"Can you trust your Bible? That is the heart of the question Steve Christie addresses in his latest work in which he makes a clear defense of the Protestant Scriptures. Have you ever wondered why the book of Genesis is included in the Bible and why 1st Enoch is not? This work clearly outlines how deuterocanonical and apocryphal books were adopted into the Catholic Canon and other versions of the Bible. While not meant to be a work of scholarship, Christie has certainly done his homework and fluidly talks us through the historical dynamics and thinking of church councils and the early Church Fathers. He carefully addresses many writings that are extra-biblical to the Protestant Bible and, without animus, argues for their exclusion.

Christie concludes his book by stating why this material is important: "this is important because this is a gospel issue, which means this is a salvation issue. As the apostle Paul warned, having the wrong gospel means you do not have the truth (Galatians 2:14). If a church does not have the 'true' and complete canon of Scripture, they cannot be the 'the church of the living God, the pillar and support of the truth' Jesus built, because they are not teaching the truth of the gospel."

Christie's book boils down to trust. Can you trust the Bible you are holding in your hand? It is an important question worth a careful study and Christie's book is a great place to start.

Paul Davis, President of the ABWE International (The American Baptists for World Evangelism)

~~~~~~~~~~~~~~~~~~~~~~~~~~~

"As Christians it is important for us to know that the Bible, we have is truly God's Word and that we can trust it. Steve Christie does an excellent job with his detailed research of Scripture, early Church Councils and Church History to show why we as Protestants can be assured that the 66 books of the Bible, specifically the 39 books of the Old Testament, we have are the inspired Word of God and how the New Testament, Jesus, and the disciples gives support of this fact."

Bob Dutko, host of "The Bob Dutko" show, the nationally syndicated "Fearlessly Defending the Faith," WMUZ-103.5 FM, Detroit, Michigan

~~~~~~~~~~~~~~~~~~~~~~~~~~~

"This is a well written, documented book explaining why the Protestant Bible is smaller than the Catholic Bible. It is a MUST-READ book to all. I highly recommend this book to be read by Bible students, seminarians, pastors, church workers and all believers in Christ, as well as non-believers who are curious why the Protestant Bible is smaller, especially, to those who are doubtful that it is complete."

Bishop Nelson Go, D.D, Touching Heart Christian Assembly, San Jose del Monte, Bulacan, The Philippines

~~~~~~~~~~~~~~~~~~~~~~~~~~

"Steve has a boundless curiosity and a desire to discover the answers to questions that others would otherwise go unanswered. The pursuit of these answers is part of a very personal quest. A quest to explore the boundaries of the canon of scripture and the foundations of the Christian faith itself."

The Rev. Daniel W. Bellavia, Senior Pastor, First Baptist Church of Greater Toledo; Foreword to *"Dying: Book I (from my head) What the Bible Reveals About Life After Death Book II (from my heart) How I feel about Dying"*

~~~~~~~~~~~~~~~~~~~~~~~

"Steve Christie has once again written a wonderful book to help Christians. *'Why Protestant Bibles Are Smaller'* is a very thorough and understandable explanation of a foundational difference between Protestants and Catholics - the Bible. The Catholic Bible is not the same as the Protestant Bible and most people do not really know why. Growing up a devout Catholic, Steve has a unique perspective and understanding of the issues and presents facts in a compelling manner. This book will be most helpful to those who consider the Bible as the final authority and will offer considerations for those who do not. I highly recommend it."

Greg Burdine, Senior Pastor of Faith Baptist Church, Adrian, Michigan

~~~~~~~~~~~~~~~~~~~~~~~~

"Based on scripture and fact, *'Why Protestant Bibles are smaller'* is truly the most informative and researched book on the subject of why Protestant Bibles have less books in them than Catholic Bibles. As a former Catholic myself, it was something I researched. I wish I had Steve's book back then! It would have been so much easier to have all the facts in one book like this has. 'Why Protestant Bibles are smaller' leaves no stone unturned and lays it all out there. It's a great reference and should be in every church library."

Chuck Guerber, Grace Hill Ministries *"Serving those in remote regions of Haiti"*

~~~~~~~~~~~~~~~~~~~~~~~~

vi

"I would recommend the book to all students of the Bible and those wishing to dig deeper into its translation history to include it in their library."

Jose R. Ruiz, CEO & Host of "Straight Talk: Earnestly Contending for the Faith," studying Biblical & Theological Studies at Liberty University, Lynchburg, Virginia, & Manager of "Scripture Plain & Simple: A Reformed Bible Society Project"

~~~~~~~~~~~~~~~~~~~~~~~~

"Steve Christie's thorough and exhaustive comparative study of the Protestant and Catholic Bibles is well worth reading. The detail to which topics are handled on this delicate yet vital study is necessary reading for any serious Christian seeking to sort out the differences. The author covers translations, books of the Bible included and excluded and the reasons for it.

Steve defines his terminology which helps in clarifying the text, a vital part of communicating ideas. A masterful job was done in the interweaving of written books, their time frames, their significance, their relationship to other books, and whether determined to be inspired or not, and the reasons why.

The comprehensive study also includes the great writers of the time, including historian Flavius Josephus and others, philosophers Hillel the Elder, Confucius and Isocrates, comparing and contrasting words, thoughts and statements versus the Biblical text, complementing the thoroughness of his research.

'Why Protestant Bibles Are Smaller' is a complex and needed dissertation, unpacking the doctrines which comparatively separates and joins the similarities and differences surrounding the Protestant and Catholic Bibles, and with the studies, the reader is taken on a journey through all of Biblical history.

This book will serve the novice and the scholarly, the faithful church attendee and the apologist, it is written in a fashion to be explanatory in nature and should serve as a helpful reference book for Catholics, Evangelicals and all others seeking clarification on the Biblical text."

Cathy Pia, member of Grace Community Church, Sun Valley, California

~~~~~~~~~~~~~~~~~~~~~~~~

"In 'Why Protestant Bibles are Smaller,' author Steve Christie provides a detailed, interesting, and very useful study defending the Protestant Old Testament. This comprehensive apologetic work provides an exhaustive analysis of the Deuterocanonical, Septuagint, Apocryphal, historical, and scriptural evidences to support its thesis. The reader is taken on a journey through the testimony of the New and Old Testaments and the relevant historical church events, including inconsistencies and errors within the Roman Catholic canon, so that he or she may be provided with the extensive and far-reaching proofs that the Protestant Old Testament canon is indeed the true canon. I recommend this very thorough and accessible book as an important resource for church and home study on the subject."

John Anthony Malone, Lead Pastor of Sovereign Grace Community Church Brooklyn, NY.; MA Biblical Literature Old Testament, Alliance Theological Seminary, JD University of Miami School of Law.

~~~~~~~~~~~~~~~~~~~~~~~~~~~~

"Steve Christie, author of 'Not Really 'Of' Us: Why Do Children of Christian Parents Abandon the Faith?,' has written a new book that examines the origin of the Bible and why some Christian denominations include more books in their versions. Christie examines this question by looking at what the writers of Scripture (including Paul, Peter, and others) say about what they considered to be Scripture. These writers, along with Jesus Himself, defined Scripture as referring to 'the law and the prophets,' which included the entire Old Testament canon (the Hebrew Bible). Writers of the New Testament also referred to writings of the New Testament as Scripture, even before those writings had been completed at the time.

The Roman Catholic Bible contains not only the books of the Hebrew Bible, but additional books, including the deuterocanonical books of the Apocrypha (Sirach, Baruch, Tobit, Judith, Wisdom, 1 Maccabees, and 2 Maccabees). However, as early as the fourth century, Cyril of Jerusalem had listed the canon of the Old Testament as being identical to the Protestant understanding and had excluded the Deuterocanonical books as "apocryphal writings" and not part of the Old Testament. That these apocryphal writings were never considered as Scripture can be inferred by the lack of any specific citations of those texts by any New or Old Testament writer.

Christie goes on to explain in detail about how the early church councils did not include the Apocrypha in their lists of canonical books of the Bible. In addition, there is no biblical support for the claims that the Deuterocanonical books are cited in any New Testament texts. For the New Testament books, the criteria for including them as an inspired writing was that they were written by one of the apostles or their close associates within the first century. Secondhand, non-eyewitness accounts were never included as Scripture. Besides these criteria, many of the later works claiming to be inspired are clearly not, since they contradict the writings within the canonical New Testament books.

Christie concludes with a discussion of what the gospel is and how it is that we are saved. The Bible makes it clear that we are saved through God's grace through faith in Jesus Christ, apart from anything we can do to earn God's favor. Apocryphal writings that claim we must perform certain acts of penance or works in order to be saved are clearly out of line with the teachings of the New Testament books.

Steve Christie's book is a thorough, but not too technical examination and apologetic for the voracity of the canon of Scripture, as contained within Protestant Bibles. It is highly recommended for serious students of the Bible who are interested in how our modern Bibles came to be or for those who are uncertain about the Roman Catholic Church's inclusion of the Apocrypha within Catholic Bibles. Christie's Roman Catholic background gives us great insight into the differences between Roman Catholicism and Protestantism. More importantly, it clarifies Scripture's path to salvation, so that one can live victoriously in Christ and rest upon His completed work to obtain our salvation."

Rich Deem, founder of GodandScience.org

In Appreciation

I would like to begin by humbly thanking my Savior and Lord Jesus Christ for mercifully sacrificing Himself as an atonement for my sins, to the Holy Spirit for convicting my heart and guiding me through this project, and to the Father for sending His only begotten Son to die for me and for all who would ever believe in His name.

Special thanks to BookMark Press, for taking a leap of faith in me by agreeing to publish this book so our Lord would be glorified.

To my dear friend and brother in Christ, the Rev. Daniel W. Bellavia, the Senior Pastor of First Baptist Church of Greater Toledo, who was raised Catholic and also converted to Protestantism. I would like to thank you for writing the Foreword to this book, as well as writing a review. Pastor Dan graciously agreed to work with me on a number of projects together to advance the gospel, including allowing me to speak at his church during the five-hundred-year anniversary of the Protestant Reformation.

To my beloved wife of five years and best friend, Lucia, who immigrated from Romania – a predominately Eastern Orthodox country but was raised Protestant. Thank you for encouraging me to write this book to advance His Kingdom on earth, and for allowing me the time to write it, including those late nights when I was burning the midnight oil, as well as the contributions you made towards the end of this book. Thank you for your love and your loyalty especially with my numerous projects, including recording the various public speeches I made and uploading our home Bible studies for others to see. Te iubesc, Pușa!

To my amazing, loving mother, Darlene, who was also raised Catholic and also converted. You have always been there when I needed you throughout my life, even during those times when no one else was, and for the wisdom, I have received from your advice over my life. Thank you for proofreading my rough draft – twice – checking for spelling and grammatical errors, and for making contributions to my book as well. Much thanks to you also for coming with Lucia and me to all those early morning church events showing your unconditional love and support. I love you, Mom!

My appreciation to the numerous godly men and women who took time out of their busy schedules to read the rough draft of my book and who wrote reviews encouraging others to read it, and to those who recommended suggestions to improve the quality of my book.

Lastly, I am indebted to Jimmy Akin from *Catholic Answers* who convinced me the Protestant Old Testament is the complete Christian Old Testament canon...which is why Protestant Bibles are smaller.

"There were Jews, such as the Sadducees, who acknowledged only the first five books of the Bible – the so-called Law of Moses. The Pharisees honored a much broader canon of Scripture that includes everything that we today would find in the Protestant Old Testament." – Jimmy Akin, Catholic Answers

"Now the Pharisees, who were lovers of money, were listening to all these things and were scoffing at Him.... 'They have Moses and the Prophets; let them hear them.'" – Jesus Christ, Luke 16:14,29

Table of Contents

FOREWORD

Steve Christie is weird.

Many people would consider this to be a slight, a jab, and perhaps a dig. To call someone weird is to say that they are not like other people. This typically has the connotation that they are less than other people so that when I say that Steve Christie is weird, you immediately think that I am saying that something is *wrong* with him.

I am not saying that.

Someone who is weird is different from their peers. Someone who is weird can also be known as unique or uncommon. In the fallen world that we live normal people do not write books about the Bible. In my life, I have met only one nurse who also has written a book about the Biblical Canon. I also must admit that when I count the number of people that I personally know that have written a book concerning the Apocrypha, the number stagnates at one. Steve is unique. He is special. He is... weird.

That's why I enjoy spending time with Steve because I also aspire to be weird.

Steve and I share many common bonds. We both grew up Roman Catholic. We both were highly engaged in the Church as young people, and both of us found ourselves estranged from the Roman Catholic Church later in life. Steve went through years of doubt and struggle that left him seeking the truth as an adult. My path involved a more cordial separation, one which never involved a separation from the Church, just a change in perspective and denomination.

We both began our journey as Altar boys with visions of serving in the Church.. We were both called away from the Church seeking to serve in the world of medicine. Steve completed his training and serves as a nurse. I eventually stepped away from my medical/dental training in order to follow my call into Pastoral ministry (a path which I anticipate that Steve will warm to in his autumn years).

We grew up separated by geographical States but connected by a state of being that transcends location. Once we encountered each other the connections established by common faith and experience made us brothers in Christ and fast friends. We have much in common and much that we enjoy discussing (short lunch meetings often continue into the dinner hour) and have enjoyed working together in many different projects.

What truly cements our relationship is our mutual affection for the scriptures. The Bible. The word of God. We believe in the primacy of the scripture. That scripture is the final word in how human beings can understand the truth while on this side of eternity. Our appreciation for the scriptures probably has a lot to do with our childhood experiences with the Bible. For a Roman Catholic of our generation, the Bible was a large ornate book found in every good household. The sheer size of this tome made reading it unlikely and impractical. Not exactly a book you could read snuggled in bed before sleep.

The Bible was an ornament. Something that was to be seen, but certainly not carried with you. Our Bible was filled with memorabilia and historical records. My family stuffed the Bible with birth certificates and baptismal records. It served its function as a portable lock box for a low-income family and for that reason the Bible was considered important. It was for us the book of life, but it was a book that spoke of our lives, heritage, and history. It is odd how the symbolic can provide us with every clue to the true meanings of life, yet still, leave us uninformed or unfulfilled in our search for the Truth.

I was weird. I wanted to read this old and ornate book. I wanted to know more than the birthdates of relatives and family social security numbers. I wanted to know the stories and the truths contained in its text. I would bring it to my room and look at the paintings and "plates" that intercut the text of the pages. I would start at the beginning, reading the pages of Genesis and seeking to understand the old-world English that filled the pages. For some reason, I was entranced with the book, and I wanted one of my own.

One summer when I was nine years old I co-opted an old manual typewriter that my father kept in the basement of our house and began the long process of creating my own Bible. It wasn't a pretty sight. I would guess that my skills probably would have tested out at ten words per minute with enough errors to render my pages unreadable. I was undaunted. Day after day I returned to the typewriter and meticulously copied the words from the book of Genesis. I never completed my own Bible, but for one glorious summer, I had my own copy of the book of Genesis.

Like I said... weird.

The Bible that I read was the New American translation; the Roman Catholic Bible that dominated the 1970s in American homes. It included 73 books, a number that might not square with the number of books in the Bible that your Sunday School teachers taught you. These "extra" (or deuterocanonical) books that can be found in various translations and editions are known as the Apocrypha. As a kid I never really paid much attention to them. They were wedged in the middle, between the Old and New Testaments. I would stumble over them occasionally on the way to reading the Gospels, but never really took the time to read them or to ask why they were there. Steve noticed these books, and though he asked the question of others, he never received an answer that satisfied him, which brings us back to the 21st Century.

I met Steve through an odd series of events that *normal* people might think of as happenstance or random occurrence. Weird people like us know better. That is part of what makes us weird. We believe that life is not a random set of encounters and experiences. We believe that life has meaning; in this world and eternally in the world to come. We believe that the Creator of the universe cares about how we live this life and how we anticipate life beyond and for this reason we pay attention to the details. Or at least we are supposed to pay attention.

One day when a member of my congregation told me of a man that she encountered on the campus of the University of Toledo, I promptly ignored her. She informed me that he had written a book about the reasons that the children of the Church grow up and out of the faith. My friend, Jeni Gerber, thought it might be a good idea to have Steve come and share his book with the people of First Baptist Church of Greater Toledo. Once again, I ignored her.

Those who know Jeni, know that she is not one that gives up on an inspired idea. I have been connected to the right person at the right time on many occasions due to her persistent obedience to the call of the Holy Spirit in her life. I finally relented when I realized that it would take less effort to meet Steve than it would be to continue ignoring Jeni. The rest as they say... is God's story.

I have discovered that Steve Christie is a man who has followed his call to serve Jesus Christ by praying, studying, writing, and teaching. He has a boundless curiosity and a desire to discover the answers to questions that others would simply leave unanswered. Steve does not consider these questions to be weird or strange. The pursuit of this knowledge is part of Steve's pursuit of a very personal quest. It is a part of his exploration of his intellectual origins.

Too frequently the people of God walk away from our questions without truly uncovering the truths that they might reveal to us. Too frequently we ignore the enduring questions of our youth. Steve is not one to easily leave the ghosts of his past. He has learned that we can either learn to ignore them or face them head on and explore what these specters might be trying to tell us. When Steve explores why children leave the Church, he is not just "asking for a friend." Steve is asking a question that has personal meaning. He is not only exploring an important question for the 21st Century Church; he is also exploring the choices of his own past and seeking to understand the most basic truth of his life and faith.

These same ghosts are pursuing him in his exploration of the Apocrypha. Unlike many who have traveled similar territory, Steve is unwilling to simply ignore the differences in the sacred texts that fill our Bibles. These are not academic questions for Steve. They are part of his personal exploration of the faith; of his faith.

The personal quality of his exploration has created a sense of urgency and importance that is so often missing in the academic texts on this topic. It is this urgency that makes his work so compelling and readable.

I hope you enjoy this book. It is a unique take, on a unique topic, written by a unique man. Here's to being weird.

Brother in Christ,

The Rev. Daniel W. Bellavia

Senior Pastor, First Baptist Church of Greater Toledo

CHRONOLOGY: TIMETABLE FOR THE HEBREW BIBLE, THE DEUTEROCANON, THE APOCRYPHA, AND OTHER EARLY WRITINGS, COUNCILS, AND LISTS

BEFORE 1400 B.C. – "The Law" is written.

AFTER 1400 B.C. – "The Prophets" and "The Writings" begin to be written.

~450 B.C. – "The Great Assembly" ("The Great Synagogue") convenes under Ezra the scribe to begin compiling the Hebrew Bible.

~425 TO 400 B.C. – The Hebrew Bible is completed.

~250 B.C. – "The Law" is (allegedly) translated into Greek (i.e.: the Septuagint).

~200 TO THE FIRST CENTURY B.C. – The Deuterocanon and other Old Testament Apocryphal writings are composed.

FIRST CENTURY B.C. TO EARLY FIRST CENTURY A.D. – The Hebrew Bible is translated into Aramaic (i.e.: the Targums).

~4 TO 3 B.C. – The end of the Old Testament era with the conception of John the Baptist; Jesus is born.

~A.D. 30-33 – Jesus' earthly ministry, crucifixion, burial, resurrection, and ascension; birth of the New Testament church.

~A.D. 35 – Philo of Alexandria affirms the *Letter of Aristeas* limited the Septuagint to "The Law."

~A.D. 44-96 A.D. – The New Testament is written and completed.

BEFORE A.D. 100 – The last apostle, John, dies ending the apostolic age.

LATE FIRST CENTURY TO FOURTH CENTURY A.D. – Writings of some of the early church fathers and other uninspired writings.

END OF SECOND CENTURY TO EARLY THIRD CENTURY A.D. – The remainder of the writings included in the Septuagint.

A.D. 382 – Jerome is commissioned by Pope Damasus I to begin compiling the Latin Vulgate.

A.D. 382 – COUNCIL OF ROME: the Catholic Old Testament = the Hebrew Bible + the Deuterocanon (minus Baruch and the epistle of Jeremiah). New Testament = same twenty-seven books as today.

A.D. 393 – COUNCIL OF HIPPO: the Catholic Old Testament = the Hebrew Bible + the Deuterocanon (minus Baruch and the epistle of Jeremiah). New Testament = same twenty-seven books as today.

A.D. 397 – COUNCIL OF CARTHAGE: the Catholic Old Testament = the Hebrew Bible + the Deuterocanon (minus Baruch and the epistle of Jeremiah). Revelation removed from the New Testament.

A.D. 405 – Jerome completes the Latin Vulgate = the Hebrew Bible + the Deuterocanon (minus Baruch and the epistle of Jeremiah). New Testament = same twenty-seven books as today.

A.D. 419 – COUNCIL OF CARTHAGE: the Catholic Old Testament = the Hebrew Bible + the Deuterocanon (minus Baruch and the epistle of Jeremiah). New Testament = same twenty-seven books as today (Revelation added back in the New Testament).

A.D. 451 – ECUMENICAL COUNCIL OF CHALCEDON: schism of the Oriental Orthodox Church from the Eastern Orthodox Church.[1] The Oriental Orthodox Old Testament = the Hebrew Bible + the Deuterocanon + some Apocryphal writings.

~A.D. 700 – CODEX AMIATINUS: the Catholic Old Testament = the Hebrew Bible + the Deuterocanon (minus Baruch. The epistle of Jeremiah was an "appendage" to the book of Jeremiah in this codex). New Testament = same twenty-seven books as today.

A.D. NINTH CENTURY – Baruch and the epistle of Jeremiah added to the Latin Vulgate.

AFTER 1000 – Revelation universally accepted in the church in both the East and the West.

1054 – THE GREAT SCHISM: schism of the Eastern Orthodox Church from the Catholic Church. The Eastern Orthodox Old Testament = the Hebrew Bible + the Deuterocanon + some Apocryphal writings.

1441 – ECUMENICAL COUNCIL OF FLORENCE: the Catholic Old Testament = the Hebrew Bible + the Deuterocanon (Sirach questioned until

---

[1] EWTN.com. *EWTN Catholic Q&A: Syriac orthodox church of Antioch.* Question from Monique Baxter on 7/17/2002. Answer by Anthony Dragani on 8/1/2002. Accessed from the Internet http://www.ewtn.com/v/experts/showmessage.asp?number=311876&Pg=&Pgnu=&recnu=

the Ecumenical Council of Trent). New Testament = same twenty-seven books as today.

1534 – LUTHER'S TRANSLATION: Catholic priest and Protestant Reformer, Martin Luther, translated the Bible into German, grouping the Deuterocanon in a separate uninspired "Apocrypha" section.[2] The Inspired sections include the Hebrew Bible and the same twenty-seven New Testament books as today.

1546 – ECUMENICAL COUNCIL OF TRENT: the Catholic Bible "defined" for the first time. The Catholic Old Testament = the Hebrew Bible + the Deuterocanon. New Testament = same twenty-seven books as today.

1610 – DOUAY-RHEIMS: English Catholic Bible includes same books defined at the Council of Trent.

1611 – KING JAMES VERSION: an early English Protestant translation = the Hebrew Bible + the Deuterocanon in a separate, uninspired Addendum in-between the Hebrew Bible and the same twenty-seven-book New Testament as today.

1647 – THE WESTMINSTER CONFESSION: affirms the Deuterocanon "not being of divine inspiration"[3] confirming the Inspired Old Testament is limited to the Hebrew Bible.

1827 – THE BRITISH AND FOREIGN BIBLE SOCIETY: permanently removed the Deuterocanon from the uninspired "Apocrypha" section of the Protestant Bible.[4]

TODAY: Protestant Old Testaments = the Hebrew Bible; Catholic Old Testaments = the Hebrew Bible + the Deuterocanon; Eastern and Oriental Orthodox Old Testaments = the Hebrew Bible + the Deuterocanon + some Apocryphal writings.

---

[2] EWTN.com. Father William Saunders. *PROTESTANT AND CATHOLIC BIBLES.* Accessed from the Internet https://www.ewtn.com/library/ANSWERS/PCBIB.HTM

[3] Ibid.

[4] Ibid.

INTRODUCTION

"For assuredly, I say to you, till heaven and earth pass away, one jot or one tittle will by no means pass from the law till all is fulfilled."
(Matthew 5:18 NKJV)

1984 was a very significant and historic year. The novel *Nineteen Eighty-Four* written by George Orwell, published in 1949, was set in this year. Bishop Desmond Tutu won the Nobel Peace Prize. Movies such as *The Terminator, Ghostbusters,* and *Gremlins* made their cinematic debuts. Martin Luther King, Sr. (the father of the famous civil rights activist, Martin Luther King, Jr.) passed away. The first World Youth Day was held in Rome, Italy. The United States and the Vatican restored full diplomatic relations. The longest game in Major League Baseball history took place between the Chicago White Sox and the Milwaukee Brewers. Bruce Springsteen's "Born in the U.S.A." came out, and Ronald Reagan won a landslide victory against Walter Mondale in November securing his second term to be reelected as the President of the United States of America.

It was also the year I entered my final year of parochial elementary school. I had been elected Treasurer of the Knights of the Altar of my local parish by my peers. As a dedicated altar boy, this was an extreme privilege. This meant I was considered fourth in rank among all the altar boys in my entire parish, just below the President, Vice-President, and Secretary. I would have the right to serve not only at weddings and funerals but also for the bishop of our local diocese. In fact, I did serve before the Bishop of the Diocese of Toledo, Ohio at Rosary Cathedral, where I would graduate from nursing school twenty years later. As a young, devout, Catholic altar boy it was quite the honor. I would go on to lead in our annual Corpus Christi parade, and I also performed as the apostle John in our annual Passion Play.

Just as the apostle Paul described himself as "a Hebrew of Hebrews" (Philippians 3:5), who "lived as a Pharisee according to the strictest sect of our religion" (Acts 26:5), I considered myself to be "a Catholic of Catholics." Even after I graduated from parochial school, I would go on to graduate from both a Catholic high school and a Catholic college.

Among some of my duties of being an altar boy were lighting the altar candles, and you were given the responsibility of being either a cross-bearer or a candle-bearer during the processional at the start of the Mass. If you were really lucky, you might even be privileged to hold the thurible – the metal vessel hung by chains used to burn incense. Behind the altar boys was the priest, who carried one of the liturgical books he read from during the service. I assumed this was the Bible he read out of at the pulpit.

I assumed wrong.

There were actually two books used during the service. The first was called a Missal[5] (similar to a Sacramentary, but not the same[6]), which contained texts for the celebration of the Mass, which the priest read at the altar. The second was called the Lectionary[7], which contained a "collection" of Scripture readings he read at the pulpit during the Homily. These readings were organized into three-year cycles. However, it was not the "actual" Bible *itself* because it did not contain the "whole" Bible. There were parts of the Bible that were "missing," which were never read during the Mass.

As I mentioned in my previous book, *"Not Really 'Of' Us: Why Do Children of Christian Parents Abandon the Faith?"* I remember having "my great-grandmother's Bible in our home stored away neatly in a shiny, wooden-like box"[8] – the New Catholic Version. Somewhere along the line, we also acquired a "Gideon Bible" in our home too. Despite the wording being slightly different, I just assumed they contained the exact same writings, similar to the NASB versus the ESV.

I assumed wrong...again.

As I began to compare the two translations, I discovered there were some books from the Old Testament in our New Catholic Version which were "missing" from the Gideon Bible. I found this odd. Was there more than one Bible? Did the Catholic Bible have "additional" books? Did the Gideon Bible have books which were "missing" or were "removed"?

Whatever the answer was, I knew at the bare minimum the "One True Church" of Christ, which He built (Matthew 16:18), needed to have the <u>complete</u> Scriptural texts of the Bible – no less, but also no more. I also realized "although opinion is valuable, Truth is necessary,"[9] because Jesus is "the author and perfecter of [our] faith" (Hebrew 12:2). For Christians, our "faith comes from hearing, and hearing by the word of Christ" (Romans

---

[5] NewAdvent.org. *Missal.* Accessed from the Internet http://www.newadvent.org/cathen/10354c.htm

[6] NewAdvent.org. *Liturgical Books, History of the Roman liturgical books.* Accessed from the Internet http://www.newadvent.org/cathen/09296a.htm

[7] NewAdvent.org. *Lectionary.* Accessed from the Internet http://www.newadvent.org/cathen/09110b.htm

[8] Christie, Steve. *Not Really 'Of' Us: Why Do Children of Christian Parents Abandon the Faith?* Introduction, p. xviii. Bloomington, IN: WestBow Press, A Division of Thomas Nelson & Zondervan, 2014.

[9] Ibid, p.82.

10:17) – i.e., Scripture. This includes not merely the *New* Testament, but also the *Old* Testament.

THE BIBLE, A BOOKSTORE, AND A MONK

Not long after I converted to Protestantism, I was strolling through the Christian section of my local Barnes and Noble bookstore. I met a man who described himself as a "pre-Vatican II Catholic monk." He explained he did not embrace the changes in the Catholic Church made after Vatican II, nor did he accept popes who were elected after this time, describing them as "antipopes."[10]

When we discussed the Old Testament, he mentioned Protestants had "removed" some books which were in the Bible for over a thousand years. Since all Scripture is Inspired by God (2 Timothy 3:16), I mentioned they were removed because each of them contained errors or contradicted other books in the Bible. Therefore, they were not Inspired, and they did not belong in the Bible to begin with.

This monk asked me for an example. When I mentioned that while Old Testament books like Daniel correctly described Nebuchadnezzar as the king of Babylon (Daniel 1:1), the book of Judith incorrectly defined him as the king of the Assyrians (Judith 1:1 NAB). He attempted to explain away this blatant contradiction by assuming this "might" have been a different Nebuchadnezzar, despite both Scripture and history not supporting this assumption (see Appendix B).

I mentioned Protestant Bibles were based on a *direct* translation from the original Biblical languages of Hebrew, Aramaic, and Greek. He recommended I seek out a Douay-Rheims Bible. Not only was the Old Testament of this seventeenth century version of the Latin Vulgate a translation from Hebrew to Greek to Latin to English, it had other problems (see Chapter Five).

Most people, including many Christians, are unaware that Catholic and Protestant Bibles are different. The goal of this book is to explain the theological and historical reasons for this, and why we can trust the Protestant Bible contains the complete Christian canon.

---

[10] NewAdvent.org defines an "antipope" as "A false claimant of the Holy See in opposition to a pontiff canonically elected" and that "illegal pretenders to the Papal Chair have arisen, and frequently exercised pontifical functions in defiance of the true occupant." Accessed from the Internet http://www.newadvent.org/cathen/01582a.htm which gives a list of thirty antipopes throughout Catholic Church history.

WHAT IS A "CANON"?

In regard to the Bible, the word "canon" refers to a list of books accepted as Inspired Scripture. NewAdvent.org (an online Catholic encyclopedia) defines it as:

> "The Greek *kanon* means primarily a reed or measuring-rod: by a natural figure it was employed by ancient writers both profane and religious to denote a rule or standard. We find the substantive *first applied to the Sacred Scriptures in the fourth century, by St. Athanasius*; for its derivatives, *the Council of Laodicea of the same period speaks of the kanonika biblia and Athanasius of the biblia kanonizomena.* The latter phrase proves that the passive sense of canon — that of *a regulated and defined collection* — *was already in use*, and this has remained the prevailing connotation of the word in ecclesiastical literature."[11] (emphasis added)

This term was "already in use" as early as the fourth century specifically by early church fathers like Athanasius and early councils like Laodicea to define the Christian Old Testament parameters. Their specific "canons" of Scripture are significant, which will be discussed in more detail in Chapters Four and Five, since they were "a regulated and defined collection" closer to the Protestant Old Testament. God revealed specific criteria to define the Old Testament canon to the ancient Jews, which He later revealed to the early church in defining the New Testament canon. These godly criteria will be discussed in detail in Chapter Ten.

"THE WHITE QUESTION"

During the 2018 G3 Conference, Protestant author and apologist Dr. James White discussed the canon of Scripture with Dr. Michael Kruger. Dr. White recalled a 1993 radio debate he had with Catholic apologist Gerry Matatics on the establishment of the Old Testament canon. During the debate Dr. White asked Mr. Matatics a question, which affectionally came to be known as "The White Question":

> "How did the believing Jewish person know that Isaiah and 2 Chronicles were Scripture fifty years before Christ?...You don't have a Magisterium to answer that question at that point in time. Jesus plainly held men accountable to what was in Scripture.... He [Matatics] can't go 'Jewish Magisterium' because he knows

---

[11] NewAdvent.org. *Canon of the Old Testament: Overview.* Accessed from the Internet http://www.newadvent.org/cathen/03267a.htm. Italics in the word "*kanon*" are in the original text, while the other italicized words were done by me for emphasis.

the Jewish Magisterium never accepted what Trent accepted as canonical Scripture. So, then you'd have a contradiction between two allegedly infallible sources."[12]

Dr. White also discussed his concerns about the lack of discernment the average Christian sitting in the pew has in knowing which books belong in the Bible versus those which do not:

"...long before we're having discussions about end times prophecies or anything else... the understanding of [the canon of Scripture] ... should be more fundamental to us than the discussion of prophetic things and stuff like that. Why? Because everything else depends on us having an agreed-upon text from which we are deriving our theology, and if we don't have that agreed-upon text, and if you say 'well we do have an agreed-upon text,' yes, but do you know why we only have the number of books in our Bibles that we have?"[13]

I realized while this is problematic for the Catholic to answer, it is significantly less challenging for the Protestant. I also learned there *is* only one Bible. Both Catholics and Protestants agree on this point. Where they *dis*agree is whether books were "added to" or "removed from" the Old Testament by Catholics or Protestants. It would not be until over two decades after I was elected Treasurer when I discovered – from a *Catholic* source – why the Protestant Bible contains the complete Christian Old Testament. This discovery had been affirmed by the writers of the New Testament, particularly from the apostle Paul, as well as from the very words of our Lord.

~~~~~~~~~~~~~~~~~~~~~~~~

What about the Septuagint (the Greek translation of the Old Testament), as well as the Latin Vulgate, the Douay-Rheims, the Dead Sea Scrolls, and Eastern Orthodox Bibles, which all include the same "missing" books not found in Protestant Old Testaments? Do they all contain the exact same writings?

What about the claims from the Catholic Church that it is "the church of the living God, the pillar and support of the truth" (1 Timothy 3:15), which "gave us our Bible"?

---

[12] White, James. *James White & Michael Kruger on the Biblical Canon.* "Alpha & Omega Ministries." Published on YouTube, Feb 27, 2018. Accessed from the Internet https://www.youtube.com/watch?v=LVVRfu1eLSU (Begins around the 42:17 mark.) Brackets included by me for clarity.

[13] Ibid. (Begins around the 16:45 mark.) Brackets inserted by me for clarity.

What about the fact that even the King James Version of the Bible originally had these "missing books," as well as being in the German translation of the Bible of Martin Luther itself and those of the other Reformers? Or did Luther "remove" them?

What about all the references to these "missing" books alluded to by Jesus and the New Testament writers?

What about the Eastern Orthodox Old Testament which not only includes these "missing books" too, but also books not found in the Catholic Old Testament?

What about the (supposed) "prophecies" about Jesus in some of these "missing" books that are found in the Catholic Old Testament?

I will be covering all this, and much more, in the following chapters regarding why Protestant Bibles are smaller.

CHAPTER ONE: What is "Scripture"?

"But now apart from the Law the righteousness of God has been manifested, being witnessed by the Law and the Prophets" (Romans 3:21)

1517 was another very significant and historic year, particularly for Protestants. On October 31, 1517, a German Augustinian monk, named Martin Luther, nailed his *"95 Theses"* (or *Disputation on the Power of Indulgences*) to the door of All Saints' Church (also known as Castle Church) in Wittenberg, Germany. This marked the birth of the Protestant Reformation. On the quincentennial, Tuesday, October 31, 2017, Protestants literally all over the world commemorated the anniversary of the Reformation.

On Sunday, October 29 ("Reformation Sunday") of this same year, I had the privilege to speak on the Reformation anniversary at First Baptist Church of Greater Toledo in Holland, Ohio. Pastor Daniel Bellavia and I discussed the positive effects and reforms that were made in the church, as well as in society, which resulted from the Reformation. One of those positive effects was the recovery of the true gospel of salvation by grace alone, through faith alone, by Christ alone, based on Scripture alone, for the glory of God alone. Another was the rediscovery of the canon of the Christian Old Testament Scriptures.

But what is classified as "Scripture"?

The apostle Paul wrote "All Scripture is inspired by God" (2 Timothy 3:16). The Greek word for "Inspired" *("theopneustos")* comes from two separate Greek words: *"theos"* ("God") and *"pneō"* ("to breathe"). In other words, Scripture is "God-breathed." When Paul wrote his second epistle to his young protégé Timothy, he told him "that from childhood you have known the *sacred writings* which are able to give you the wisdom that leads to salvation through faith which is in Christ Jesus" (v.15, emphasis added).

For Timothy this would refer, specifically, to the *Old* Testament Scriptures, since the New Testament Scriptures were still being written in the first century. However, both the apostles Paul and Peter would also classify the *New* Testament writings as "Scripture" as well. For example, Paul quoted Luke's gospel by calling it "Scripture," and Peter referred to "all" of Paul's "letters" by comparing them to *"the rest of the Scriptures"*:

"For the *Scripture* says... '*The laborer is worthy of his wages*'" (1 Timothy 5:18, cf. Luke 10:7, emphasis added)

"as also in *all his* [Paul's] *letters*, speaking in them of these things, in which are some things hard to understand, which the untaught and unstable distort, as they do also *the rest of the Scriptures*, to their own destruction" (2 Peter 3:16, emphasis added)

The epistle of Jude quoted Peter's second epistle extensively (ex: Jude v.18, cf. 2 Peter 3:3), which Jude stated he wrote about our "common salvation...appealing that you contend earnestly for the faith which was once for all handed down to the saints," which "were spoken beforehand by the apostles of our Lord Jesus Christ" (Jude v.3,17). Jude affirmed the Inspiration of both of Peter's epistles, because Peter wrote that he penned *two* epistles (2 Peter 3:1, cf. 1 Peter 1:1).

The evangelist Luke also wrote he had "compiled an account of the things" which "were handed down to us by those who from the beginning were eyewitnesses" (Luke 1:1-2). Much of Luke's gospel is "synoptic" to Matthew's and Mark's gospels, and Matthew was an "eyewitness" of the events recorded in his gospel. When Paul affirmed Luke's gospel by calling it "Scripture," this also included the book of Acts, since Luke affirmed he wrote *two* Inspired writings to a man named "Theophilus" (Acts 1:1, cf. Luke 1:3).

Peter and Paul affirmed the reliability of Mark and his gospel. Paul wrote to Timothy that Mark was "useful to me for service" (2 Timothy 4:11). Peter referred to him as "my son, Mark" (1 Peter 5:13). Eusebius affirmed from the authority of Papias (an alleged disciple of the apostle John) that Mark's gospel was essentially the words of Peter:

"Mark became Peter's interpreter and wrote down accurately, but not in order, all that he remembered of the things done by the Lord. ...Mark did not err in writing down some things just as he recalled them. For he had one overriding purpose: to omit nothing he had heard and to make no false statements in his account."[14]

By the mid-first century A.D., most of the New Testament Scriptures, which had been written, were considered just as "God-breathed" as the Old Testament Scriptures by those in the early church, like the apostles Paul and Peter, as well as others, like Jude. Unlike the Old Testament canon,

---

[14] *Eusebius: The Church History.* Translation and commentary by Paul L. Maier. Published by Kregel Publications, a division of Kregel, Inc.: Grand Rapids, MI, 1999, 2007. Book 3.39, p.114.

Catholics and Protestants *agree* with each other on the exact same twenty-seven-book New Testament canon. This is not in dispute. Since they agree with each other, then what does the *New* Testament canon reveal about the *Old* Testament canon? (I will be covering the godly criteria revealed by God to the later church in discerning the Inspiration of the New Testament books in Chapter Ten.)

HOW DID THE APOSTLE PAUL DEFINE THE OLD TESTAMENT CANON?

Shortly after I became a Protestant, I came across a YouTube video by *Catholic Answers* titled, "How did the Old Testament canon develop?" Jimmy Akin, who is a Catholic author, church historian, and their senior apologist, stated in the video:

> "There were Jews, such as the Sadducees, who acknowledged only the first five books of the Bible – the so-called Law of Moses. The *Pharisees* honored *a much broader canon of Scripture* that *includes everything* that we today would find *in the Protestant Old Testament.*"[15] (emphasis added)

As mentioned in the Introduction, the apostle Paul stated he "lived as a *Pharisee* according to *the strictest sect of our religion*" (Acts 26:5, emphasis added). He was originally the notorious Pharisee, Saul of Tarsus, who persecuted and murdered Christians prior to his conversion to Christianity (Acts 9:1). He also stated he was "a *Hebrew of Hebrews;* as to *the Law,* a *Pharisee*" (Philippians 3:5, emphasis added).

By "the Law," Paul was not limiting this to the five books of Moses, i.e.: the Pentateuch (see Chapter Two). Here, Paul was including "the Law" to refer to the *entire* Old Testament canon (ex: 1 Corinthians 14:21, cf. Isaiah 28:11-12). During Jesus' ministry, He would also expand "the Law" to include "the Prophets" (Matthew 12:4-5, cf. 1 Samuel 21:4-6) and "the Writings" (John 10:34, cf. Psalm 82:6).

What made Paul a "Hebrew of Hebrews" was not merely because he was Jewish, or because he was a member of the Sanhedrin. It was because Paul was a *Pharisee*, which he proclaimed was the "*strictest* sect of our religion" (Acts 26:5). You could not be any higher up the ranks of Judaism than being a Pharisee, like Paul. Paul had the authority to discern what "the Law" (the Old Testament) was because he was *specifically* a Pharisee, rather than belonging to another Jewish sect which did not have this

---

[15] Akin, Jimmy. *How did the Old Testament canon develop?* "Catholic Answers." Published on YouTube, Nov 18, 2010. Accessed from the Internet https://www.youtube.com/watch?v=dF5NYPENhp4 (Begins around the 0:50 mark.)

Pharisaic authority. On other occasions, Paul would use the more broader term "the Law and the Prophets" to refer the Old Testament canon (see below).

As Jimmy Akin admitted, "The Pharisees honored a much broader canon of Scripture that includes everything that we today would find in the Protestant Old Testament."[16] When the apostle Paul wrote his Inspired letter to the church of Rome around A.D. 56, he used the term "the Law and the Prophets" to refer to the Old Testament Scriptures:

> "But now apart from the Law the righteousness of God has been manifested, being witnessed by *the Law and the Prophets*" (Romans 3:21, emphasis added).

As a Pharisee, the apostle Paul would have understood "the Law and the Prophets" to refer to *only* those writings found in Protestant Old Testaments today, like Jimmy Akin mentioned earlier. When Paul stood before the Jewish Sanhedrin (i.e.: "the Council"), which was made up of Pharisees and Sadducees, he quoted Exodus 22:28: "for it is written, 'YOU SHALL NOT SPEAK EVIL OF A RULER OF YOUR PEOPLE'" (Acts 23:5). This common New Testament expression – "it is written" – is used to refer to Old Testament Biblical citations. In his book *"The Gospel According to Paul,"* Pastor John MacArthur comments on the significance of this particular phrase:

> "The phrase 'it is written'...is a formal appeal to the highest of all authorities, an explicit recognition that when Scripture speaks, God has spoken. The idea it conveys is, 'This stands written as an eternal truth.' In this expression, the tense serves to underscore the finality and continuing authority of Scripture as the unchanging and eternal Word of God."[17]

This phrase has always been understood in both the church, as well as in ancient Judaism in the Old Testament era, to be a reference to an eternal written truth and an unchanging continual authority from the Word of God. As far back as the days of Joshua, he used it to describe the godly authority of Moses' writings (Joshua 8:31, cf. Exodus 20:23-25).[18]

---

[16] Ibid.

[17] MacArthur, John. *The Gospel According to Paul: embracing the good news at the heart of Paul's teachings*, p. 34. Nashville, Tennessee: Nelson Books, 2017.

[18] See also, 2 Kings 23:21, *cf. Deuteronomy 16:2-8*; 2 Chronicles 23:18, *cf. Numbers 28:2*; 2 Chronicles 25:4, *cf. Deuteronomy 24:16*; 2 Chronicles 31:3, *cf. Numbers 28:1-29,40*; 2 Chronicles 35:12, *cf. Leviticus 3:3*; Ezra 3:2, *cf. Leviticus 1:3-17*; Ezra 3:4, *cf. Numbers 29:12-38*; Ezra 6:18, *cf. Numbers 3:6 and 8:9*; Nehemiah 8:15, *cf. Leviticus 23:40-42*; Nehemiah 10:34, *cf. Leviticus 6:12*; Nehemiah 10:35-38, *cf. Exodus 13:12; 23:19; 34:26*;

Jesus used this same phrase "it is written" when He quoted the Old Testament prophet Isaiah (Luke 4:17-19, cf. Isaiah 61:1-2). He declared He was the fulfillment of this prophecy when He stated, "Today this Scripture has been fulfilled in your hearing" (v.21).

One of these "eternal truths" Paul cited from the "eternal Word of God" is from the Old Testament book of Ezekiel. Although the Sadducees did not accept the prophetic book of Ezekiel in their canon, the Pharisees did. Luke went on to write:

> "The high priest Ananias commanded those standing beside him to strike him [Paul] on the mouth. Then Paul said to him, *'God is going to strike you, you whitewashed wall!* Do you sit to try me according to the Law, and in violation of the Law order me to be struck?'... But perceiving that one group were Sadducees and the other Pharisees, Paul began crying out in the Council, 'Brethren, *I am a Pharisee*, a son of Pharisees; I am on trial for the hope and resurrection of the dead!' As he said this, there occurred a dissension between the Pharisees and Sadducees, and the assembly was divided. For the Sadducees say that there is no resurrection, nor an angel, nor a spirit, but the Pharisees acknowledge them all. And there occurred a great uproar; and some of the scribes of *the Pharisaic party* stood up and began to argue heatedly, saying, 'We find nothing wrong with this man; suppose a spirit or an angel has spoken to him?'" (Acts 23:2-3,6-9, emphasis added)

After Paul was struck on the mouth by the order of the high priest Ananias (v.3), he lashed back by calling him a "whitewashed wall" who God was "going to strike" (v.4). Here, Paul was referencing the prophetic book of Ezekiel. God had rebuked the false prophets of Israel for erecting a false "wall" of peace "whitewashing" it to make it appear genuine (Ezekiel 13:10-16). When Paul said this, he proclaimed it before the Jewish sects of the Pharisees who accepted Ezekiel as a prophetic book in their canon, and the Sadducees who rejected it (Acts 23:7-9).

The Pharisees would have recognized and took this as a prophetic rebuke since they had the book of Ezekiel in their canon, while the Sadducees would not have since they rejected it. This explains why the Pharisees found no fault in Paul (v.9). Paul affirmed the Pharisaic beliefs in angels, spirits, and the resurrection of the dead (v.8) – which Sadducees rejected – as well as their Old Testament canon by citing the book of Ezekiel.

Leviticus 19:24; Numbers 18:13,15,26 and Deuteronomy 26:2; Psalm 40:7, cf. Deuteronomy 17:14-20; Isaiah 65:6-7, cf. Exodus 20:5; Daniel 9:10-13, cf. Leviticus 26:21-42 and 28:15-69.

Earlier, Jesus rebuked the Pharisees by calling them "whitewashed tombs" (Matthew 23:27). However, just prior to this, He described them as having "seated themselves in the chair of Moses; therefore all that they tell you, do and observe, but do not do according to their deeds; for they say things and do not do them" (v.2-3). By saying this, Jesus was reinforcing what the Pharisees had "told" others, which was based on their canon, while rejecting their evil "deeds" which conflicted with it.

Despite the Pharisees rejecting the Christian sect Paul converted to, their disdain for the faction of the Sadducees resulted in the Pharisees actually *defending* Paul! Not only was Paul affirming their specific beliefs, but *also* their acceptance of the writings of "the Prophets" – such as Ezekiel – which Paul shared with them and the Sadducees rejected.

In essence, Paul was affirming their canon of Scripture, by citing Ezekiel and by declaring that, he too, was *still* a Pharisee ("*I am* a Pharisee" – v.6, emphasis added). This *present tense* admission by Paul ("I am") indicates while he had converted to Christianity, he still embraced their *Scriptural* beliefs, based on *their canon*. Paul rejected their legalistic, extra-scriptural man-made traditions, which conflicted with their canon, such as their rejection of Jesus as their Messiah, which Jesus "fulfilled" through "the Law [and] the Prophets" (Matthew 5:17) – i.e.: *their* Old Testament canon.

Paul repeated this Pharisaic belief of the resurrection of the dead, based on their Old Testament canon, when he spoke before Felix, the governor of Judea:

> "But this I admit to you, that according to the Way which they call a sect *I do serve the God of our fathers, believing everything that is in accordance with the Law and that is written in the Prophets*; having a hope in God, which these men cherish themselves, that there shall certainly be *a resurrection of both the righteous and the wicked*.... '*For the resurrection of the dead* I am on trial before you today'" (Acts 24:14-15,21, emphasis added).

Paul declared his "hope in God" was based on "believing *everything*" which was written in "the Law and that is written in the Prophets" (v.14). "Everything" from the perspective of a Pharisee, like Paul, would include "everything" written in the boundaries of the canon of the Pharisees.

Earlier, when Paul traveled to Pisidian Antioch with Barnabas, they entered a synagogue on the Sabbath to hear "the reading of the Law and the Prophets" (Acts 13:14-15). Paul then declared "those who live in Jerusalem, and their rulers, recognizing neither Him [Jesus] nor the utterances of *the prophets which are read* every Sabbath, fulfilled these by condemning Him" (v.27, emphasis added). The "prophets which were read" on the Sabbath in Jerusalem would have been from the same writings, which were read in Pisidian Antioch on the Sabbath ("the Law and the Prophets" – v.15).

The term "the Law and the Prophets" would have meant the same thing to those living in Jerusalem, as in Pisidian Antioch, as well as to Paul and Barnabas – the canon of the Pharisees. Not surprisingly, God chose a Pharisee (Paul) to write one-third of the *New* Testament canon, just as the Pharisees adopted the same *Old* Testament canon which Protestants would embrace centuries later. This means when Paul wrote "the Law and the Prophets" in his epistle to the Romans, *the church of Rome would have understood this to be limited to this Old Testament canon!*

HOW DID JESUS DEFINE THE OLD TESTAMENT CANON?

Jesus Himself used this same metonym ("the Law and the Prophets") to refer to the Old Testament canon as Paul did when He spoke to the Pharisees:

> "Now *the Pharisees*, who were lovers of money, were listening to all these things and were scoffing at Him. And He said to them… '*The Law and the Prophets* were proclaimed until John [the Baptist]'" (Luke 6:14-16, emphasis added).

Merriam-Webster's Dictionary defines metonymy as "a figure of speech consisting of the use of the name of one thing for that of another of which it is an attribute or with which it is associated (such as 'crown' in 'lands belonging to the crown')."[19] For example, "plastic" is a metonym for "credit card." Likewise, "the Law and the Prophets" is a metonym for the Old Testament Scriptures. When Jesus and others used this term, none of the New Testament had been written. They would not have described it as the "*Old* Testament," like we do today, since there was no *New* Testament yet. They used the metonym "the Law and the Prophets" to describe the same canon of Scripture which Protestants today designate with the term "Old Testament."

The significance of this passage in Luke 6:14-16 was "who" Jesus was speaking to – *the Pharisees*. What would the Pharisees have understood "the Law and the Prophets" to mean when they heard Jesus use this term? They would have understood it to be limited to <u>only</u> those writings found

---

[19] Merriam-Webster.com. "Metonymy." Accessed from the Internet https://www.merriam-webster.com/dictionary/metonymy

in Protestant Old Testaments today. This is how Jesus – and later, Paul – would have understood it as well.

Since Paul was a Pharisee, he *might* have been one of the Pharisees who Jesus was addressing. This would explain why Paul used the same term – "the Law and the Prophets" – later in his epistle to the church of Rome. The term "the Law and the Prophets" (or a variation of it) is used in the New Testament eleven times to describe the Old Testament canon – six times by Jesus. When this term cites Old Testament Scriptures, the *earliest* and most direct references are found in the books from the Protestant Old Testament canon (see Appendix A).

What is often overlooked in Luke 16:19-31 is the wording Jesus used when He discussed the eternal fates of the rich man and Lazarus with the Pharisees. After they both died, Lazarus ended up in the "good" part of Hades, which Jesus refers to as "Abraham's bosom" (v.22). However, the rich man ended up in endless "torment," eternally separated from Lazarus and Abraham by "a great chasm fixed" (v.23-26). In agony, the rich man begged "Father Abraham" to send Lazarus back to his father's house to warn his five brothers of "this place of torment" he was experiencing (v.27-28). Abraham's response was, "They *have Moses and the Prophets*; let them hear them" (v.29, emphasis added).

Although the immediate context of this event is referring to the rich man's five brothers, the application of the lesson is addressed to "the Pharisees, who were lovers of money, [who] were listening to all these things" (v.14). When Jesus said, "They *have* Moses and the Prophets" (v.29), He was indicating the Pharisees "have possession of" (Greek: *"echō"*) the *complete* Old Testament Scriptures at their disposal to refer to – not just "part" or "most" of it.

Some would object to this conclusion since not all Jews believed in the exact same Old Testament canon. In his book *"The Jesus You Can't Ignore,"* Pastor John MacArthur quotes from William Wiston's 1737 translation of Josephus' *Antiquities of the Jews,* book 18, chapter 1, paragraph 2-6.[20] In it, he mentions four prominent Jewish sects in the first century A.D.: the Sadducees, the Pharisees, the Essenes, and followers of Judas the Galilean – none of which agreed on the exact same canon of the Old Testament.

The New Testament mentions two other Jewish sects: the Samaritans (Matthew 10:5) who only espoused to the five books of Moses, and the Herodians (Matthew 22:16) who also accepted them and at least *some* of

---

[20] MacArthur, John. *The Jesus You Can't Ignore: what you must learn from the bold confrontations of Christ.* Appendix, pp. 209-212. Nashville, Tennessee: Thomas Nelson, Inc., 2008.

the Old Testament prophets, but not necessarily all of them. When Herod asked the scribes (who were also Pharisees – Acts 23:9) and the chief priests about the magi's claims, "He who has been born King of the Jews" (Matthew 2:1-4), they quoted from the prophetic book of Micah (v.5-6, cf. Micah 5:2). The magi stated, "we saw His star in the east" (v.2). Regarding these "magi from the east" (v.1), GotQuestions.org states:

"Most likely, the magi knew of the writings of the prophet Daniel, who in time past had been the chief of the court seers in Persia. Daniel 9:24-27 includes a prophecy which gives a timeline for the birth of the Messiah. Also, the magi may have been aware of the prophecy of Balaam (who was from the town of Pethor on the Euphrates River near Persia) in Numbers 24:17. Balaam's prophecy specifically mentions a 'star coming out of Jacob.'"[21]

The magi brought the Child Jesus "gold, frankincense, and myrrh" (Matthew 2:11). Gold and frankincense were gifts suitable for a king (Isaiah 60:6). The ark of the covenant was overlaid with gold (Exodus 25:10-17), and frankincense was used in worship in Israel (Exodus 30:34). Jesus refused to drink myrrh, or gall, when He was on the cross (Matthew 27:34, cf. Mark 15:23). Myrrh symbolized the future Messiah's suffering and affliction which was prophesied by King David (Psalm 69:21). Gall was a term used by Moses as a warning to Israel against practicing idolatry (Deuteronomy 29:18 KJV). The meaning of all three gifts can be found in "the Law," as well as some of the books of "the Prophets," which the magi brought to worship Jesus (Matthew 2:2).

Herod would have understood these as fulfilled Old Testament prophecies of the coming Jewish Messiah. This explains Herod's fear of being overthrown as king of Israel (Matthew 2:3), spawning his evil intention to murder Him. This resulted in his order to slay "all the male children who were in Bethlehem and all its vicinity, from two years old and under, according to the time which he had determined from the magi" (v.16). It also explains why the Pharisees were "conspiring with the Herodians against Him, as to how they might destroy Him" (Mark 3:6). They both realized Jesus was fulfilling the Messianic prophecies based on the Old Testament.

The Samaritans were despised by the Jews (John 8:48), who did not even drink out of the same cup (John 4:9). Although they believed in the same five books of Moses as the Sadducees[22] (or at least a modified version

---

21 GotQuestions.org. "What does the Bible say about the three wise men (Magi)?" Accessed from the Internet https://www.gotquestions.org/three-wise-men.html

22 Catholic Answers Staff. "Who were the Samaritans and why were they important?" Published August 04, 2011. Accessed from the Internet https://www.catholic.com/qa/who-were-the-samaritans-and-why-were-they-important

of it), they did not espouse to the rest of the Old Testament, which explains why Jesus told the Samaritan woman at the well, "You worship what you do not know; we worship what we know, for salvation is from the Jews" (v.22). Unlike the Jews – specifically the Pharisees – the Samaritan Old Testament canon was incomplete, because it lacked "the Prophets."

As previously mentioned, the term – "the Law and the Prophets" – was used by Jesus and Paul to refer to the Old Testament canon of the Pharisees, but not of these other Jewish sects. Although there was no formal established *Jewish* Old Testament canon in the first century all Jews agreed on, there was indeed a formal *Pharisaic* Old Testament canon, which Jesus and Paul would have accepted (see Chapter Seven).

Some may argue even though Jesus affirmed the writings found in the canon of the Pharisees, He never explicitly rejected the canon of the Sadducees as being "incomplete" in favor of the Pharisaic canon. After Jesus miraculously fed the four-thousand, both the Pharisees *and the Sadducees* came to Jesus attempting to test Him to show them a sign from Heaven (Matthew 16:1). Jesus' response to them was, "'An evil and adulterous generation seeks after a sign; and a sign will not be given it, except the sign of Jonah.' And He left them and went away" (v.4). The NKJV adds "*the prophet* Jonah." This is how Jonah is referred to in the Old Testament ("Jonah, the son of Amittai, *the prophet*" – 2 Kings 14:25, cf. Jonah 1:1).

Elsewhere in a similar, but different, account when the Pharisees and scribes asked Jesus for a sign, Jesus said the same thing: "no sign will be given to it but the sign of *Jonah the prophet*" (Matthew 12:39 – NASB, emphasis added, cf. Luke 11:29 – NKJV). The significance is when Jesus referred to Jonah as a "prophet" by referencing Jonah 1:17 (cf. Matthew 16:4). When the Sadducees heard this, they understood Jesus was asserting Jonah was a genuine prophet of God, and his writing was Inspired Old Testament Scripture. Hence, Jesus was declaring their canon was incomplete. When the Pharisees heard it, they would not have come to that conclusion about their canon, since *they accepted Jonah as a prophet and his writing* as Inspired Scripture.

Jesus summed up all His teachings and commands with "The Golden Rule" by attributing them to the Old Testament canon: "In everything, therefore, treat people the same way you want them to treat you, for this is *the Law and the Prophets*" (Matthew 7:12, emphasis added).

Some would question if this declaration is evidence for the Pharisaic canon. After all, various "golden rules" of reciprocity towards others existed even prior to the time of Jesus. Unlike Jesus' *positively*-commanded

"Golden Rule" to do "good" unto others, these were *negatively-*commanded to prevent doing "bad" deeds to others. For example:

"What is *hateful* to yourself, *do not to* someone else." – Hillel the Elder (Jerusalem) (110 B.C. to A.D. 10)[23]

"*Never impose* on others what you would *not choose* for yourself." – Confucius (China) (551 to 479 B.C.)[24]

"*Do not do* to others that which *angers you* when they do it to you." – Isocrates (Greece) (436 to 338 B.C.)[25]

Jesus' *positively-*commanded "Golden Rule" predates these *negatively-*commanded "golden rules" by centuries, because it was based on "the Law and the Prophets" (Matthew 7:12), i.e.: the Old Testament Scriptures. Later, when Jesus was asked, "Teacher, which is the great commandment in the Law?" (Matthew 22:36), His response was:

"'YOU SHALL LOVE THE LORD YOUR GOD WITH ALL YOUR HEART, AND WITH ALL YOUR SOUL, AND WITH ALL YOUR MIND.' This is the great and foremost commandment. The second is like it, 'YOU SHALL LOVE YOUR NEIGHBOR AS YOURSELF.' On these *two commandments* depend *the whole Law and the Prophets*." (vv.37-40, emphasis added)

Here, Jesus quoted from Deuteronomy 6:5 and Leviticus 19:18 from "the Law," which commands us not only to "love the LORD your God," but also to "love your neighbor as yourself" (Matthew 22:37,39). Jesus also corrected some of the teachings of the scribes and the Pharisees. Although they taught correctly to "love your neighbor" (Leviticus 19:18), they *incorrectly* taught to "hate your enemies" (Matthew 5:43). Jesus, however, taught to "love your enemies and pray for those who persecute you" (Matthew 5:44). Jesus' "Golden Rule" commands us to "love one another, even as I have loved you" so "all men will know that you are My disciples" (John 13:34-35).

So, earlier when Jesus preached "treat people the same way you want them to treat you, for this is *the Law and the Prophets*" (Matthew 7:12, emphasis added), Jesus was referring to the passages commanded in Leviticus 19:18 and Deuteronomy 6:5 in "the Law." Later, He repeated in

---

[23] JewishEncyclopedia (1906). Hillel, by Solomon Schechter, William Bacher. Accessed from the Internet http://www.jewishencyclopedia.com/articles/7698-hillel

[24] Chinese Text Project #24. Confucianism, The Analects, Section 15: Wei Ling Gong. Accessed from the Internet http://ctext.org/analects/wei-ling-gong

[25] Isocrates, Nicocles or the Cyprians, Isoc 3.61, George Norlin, Ed. Accessed from the Internet http://www.perseus.tufts.edu/hopper/text?doc=Perseus%3Atext%3A1999.01.0144%3Aspeech%3D3%3Asection%3D61

Matthew 22:40: "On these *two commandments* depend *the whole Law and the Prophets*" (emphasis added) – the entire Old Testament canon of the Pharisees.

Still, some will point out Jesus was simply "restating" the negative form of "The Golden Rule" in passages in Catholic Old Testaments. For example, from the New American Bible (a Catholic translation):

"*Do to no one* what you yourself *dislike*" (Tobit 4:15 NAB)

"Recognize that your neighbor feels as you do, and *keep to your own dislikes*" (Sirach 31:15 NAB)

However, just as the other *negatively*-commanded "golden rules" prior to the time of Jesus were not what He was referring to, likewise, Jesus was <u>not</u> simply "restating" these *negatively*-commanded "golden rules" found in the writings of Catholic Old Testaments either. He was referring *specifically* to the two passages in Leviticus and Deuteronomy in "the Law," which summed up "the Law and the Prophets."

Just as those other *negatively*-commanded "golden rules" from the Old Testament *era* do not belong in the Old Testament (like those of Hillel, Confucius, and Isocrates), neither do those from the Catholic Old Testament for the same reason. Jesus would not have accepted those writings as being part of "the Law and the Prophets" no more than Paul would have, since they were not part of the Old Testament canon of the Pharisees. In his book *"The Canon of Scripture,"* F.F. Bruce wrote:

> "Our Lord and his apostles differ from the religious leaders of Israel about the *meaning* of the scriptures; there is no suggestion that they differed about the *limits* of the scriptures."[26] (emphasis added)

I will cover why the writings of Tobit and Sirach, and others in the Catholic Old Testament, are not considered Inspired Scripture in later chapters.

HOW DID THE DISCIPLES DEFINE THE OLD TESTAMENT CANON?

After Jesus found and called Philip in Galilee to follow Him, Philip went and found Nathanael and told him, "We have found Him of whom *Moses in the Law and also the Prophets* wrote—Jesus of Nazareth, the son of Joseph" (John 1:45, emphasis added). The term "Moses and the

---

[26] Bruce, F.F. *The Canon of Scripture.* Chapter Two: The Law and the Prophets, The Canon of the Old Testament. Downers Grove, IL: IVP Academic, An imprint of Intervarsity Press, December 18, 2018.

Prophets," and "the Law of Moses and the Prophets," were other metonyms used in the New Testament to describe the same Old Testament canon of the Pharisees.

For example, Luke quoted Jesus by using the term "Moses and the Prophets" or "the Law of Moses and the Prophets" to describe the Old Testament (Luke 16:29,31; 24:27,44). Luke also quoted the apostle Paul who used these same terms (Acts 26:22; 28:23).

When Nathanael heard from Philip the alleged Messiah was from Nazareth, his initial response was "Can any good thing come out of Nazareth?" (John 1:46). Nazareth was despised as a city in Israel, even among other Galileans like Nathanael. Christians would later be addressed with contempt being referred to as "of the sect of the Nazarenes" (Acts 24:5). Yet, when Nathanael actually met Jesus, his response was "Rabbi, You are the Son of God; You are the King of Israel" (John 1:49).

Nathanael recognized Jesus was the promised Messiah from the Old Testament Who Philip spoke of (v.45), based on Jesus revealing His Omniscience about Nathanael, which He should not have been able to know if Jesus was not the Son of God (v.47-48). Nathanael's description of Jesus as "the King of Israel" was a Messianic term used in the Old Testament prophetic writings to describe the ruler of Israel from the Davidic line, who was "anointed" by God Himself (2 Samuel 12:7). The Hebrew word "anointed" (*"mashach"*) is translated into the Greek root (*"chriō"*), which is where we get *"Christos"* or "Christ" in the New Testament to describe the Messianic title of Jesus. Nathanael would have based this title from "the Law and the Prophets" from the Pharisaic Old Testament.

Nathanael used the Messianic title "the Son of God" which was used in the Old Testament to describe a heavenly, Divine Being. After King Nebuchadnezzar ordered Daniel's three friends – Shadrach, Meshach, and Abed-Nego – into the burning furnace for disobeying his decree, he described a fourth man in the midst of the fire "like the Son of God" (Daniel 3:25 NKJV; Daniel 3:92 New Catholic Version). Although Nebuchadnezzar might not have completely understood who this fourth man was, he undoubtedly knew He was a supernatural, heavenly being. (See also Psalm 2:7-8, cf. 2 Samuel 7:12-14.)

Jesus used this term "the Son of God" later to equate Himself with the One True God of Israel, based on the Old Testament Scriptures (John 10:34-36). Jesus' other disciples, like Peter, John, and Martha – and later Paul, Mark, and the Ethiopian eunuch – would use these same Messianic titles for

Jesus ("the Christ, the Son of God" – Matthew 16:16; Mark 1:1; John 11:27; 20:31; Acts 8:37[27]; 2 Corinthians 1:19).

Nathanael was from Bethsaida, the same town in Galilee where Peter and Andrew were from (John 1:44). When Philip and the other disciples utilized and heard the Lord use the term "the Law and the Prophets," they too would have understood it to mean how Nathanael understood it – the Old Testament canon of the Pharisees.

It would be no different than an unbelieving Jew today referring to the Old Testament of Protestants as "the Hebrew Bible." When heard by other non-Christian Jews, this term would be understood to refer to only those *writings* found in Protestant Old Testaments today. Likewise, when the disciples heard or used the term "the Law and the Prophets" (or a similar metonym) to describe the Old Testament Scriptures, they too would have understood it to be limited to those exact same writings.

Lastly, because Peter acknowledged "all" of Paul's epistles by comparing them to the "rest of the Scriptures" (2 Peter 3:15-16), Peter believed in the same Old Testament canon Paul did who referred to it as "the Law and the Prophets" (Romans 3:21). As a Pharisee, since Paul limited this to the boundaries of the Protestant Old Testament, so would Peter based on his affirmation of Paul's epistles – which would include his epistle to the Romans.

The Jewish leaders rejected Jesus as their long-awaited Messiah because of their extra-scriptural man-made "traditions" (Matthew 15:1-2), which either exceeded or "transgressed" the Old Testament "commandment of God" (v.3). In contrast, the disciples accepted Jesus as their Messiah based *solely* on "the Law and also the Prophets" (John 1:45) – i.e.: *sola scriptura*.

WHAT ABOUT PAUL'S "LOST LETTERS"?

Paul referenced two letters he composed allegedly not found in the New Testament. He wrote a previous letter to the church of Corinth warning "I wrote you in my letter not to associate with immoral people" (1 Corinthians 5:9). He also wrote to the church of Colossae "When this letter is read among you, have it also read in the church of the Laodiceans; and you, for your part read my letter that is coming from Laodicea" (Colossians 5:9). Since Peter affirmed *all* of Paul's epistles to be Inspired

---

[27] This verse is not found in the earliest and most reliable Greek manuscripts. However, the Messianic title, "the Son of God," to describe Jesus is found in these other verses, as well as in numerous others in the New Testament.

Scripture (2 Peter 3:15-16) would that include these two "lost" letters of Paul as well? If so, why are they not in the New Testament?

We tend to assume if someone writes Inspired Scripture then *everything*, they write is likewise Inspired. However, Paul also quoted uninspired writings (Acts 17:28; 1 Corinthians 15:33; Titus 1:2), which are not in our Bibles. The Old Testament, likewise, references unknown texts like "the Book of the Wars of the LORD" (Numbers 21:14), but they are not in the Old Testament canon either. Simply referencing them does not equate with them being Inspired. Otherwise, God would have included them in the Bible, and they would not be "lost." However, it goes without saying that the portion that is quoted is inspired by the simple fact the author was moved by the Holy Spirit to include it.

When Peter became influenced by the Judaizers (supposedly) sent by James, "he began to withdraw and hold himself aloof" from eating with the uncircumcised Gentiles (Galatians 2:12). Paul immediately "opposed him to his face, because he stood condemned" (v.11). Although Peter was the author of two Inspired New Testament epistles (1 Peter 1:1; 2 Peter 1:1; 3:1), this does not mean *everything* Peter wrote, said, and did was Inspired.

Some have surmised Paul's letter to the church of Laodicea (Colossians 5:9) was actually the epistle to the Ephesians.[28] The words "at Ephesus" (Ephesians 1:1) are not found in the earliest Greek manuscripts of the text. It is believed by some Paul's epistle to the Ephesians was a circular letter meant to be spread throughout the church, including the church of Laodicea.

Paul's "first" letter to the church of Corinth (1 Corinthians 5:9) *may* have been an uninspired, personal letter intended *strictly* for this particular church in the first century. It may not have been meant for the future body of Christ at large throughout the millennia, such as 1 and 2 Corinthians and the rest of the New Testament. If it was, God would have preserved this "lost" text, which He did not.

The apostle John wrote in his gospel there were "many other signs Jesus also performed in the presence of the disciples, which are not written in this book" (John 20:30), and "many other things which Jesus did" (John 21:25). John did not write everything down since "the world itself would not contain the books that would be written" (v.25). If it were vital for us to know these unwritten details of what Jesus did, God would have included them in the pages of Scripture, but He did not because He did not

---

[28] EWTN.com | Global Catholic Network. *EWTN Catholic Q&A. RE: Laodiceans.* Question from Edward Pothier on 03-03-2002. Answer by Dr. Warren Carroll on 03-03-2002. COPYRIGHT 2002. Accessed from the Internet http://www.ewtn.com/v/experts/showmessage_print.asp?number=313409&language=en

consider it necessary for us to know. Therefore, Peter was not referring to these two "missing" uninspired letters of Paul. Peter was only referring to Paul's Inspired texts contained in the twenty-seven-book New Testament canon.

What about Jesus and the New Testament writers who seem to allude to books found in Catholic Old Testaments (called "Deuterocanonical" by Catholics and "Apocryphal" by Protestants)? How do we address the New Testament quoting from the Greek translation of the Catholic Old Testament, i.e.: the Septuagint?

Before I can further address why Protestant Bibles are smaller, I need to first address why Catholic Bibles *"really"* are bigger. I will accomplish this by discussing the history of the Septuagint, the Vulgate, the various councils, and the English translation of the Catholic Bible – the Douay-Rheims. These, and other questions, will be addressed in the next few chapters. For now, it should be clear and obvious from the *New* Testament Scriptures: when Jesus, His disciples, the apostle Paul, and others referred to the Old Testament canon as "the Law and the Prophets" it referred to the canon of the Pharisees and that of later Protestants.

CHAPTER TWO: What about the Septuagint?

"they will look on Me whom they have pierced" (Zechariah 12:10)

2017 involved me calling into a well-known, nationally syndicated Catholic radio station called *Catholic Answers Live*. On June 26, 2017, they were having their monthly call-in show called, "Why Aren't You Catholic?" I had just finished uploading a detailed three-part video on YouTube, covering the Protestant Reformation. Most of the video, however, was on defending why the Protestant Old Testament was the complete Christian Old Testament which Jesus and the early first century church would have accepted. In total, it is approximately one and one-half hours, broken up into three separate parts. It can be viewed by going to my YouTube channel (BornAgainRN) and typing in the search engine: "Protestant Reformation" and clicking the video titled: "The Protestant Reformation – 500 Year Anniversary (Part 1 of 3)," or you can simply go to the link in the reference section of this book.[29] (Parts two and three follow immediately afterwards.)

The hosts on the show that day were Cy Kellett and Trent Horn. Mr. Horn was fielding the callers' comments and questions as they came in. I was the second caller. When Mr. Kellett asked me "Why aren't you Catholic?" I immediately began with the defense of the Protestant Old Testament being the same canon the apostle Paul, as a Pharisee, would have accepted. I also reiterated Jimmy Akin's comment about the Pharisaic canon being the same as Protestant Old Testaments. Since Paul was a Pharisee, when he used the term "the Law and the Prophets" to refer to the Old Testament canon that would have included everything we find in Protestant Old Testaments today.

You can view my call-in in its entirety by going to their YouTube channel (Catholic Answers), and in their search engine type in: "Trent Horn: Why Aren't You Catholic? - Catholic Answers Live - 06/26/17," or you can simply go to the link in the reference section of this book.[30]

---

[29] Christie, Steve. *The Protestant Reformation - 500 Year Anniversary (Part 1 of 3)*. "BornAgainRN." Published on YouTube, May 6, 2017. Accessed from the Internet https://www.youtube.com/watch?v=mStL5_wGrYk&index=14&list=PLjfXQw6fZto7R2Us4g jbLt5IJqlkDz1YP

[30] Horn, Trent and Kellett, Cy. *Why Aren't You Catholic? - Catholic Answers Live - 06/26/17*. "Catholic Answers." Published on YouTube, June 26, 2017. Accessed from the Internet https://www.youtube.com/watch?v=9cAaa77upBo (My call-in begins around

One of the questions Mr. Horn brought up when he responded to the common Protestant challenge of "why Catholic Bibles are bigger than Protestant Bibles" was: "we should rather ask, 'why are Protestant Bibles smaller than Catholic Bibles?'"[31] Unfortunately, I did not get the chance to respond to his question, since they had to get to other callers. However, this book should be adequate in answering Mr. Horn's question from both a New Testament and a historical position.

One of the common defenses for why Catholic Bibles are "bigger" than Protestant Bibles – particularly the Old Testament – is Jesus and the New Testament writers quoted frequently from the Septuagint. However, Eastern Orthodox Bibles are *also* based on the Septuagint, yet their Old Testament is "bigger" than Catholic ones.

The Septuagint is believed in Catholicism (and Eastern Orthodoxy) to be the Greek translation of the complete Old Testament Jesus and the New Testament writers used, which includes writings not found in Protestant Old Testaments. Before I go into more detail, I think it is important to define a few terms first, which I will be using throughout this book.

DEFINING TERMS

THE LAW: unless otherwise specified in this book, in regard to the Old Testament canon, this term refers to the five books attributed to Moses found at the very beginning of the Bible. It is sometimes referred to as the TORAH or the PENTATEUCH.

THE PROPHETS: a term to describe the rest of the Old Testament writings which are not included in THE LAW. It can also refer more specifically to the second division of the Old Testament separate from THE LAW and THE WRITINGS (ex.: Luke 24:44). (This distinction will be discussed in more detail in later chapters.)

THE WRITINGS: believed by both Catholics and Protestants to be Inspired writings in the Old Testament distinct from THE LAW and THE PROPHETS, such as "The Psalms."

THE LAW AND THE PROPHETS: a term used by Jews and Protestants to refer to the books from the Old Testament era, which are limited to THE LAW and THE PROPHETS, which include THE WRITINGS, that make up the complete Old Testament. Jews and Protestants call this the HEBREW BIBLE.   Catholics   sometimes   call   these   group   of   writings   the

---

35:54 and picks up again after the break with Mr. Horn around 41:20, followed by me clarifying my position around the 44:11 mark.)

[31] Ibid. Horn, Trent. *Catholic Answers Live – 06/26/17.* YouTube.com. (Begins around the 41:38 mark.)

PROTOCANON ("first canon"). However, this excludes those writings Catholics call DEUTEROCANON and Protestants call APOCRYPHA.

HEBREW BIBLE: synonymous with THE LAW AND THE PROPHETS, except the books in the Hebrew Bible are arranged somewhat differently from those in the Protestant Old Testament, but they still contain the exact same writings.

DEUTEROCANON: "second canon"; a set of seven books (Sirach, Baruch, Tobit, Judith, Wisdom, 1 Maccabees, and 2 Maccabees), as well as "additions" to the books of Daniel and Esther not found in Protestant Old Testaments. Protestants consider these books to be APOCRYPHA.

APOCRYPHA: "hidden," or "spurious"; used by Protestants to refer to those set of writings found in Catholic Old Testaments (i.e.: DEUTEROCANON) which are not found in Protestant Old Testaments, as well as other writings not found in either Protestant or Catholic Old Testaments. Used by Catholics to refer to only those writings not found in the Catholic Old Testament.

SEPTUAGINT: "seventy"; originally applied to *only* the Greek translation of THE LAW,[32] but later believed by Catholics to be the complete Greek translation of the Old Testament, which also includes not only THE PROPHETS and THE WRITINGS, but also the DEUTEROCANON. It is sometimes abbreviated LXX.

~~~~~~~~~~~~~~~~~~~~~~~~~~~~~~

So as not to confuse readers, I will only be using the term "the Hebrew Bible," instead of "the Law and the Prophets," to refer to the Protestant Old Testament canon, unless otherwise specified. By "Hebrew Bible," this does not refer to the *Hebrew language choices* in it (like those used for the later Masoretic Text). It simply refers to *the specific writings* that are contained in the boundaries of the canon of the Hebrew Bible. Likewise, I will only use the term "Apocrypha" when discussing those books Catholics and Protestants agree are not Inspired Old Testament Scriptures.

---

[32] McDonald, Lee Martin. *The Biblical Canon: Its Origin, Transmission, and Authority.* [Updated & rev. 3rd ed.]. Published by Baker Academic, a division of Baker Publishing Group: Grand Rapids, Michigan, 2007. On page 119, McDonald points out "The original translation was of only the Pentateuch," and then states in footnote #2 "the Septuagint (LXX), which should technically be applied to only the Pentateuch and not to the rest of the OT Scriptures." For more historical evidence the Septuagint was originally limited to "the Law," see pages 44-45 where McDonald quotes from the legendary *Letter of Aristeas*, which states "...the lawbooks of the Jews were worth translation..." and on page 75 where it declares "Scrolls of the Law of the Jews...are written in Hebrew characters and language.... These (books) also must be in your library in an accurate version" (parentheses in original quote from McDonald).

Furthermore, I will use the term "Deuterocanonical" (or "Deuterocanon") to refer to the seven writings (and the "additions" to Daniel and Esther) from the Old Testament era which are in dispute between Catholics and Protestants. It is worth noting the term "Deuterocanon" did not come into existence to describe these writings until the seventeenth century in response to the Protestant Reformers questioning their Inspiration and canonicity.

It is also worth mentioning by using the term "Deuterocanon," this demonstrates Catholics during the Reformation recognized and acknowledged there was an earlier unified and organized "Protocanon" ("first canon") of books. This "Protocanon," which was strictly made up of the books of the Hebrew Bible, was distinct and separate from this later collection of writings. Even Catholics used the term "Apocrypha" to describe the Deuterocanonical books centuries prior to the Reformation, such as Cyril of Jerusalem (A.D. 315 to 386):

> "Of these read the two and twenty books but have nothing to do with *the apocryphal writings*. And *of the Old Testament*, as we have said, study the two and twenty books, Genesis, Exodus, Leviticus, Numbers, Deuteronomy, Joshua, Judges, Ruth, the first and second books of Kings [1 and 2 Samuel]; also the third and fourth one book [1 and 2 Kings], the first and second of Chronicles, the first and second of Esdras [Ezra-Nehemiah], Esther, Job, Psalms, Proverbs, Ecclesiastes, Song of Songs, of the Twelve Prophets one book[33], Isaiah, Jeremiah, Baruch, Lamentations and the Epistle; Ezekiel, Daniel."[34] (emphasis added).

With the exception of including the Deuterocanonical book of Baruch and "the Epistle" (which is possibly chapter six of Baruch – "the Letter of Jeremiah"[35]), Cyril does not record *any* of the other Deuterocanonical books in his list. So, Cyril – the bishop of Jerusalem and Doctor of the

---

[33] The "Twelve Prophets" Cyril is referring to are: Hosea, Joel, Amos, Obadiah, Jonah, Micah, Nahum, Habakkuk, Zephaniah, Haggai, Zechariah, Malachi, which he grouped into "one book," which Christians refer to as "the Minor Prophets."

[34] Cyril of Jerusalem, 615-386, Catechetical Lectures, 4:34-35. Accessed from the Internet and summarized for lucidity from the Christian Apologetics and Research Ministry https://carm.org/early-church-fathers-canon, *Not all Church Fathers agree with the Catholic Church's view of the Canon*. Brackets added by me for clarification: "the first and second books of Kings" refers to 1 and 2 Samuel, "the third and fourth one book" refers to 1 and 2 Kings, and the "first and second of Esdras" refers to Ezra-Nehemiah. Matt Slick is the President and Founder of the Christian Apologetics and Research Ministry (CARM.org).

[35] New American Bible, St. Joseph Medium Size Edition, Catholic Book Publishing Corp: New York, 1970. Introduction to Baruch. *"The final chapter is really a separate work, with a title of its own (6:1),"* p.964. Baruch: Chapter Six, *"The Letter of Jeremiah Against Idolatry,"* pp. 969-971.

Church[36] – would have classified at least the other six Deuterocanonical books as "apocryphal writings" and *not* part "of the Old Testament."[37] However, he does include *every book* from the Protestant Old Testament canon (i.e.: the Hebrew Bible), despite being assembled differently.

JESUS, THE APOSTLES, AND THE SEPTUAGINT

One of the arguments in favor of the Deuterocanon being included in the Old Testament is Jesus and His disciples used, and even quoted from, the Septuagint. Catholic apologists, like Trent Horn from Catholic Answers in his podcast, will be quick to point out "the New Testament *alludes* to the Deuterocanonical books"[38] (emphasis added). However, Mr. Horn later admitted "Jesus and the apostles quote the Old Testament a lot, and, no, *there's no direct quotation from the Deuterocanonical books in Scripture*,"[39] and "there's also *direct quotations from other Apocryphal works* and non-Biblical works"[40] (emphasis added – see Chapter Six). Although there are books from the Hebrew Bible which the New Testament neither quotes nor alludes to, simply quoting or alluding to a piece of literature is not the godly criteria used to discern if it is Inspired or not. There are other writings the New Testament also quotes and alludes to, which are not in Catholic nor Protestant Old Testaments, as I will illustrate in this and later chapters.

It must also be acknowledged that even the apostle Paul, as well as some of the other New Testament writers (like the apostle John), also quoted from the Septuagint. This fact is not disputed, even by Protestants. However, even Mr. Horn affirmed it was the *Hebrew Bible* which was the first "canon" initially translated into the Septuagint:

---

[36] "St. Cyril of Jerusalem, BISHOP OF JERUSALEM, DOCTOR OF THE CHURCH." Accessed from the Internet https://www.ewtn.com/saintsHoly/saints/C/stcyrilofjerusalem.asp. EWTN.com defines "Doctors of the Church" as "men and women who are revered by the Church for the special value of their writings and preaching and the sanctity of their lives. A Doctor is named by a special decree of the Pope or an Ecumenical Council. They each made important and lasting contributions to the faith and are to be recognized for their great merits." Accessed from the Internet http://www.ewtn.com/doctors/ where Pope Benedict XVI in 2012 further makes "The declaration that a saint is a Doctor of the Universal Church implies the recognition of a charism of wisdom bestowed by the Holy Spirit for the good of the Church and evidenced by the beneficial influence of his or her teaching among the People of God."

[37] Ibid. CARM.org. *Not all Church Fathers agree with the Catholic Church's view of the Canon.*

[38] Horn, Trent. *Why Catholic Bibles Are Bigger.* August 16, 2018. Counsel of Trent (Audio podcast) Accessed from the Internet https://www.catholic.com/audio/cot/25 (Begins around the 10:28 mark.)

[39] Ibid. (Begins around the 19:47 mark.)

[40] Ibid. (Begins around the 22:01 mark.)

"This [the Septuagint] is the Bible that Jesus and the apostles used…. It comes from the story that King Ptolemy II of Egypt, he had asked for *the Hebrew Bible for the Old Testament to be translated into Greek* to be put into the library of Alexandria."[41] (emphasis added)

It was the books of the *Hebrew Bible*, specifically, from the Septuagint which Jesus and the apostles used and considered Inspired Old Testament Scripture. Lee Martin McDonald (*"The Biblical Canon: Its Origin, Transmission, and Authority"*) further reveals the Septuagint "initially included only the Law of Moses," and then cites N. Fernandez Marcos (*"The Septuagint in Context: Introduction to the Greek Versions of the Bible"*): "by the end of the second or third century C.E., the term LXX was transferred to all of the literature that comprised the Greek Bible."[42] This demonstrates the version of the Septuagint which included the so-called Deuterocanon was a much later edition well into the future church age.

Mr. Horn also admitted "sometimes *they* [Jesus and the apostles] *do quote from Hebrew manuscripts* or Hebrew traditions"[43] (emphasis added), meaning they did not strictly use the Septuagint, nor all of it. Mr. Horn also erred when he said "these books [Deuterocanon] were *in the Bible before…the time of Christ*"[44] (emphasis added). Rather, it was the books of THE LAW – not the Deuterocanon – which was initially translated into the Septuagint.

Mr. Horn further acknowledged there was a "three-tiered system" the ancient Jews used to discern between the "Protocanon" versus the "Deuterocanon" and other Apocryphal writings. He referenced Sixtus of Sienna, a Jewish convert to Catholicism in the sixteenth century, who was the first to refer to the "disputed" books as "Deuterocanon":

"…he [Sixtus of Sienna] had a *three-tiered classification system* for understanding *the different books of the Bible*. So, the first was the Protocanon. These were the books of the Bible, that both Catholics and Protestants agree are Inspired Scripture…. At the bottom of this three-tiered system, *the third tier, you had the Apocrypha*. You had those writings that Catholics and Protestants agree are not sacred Scripture…. *The second tier*, the middle tier, is *the area that's disputed, the Deuterocanonical*

---

[41] Ibid. (Begins around the 7:36 mark.) Brackets inserted by me for clarity.

[42] Ibid. McDonald, *The Biblical Canon*, p.120 citing N. Fernandez Marcos (*The Septuagint in Context: Introduction to the Greek Versions of the Bible*, pp. 48-51. Translated by W. G. W. Watson. Watson. Leiden: Brill, 2001).

[43] Ibid. Horn. *Why Catholic Bibles Are Bigger*. (Podcast) (Begins around the 10:13 mark.) Brackets inserted by me for clarity.

[44] Ibid. (Begins around the 5:35 mark.) Brackets inserted by me for clarity.

books. Protocanon is first canon. Deuterocanon...are the second canon."[45] (emphasis added)

Even Sixtus of Sienna's "three-tiered system" listed the Deuterocanon and the Apocrypha as separate "tiers" which were not on par with the first "tier" of the Hebrew Bible. If they were, the books of the Deuterocanon and the Apocrypha would have been intermingled with the books of the Hebrew Bible. Just as the Deuterocanon is intermingled in Catholic Bibles now, if it was considered Inspired in the early church, it too would have been intermingled rather than in its own separate "tier." Mr. Horn also acknowledged the book of Baruch was <u>not</u> part of the second section of the Hebrew Bible ("the Prophets"), because it was written *afterwards*:

> "They [Deuterocanonal books] were written before the time of Jesus, *but after the time of 'The Prophets' and the other books that make up* the end of the Protestant Old Testament, as well as *the end of Hebrew Bibles* that we have today."[46] (emphasis added)

Since the Deuterocanonical book of Baruch was written "<u>after</u> the time of *'The Prophets'* and the other books that make up...the end of Hebrew Bibles," then "why" is it included under *"the Prophets"* in Catholic Old Testaments?

There are two important points which need to be interjected into the defense of including the Deuterocanon into the Old Testament: 1) the Septuagint was not limited to the Hebrew Bible and the Deuterocanon; and 2) the Septuagint was not the only Greek translation used in the early church.

1. <u>The Septuagint was not limited to the Hebrew Bible and the Deuterocanon.</u>

Contrary to popular belief, the Septuagint was <u>not</u> limited to *only* those writings found in Catholic Old Testaments (i.e.: the Hebrew Bible and the Deuterocanon). There was more than one "version" of the Septuagint in the church age, which contained writings such as: *3 Maccabees, 4 Maccabees, 1 Esdras* (sometimes referred to as *3 Esdras*), *Odes* (including the *Prayer of Manasseh*), the *Psalms of Solomon*, and *Psalm 151*.[47] McDonald cites E. J. Epp (*"The Oxyrhynchus New Testament Papyri"*), "Epp further notes (18-20) the discovery at Oxyrhynchus of one Old Latin

---

[45] Ibid. (Begins around the 3:40 mark.) Brackets inserted by me for clarity.

[46] Ibid. (Begins around the 2:14 mark.) Brackets inserted by me for clarity.

[47] Bible Research: Internet Resources for Students of Scripture. *The Old Testament Canon and Apocrypha.* Accessed from the Internet http://www.bible-researcher.com/canon2.html

and twenty-three Greek manuscripts of the LXX that included portions of Wisdom of Solomon, Tobit, *Apocalypse of Baruch* [i.e.: *2 Baruch*], and *1 Enoch*."[48] Later, McDonald lists in Appendix D of his book (*"The Biblical Canon"*) where *2 Baruch* and *1 Enoch* (and several other Apocryphal literature) are even cited and/or alluded to several times in the New Testament.[49]

None of these Apocryphal writings are found in either Catholic or Protestant Old Testaments, despite them being in some early versions of the Septuagint. According to the Ethiopian Orthodox Tewahedo Church, their Old Testament also includes additional writings, such as *4 Esdras* and the book of *Jubilees*, as well as *1 Enoch* which "The Ethiopic version of the Old and New Testament was *made from the Septuagint*"[50] (emphasis added). It also includes the other non-Catholic writings from the Septuagint listed above (*3 and 4 Maccabees, 2 Baruch*, etc.), as well as those in the Hebrew Bible and the Deuterocanon.

Catholic author, Gary Michuta, admits "The Septuagint never actually stopped. It was a liturgical text, and so more and more books were added to the Septuagint. So, the Septuagint today is much bigger than before."[51] Although Mr. Michuta attempts to justify the inclusion of the Deuterocanon in the Old Testament because "the New Testament uses these books as Scripture and they use the Septuagint,"[52] the same could be said about Apocryphal literature which was *also* used in the Septuagint and quoted in the New Testament. Mr. Michuta acknowledges:

> "...the same thing's true with the [Eastern] Orthodox, *they used the Septuagint*, that Greek translation, and *that became their Bible* that's read in the liturgy. So, they include books written after the first century."[53] (emphasis added)

---

[48] Ibid. McDonald, p.356, footnote #9. McDonald's citation from Epp, E. J. "The Oxyrhynchus New Testament Papyri: 'Not without Honor Except in Their Hometown?" *Journal of Biblical Literature* 123 (2004): 5-55. Words in brackets added by me for clarification.

[49] Ibid, McDonald, Appendix D: New Testament Citations of and Allusions to Apocryphal and Pseudepigraphical Writings, pp.452-464.

[50] *Ethiopian Orthodox Tewahedo Church Faith and Order: The Bible.* Accessed from the Internet http://www.ethiopianorthodox.org/english/canonical/books.html

[51] Michuta, Gary. *Gary Michuta & Fr. Hugh Barbour - Catholic Answers Live - 10/23/17.* "Catholic Answers." Published on YouTube, October 23, 2017. Accessed from the Internet https://www.youtube.com/watch?v=7YlzLYjvxto (Begins around the 30:12 mark.)

[52] Ibid (Begins around 30:32 mark.)

[53] Michuta, Gary. *Why Catholic Bibles Are Bigger.* October 08, 2018 – 7pm (Radio). Catholic Answers Live. Accessed from the Internet https://www.catholic.com/audio/cal/8747 (Begins around the 48:41 mark.) Brackets inserted by me for clarity.

The New Testament never actually "uses these books [i.e.: the Deuterocanon] as *Scripture*" (see Appendix A). So why does the Catholic Old Testament only base its canon on "part" of the Septuagint, but not all of it? Why are some of these writings from the Septuagint "missing" from their canon?

The answer is based – at least in part – on the belief the New Testament only quotes from certain books from the Septuagint, like those from the Hebrew Bible and the Deuterocanon, but not others. For example, Jimmy Akin, who was mentioned in Chapter One, gives a list of self-admitted "proposed references" of Deuterocanonical verses from the New Testament.[54]

However, Mr. Akin acknowledges "giving a list is not such a simple affair since it is not always obvious whether something is a genuine reference."[55] Is a certain New Testament verse a genuine reference to a Deuterocanonical writing, or is it a quote or reference to an *earlier* writing from the Hebrew Bible which the *later* Deuterocanonical writing is simply alluding to?

In his very first reference, Mr. Akin lists Matthew 4:4 where Jesus is in the wilderness for forty days, and He responds to Satan who is tempting Him by quoting the Old Testament: "But He answered and said, 'It is written, "MAN SHALL NOT LIVE ON BREAD ALONE, BUT ON EVERY WORD THAT PROCEEDS OUT OF THE MOUTH OF GOD."'" In Mr. Akin's list, he attempts to link Jesus' words from Matthew 4:4 to Wisdom 16:26[56], which states: "...it is not the various kinds of fruits that nourish a man, but it is your word that preserves those who believe you" (NAB). Is Jesus referencing *that* verse from Wisdom, or is He quoting an *earlier* verse from the Hebrew Bible?

In Deuteronomy 8:3, Moses wrote: "man does not live by bread alone, but man lives by everything that proceeds out of the mouth of the LORD." Jesus is clearly quoting from the *earlier* Deuteronomy passage from "the Law," rather than from the *much later* Wisdom passage. In the Catholic New American Bible (NAB), Matthew 4:4 *references*

---

[54] Akin, James. Jimmyakin.com. *Deuterocanonical References in the New Testament.* Accessed from the Internet http://jimmyakin.com/deuterocanonical-references-in-the-new-testament

[55] Ibid.

[56] Ibid.

Deuteronomy 8:3 – not Wisdom 16:26.[57] Wisdom 16:26 *itself* references the earlier Deuteronomy passage as the original source![58]

We even see this in the New Testament references from the Hebrew Bible. In Matthew 2:6 the chief priests and scribes gather before King Herod to explain from the Old Testament where the Messiah is to be born: "FOR OUT OF YOU SHALL COME FORTH A RULER WHO WILL SHEPHERD MY PEOPLE ISRAEL." Is this from the earlier Old Testament passage from 2 Samuel 5:2 ("And the LORD said to you, 'You will shepherd My people Israel, and you will be a ruler over Israel'") or from the later Old Testament passage from 1 Chronicles 11:2 ("You shall shepherd My people Israel, and you shall be prince [ruler] over My people Israel")? Both passages are from the Inspired Hebrew Bible, but the New Testament quote is actually referencing the *earlier* passage from 2 Samuel 5:2, not 1 Chronicles 11:2. In fact, 1 Chronicles 11:2 quotes 2 Samuel 5:2. (I will cover in a later chapter more specifically why 1 Chronicles is God-breathed Scripture, while Wisdom is not.)

In his book, "Why Catholic Bibles are Bigger," Michuta also attempts to cross-reference New Testament writings to the Deuterocanonical books in the Septuagint. For example, he attempts to link Matthew 27:43 to Wisdom 2:17-18, but he admits the *earlier* writing from Psalm 22:8-9 in the Hebrew Bible is *a direct quote of Matthew 27:43!*[59] The New American Bible also references Psalm 22:9 as the *earlier* source for Matthew 27:43.[60]

Mr. Michuta also attempts to cross-reference 2 Corinthians 9:7 to Sirach 35:8. However, he admits once again this New Testament reference is from an *earlier* verse found in the Hebrew Bible: "The Septuagint version of *Proverbs 22:8a* and Sirach 35:8 (KJV 35:9) *echoes Paul's thoughts in 2 Corinthians 9:7*"[61] (emphasis added), as does the New American Bible. Even though this Old Testament "echo" is from the book of Proverbs in the Septuagint, its *earliest* reference is from a book from the boundaries of the Hebrew Bible, not from the *much later* Deuterocanonical book of Sirach. Furthermore, the Hebrew Bible verse Paul "actually" quotes – just two verses later – is a direct quote from Psalm 112:9:

---

[57] Ibid. New American Bible, footnote and cross-reference section for Matthew 4:4, p.15.

[58] Ibid. p.767 cross-reference section for Wisdom 16:26.

[59] Michuta, Gary G. *Why Catholic Bibles are Bigger: the untold story of the lost books of the Protestant Bible.*, Chapter One *"A Closed Pre-Christian Canon?"* Published by the Grotto Press: Port Huron, Michigan, 2007.

[60] Ibid. New American Bible, footnote for Matthew 27:43, p.64.

[61] Ibid. Michuta. *Why Catholic Bibles are Bigger.*

"as it is written, 'HE SCATTERED ABROAD, HE GAVE TO THE POOR, HIS RIGHTEOUSNESS ENDURES FOREVER.'" (2 Corinthians 9:9)

"He has given freely to the poor, His righteousness endures forever." (Psalm 112:9)

Even when a passage from the New Testament appears to be referencing or alluding to a passage from the Old Testament era, we have to discern what is the *original* source it is actually referencing. We also have to be careful about discerning if a particular passage is an actual reference or not. Even Mr. Akin admits to this stating, "How many New Testament references there are to the Old Testament depends in large measure on what you are going to count as a reference."[62]

Even though a particular writing *may* be a bona fide Inspired Old Testament Scripture, we must not automatically assume it is, simply because the New Testament "appears" to be alluding to the Septuagint. As mentioned earlier, the New Testament quotes *1 Enoch* (Jude v.14) which was in early versions of the Septuagint. However, *1 Enoch* is not an Inspired Old Testament writing, despite being in the Septuagint and Jude quoting from it.

Another point to consider: if a book from the Septuagint is *not* quoted, or even alluded to, in the New Testament, does that mean it is not Inspired?

Should the book of Esther "not" be included in the Old Testament, since the New Testament never even alludes to it? In his enormous list of (alleged) references, Mr. Akin does not list any supposed allusions from the New Testament to the Septuagint's Deuterocanonical "additions" to Esther either.[63]

Should one conclude the "additions" to Esther are not God-breathed Scripture and *also* does not belong in the Old Testament, despite the "additions" to Esther being in the Septuagint? The Song of Solomon, Obadiah, and possibly Nahum would have to be removed from the Old Testament too, since these writings from the Septuagint are neither quoted, nor alluded to, in the New Testament.

If the Deuterocanonical books alluded to in the New Testament are validation for being included in the Old Testament, would that mean any other writings the New Testament quotes from or alludes to would have to be included in the Old Testament as well? If so, we would have to include the Greek poet Epimenides, since Paul quotes him (Acts 17:28; Titus

---

[62] Ibid. Akin. Jimmyakin.com.
[63] Ibid.

1:12), as well as the entire play "Thais" by Menander (1 Corinthians 15:33). While a particular *quote or allusion* in the New Testament may be Inspired, that does not necessarily equate with the *entire writing* it came from as being Inspired and belonging in Scripture.

Given Jesus, His disciples, and even the apostle Paul "used" the Septuagint, and because they referenced and even quoted from the Septuagint, does that not make it authoritative since it is *"the"* Greek translation of the Old Testament?

2. The Septuagint was not the only Greek translation used in the early church.

Another common misconception is the Septuagint was the only authoritative Greek translation of the Old Testament in Judaism and the early church. It would be similar to a Protestant today who only uses the King James Version of the Bible, i.e.: the "Authorized Version". This assumption overlooks the historical background from antiquity of "why" the Septuagint was created.

At the close of the Hebrew Bible with the book of Nehemiah (around 400 B.C.), the Jewish people had been ruled by the Medo-Persian Empire (Ezra 9:9). During what Protestants refer to as the "Intertestamental Period" (around 400 B.C. to the New Testament), the Medo-Persians were conquered by Greece under the rule of Alexander the Great. After his death (323 B.C.), the Greek culture not only had a profound effect on Israel's culture, but also their language. This "Hellenization" of the Greek culture and language was so penetrating it continued to flourish in Israel, even after Rome conquered the Greek Empire. Hellenism is clearly seen in the infancy of the early church in the first century in the New Testament (Acts 6:1; 9:29).

During this time, many Jews lost the ability to speak their native Hebrew tongue due to this Greek cultural influence. As a result, there was a need for the Old Testament Scriptures to be translated into the Greek language, which even Jews were speaking. This began with the translation of "the Law," and it eventually led to the rest of the Old Testament Scriptures. This is why the New Testament was written in Greek. The translation of the Old Testament into Greek was based strictly on a need for the Jewish people to comprehend their Scriptures in the fairly new Greek language they were speaking, rather than the ancient Hebrew they no longer understood.

Over time, the Septuagint was not limited to the Greek translation of Old Testament, but also a translation of uninspired writings, such as those mentioned earlier like *1 Enoch*, *3 Maccabees*, *4 Maccabees*, *Psalm 151*, etc. as well as the so-called Deuterocanonical books. Despite these uninspired writings being included in the Septuagint, it was used throughout Israel, just as the King James Version was used in England centuries later, which also included the uninspired Deuterocanonical books. The assumption the Jews and later Christians used the Septuagint as a sort of "Septuagint-only" Old Testament canon cannot be proved either Scripturally nor historically.

Enter Origen of Alexandria.

ORIGEN OF ALEXANDRIA

The early Christian theologian and Greek scholar, Origen of Alexandria (c. A.D. 186 to 254) produced a body of work referred to as the *Hexapla* (Greek: "sixfold"). Eusebius states in his "Church History" (translation and commentary by Paul L. Maier):

> "He [Origen] also sought out *other translations of the sacred writings besides the Septuagint*, and in addition to the common versions – those of Aquila, Symmachus, and Theodotion – *he discovered others* that had been long lost and brought to light."[64] (emphasis added)

In the footnotes, Maier explains the *Hexapla* was "So named because it was arranged in six columns in the following order: Hebrew, a Greek transliteration of the Hebrew, as well as the versions of Aquilla, Symmachus, the Septuagint, and Theodotion."[65] Eusebius goes on to say: "All these he included in one volume, placing them in adjacent parallel columns next to the Hebrew text, producing the *Hexapla* as it is called."[66]

Contrary to popular belief, the Vulgate did not use the Septuagint as its sole source for its Greek-to-Latin translation, but rather other Greek translations as well, including Aquila and others. Jerome's "extensive use of the Aquiline and Theodotiontic texts of the Hexapla"[67] were fundamental for his work on the Vulgate (the Latin translation of the Catholic Bible). Jerome "translated...from the Greek, the additions to Esther from the Septuagint, and the additions to Daniel from Theodotion."[68] Symmachus' "version of the Old Testament was largely used by Jerome."[69] "[Aquila's] was followed extensively by Jerome in his

---

[64] Ibid. Maier. *Eusebius: The Church History*. Book 6.16, p.200. Brackets inserted by me for clarity.

[65] Ibid. Footnote, #9.

[66] Ibid.

[67] The Latin Vulgate Bible. *Vulgate: The Holy Bible In Latin Language With Douay-Rheims English Translation*. Accessed from the Internet www.Vulgate.org

[68] Ibid.

[69] NewAdvent.org. *Symmachus the Ebionite*. Accessed from the Internet http://www.newadvent.org/cathen/14378a.htm

own work as a translator of the Old Testament,"[70] and "Theodotion...gave a version much closer than the others."[71]

We can see from the testimonies of Origen, Eusebius, Jerome, and others the early church did not use the Septuagint as their "only" Greek translation or sole authority for the Old Testament.

We can even see this in the early first century church from the Inspired Greek New Testament. Although it is admitted when the New Testament references the Old Testament, it overwhelmingly alludes to or quotes from the Septuagint. Jimmy Akin speculates "by some reckonings as many as eighty-or-so percent" the New Testament references the Septuagint over a different Greek translation.[72] (Elsewhere, Mr. Akin wrote it is really closer to "Two thirds of the Old Testament quotations in the New are from the Septuagint."[73])

Of course, this would lead to an obvious question: "Why *only* eighty percent, or even two-thirds? Why not one-hundred percent if Jesus and the first century church viewed the Septuagint as being authoritative and *'the'* complete Greek translation of the Old Testament?"

Enter the apostle John.

THE APOSTLE JOHN AND THE SEPTUAGINT

In John's gospel and Revelation, when he quotes the prophet Zechariah from the Old Testament, he *does not* use the Septuagint, but rather his own Greek translation. When John translates it in both of these New Testament writings, he translates it the *same way in both texts*, but *both differently from the Septuagint*. For example, take a look at John's translation of Zechariah 12:10 in both texts and compare them to the Septuagint:

(Septuagint): "they will look on Me whom they have **pierced**"

καὶ ἐπιβλέψονται πρός με ἀνθ' ὧν **κατωρχήσαντο**[74]

---

[70] NewAdvent.org. *Hexapla*. Accessed from the Internet http://www.newadvent.org/cathen/07316a.htm. Brackets inserted by me for clarity.

[71] Ibid.

[72] Ibid. Akin. "Catholic Answers." YouTube.com. *How did the Old Testament canon develop?*

[73] Akin, James. *Defending the Deuterocanonicals, The Apostles & the Deuteros.* Accessed from the Internet http://www.ewtn.com/library/answers/deuteros.htm

[74] Blue Letter Bible. "The Minor Prophet Zechariah 12 - (NASB - New American Standard Bible)." Blue Letter Bible. 1996-2017. 12 Dec 2017. Accessed from the Internet <http://www.blbclassic.org/Bible.cfm?b=Zec&c=12&t=NASB >

(John 19:37): "THEY SHALL LOOK ON HIM WHOM THEY PIERCED."

καὶ πάλιν ἑτέρα γραφὴ λέγει ὄψονται εἰς ὃν **ἐξεκέντησαν**[75]

(Revelation 1:7): "and every eye will see Him, even those who **pierced** Him"

καὶ ὄψεται αὐτὸν πᾶς ὀφθαλμὸς καὶ οἵτινες αὐτὸν **ἐξεκέντησαν**[76]

Notice, the apostle John chooses the same Greek word translated "pierced" ("**ἐξεκέντησαν**") in both his gospel and Revelation, from the Greek root verb ("*ekkenteō*"), which means "to dig out" or "to dig through; to pierce." The base of this verb comes from the neuter noun ("*kentron*"), which means "a sting, as that of bees, scorpions, locusts." It is used by the apostle Paul, in passages like: "O DEATH, WHERE IS YOUR STING?" (1 Corinthians 15:55), and "The sting of death is sin" (v.56). The apostle John also uses it in Revelation 9:10 to describe the locusts which were released out of the bottomless pit: "They have tails like scorpions, and stings."

The Septuagint uses a different Greek word that means "to mock, or to insult" ("**κατωρχήσαντο**"), rather than "to pierce" ("**ἐξεκέντησαν**"). This latter meaning "to pierce" is a more accurate translation from the Hebrew language of Zechariah 12:10, as well as in John's Greek translation in his writings. Ellicott's Commentary from BibleHub.com illustrates this:

> "The Greek translation (LXX.) of the prophet avoided the strong word 'pierced,' as applied to Jehovah, and substituted for it 'insulted.' *St. John translates the original Hebrew freely for himself* (comp. Revelation 1:7), and gives the undoubted meaning of the Hebrew word, translating it *by the same Greek word, which is used by Aquila, Theodotion, and Symmachus.* He thinks of the prophecy which spoke of Jehovah as pierced by His people, and sees it fulfilled in the Messiah pierced on the cross."[77] (emphasis added)

and regarding Revelation 1:7:

[75] Blue Letter Bible. "Gospel of John 19 - (NASB - New American Standard Bible)." Blue Letter Bible. 1996-2017. 12 Dec 2017. Accessed from the Internet <http://www.blbclassic.org/Bible.cfm?b=Jhn&c=19&t=NASB >

[76] Blue Letter Bible. "Revelation of Jesus Christ 1 - (NASB - New American Standard Bible)." Blue Letter Bible. 1996-2017. 12 Dec 2017. Accessed from the Internet <http://www.blbclassic.org/Bible.cfm?b=Rev&c=1&t=NASB >

[77] Bible Hub. (John 19:37). "Ellicott's Commentary for English Readers." (37) *They shall look on him who they pierced.* Accessed from the Internet https://biblehub.com/commentaries/ellicott/john/19.htm

"Here and in John 19:37 the writer, in quoting Zechariah 12:10, *deserts the LXX.* and follows the Masoretic Hebrew text. *The LXX. softens down 'pierced' into 'insulted'* (κάτωρχήσατο), 'piercing' appearing a violent expression to use respecting men's treatment of Jehovah.... Here and in John 19:37 the writer, *in translating from the Hebrew*, uses the uncommon Greek word ἐκκεντᾷν."[78] (emphasis added)

Although John did quote from the Septuagint in his writings, he deviated from it and instead provided his own Greek translation of Zechariah 12:10, which is a more faithful translation from the Hebrew Old Testament than the Septuagint. Also, notice John's Greek word choice for "pierce" is the *exact same word* used by Aquila, Theodotion, and Symmachus, whose translations were mentioned earlier by Eusebius. As previously mentioned, they were used alongside the Septuagint in Origen's *Hexapla* translations of the Old Testament. John's word choice is in *agreement* with Aquila, Theodotion, and Symmachus, while the Septuagint's is in *disagreement* with all of them.

The significance is John's writings are Inspired since they are part of the New Testament. So, if *all* of the Septuagint was just as authoritative as John's Inspired writings (as well as the original Hebrew text), it should *agree* with his Greek translation of Zechariah 12:10.

But it does not.

Even though the New Testament quotes from and alludes to the Septuagint most of the time, it is incorrect to say the Septuagint is *"the"* authoritative Greek translation of the Old Testament, just because Jesus and the New Testament writers referenced it. It was not even the same version we have today. Theodotion's version was a "free revision of the Septuagint" including "the omissions and erroneous renderings of which it corrected"[79]:

"[Theodotion's version] also showed parts *not appearing in the original*, as the deuterocanonical fragments of Daniel, the postscript of Job, the Book of Baruch, but not the Book of Esther. It was not approved by the Jews but was favourably received by the Christians. Origin [sic] gave it a place in his 'Hexapla' and

---

[78] Bible Hub. (Revelation 1:7). "Pulpit Commentary," Verses 7,8 (points #2 and #3). Accessed from the Internet https://biblehub.com/commentaries/pulpit/revelation/1.htm

[79] NewAdvent.org. *Versions of the Bible: Greek: Version of Theodotion.* Accessed from the Internet http://www.newadvent.org/cathen/15367a.htm#greek

from it *supplied parts missing in the Septuagint.*"[80] (emphasis added).

This demonstrates the version of the Septuagint Jesus and the apostles used was <u>not</u> the same as the version Theodotion "corrected," which mirrored the apostle John's earlier "correction" from the Septuagint of Zechariah's prophecy. Like John before him, Theodotion realized the Septuagint was not the *"sole"* authority of Jesus and the apostles for their understanding of the Old Testament.

Enter the apostle Matthew.

THE APOSTLE MATTHEW AND THE SEPTUAGINT

According to Eusebius, *"Matthew* at first preached to Hebrews, and when he planned to go to others also, he *wrote his Gospel in his own native language"*[81] (emphasis added). Centuries earlier, Papias, an alleged disciple of the apostle John, affirmed "Matthew compiled the sayings [*logia* of Christ] in the Hebrew language."[82] This means when Matthew wrote his original Inspired gospel in "his own native Hebrew language," obviously he would not have used the Septuagint when he quoted from the Old Testament, which was written in *Greek.*

It would not be until later when Matthew or a scribe would translate his Inspired writing into Greek.[83] Even when Matthew's gospel was translated into Greek, it did not always follow the Septuagint. Compare Matthew 2:15 to Hosea 11:1 from the Septuagint:

(<u>Septuagint</u>): "And out of Egypt I called <u>My</u> <u>son</u>."

εξ αιγυπτου μετεκαλεσα <u>τα</u> <u>τεκνα</u> <u>αυτου</u>[84]

(<u>Matthew 2:15</u>): "OUT OF EGYPT I CALLED <u>MY</u> <u>SON</u>."

---

[80] Ibid. Brackets inserted by me for clarity.

[81] Ibid, Maier. *Eusebius: The Church History.* Book 3:24, p.99.

[82] Ibid, Book 3:39, p.114. Maier's footnote assumes "Probably Aramaic is intended, just as in the New Testament." Brackets and italics in the original text.

[83] It is the position of BookMark Press that it was Matthew who gave us his Gospel in Greek, not a scribe. If it were a scribe, the Greek original would not be inspired. Scribes and copyists were not inspired while carrying out their work.

[84] Blue Letter Bible. "The Minor Prophet Hosea 11 - (NASB - New American Standard Bible)." Blue Letter Bible. 1996-2019. 12 Feb 2019. Accessed from the Internet <http://www.blbclassic.org/Bible.cfm?b=Hos&c=11&t=NASB >

εξ αιγυπτου εκαλεσα **τον υιον μου**[85]

Although the English translations appear identical, like the apostle John, Matthew deviated from the Septuagint. Matthew chose the Greek words ("**τον υιον μου**"), which literally translates "My son" and is a more accurate translation from the Hebrew. In contrast, the Septuagint used the Greek words ("**τα τεκνα αυτου**"), which better translates "his children." Ellicott's Commentary on Matthew 2:15 from BibleHub.com confirms:

> "…the words 'Out of Egypt did I call my Son' (he translated from the Hebrew instead of reproducing the Greek version of the LXX.)"[86]

While Matthew did quote from the Septuagint in his gospel, like the apostle John he did not do so consistently. Since Matthew originally wrote his gospel in Hebrew, once it was translated into Greek it needed to be a faithful rendition of the Hebrew when it quoted the Old Testament. Where Matthew departed from the Septuagint, the latter was not as precise of a translation from the original Old Testament text. Like John, Matthew did not consider the Septuagint to be as authoritative as the original Old Testament languages, otherwise Matthew would have quoted from it consistently instead of using his own Greek adaptation.

Like John, he did not.

THE PHARISEES AND THE SEPTUAGINT

As Jimmy Akin mentioned in Chapter One, the Pharisees only acknowledged the same books which are in Protestant Old Testaments today. Whenever the Pharisees tested Jesus from the Septuagint, they *only* challenged Him from writings from the boundaries of the Hebrew Bible, which Jesus responded from these *same* boundaries:

> "They [the Pharisees] said, 'Moses permitted a man TO WRITE A CERTIFICATE OF DIVORCE AND SEND her AWAY. But Jesus said to them, 'Because of your hardness of heart he wrote you this commandment. But from the beginning of creation, God MADE THEM MALE AND FEMALE. FOR THIS REASON A MAN SHALL LEAVE HIS FATHER AND MOTHER, AND THE TWO SHALL BECOME ONE FLESH; so they are no

---

[85] Blue Letter Bible. "Gospel of Matthew 2 - (NASB - New American Standard Bible)." Blue Letter Bible. 1996-2019. 12 Feb 2019. Accessed from the Internet <http://www.blbclassic.org/Bible.cfm?b=Mat&c=2&t=NASB >

[86] Bible Hub. (Matthew 2:15). "Ellicott's Commentary for English Readers." (15) *Out of Egypt have I called my son*. Accessed from the Internet https://biblehub.com/commentaries/ellicott/matthew/2.htm. Parentheses in original text.

longer two, but one flesh. What therefore God has joined together, let no man separate." (Mark 10:4-9)

The Pharisees were quoting from Deuteronomy 24:1 from the Septuagint:

(Septuagint): "he writes her a certificate of divorce"

γράψει αὐτῇ **βιβλίον ἀποστασίου** [87]

(Mark 10:4): "TO WRITE A CERTIFICATE OF DIVORCE"

βιβλίον ἀποστασίου γράψαι[88]

Jesus' response to the Pharisees from the Septuagint came from Genesis 1:27 and Genesis 2:24:

(Septuagint): "male and female He created them"

ἄρσεν καὶ θῆλυ ἐποίησεν αὐτούς[89]

(Mark 10:6): "MADE THEM MALE AND FEMALE"

ἄρσεν καὶ θῆλυ ἐποίησεν αὐτούς[90]

(Septuagint): "For this reason a man shall leave his father and his mother, and be joined to his wife; and they shall become one flesh."

ἕνεκεν τούτου καταλείψει ἄνθρωπος τὸν πατέρα αὐτοῦ καὶ τὴν μητέρα αὐτοῦ καὶ προσκολληθήσεται πρὸς τὴν γυναῖκα αὐτοῦ καὶ ἔσονται οἱ δύο εἰς σάρκα μίαν[91]

(Mark 10:7): "FOR THIS REASON A MAN SHALL LEAVE HIS FATHER AND MOTHER"

---

[87] Blue Letter Bible. "Book of Deuteronomy 24 - (NASB - New American Standard Bible)." Blue Letter Bible. 1996-2019. 22 Apr 2019. Accessed from the Internet < http://www.blbclassic.org/Bible.cfm?b=Deu&c=24&t=NASB >

[88] Blue Letter Bible. "Gospel of Mark 10 - (NASB - New American Standard Bible)." Blue Letter Bible. 1996-2019. 22 Apr 2019. Accessed from the Internet < http://www.blbclassic.org/Bible.cfm?b=Mar&c=10&t=NASB >

[89] Blue Letter Bible. "Book of Beginnings - Genesis 1 - (NASB - New American Standard Bible)." Blue Letter Bible. 1996-2019. 22 Apr 2019. Accessed from the Internet < http://www.blbclassic.org/Bible.cfm?b=Gen&c=1&t=NASB >

[90] Ibid. Blue Letter Bible. "Gospel of Mark 10 - (NASB - New American Standard Bible)."

[91] Blue Letter Bible. "Book of Beginnings - Genesis 2 - (NASB - New American Standard Bible)." Blue Letter Bible. 1996-2019. 22 Apr 2019. Accessed from the Internet < http://www.blbclassic.org/Bible.cfm?b=Gen&c=2&t=NASB >

ἕνεκεν τούτου καταλείψει ἄνθρωπος τὸν πατέρα αὐτοῦ καὶ τὴν μητέρα καὶ προσκολληθήσεται πρὸς τὴν γυναῖκα αὐτοῦ[92]

(Mark 10:8): "AND THE TWO SHALL BECOME ONE FLESH"

καὶ ἔσονται οἱ δύο εἰς σάρκα μίαν[93]

Both the Pharisees and Jesus quoted from "the Law" from the same version of the Septuagint. Since the Pharisees espoused to the boundaries of the Hebrew Bible, the version of the Septuagint they would have used would not have included the Deuterocanon. Jesus responded to the Pharisees using this same version. This means the version of the Septuagint, which Jesus espoused to, also *excluded* the Deuterocanon.

As Trent Horn stated earlier, the Septuagint "that Jesus and the apostles used [was] the Hebrew Bible for the Old Testament [which was] translated into Greek,"[94] and as Gary Michuta revealed "more and more books were added to the Septuagint. So, the Septuagint today is much bigger than before."[95] This means the version of the Septuagint used by the Pharisees and Jesus was not the same version used in the later church. Later versions of the Septuagint had "more and more books" which were added to it.

In Matthew's version of Jesus' encounter with the Pharisees, Jesus asked them, "Have you not read that He who created them from the beginning MADE THEM MALE AND FEMALE?" (Matthew 19:4). "Have you not read" is a metonym to describe a passage from the Old Testament. Jesus was indicating the Pharisees would have "read" from the version of the Septuagint that *excluded* the Deuterocanon, which was the same version Jesus and His disciples "read" from.

The Septuagint was simply used as a good translation of the Hebrew Bible, and then later the Deuterocanon and other Apocryphal writings. However, it does not support the validation that "all" of its writings are Inspired. Instead, only the specific *verses* referenced from the Septuagint are Inspired whenever the New Testament merely quotes from them, just as when Jude directly quotes from the book of *1 Enoch* (Jude v.14), even though the *book itself* is not Inspired.

---

[92] Blue Letter Bible. "Gospel of Mark 10 - (NASB - New American Standard Bible)." Blue Letter Bible. 1996-2019. 22 Apr 2019. Accessed from the Internet < http://www.blbclassic.org/Bible.cfm?b=Mar&c=10&t=NASB >

[93] Ibid.

[94] Ibid. Horn, Trent. *Why Catholic Bibles Are Bigger.* August 16, 2018. Counsel of Trent. Catholic.com. (Audio podcast – Begins around the 7:36 mark.) Brackets inserted by me for clarity.

[95] Ibid. Michuta, Gary. *Gary Michuta & Fr. Hugh Barbour - Catholic Answers Live - 10/23/17.* "Catholic Answers." YouTube. (Begins around the 30:12 mark.)

Since the *original* autographs of the Hebrew Bible no longer exist, it is inaccurate to say the Septuagint is a "better" Greek translation from the original Hebrew. For all we know, where the Septuagint and the Greek New Testament disagree, it *may* be because the Greek New Testament is a more direct translation from the Hebrew Bible than the Septuagint. This would have to be true, since the Inspired New Testament was originally penned in Greek, while the Inspired Old Testament was originally written in Hebrew and Aramaic. Where the Septuagint disagrees with both the New Testament and the later Masoretic Text (a later Hebrew version of the Old Testament), it is more likely the Septuagint did not translate from the original Hebrew as accurately.

THE DEAD SEA SCROLLS

On the Catholic.com online *Magazine*, Cale Clarke wrote: "Sometime in either late 1946 or early 1947, a Bedouin shepherd accidentally discovered a cave containing ancient manuscripts in the desert region near the shores of the Dead Sea."[96] They were "generally composed between the third century B.C. and first century A.D."[97] Clark continued: "In total, eleven caves were found in the region (with a twelfth and possibly a thirteenth discovered in 2017), containing copies of many biblical books, along with other religious writings and communal documents belonging to the Jewish sect that compiled them. In all likelihood, this group was the Essenes."[98]

Matthew Bunson from EWTN.com (the Global Catholic Network), revealed they were "mostly Hebrew, manuscripts,"[99] which "Virtually all of the books of the Canonical OT [Old Testament] are found in the collection, as well as various apocryphal and Pseudoepigraphical books."[100] Included in these manuscripts found at the Dead Sea were "Fragments of two deuterocanonical works: ...Tobit and Sirach."[101] McDonald also

---

[96] Clark, Cale. "The Ever-Deepening Mystery of the Dead Sea Scrolls." February 08, 2018. Accessed from the Internet https://www.catholic.com/magazine/online-edition/the-ever-deepening-mystery-of-the-dead-sea-scrolls

[97] Ibid.

[98] Ibid.

[99] EWTN.com. *Catholic Q & A. Dead Sea scrolls.* Question from Anna Marie M. on 6/14/2004: Answer by Matthew Bunson on 6/18/2004. Accessed from the Internet http://www.ewtn.com/v/experts/showmessage.asp?number=403554&Pg=&Pgnu=&recnu=

[100] Ibid. Brackets inserted by me for clarity.

[101] EWTN.com. *Catholic Q & A. The Dead Sea Scrolls - Books missing from Protestant Bible.* Question from Ed Gross on 10-28-2002: Answer by Fr. John Echert on 10-28-2002. Accessed from the Internet http://www.ewtn.com/v/experts/showresult.asp?RecNum=307567&Forums=0&Experts=0&Days=2002&Author=&Keyword=&pgnu=5&groupnum=297&record_bookmark=74457

mentions "a Greek version of the Epistle of Jeremiah."[102] Bunson added "other non-biblical works were also discovered at Qumran."[103]

Comprising the "non-biblical works" discovered were the "Melchizedek Scroll,"[104] the "Copper Scroll,"[105] the "War Scroll," the "Hymn Scroll," and the "Temple Scroll" among "Some 650 nonbiblical scrolls or manuscripts...discovered at Qumran and elsewhere in the Judean desert."[106] McDonald cites Yadin who "argues convincingly that the *Temple Scroll* was venerated as the Essene Torah and held to be equal in importance to the traditional Torah."[107] They also included writings such as *1 Enoch*, the book of *Jubilees*, and *4 Enoch*[108] which are all included in the canon of the Ethiopian Orthodox Tewahedo Old Testament.[109]

McDonald states, "4QMMT, a fragmented text (4Q394-99) discovered among the Dead Sea Scrolls at Qumran...dated by some scholars as early as 150 B.C.E....is frequently cited as evidence for a three-tiered biblical canon in the century before Jesus...'the book of Moses, the books[s of the Pr]ophets, and Davi[d...]'."[110] (For Scriptural and historical evidence for a three-tiered Biblical canon see Chapter Seven.)

McDonald further comments: "All of the OT [Old Testament] books, except perhaps Esther and Nehemiah, have been found at Qumran.... While no part of the biblical book of Esther has been found to date at Qumran, several fragments of a loosely parallel work called proto-Esther were discovered and should cause some hesitation in concluding that the

---

[102] EWTN.com. *Catholic Q & A. The Dead Sea Scrolls - Books missing from Protestant Bible*. Question from Ed Gross on 10-28-2002: Answer by Fr. John Echert on 10-28-2002. Accessed from the Internet
http://www.ewtn.com/v/experts/showresult.asp?RecNum=307567&Forums=0&Experts=0&Days=2002&Author=&Keyword=&pgnu=5&groupnum=297&record_bookmark=74457

[103] Ibid. EWTN.com. *Catholic Q & A. The Dead Sea Scrolls - Books missing from Protestant Bible*

[104] Ibid. Clark. "The Ever-Deepening Mystery of the Dead Sea Scrolls."

[105] Most, Fr. William. "DEAD SEA SCROLLS: THREAT TO CHRISTIANITY?" Accessed from the Internet https://www.ewtn.com/library/SCRIPTUR/DEADSEA.HTM

[106] Ibid. McDonald. *The Biblical Canon*, p.128-130.

[107] Ibid, p. 134 cites Yadin, Y. "The Temple Scroll, the Longest and Most Recently Discovered Dead Sea Scroll," Pages 161-77 in vol. 2 of *Archaeology and the Bible: The Best of BAR: Archaeology in the World of Herod, Jesus, and Paul*. Edited by H. Shanks and D. P. Cole. Washington, D.C.: Biblical Archaeology Society, 1990; and idem, *The Temple Scroll*. 3 vols. Jerusalem: Israel Exploration Society, 1983.

[108] Ibid, p.133.

[109] Ibid. *Ethiopian Orthodox Tewahedo Church Faith and Order: The Bible*.

[110] Ibid. McDonald. *The Biblical Canon*, p.90. Brackets included in the original text.

Qumran community did not know Esther."[111] Since the books of Ezra and Nehemiah were originally one book (see Appendix A), the Essene community did espouse to all of the books from the Hebrew Bible. Even though they accepted *some* of the so-called Deuterocanonal, Apocryphal, and other uninspired writings, they did not include others.

Despite the discovery of Tobit, Sirach, and the epistle of Jeremiah among the Dead Sea Scrolls, none of these other writings (including the highly venerated *Temple Scroll*) are included in the Catholic, Protestant, or Eastern Orthodox Old Testaments.   Although *only three* so-called Deuterocanonical writings were discovered among of the Dead Sea Scrolls, this does not justify including them into the Christian Old Testament – otherwise, ALL of the Dead Sea Scrolls would have to be included as well.

What about the Vulgate?   Was not the Vulgate a direct Latin translation of the Septuagint, which contained the exact same writings – including the Deuterocanon?   As mentioned earlier, it was actually the Greek translation of the Old Testament of Theodotion and others – which *differed* from the Septuagint – that Jerome used to compile the Vulgate, along with the Septuagint and the rest of the *Hexapla*.[112] As I will demonstrate in the next chapter, just as there were different versions of the Septuagint in the early church with different books, likewise there were also different versions of the Vulgate with different books as well.

---

[111] Ibid, p.128, and footnote #32. McDonald asserts "this is not the same thing as saying that the canon of Qumran is equal to the biblical canon of later Judaism or the Protestant OT [Old Testament] canon," p.129. Brackets inserted by me for clarity.

[112] Ibid. Vulgate.org.

CHAPTER THREE: What about the Vulgate?

"Therefore many of the Jews read this inscription, for the place where Jesus was crucified was near the city; and it was written in Hebrew, Latin and in Greek" (John 19:20)

382 was the beginning of a very historic undertaking in the church in the late fourth century A.D. Since the first century, the culture of the church had changed dramatically from Greek-speaking Jews, like Peter and Paul, to Latin-speaking Gentiles, like Augustine and Jerome. This was largely due to the impact of the Latin language and influence of the Roman Empire in Israel, which started prior to the time of Christ. This impact extended well into the church age, just as the Greek culture had influenced Israel after the death of Alexander the Great. In fact, the Greek word for "Latin" (*"Rhōmaïstí"*) means "of Rome's strength."

This influence is even found in the early church in the New Testament, like when the Romans nailed the inscription on Jesus' cross "in Hebrew, Latin, and in Greek" (John 19:20), for different ethnic groups to read. Mark used some common terms in his gospel from the Latin origin, rather than their Greek equivalents (i.e.: "Legion" – Mark 5:9; "executioner" – 6:27; "denarius" – 12:15; "two mites" and "quadrans" – 12:42 [NKJV]; "Praetorium" and "garrison" – 15:16 [NKJV]; "centurion" – 15:39).[113]

In the first few centuries of the church, its language shifted from Greek to Latin. This resulted in a need for the Bible to be translated into the "common" language of the church, just as the Jews had previously needed to have the Word of God in their "common" language prior to, and contemporary with, the time of Christ. The Latin-speaking Gentiles needed a "common" Latin-based Bible to read and understand.

Our Lord has always had a desire for His children to understand His Word in the "common" language of His people. First, with Hebrew and Aramaic, and then with Greek and Latin, as well as countless others. Our Lord even promises to give a blessing to anyone who "heeds" the words in the book of Revelation, which requires the believer to be able to *"read"* it (Revelation 1:3). Centuries later, this was also the desire of the Protestant Reformers, such as Martin Luther with his German translation and William Tyndale with his English translation.

---

[113] The MacArthur Study Bible (New King James Version). *The Gospel According to Mark: Background and Setting*, p.1453. Word Publishing, a division of Thomas Nelson, Inc.: Nashville, Tennessee. All rights reserved, 1997.

Although there were Latin translations of the Bible prior to A.D. 382 – just as there would be German and English translations before Luther and Tyndale – there was a need to develop a more accurate Latin translation for the Latin-speaking church. The church's desire in the late fourth century was for the average person to be able to hear and read the Word of God for themselves, by making it available to them in their own language so they could understand the gospel of Jesus Christ more clearly.

Enter Jerome.

JEROME AND THE VULGATE

Jerome, another Doctor of the Church[114], is attributed for being commissioned by Pope Damasus I to translate the Bible into Latin. His Latin translation came to be known as the "Vulgate." EWTN.com indicates "The word 'vulgate' signifies that this was the *common language* of the people of the time. This version served as the official text of the Bible for the Church from its inception until the twentieth century"[115] (emphasis added).

Jerome translated the Bible into the "common" ("vulgar") language of the Latin-speaking church. More specifically, it is generally believed by many that he *directly* translated the Septuagint into the Vulgate. However, Jerome was neither the sole translator of the Vulgate, nor was the Septuagint the only Greek version he used in his translation.

As mentioned in Chapter Two, Jerome used the Greek translation of the Old Testament of Theodotion and others, as well as the Septuagint, to compile the Vulgate. According to EWTN.com "between 386 and 391 a second revision of the Latin Psalter, this time according to the text of the *'Hexapla'* of Origen (Gallican Psalter, embodied in the Vulgate). It is doubtful whether he [Jerome] revised the entire version of the Old Testament according to the Greek of the Septuagint."[116]

Although the first part of Jerome's life, "until about 391-2, he considered the Septuagint translation as inspired. But the progress of his Hebraistic studies and his intercourse with the rabbis made him give up that idea, and he recognized as inspired the original text only. It was about this

---

114 NewAdvent.org. *Doctors of the Church*. Accessed from the Internet http://www.newadvent.org/cathen/05075a.htm

115 EWTN.com. *Catholic Q & A*. Latin Vulgate, Question from Don Howe on 4/23/2003, Answer by Fr. John Echert on 4/24/2003. Accessed from the Internet http://www.ewtn.com/v/experts/showmessage.asp?number=289736

116 EWTN.com. *St. Jerome, Doctor of the Church, Chronology*. Accessed from the Internet https://www.ewtn.com/saintsholy/saints/J/stjerome.asp. Brackets inserted by me for clarity.

period that he undertook the translation of the Old Testament from the Hebrew."[117]

Just as Jerome's desire was to translate the gospels from the Greek of the New Testament, his desire was to translate as much as he could from the Hebrew of the Old Testament. Although Jerome was able to translate the books from the Hebrew Bible, he was unable to translate the Deuterocanonical books from the Hebrew language. Furthermore, he did not translate them entirely from the Septuagint. For instance, Jerome translated Tobit and Judith from the Aramaic, and the "additions" to Daniel from Theodotion.[118]

CODEX AMIATINUS (~A.D. 700)

The Deuterocanonical "additions" to Jeremiah, which later came to be known as Baruch and the epistle of Jeremiah, remained excluded from the Vulgate for four-hundred years. The Codex Amiatinus "dates to the end of the 7th century AD; making it the oldest known surviving complete Catholic Bible written in the Latin Vulgate,"[119] which "was based on St. Jerome's Latin Vulgate version."[120] Both Catholic.com[121] and NewAdvent.org[122] describe the Codex Amiatinus as:

> "the most celebrated manuscript of the Latin Vulgate Bible, remarkable as *the best witness to the true text of St. Jerome....* The codex (or pandect) is usually said to contain the whole Bible; but it should be noted that *the Book of Baruch is missing*, though *the Epistle of Jeremias*, usually incorporated with it, is here *appended to the Book of Jeremias*." (emphasis added)

As late as *three-hundred years* after Jerome's Latin Vulgate was translated, the Deuterocanonical book of Baruch was still not in the Catholic Bible. When Pope Leo III crowned King Charlemagne Emperor of the Holy Roman Empire in A.D. 800, neither of them had the book of Baruch in their Bibles. It would not be until sometime later in the ninth

---

[117] Ibid. *St. Jerome, Characteristics of St. Jerome's Work.*

[118] Ibid. Vulgate.org.

[119] AncientOrigins.net. "Reconstructing the Story of Humanity's Past." *The Codex Amiatinus: The Skins of 500 Calves Were Used to Create this Monumental Manuscript,* 7 December 2017 – 18:53 DHWTY. Ancient Origins Copyright 2013-2018. Accessed from the Internet https://www.ancient-origins.net/artifacts-ancient-writings/codex-amiatinus-skins-500-calves-were-used-create-monumental-manuscript-021745

[120] Ibid.

[121] Catholic Answers. *Codex Amiatinus.* Accessed from the Internet https://www.catholic.com/encyclopedia/codex-amiatinus

[122] NewAdvent.org. *Codex Amiatinus.* Accessed from the Internet http://www.newadvent.org/cathen/04081a.htm

century when it was "added" to Scripture. This means the Vulgate of the Holy Roman Empire during the Reformation was not the same Vulgate of the Holy Roman Empire during the reign of Emperor Charlemagne, nor the same Vulgate of Jerome.

So, later Protestants did not actually "remove" the book of Baruch and the epistle of Jeremiah *from* the Bible since they were not in the Vulgate to begin with. Rather, it was later Catholics who "added" them *to* the Bible. This was no different than the Church of Jesus Christ of Latter-Day Saints who "added" the Book of Mormon, which was also not Inspired Scripture.

Moreover, additional writings like the *Prayer of Manasseh* have been found in other Vulgate manuscripts along with other non-deuterocanonical books, like *4 Esdras* (sometimes called *2 Esdras*)[123] and *the epistle to the Laodiceans* in Codex Dublinensis (eighth century) and Codex Fuldensis (sixth century).[124] Just as there were different early versions of the Septuagint, there were different early versions of the Vulgate – the earliest of which did not contain the exact same books found in today's Catholic Old Testaments.

JEROME AND THE DEUTEROCANON

The authority of the Hebrew Bible was present even in Jerome's day. Commenting on the canonicity of the Old Testament Scriptures, Jerome himself stated:

> "As, then, the Church reads Judith, Tobit, and the books of Maccabees, but does *not admit them among the canonical Scriptures*, so let it read these two volumes for the edification of the people, *not to give authority to doctrines of the Church*."[125] (emphasis added)

Even though Jerome did end up translating "most" of the Deuterocanonical books into his Latin Vulgate, he stated even the church in his time did not consider the Deuterocanon to be either "canonical" nor "Scriptures," nor "doctrines of the Church" were to be based on them. They were simply good for reading for "edification" – just as they would be centuries later in early Protestant translations.

---

[123] Ibid. Bible Research. *The Old Testament Canon and Apocrypha.*

[124] Ibid. McDonald. *The Biblical Canon*, p.361.

[125] Bible Study Tools, Grow deeper in the Word: *Jerome, Prefaces to the Books of the Vulgate Version of the Old Testament. Proverbs, Ecclesiastes, and the Song of Songs.* Accessed from the Internet https://www.biblestudytools.com/history/early-church-fathers/post-nicene/vol-6-jerome/jerome/prefaces-books-vulgate-version-old-testament.html

Jerome translating them and placing them in the Vulgate does not equate with them being Inspired Scripture, no more than when the later versions of the Vulgate would include non-deuterocanonical books, like *4 Esdras* and *the epistle to the Laodiceans.* EWTN.com declares Jerome "never either categorically acknowledged or rejected the deuterocanonical books as part of the Canon of Scripture."[126] Although Jerome may not have *personally* rejected them publicly, he admits the church in his time did not consider the Deuterocanon as "canonical Scriptures," despite them being in his Latin translation.

Jerome's discernment on the Inspiration and canonicity of the Scriptures, as well as his personal life, mirrored the later Reformers. EWTN.com describes Jerome as "a monk addressing monks,"[127] just as Martin Luther would be centuries later. Jerome had also planned to become a lawyer and became fluent in several languages before entering the monastery,[128] just as Luther would plan on doing in the future before deciding to become an Augustinian monk. It was Luther's study of Jerome's discernment of the Old Testament canon as one of the many reasons which led him to eventually reject the Deuterocanon, as well as some of the other reasons explained in this book.

As mentioned earlier, Jerome was not the sole translator of the Vulgate: "Although the Latin Vulgate is attributed to Jerome, he did not translate the entire Bible himself.... But the Latin Vulgate used today includes New Testament books translated by other scholars."[129]

While Jerome translated the Old Testament into Latin from different sources and languages (as well as "most" of the Deuterocanonical books), he only translated the four New Testament gospels into the Vulgate.[130] It is unknown who translated the rest of the New Testament from Greek to Latin.[131] So, it is just as imprecise to assume Jerome was the *sole* translator of the Vulgate, as it is to say "...the official Latin Vulgate retained the forms of the Septuagint."[132] The Vulgate, like the Septuagint before it, had more

---

[126] Ibid. ETWN.com. *St Jerome.*

[127] Ibid.

[128] GotQuestions.org. *Who was St. Jerome?* Accessed from the Internet https://www.gotquestions.org/Saint-Jerome.html

[129] Ibid.

[130] Ibid.

[131] Plater, William Edward; Henry Julian White (1926). *A grammar of the Vulgate, being an introduction to the study of the latinity of the Vulgate Bible.* Oxford: Clarendon Press.

[132] NewAdvent.org. *Canon of the Old Testament: The canon of the Old Testament in the Catholic Church.* Accessed from the Internet http://www.newadvent.org/cathen/03267a.htm

than one version comprising different books in their respective Old Testament canons.

"REPENT" VERSUS "DO PENANCE"

It cannot be deduced historically – nor Scripturally (based on the Biblical languages) – that Jerome's Vulgate, which was completed by A.D. 405, was a direct translation from the Septuagint. It can also not be concluded it was a translation from the original Biblical texts to the Septuagint and then to the Vulgate.

The Vulgate was incorrectly translated into Latin we must "*do penance*" (Acts 2:38) before our sins can be forgiven,[133] which was then translated incorrectly into English in the Douay-Rheims.[134] The correct translation from the Greek word ("*metanoeō* ") means to "repent" or "to change one's mind for better, heartily to amend with abhorrence of one's past sins."[135] It "involves a turning with contrition from sin to God; the repentant sinner is in the proper condition to accept the divine forgiveness."[136]

Contrary to the Vulgate and the Douay-Rheims, both the New Catholic Version and the New American Bible correctly translated this Greek word into English as "repent" in Acts 2:38 instead of "do penance." Luther also correctly translated "Repent" into Latin in the first of his *95 Theses*: "When our Lord and Master Jesus Christ said, 'Repent' (Mt 4:17), he willed the entire life of believers to be one of repentance."[137] This is important because the English translation of the Catholic Bible – the Douay-Rheims – is the version virtually all English Catholic Bibles today are based on. It is also believed to be a direct English translation of the Vulgate. This too is an erroneous assumption, which I will demonstrate in Chapter Five.

---

[133] LatinVulgate.com: *Helping You Understand Difficult Verses, The Acts of the Apostles: Chapter 2*. Accessed from the Internet http://www.latinvulgate.com/lv/verse.aspx?t=1&b=5&c=2

[134] Ibid. DRBO.ORG. *The Acts Of The Apostles Chapter 2*. Accessed from the Internet http://drbo.org/chapter/51002.htm

[135] Blue Letter Bible. "Dictionary and Word Search for *metanoeō (Strong's 3340)*". Blue Letter Bible. 1996-2018. 16 Feb 2018. Accessed from the Internet < http://www.blbclassic.org/lang/lexicon/lexicon.cfm?Strongs=G3340&t=NASB >

[136] Ibid. Taken from F.F. Bruce. The Acts of the Apostles [Greek Text Commentary], London: Tyndale, 1952, p. 97.

[137] Luther.de. *The 95 Theses*. Accessed from the Internet http://www.luther.de/en/95thesen.html

THE PRAYER OF MANASSEH

As mentioned in Chapter Two, the *Prayer of Manasseh* was included in some early versions of the Septuagint. This has been confirmed by EWTN.com, which states this writing does "appear in some manuscripts of the ancient Septuagint."[138] The article goes on to say "It was included as an appendix in the ancient Vulgate."[139] However, it was neither included in any of the third or fourth century church councils (see Chapter Four), nor the English Catholic translation of the Bible – the Douay-Rheims (see Chapter Five), nor in any modern English Catholic translations today, such as the New Catholic Version or the New American Bible. If modern English Catholic Old Testaments are supposed to be faithful translations from the Septuagint and the Vulgate, why do none of these later Catholic translations include the *Prayer of Manasseh*?

Does not the completion of the Vulgate *post*-date the fourth century church councils, i.e.: Rome, Hippo, and Carthage, which all (allegedly) "universally" agreed on the exact same canon of Scripture found in Jerome's translation, including the Deuterocanon? Did not the Council of Trent in the sixteenth century simply "reaffirm" the Old Testament canon of these much earlier fourth century church councils? Since the canon of the Douay-Rheims (supposedly) "agrees" with all these earlier councils, does this not make it *"the"* authoritative translation for all other English Bibles, based on the authority of these councils?

These councils also included the exact same *New* Testament books both Catholics and Protestant "agree" are canonical and Inspired. Should Protestants not *also* agree on the exact same *Old* Testament books as well, based on the authority and settlement of the canon of these early church councils too? Why would Protestants "agree" on the same *New* Testament canon, but not the same *Old* Testament canon? These questions, as well as others, will also be covered in the next two chapters.

---

[138] EWTN.com. *"Catholic Q&A."* Prayer of Manasseh Question from Bill Tooke on 12/16/2001. Answer by Fr. John Echert on 12/17/2001. Accessed from the Internet http://www.ewtn.com/v/experts/showmessage.asp?number=339293
[139] Ibid.

CHAPTER FOUR: What about the church councils?

"Jesus, who, having devoted himself for a long time to the diligent study of the law, and the prophets, and the rest of the books of our ancestors" (Foreword to Sirach NAB)

382, 393, and 397 are all significant and familiar dates to anyone who is a student of church history. These are the starting dates of the fourth century church councils of Rome, Hippo, and Carthage, respectively. Among other things, they addressed the canon of Scripture including the Old Testament. A.D. 382 was the same year Pope Damasus I commissioned Jerome to translate the Bible into the Latin Vulgate, which we covered in the previous chapter. It was imperative to the Pope that Jerome's Latin translation be reflective of (and in complete agreement with) the Council of Rome which he convened over, as well as the subsequent councils. Later church councils, like Florence (1441) and Trent (1545), would attempt to "reaffirm" these earlier councils on the canon of Scripture.

Did each of these three councils carry the same authoritative "weight" as others did, and did they all agree on the <u>exact</u> same writings? Did they reflect the "universal" belief of the canon of Scripture in the early church, as well as the other councils during that time?

I will begin with the councils themselves. When examining the individual books listed in these three church councils, there is nearly universal consistency in their canon, including the Old Testament. One of these consistencies is the *exclusion* of the Deuterocanonical writings of Baruch and the epistle of Jeremiah. Below is a list of these books from each of these three church councils. For clarity, I have put in brackets the modern names and spelling of some of these writings, as well as the name of the particular council at the end:

"Decree of the Council of Rome (AD 382) on the Canon of Scripture during the reign of Pope Damasus I (AD 366-384).

"Now indeed we must treat of the divine Scriptures, what the universal Catholic Church accepts and what she ought to shun. The order of the Old Testament begins here: Genesis one book, Exodus one book, Leviticus one book, Numbers one book, Deuteronomy one book, Josue Nave [Joshua] one book, Judges one book, Ruth one book, Kings [1 and 2 Samuel, 1 and 2 Kings] four books, Paralipomenon [1 and 2 Chronicles] two books, Psalms one book, Solomon three books, Proverbs one book,

Ecclesiastes one book, Canticle of Canticles [Song of Solomon] one book, likewise Wisdom one book, Ecclesiasticus [Sirach] one book.

Likewise, the order of the Prophets. Isaias [Isaiah] one book, Jeremias [Jeremiah] one book, with Ginoth, that is, with his Lamentations, Ezechiel [Ezekiel] one book, Daniel one book, Osee [Hosea] one book, Micheas [Micah] one book, Joel one book, Abdias [Obadiah] one book, Jonas [Jonah] one book, Nahum one book, Habacuc [Habakkuk] one book, Sophonias [Zephaniah] one book, Aggeus [Haggai] one book, Zacharias [Zachariah] one book, Malachias [Malachi] one book. Likewise the order of the histories. Job one book, Tobias [Tobit] one book, Esdras two books [Ezra and Nehemiah], Esther one book, Judith one book, Machabees [1 and 2 Maccabees] two books.

Likewise, the order of the writings of the New and Eternal Testament, which only the holy and Catholic Church supports. Of the Gospels, according to Matthew one book, according to Mark one book, according to Luke one book, according to John one book.

The Epistles of Paul the Apostle in number fourteen. To the Romans one, to the Corinthians two, to the Ephesians one, to the Thessalonians two, to the Galatians one, to the Philippians one, to the Colossians one, to Timothy two, to Titus one, to Philemon one, to the Hebrews one.

Likewise, the Apocalypse of John, one book. And the Acts of the Apostles one book. Likewise, the canonical epistles in number seven. Of Peter the Apostle two epistles, of James the Apostle one epistle, of John the Apostle one epistle, of another John, the presbyter, two epistles, of Jude the Zealut, the Apostle one epistle."[140] **[Council of Rome, A.D. 382]**

~~~~~~~~~~~~~~~~

"This is Canon xxxvj. of Hippo., 393.

Canon XXIV. (Greek xxvii.) Item, that besides the Canonical Scriptures nothing be read in church under the name of divine Scripture. But the Canonical Scriptures are as follows:

---

[140] Mitchell, Taylor. *Decree of Council of Rome (AD 382) on the Biblical Canon.* Accessed from the Internet http://taylormarshall.com/2008/08/decree-of-council-of-rome-ad-382-on.html

Genesis. Exodus. Leviticus. Numbers. Deuteronomy. Joshua the Son of Nun. The Judges. Ruth. The Kings, iv. books. The Chronicles, ij. books. Job. The Psalter. The Five books of Solomon. The Twelve Books of the Prophets. Isaiah. Jeremiah. Ezechiel [Ezekiel]. Daniel. Tobit. Judith. Esther. Ezra [Ezra and Nehemiah], ij. books. Macchabees [1 and 2 Maccabees], ij. books. The New Testament. The Gospels, iv. books. The Acts of the Apostles, j. book. The Epistles of Paul, xiv. The Epistles of Peter, the Apostle, ij. The Epistles of John the Apostle, iij. The Epistles of James the Apostle, j. The Epistle of Jude the Apostle, j. The Revelation of John, j. book.

Let this be sent to our brother and fellow bishop, Boniface, and to the other bishops of those parts, that they may confirm this canon, for these are the things which we have received from our fathers to be read in church."[141] **[Council of Hippo, A.D. 393]**

~~~~~~~~~~~~~~~~~

"Canon 24. (Greek xxvii.) That nothing be read in church besides the Canonical Scripture. Item, that besides the Canonical Scriptures nothing be read in church under the name of divine Scripture. But the Canonical Scriptures are as follows:

Genesis. Exodus. Leviticus. Numbers. Deuteronomy. Joshua the Son of Nun. The Judges. Ruth. The Kings, iv. books. The Chronicles, ij. books. Job. The Psalter. The Five books of Solomon. The Twelve Books of the Prophets. Isaiah. Jeremiah. Ezechiel [Ezekiel]. Daniel. Tobit. Judith. Esther. Ezra [Ezra and Nehemiah], ij. books. Macchabees [1 and 2 Maccabees], ij. books. The New Testament. The Gospels, iv. books. The Acts of the Apostles, j. book. The Epistles of Paul, xiv. The Epistles of Peter, the Apostle, ij. The Epistles of John the Apostle, iij. The Epistles of James the Apostle, j. The Epistle of Jude the Apostle, j. The Revelation of John, j. book.

Let this be sent to our brother and fellow bishop, Boniface, and to the other bishops of those parts, that they may confirm this canon, for these are the things which we have received from our fathers to be read in church."[142] **[Council of Carthage, A.D. 419]**

---

[141] Christian Classics Ethereal Library. 1993-2015. Harry Plantinga. Accessed from the Internet http://www.ccel.org/ccel/schaff/npnf214.xv.iv.iv.xxv.html

[142] NewAdvent.org. *Council of Carthage (A.D. 419): The Canons, Canon 24. (Greek xxvii.)* Accessed from the Internet http://www.newadvent.org/fathers/3816.htm

I will be discussing why the Council of Carthage is dated at A.D. 419 rather than A.D. 397 later in this chapter. I will also cover why the listed books and, curiously, even the wording and the order of books itself between the Council of Hippo and the Council of Carthage are verbatim, including both councils mentioning Boniface. I will address the Council of Rome first.

THE COUNCIL OF ROME (A.D. 382)

As with the other two councils, the Council of Rome specifically mentioned the Deuterocanonical books of Tobit, Judith, and the two books of Maccabees by name. Unlike the two later councils, it also *specifically* mentions Wisdom and Sirach. Pope Damascus I who reigned over this first council lists Solomon's books as only being *three* (Proverbs, Ecclesiastes, and Song of Solomon), while listing Wisdom and Sirach as separate non-Solomonic books. The latter two councils' conflict with Rome and Damasus by including Wisdom and Sirach as being part of the *five* books of Solomon. Despite all three councils accepting these same books, they were not "universal" in their agreement of which ones were attributed to Solomon.

The disagreement between the three councils with regard to whether Wisdom and Sirach are attributed or not to Solomon – as well as Augustine himself dissenting with the two latter councils he was present at (see below) – demonstrates the lack of "universal" consensus between these three early councils. This disunity regarding authorship of two supposed Inspired texts, or at least attribution to an Inspired writer, is problematic since these councils were used as evidence of "universal" agreement in the Catholic Church for their Old Testament canon.[143]

The epistles of James and Jude were included in the New Testament at the Council of Rome and the subsequent councils, since it was believed they were two of the original twelve disciples of Jesus.[144,145] Apostolic authorship was used to validate their epistles into the New Testament canon.

---

[143] EWTN.com. Akin, Jimmy. *The Two Canons: Scripture and Tradition, 3. The Key To Canonicity.* Accessed from the Internet
http://www.ewtn.com/library/answers/2canons.htm

[144] EWTN.com. *St. James the Less, Apostle. Feast: May 3.* Accessed from the Internet
https://www.ewtn.com/library/MARY/JAMES.HTM

[145] ETWN.com. *St. Jude, Apostle.* Accessed from the Internet
https://www.ewtn.com/library/MARY/STJUDE.HTM

Early Christian writers, such as Eusebius, described them as brothers of the Lord "humanly speaking,"[146,147] and Hegesippus referred to James as "the brother of the Lord" who "was consecrated from his mother's womb."[148] Hegesippus also referred to Jude as "the Lord's...brother according to the flesh"[149] and referred to one of the "descendants of one of the Savior's brothers named Jude."[150] Although not an early church father, Josephus also referred to James in the first century A.D. as "the brother of Jesus who was called Christ, whose name was James."[151] Even though they were not part of "The Twelve" (Mark 3:16-19), their epistles are just as God-breathed since they were close associates of the apostles, like Mark and Luke were, so they belong in the New Testament canon.

Even the "key participants" of this council,[152] did not agree with each other on the Old Testament canon. Jerome preferred the Hebrew Bible (see Chapter Three), as did Epiphanius of Salamis (ca. 315-405) who produced "a twenty-two-book catalogue" which "parallels the current Protestant OT [Old Testament] canon."[153] Not enough is known about Acholius of Thessalonica and Paulinus of Antioch. Since they were Eastern Church Fathers, they most likely embraced the canon of the Hebrew Bible (see Chapter Five).

As previously mentioned, the Deuterocanonical book of Baruch and the epistle of Jeremiah were also *not* in the list at the Council of Rome, despite listing the other six Deuterocanonical books explicitly. The Council of Rome is more exhaustive than the two latter councils given it lists all the individual books of the canon by name, such as naming the twelve "minor prophets" separately. The two latter councils simply refer to them as "the books of the twelve prophets." Yet, both Baruch and the epistle of Jeremiah are omitted – individually – from the lists of *all three councils*.

---

[146] Ibid. Maier. *Eusebius: The Church History*, Book 3:11, p.92.

[147] Ibid, Book 3:19, p.94. See also Book 1:13, p.45; Book 2:1, p.52; Book 3:7, p.88; Book 4:5, p.120; and Book 7:19, p.238.

[148] Ibid, Book 2:23, p.71.

[149] Ibid, Book 3:20, p.94.

[150] Ibid, Book 3:32, p.106

[151] Ibid, Book 2:23, p.72. For a more detailed explanation from the New Testament, which affirms Jesus' "brothers" were indeed His younger half-siblings, view my YouTube video: Christie, Steve. *Did Mary & Joseph have children, & did Jesus have brothers & sisters?* "BornAgainRN." Published on YouTube, July 2, 2012. Accessed from the Internet https://www.youtube.com/watch?v=NyiGw4cl95E

[152] FourthCenturyChristianity.com. *The Council of Rome (AD 382).* Wisconsin Lutheran College © 2018. Last updated: 10-13-2010. Accessed from the Internet https://www.fourthcentury.com/the-council-of-rome-ad-382/

[153] Ibid. McDonald, Lee Martin. *The Biblical Canon*, p.204. Brackets inserted by me for clarity.

In a letter addressed to Anthony Houston on EWTN.com, "It is to be noted that the book of Baruch was considered by some Church Fathers to be a part of the book of Jeremiah and as such was not listed separately by them."[154] This is arguably a reason why the Council of Rome did not list them individually, despite listing *all* of the other Deuterocanonical books and the individual "minor prophets" separately.

However, as mentioned in Chapter Two, Cyril of Jerusalem who lived during this time (A.D. 315 to 386) *did* list Baruch and the epistle of Jeremiah *as separate writings* from the book of Jeremiah, as well as Lamentations. Origen of Alexandria listed "The Letter" of Jeremiah, as well as Lamentations, separately from the book of Jeremiah.[155] Even the New Testament references the epistle of Jeremiah as a separate writing (1 John 5:21, cf. Epistle of Jeremiah v.72 NAB), distinct from the book of Baruch (Matthew 5:18, cf. Baruch 4:1 NAB). NewAdvent.org also declares the epistle of Jeremiah is a *separate* work from the book of Baruch stating, "it does not belong in the book proper."[156] Even *if* the book of Baruch was included in the fourth and fifth century councils, the epistle of Jeremiah was not, since it was a separate work from Baruch, Jeremiah, and Lamentations.

The Introduction to the book of Baruch discloses a historical error mentioned in it regarding the practice of a Jewish feast, which would have been impossible to observe in Baruch's day: "And observance of the feast of Booths...would not have been possible during the lifetime of Baruch after the fall of Jerusalem."[157] Regarding the epistle of Jeremiah it attests, "in restating previous inspired teachings at a later day, it does so with no special literary grace."[158] This demonstrates the events recorded in Baruch and the epistle of Jeremiah did not occur, nor were they written, during the time Baruch was alive. They were penned centuries later.

Unlike the Deuterocanonical book of Baruch and the epistle of Jeremiah, the Old Testament prophet Jeremiah was clearly the author of the book of Jeremiah (Jeremiah 1:1), written sometime between the sixth and seventh centuries B.C. He was also the author of Lamentations around the fall of Jerusalem in the sixth century B.C., originally one book with Jeremiah. MacArthur points out in his Study Bible:

---

[154] *EWTN Catholic Q&A.* For Anthony Houston, Origins of the Bible. Question from Doria2 on 05-18-2001. Accessed from the Internet
http://www.ewtn.com/v/experts/showmessage_print.asp?number=367573&language=en

[155] Ibid. Maier. *Eusebius: The Church History.* Book 6.25, p.205-206.

[156] NewAdvent.org. *Baruch.* Accessed from the Internet
http://www.newadvent.org/cathen/02319c.htm

[157] Ibid. New American Bible, Introduction to Baruch, p.964.

[158] Ibid.

"The author of Lamentations is not named within the book, but there are internal and historical indications that it was Jeremiah. The LXX introduces Lam. 1:1, 'And it came to pass, after Israel had been carried away captive...Jeremiah sat weeping [cf. 3:48,49, etc.]...lamented...and said....' Jeremiah wrote Lamentations as an eyewitness (cf. 1:13-15; 2:6,9; 4:1-12), possibly with Baruch's secretarial help (cf. Jer. 26:4; 45:1), during or soon after Jerusalem's fall in 586 B.C."[159]

Although Baruch was instrumental with assisting Jeremiah with at least some of his writings in the books of Jeremiah and Lamentations (Jeremiah 36:4), the Deuterocanonical book of Baruch and the epistle of Jeremiah were not among them. The book of Baruch was most likely written "later than 164 B.C. The appended Letter of Jeremiah which can hardly be earlier than the first century B.C."[160]

Even if some would assume the fourth century councils "considered" the Deuterocanonical book of Baruch and the epistle of Jeremiah to be "part" of the book of Jeremiah, Scripturally and historically this assumption cannot be supported. The "Baruch" who is mentioned in the book of Jeremiah (Jeremiah 45:1-2) in no way had anything to do with the much later written Deuterocanonical book of Baruch, nor the epistle of Jeremiah. These two Deuterocanonical writings were written several centuries after the prophet Jeremiah and Baruch died. Like Wisdom and Sirach, these two uninspired writings were written during the Intertestamental Period long after the canon of the Hebrew Bible was closed (see Appendix B).

These, as well as other reasons, is why Jerome may not have included Baruch in his Latin translation of the Vulgate, in addition to not being able to translate it from the Hebrew language. This may also explain why it did not get "added" to later editions of the Vulgate until four centuries later. It is no wonder why Baruch and the epistle of Jeremiah were not listed individually at the Council of Rome (as well as being omitted from other councils and lists), despite the other six Deuterocanonical books, Lamentations, and the twelve "minor prophets" being listed separately and explicitly by name.

---

[159] Ibid. The MacArthur Study Bible (New King James Version). *The Book of Lamentations: Author and Date*, p.1139.

[160] *The Apocrypha: an American translation*. Translated by Edgar J. Goodspeed with an introduction by Moses Hadas. *Introduction*, p.xxi, 329. Published by Vintage Books, a division of Random House, Inc.: New York and simultaneously in Canada by Random House of Canada Limited, Toronto, 1989.

THE COUNCILS OF HIPPO (A.D 393) AND CARTHAGE (A.D. 397)

While the Council of Hippo and the Council of Carthage appear to harmonize with the Council of Rome's canonical list of books, where they differ from Rome is their verbatim order of these writings and even the wording itself in these two latter councils. If we look back at the lists and wording of Hippo and Carthage, they are eerily identical in every way.

Too identical!

They both begin with "Canon 24" and that in Greek it is "xxvii." They both refer to the *five* books of Solomon, compared to Rome attributing only *three*. They both describe the book of the Psalms as "The Psalter." They both refer to the "twelve books of the [minor] prophets" collectively instead of listing them individually like Rome did. They both agree the apostle John wrote *three* epistles, while Rome attributes only *one* to the apostle and the other two to a different "John, the presbyter." They both omit Lamentations, while Rome mentions it separately from Jeremiah. Even the *order itself* of the books listed from Genesis to Revelation does not deviate in *any way* between these two councils!

The oddest harmony between these two councils is they both mention Pope Boniface as reigning over <u>both</u> of them...even though he did not rule over <u>either</u> Hippo of 393 nor Carthage of *397*. Rather, it was Pope Siricius (A.D. 344 to 399) who ruled over both the Council of Hippo of A.D. 393 and the Council of Carthage of A.D. 397, not Boniface. Why do <u>both</u> of them list Boniface as the reigning pope over these two councils, considering he would not be elected pope until the fifth century?

As discussed earlier, the list from the Council of Carthage is actually from the year *419*, rather than 397. It also mentions the pope who reigned over the Council of Carthage of 419 was Pope Boniface, who was elected pope in A.D. 418. – one year before this second Council of Carthage convened. In his *History of the Councils of the Church*, Catholic bishop, professor, and theologian Karl Joseph von Hefele reveals the list of books from the Council of Carthage of 397 was written *retroactively* back into this earlier council, because "this compilation was done in the year 419 by Dionysius Exiguus."[161]

---

[161] Bible-Researcher.com. *Third Council of Carthage (A.D. 397)*. Accessed from the Internet http://www.bible-researcher.com/carthage.html (footnote #1, cf. the English edition, *A History of the Councils of the Church: From the Original Documents by Charles Joseph Hefele, translated from the German and edited by William R. Clark*, etc., vol. 2 (Edinburgh: T & T Clark, 1876), p. 468.)

Hefele also asserts "this canon derives from an earlier council, convened in 393 at Hippo Regius."[162] BibleResearcher.com reveals "...*we do not have the canon in its original form here. The original canon has been edited* by someone who has adapted it to churchly developments *after 418 A.D.*"[163] (emphasis added). An indication the list from the Council of Carthage of 397 was later "edited" is evident from this council mentioning Pope Boniface[164] rather than Siricius who was pope then.

The list from the Council of Carthage of 419 originated verbatim from the list of the Council of Hippo of 393, not from the Council of Carthage of 397. While the Councils of Rome, Hippo, and Carthage of 419 lists Paul's epistles as *fourteen*, the Council of Carthage of 397 lists them as *thirteen*.[165] This is further evidence this third council in the fourth century was edited.

BibleResearcher.com asserts: "We also observe the peculiar manner in which the Epistle to the Hebrews is listed: 'Epistolae Pauli Apostoli xiii., ejusdem ad Hebraeos una [thirteen Epistles of the Apostle Paul, one epistle of the same to the Hebrews].' Here *ejusdem* looks like a later addition."[166] The text without this later addition would read: "*thirteen* Epistles of the Apostle Paul, *one* to the Hebrews," clarifying Hebrews was a *separate epistle* from Paul's thirteen epistles, based on this council. This conflicts with the other councils which claim Paul wrote *fourteen* epistles.

Moreover, the *actual* canon list from the 397 Carthage council *omitted* the book of Revelation![167] In his book *The Biblical Canon: Its Origin, Transmission, and Authority*, Lee Martin McDonald stated "Revelation was *added later in 419* at the subsequent synod at Carthage"[168] (emphasis added). McDonald adds "The Council of Hippo (393 C.E.) set forth a biblical canon similar to the one produced by Augustine. Although *the deliberations of this council are now lost*, they were *summarized* in the proceedings of the Third Council of Carthage (397 C.E.)"[169] (emphasis added). Dr. Bryan Litfin, associate professor of theology at Moody Bible Institute, confirmed in his book *Getting to Know the Church Fathers: An*

---

162 Ibid. (Footnote #7, Hefele, *op. cit.*, p. 394.)

163 Ibid.

164 Ibid. Brackets with English translation inserted by me for clarity. Italics are in the original text.

165 Ibid. McDonald, Lee Martin. *The Biblical Canon. Appendix C: Lists and Catalogues of New Testament Collections. Table C-2: New Testament Lists from the Fourth Century, Carthage Synod*, p.449.

166 Ibid. Bible-Researcher.com. *Third Council of Carthage (A.D. 397)*. Italics in the original text. Brackets inserted by me for clarity.

167 Ibid. McDonald. *The Biblical Canon. Appendix C*, p.449.

168 Ibid. McDonald, footnote #19. Synod of Carthage, Canon 39 (397, North Africa).

169 Ibid., p.209.

Evangelical Introduction the Council of Carthage of 397 omitted "Revelation, which was added a few years after that."[170]

Because the list from the Council of Carthage of 419 was lifted verbatim from the Council of Hippo of 393, it could not have been taken from the Council of Carthage of 397 since it omitted Revelation from its list. Furthermore, McDonald references F.F. Bruce it was actually the Council of Hippo which was the first council to make a "formal pronouncement" on the biblical canon,[171] not the preceding Council of Rome of 382 which had a similar – but not exact – canonical list to the Council of Carthage of 397.

The omission of Revelation was not uncommon in the early church, even among bishops and Doctors of the Church, during the era of the fourth century councils. For example, Cyril of Jerusalem who was mentioned in Chapter Two, not only omitted most of the Deuterocanonical books from his list, he also omitted Revelation as well.[172] McDonald states, "Cyril of Jerusalem rejected the book altogether and forbade its use in public or private (*Catechetical Lectures* 4.36)."[173]

Since Cyril was both a respected bishop and Doctor of the Church during this time, as well as later canonized as a saint in the Catholic Church, this should not be overlooked nor dismissed. McDonald further stressed the rejection of Revelation in the church centuries after the life of Athanasius of Alexandria (ca. 296-373): "Not until almost seven hundred years later was the book of Revelation universally accepted into the canon."[174]

Jerome, Epiphanius of Salamis, etc. who attended the Council of Rome, as well as some Doctors of the Church and others, were not the only early church fathers during this time who dissented with some of the conclusions of the Old Testament canon from the fourth century church councils.

Enter Augustine.

---

[170] Litfin, Bryan M. *Getting to Know the Church Fathers: An Evangelical Introduction*, p.110. Published by Brazos Press, a division of Baker Publishing Group: Grand Rapids, MI, 2007.

[171] Ibid., McDonald, p.209. McDonald references F.F. Bruce, *Canon of Scripture*, 97.

[172] Ibid., p.381.

[173] Ibid., p.399.

[174] Ibid., p.381.

AUGUSTINE OF HIPPO

Even though Augustine was one of the "key participants" at the latter two councils of Hippo[175] (where he was later elected bishop) and Carthage[176], he did not attribute Wisdom and Sirach to Solomon either, dissenting with these councils:

> "and *three of Solomon*. . .. But as to those *two books*, one of which is entitled *Wisdom* and the other of which is entitled *Ecclesiasticus* [Sirach] and which are called 'of Solomon' because of a certain similarity to his books, it is held most certainly that *they were written by Jesus Sirach*."[177] (emphasis added)

Unlike the three books written earlier by Solomon found in the Hebrew Bible (Proverbs, Ecclesiastes, and Song of Solomon), these much later books could not have possibly been penned by Solomon himself. The three poetic writings by the former king of Israel would have been written sometime during his reign (971 to 931 B.C.). The latter two non-Solomonic writings (Wisdom and Sirach) were written centuries later during the Intertestamental Period after 400 B.C. – roughly, between seven hundred and fifty years to eight hundred and fifty years later.

The book of Sirach, which is arguably the oldest of the Deuterocanonical books, only dates back to about 200 to 175 B.C.,[178] while the book of Wisdom, the youngest of the Deuterocanon, only dates back to about a hundred years before the time of Christ.[179] These much later dates are far too late to attribute these writings to Solomon.

What is interesting is the grandson of Jesus son of Sirach, the author of Sirach (Sirach 50:27), wrote a Foreword to Sirach testifying of his grandfather's devotion of his study of "the law, the prophets, and the rest of the books":

> "Jesus, who, having devoted himself for a long time to the diligent study of *the law, and the prophets, and the rest of the*

---

[175] FourthCenturyChristianity.com. *The Council of Hippo (AD 393).* Wisconsin Lutheran College © 2018. Last updated: 4-17-2012. Accessed from the Internet https://www.fourthcentury.com/council-of-hippo-ad-393/

[176] FourthCenturyChristianity.com. *The Council of Carthage (AD 393).* Wisconsin Lutheran College © 2018. Last updated: 4-10-2012. Accessed from the Internet https://www.fourthcentury.com/council-of-carthage-ad-397/

[177] *DEFENDING THE DEUTEROCANONICALS – James Akin, THE FATHERS KNOW BEST: Old Testament Canon, Augustine* (On Christian Instruction 2:8:13 [ca. A.D. 395]). https://www.ewtn.com/library/ANSWERS/DEUTEROS.HTM. Brackets inserted by me for clarity.

[178] Ibid. New American Bible, Introduction to Sirach (Ecclesiasticus), p.771.

[179] Ibid. New American Bible, Introduction to Wisdom, p.750.

books of our ancestors" (emphasis added, Foreword to Sirach NAB)

Commenting on this, the footnotes to Sirach in the New American Bible refer to "*the law, the prophets, and the rest of the books: the Sacred Scriptures of the Old Testament written before the time of Sirach*, according to *the threefold division of the present Hebrew Bible*"[180] (emphasis added). Since this was "written *before* the time of Sirach," this means at the time of its writing, Israel had recognized this "threefold division" of the Old Testament before the first Deuterocanonical book of Sirach was even written. This "threefold division" is similar to how Jesus Christ divided the Old Testament into three divisions in Luke's gospel, as well as how the apostle Paul did later when he quoted the three divisions of the Hebrew Bible in the same passage in his epistle to the church of Rome:

> "Now He [Jesus] said to them, 'These are My words which I spoke to you while I was still with you, that all things which are written about Me in *the Law of Moses and the Prophets and the Psalms* must be fulfilled.' Then He opened their minds to understand *the Scriptures*." (emphasis added, Luke 24:44-45)

> "Again he says, 'REJOICE, O GENTILES, WITH HIS PEOPLE.' And again, 'PRAISE THE LORD ALL YOU GENTILES, AND LET ALL THE PEOPLES PRAISE HIM.' Again Isaiah says, 'THERE SHALL COME THE ROOT OF JESSE, AND HE WHO ARISES TO RULE OVER THE GENTILES, IN HIM SHALL THE GENTILES HOPE.'" (Romans 15:10-12)

In chapter fifteen of his epistle to the Romans, the apostle Paul first quotes Deuteronomy 32:43 ("the Law"), then Psalm 117:1 ("the Psalms"), and lastly Isaiah 11:10 ("the Prophets"). Notice how Paul divided *"the threefold division of the present Hebrew Bible,"* which existed before the first Deuterocanonical book of Sirach was ever penned – "the Law, the Prophets, and the Psalms" – the same way Jesus did in Luke 24:44-45. Since Paul was a Pharisee whose Old Testament canon mirrored later Protestants', and because he separated the third division with "the Psalms" the same way Jesus did, this demonstrates Jesus affirmed "the Psalms" as the first book of the third division of the Hebrew Bible.

This "threefold division" attributed to Protestant Old Testaments ("the Law and the Prophets and the Writings") is witnessed by the grandson of Sirach, the apostle Paul, and even the Lord Jesus Himself. (I will explain why Jesus broke down this threefold division of the Old Testament in

---

[180] Ibid. New American Bible, Foreword to Sirach, p.771.

Chapter Seven, rather than simply calling it "the Law and the Prophets" like He did elsewhere in the New Testament.)

Commenting on the Old Testament canon, Augustine also omitted both the book of Baruch and the epistle of Jeremiah, despite mentioning the other six Deuterocanonical writings, as well as the twelve "minor prophets" by name.[181] While the Hebrew Bible refers to Jeremiah as "the prophet," it merely refers to Baruch as "the scribe" (Jeremiah 36:8,26; 43:6; 45:1). So, according to the Hebrew Bible, Baruch was *not* a prophet. Therefore, the Deuterocanonical book of Baruch is not part of "the Prophets."

Despite given the reverent titles "the Doctor of the Church as well as the Doctor of Grace,"[182] Augustine did not hold the Deuterocanon to be at the same level as the books from the Hebrew Bible. B.F. Wescott notes:

> "In confirmation of this view of Augustine's special regard for the Hebrew Canon, it may be further urged that he appeals to the Jews, 'the librarians of the Christians,' as possessing 'all the writings in which Christ was prophesied of' (In Ps. xl., Ps. lvi.), and to 'the Law, the Psalms, and the Prophets,' which were supported by the witness of the Jews (c. Gaud, l. c.), as including 'all the canonical authorities of the Sacred books' (de Unit. Eccles. p. 16), which, as he says in another place (de Civ. xv. 23, 4), 'were preserved in the temple of the Hebrew people by the care of the successive priests.'"[183] (emphasis added)

Augustine demonstrated the inferiority of the Deuterocanonal books of the Maccabees in his work *The City of God,* Book 18, Chapter 36 contrasting them to "the Holy Scriptures":

> "...the Holy Scriptures which are called canonical, but in others, among which are also the books of the Maccabees. These

---

[181] Bible-Researcher.com. *Augustine on the Canon.* Accessed from the Internet http://www.bible-researcher.com/augustine.html

[182] NewAdvent.org. *St. Augustine of Hippo, As bishop of Hippo (360-430), The Donatist controversy and the theory of the Church.* Accessed from the Internet http://www.newadvent.org/cathen/02084a.htm

[183] Ibid. Bible-Researcher.com. *Augustine on the Canon,* footnote #4. Quote taken from Westcott, B.F. "Canon of Scripture," in vol. 1 of *Dr. William Smith's Dictionary of the Bible: Comprising Its Antiquities, Biography, Geography, and Natural History; revised and edited by Professor H.B. Hackett, D.D.,* etc. (Cambridge, 1881), pp. 362-3. Accessed from the Internet http://www.bible-researcher.com/augustine.html

are held as canonical, not by the Jews, but by the Church."[184] (emphasis added)

Although Augustine labeled the Deuterocanon as "canonical," he most likely would not have if he had known they were not part of the Hebrew Bible. Dr. James White illustrates:

"Augustine could not read Hebrew, and the manuscripts that he had contained these books...because though he accepted the Apocryphal books, he did so because *he thought they were part of the Hebrew canon.* If he had known what the Hebrew canon was he would have taken a different position than that which he took, but *he was unaware of those particular facts.*"[185] (emphasis added)

Since Augustine preferred the Hebrew Bible, had he known the Deuterocanon was not included in it, his rejection of the Deuterocanon may have influenced the Council of Hippo's inclusion of it where Augustine attended and where he was later the bishop. This awareness may have also influenced the Council of Carthage of 397 where he also attended. Not only did the canon lists differ between the councils, the participants in these councils were not "universal" (i.e.: "catholic") in their agreement of the Old Testament canon.

THE COUNCIL OF LAODICEA (~A.D. 363)

These were not the only councils from the fourth century having different lists, nor was the Council of Carthage of 397 the only council to omit Revelation. The Council of Laodicea of A.D. 363 also had a different list of canonical books, including omitting Revelation. McDonald indicates:

"Revelation did not get included in the canon list of the Council of Laodicea or in the canon 85 of the *Apostolic Constitutions.* Most scholars contend, as [R.H.] Charles shows that Revelation was ignored or rejected in many Eastern churches in the fourth century."[186]

---

[184] NewAdvent.org. *The City of God (Book XVIII), Chapter 36. — About Esdras and the Books of the Maccabees.* Accessed from the Internet http://www.newadvent.org/fathers/120118.htm

[185] White, James. *The Great Debate IX: Is The Apocrypha Scripture? (White vs Michuta).* "Alpha & Omega Ministries." Published September 24, 2014. Accessed from the Internet https://www.youtube.com/watch?v=AAoNfH1rFtE (Begins around the 55:39 mark.)

[186] Ibid., p.399. McDonald references R.H. Charles, *Revelation of St. John,* 1.xcvii-ciii. Italics in the original text. Brackets inserted by me.

The Council of Laodicea preceded these other fourth and fifth century councils. This council also omitted all of the Deuterocanonical books, except for Baruch and the epistle of Jeremiah, which it listed as *separate writings* from each other, as well as separate from the books of Jeremiah and Lamentations.[187] Although some have questioned the authenticity of Canon 60 of this list,[188] the omission of Revelation from other lists – especially from those of Cyril, the Council of Carthage of 397, and it being ignored by Eastern churches – was likely "due to a general reaction against this book in the east after excessive use was made of it by the Montanist cults."[189] Even *"if"* Canon 60 of the Council of Laodicea is inauthentic, Revelation was excluded from other lists, including those of other early councils, churches, and Christians.

Even if one wishes to assume the book of Baruch was included with the book of Jeremiah in the fourth and fifth century councils, there is an obvious problem between them and the Vulgate. The Vulgate was completed in A.D. 405, during the papacy of Pope Innocent I, which *excluded* the book of Baruch (see Chapter 3), while the Council of Carthage in A.D. 419 (allegedly) included it! If the book of Baruch was believed to be "part" of the book of Jeremiah, *why* would the Council of Carthage of A.D. 419 include it *fourteen years after* the Vulgate was completed by Jerome, during the papacy of Pope Innocent I, who excluded it?

Furthermore, Jerome was commissioned by Pope Damasus I who reigned over the Council of Rome in A.D. 382. Would not Jerome's Vulgate, which excluded Baruch, reflect the canon of Pope Damasus I who reigned over this earlier council, as well as reflect the canon of the council itself and the subsequent councils in the fourth century?

As evident from this chapter, using these fourth and fifth century church councils as being "authoritative" to define the Biblical canon – including those councils ruled over by popes – is problematic. As I demonstrated, the Council of Carthage of 397 ruled over by Pope Siricius had a different Biblical canon than those of the other councils, such as the Council of Rome by Pope Damasus I, the Council of Carthage of 419 by Pope Boniface I, and the Council of Laodicea.

The Council of Hippo which Pope Siricius *also* ruled over had a *different canon than the Council of Carthage of 397.* So, this same pope *ruled over two different councils,* which produced *two different canons of*

---

[187] NewAdvent.org. *Synod of Laodicea (4th Century). The Canons: Canon 60.* Accessed from the Internet http://www.newadvent.org/fathers/3806.htm

[188] Ibid.

[189] Bible-Researcher.com. *Cyril of Jerusalem on the Canon.* Accessed from the Internet http://www.bible-researcher.com/cyril.html

Scripture! Furthermore, Pope Innocent I, who reigned when Jerome's Vulgate was completed in 405, also had a different canon than the Council of Carthage of 397 *from just eight years earlier.*

One of the reasons for rejecting the ultimate "authority" of these councils, despite most of them being ruled over by different popes, is none of them were ecumenical councils.

WHAT IS AN ECUMENICAL COUNCIL?

NewAdvent.org defines an ecumenical council as "those to which the bishops, and others entitled to vote, are convoked from the whole world (oikoumene) under the presidency of the pope or his legates, and the decrees of which, having received papal confirmation, bind all Christians."[190] Vatican.va adds "A council is never ecumenical unless it is confirmed or at least accepted as such by the successor of Peter; and it is prerogative of the Roman Pontiff to convoke these councils, to preside over them and to confirm them."[191] NewAdvent.org goes on to list twenty ecumenical councils recognized by the Catholic Church.[192]

Although these fourth and fifth century councils with similar (but not exact) lists were ruled over by popes, none of them were ecumenical, like the First Ecumenical Council of Nicaea I of A.D. 325. Even though it was ecumenical and it settled doctrinal matters, such as the Deity of Christ, it did not deal with the Biblical canon. Rather, the first ecumenical council to even address it was the Council of Florence of 1441 under Pope Eugene IV. However, certain Deuterocanonical books, like Sirach, were still questioned in the church for well over a millennium after these fourth and fifth century councils convened. Furthermore, the Biblical canon was not officially "defined" until the Ecumenical Council of Trent in 1546 in response to the Protestant Reformation. EWTN.com confirms this:

> "But doubts about its [Sirach's] canonicity lasted into the Middle Ages, especially under the influence of St. Jerome, who preferred the Palestinian Canon, *such doubts lasted even after the Council of Florence (1441)* which included it in the list of sacred

---

[190] NewAdvent.org. *General Councils: Classification 1. Ecumenical Councils.* Accessed from the Internet http://www.newadvent.org/cathen/04423f.htm

[191] Vatican.va. *Dogmatic Constitution on the Church, Lumen Gentium, Solemnly Promulgated by his Holiness Pope Paul VI, on November 21, 1964. Chapter III: On the Hierarchical Structure of the Church and in Particular on the Episcopate,* (point 22). Accessed from the Internet http://www.vatican.va/archive/hist_councils/ii_vatican_council/documents/vat-ii_const_19641121_lumen-gentium_en.html

[192] Ibid. NewAdvent.org. *General Councils.*

books without denying its canonicity. *It's* [sic] *canonicity was finally defined at the Council of Trent.*"[193] (emphasis added)

THE SECOND ECUMENICAL COUNCIL OF NICAEA (A.D. 787)

Although Canon Two of the Second Ecumenical Council of Nicaea (A.D. 787) promulgated "Candidates for a bishop's orders must know the Psalter by heart and must have read thoroughly, not cursorily, all the sacred Scriptures,"[194] it did not explicitly define what the "sacred Scriptures" were. Additionally, the book of Baruch was still not in the Latin Vulgate at this time (see Chapter Three). This means this Second Ecumenical Council of Nicaea produced a *different Biblical canon from* what was produced at *the later Ecumenical Councils of Florence and Trent*.

It was at the Ecumenical Council of Trent, which pronounced "anathema" on *anyone* who rejected their Biblical canon even in part (see Chapter Ten). This was done to combat the "heresy" of the Protestant Reformation, which questioned the Inspiration of the Deuterocanon, which included the book of Baruch. So, you do not even have ecumenical councils agreeing with *each other* on the Old Testament canon!

As I pointed out, the book of Revelation was not included in the earlier non-ecumenical Council of Carthage of 397. This *may* explain why some Catholic sites like EWTN.com, which list the books from this fourth century council, only list the *Old* Testament books from this council. Not only does this Web site omit the book of Baruch from its Old Testament list, but it also omits listing the *New* Testament[195] since this council had removed the book of Revelation.

Hence, the first ecumenical council to "define" the canon of the Catholic Old Testament (as well as the New Testament) was not until 1546 at the Council of Trent. When Protestants state the Catholic Church did not "define" their Old Testament canon until then, this is what they are referring to – the first *ecumenical* council to define the canon. This, of course, raises an important question: if these church councils did not get

---

[193] ETWN.com. *Deuterocanonical Books in Canon of Scripture*, by Fr. William Most. Copyright © 1997 EWTN Online Services. Accessed from the Internet http://www.ewtn.com/library/SCRIPTUR/DEUTEROS.TXT Brackets inserted by me for clarity.

[194] NewAdvent.org. *The Second Council of Nicaea*. Accessed from the Internet http://www.newadvent.org/cathen/11045a.htm

[195] EWTN.com. Akin, Jimmy. *DEFENDING THE DEUTEROCANONICALS, Council of Carthage*. Accessed from the Internet http://www.ewtn.com/library/answers/deuteros.htm

the exact *Old* Testament canon right, how can we be certain these same church councils got the *New* Testament right?

Earlier I explained the Old Testament canon was *already* settled even before Christ's Incarnation in the first century. The apostle Paul, who was a Pharisee, "defined" the Old Testament canon as "the Law and the Prophets" (Romans 3:21), just as Jesus had when He spoke with the Pharisees (Luke 16:14-16). As Jimmy Akin mentioned earlier, Pharisees shared the same Old Testament canon as Protestants do today. Later in his epistle to the church of Rome, Paul broke it down into its threefold division (Romans 15:10-12), just as Jesus did earlier (Luke 24:44-45).

Unlike the Old Testament canon which was already developed by the time of Christ, the New Testament was yet to be written. God "moved [men] by the Holy Spirit spoke from God" (2 Peter 1:21) to recognize the New Testament canon, long before the fourth and fifth century church councils did. He did not need to do this with the Old Testament, since it was already written, established, and recognized by Jesus, His disciples, the Pharisees (like Paul), and the early first century church. (I will cover in more detail the same godly criteria the Reformers used to recognize the Old Testament canon, which the early church had used to recognize the New Testament canon in a later chapter.)

As highlighted in Chapters Two and Three, the *Prayer of Manasseh* was originally included in early versions of the Septuagint and the Vulgate. So, "why" does it not appear in the "lists" of the fourth and fifth century church councils, as well as the later fifteenth and sixteenth century ecumenical church councils?

What about the English translation of the Douay-Rheims Bible the Catholic Church produced in the seventeenth century? Is it not a faithful English translation of the Latin Vulgate which reflected the Biblical canon of the early church? I will be discussing this and more in the next chapter.

CHAPTER FIVE: What about the Douay-Rheims Bible?

"a son [of David] to reign upon his throne" (Jeremiah 33:21 New Catholic Version)

1610 is a year which is more significant for Catholics than for Protestants. For most Protestants, its only significance is it was the year before the first edition of the King James Version of the Bible was published. For Catholics, it was the year their seventeenth century English translation of the Bible was published – the Douay-Rheims. This was the translation virtually all other English Catholic translations would be based on, such as the New Catholic Version (NCV) and the New American Bible (NAB).

In the Introduction to the New Catholic Version, Rev. J. Edgar Bruns writes: "The Douay Bible is a very faithful translation of the Vulgate by English exiles at the Seminary of Douay who published the New Testament at Rheims in 1582 and the Old Testament at Douay in 1609 and 1610."[196] Similarly, the New American Bible asserts "we have incorporated in this Edition the very latest complete Catholic translation known as 'The New American Bible.'"[197] It attests it is "under the patronage of the Bishops' Committee of the Confraternity of Christian Doctrine."[198] The New Catholic Version makes a similar attestation of being under the Confraternity of Christian Doctrine.[199] Naturally, we would expect them both to be a faithful and complete translation of the Douay-Rheims, as well as of the Latin Vulgate from the Septuagint.

However, upon close examination of Jeremiah chapter ten, the Septuagint omits verse nine, which in the New Catholic Version reads:

> "Silver spread into plates is brought from Tharsis, and gold from Ophaz: the work of the artificer, and of the hand of the coppersmith: violet and purple is their clothing: all these things are the work of artificers" (NCV).

---

[196] Bruns, Rev. J. Edgar Bruns, S.T.D., S.S.L. St. John's University Graduate School of Theology. The New Catholic Version, Introduction, pp.iii-v. Published by Memorial Bibles: Nashville, Tennessee, 1961. P.J. Kenedy & Sons

[197] Ibid. New American Bible, Preface, p. [5], Catholic Book Publishing Corp.

[198] Ibid.

[199] Ibid. The New Catholic Version, p.ii.

It has a similar wording in the New American Bible as well. This same verse is also found in all the major Protestant versions of Jeremiah 10:9.[200] Although it is found in the Vulgate, it is *not* found in the Septuagint. Verses six, seven, eight, and ten are omitted from the Septuagint as well![201]

These are not the only omissions from the book of Jeremiah. In Jeremiah chapter thirty-three, verses fourteen through twenty-six are *also* omitted.[202] The Vulgate and the Douay-Rheims include *all* of these verses. *This is HALF of the chapter*...not just a single verse or two! The footnotes of the New American Bible (NAB) attempt to explain the absence of these thirteen verses from the Septuagint:

> "This is the longest continuous passage in the Book of Jeremiah that is lacking in the Greek. It appears to be a post-exilic composition of an inspired writer who used parts of the prophecies of Jeremiah — often, however, in a sense different from the prophet's."[203]

Yet, the New American Bible includes them, as does the New Catholic Version, despite them not being in the Septuagint. Despite this, the Septuagint is claimed by the Catholic Church to be *"the"* Greek translation of the Old Testament — including the Deuterocanon — which Jesus and the New Testament writers used.

These thirteen omitted passages are significant prophetic passages that were fulfilled in the New Testament. For example, "a son [of David] to reign upon his throne" (Jeremiah 33:21 NCV) was fulfilled by Jesus (Luke 1:32-33). The apostle Paul referenced verse twenty-four when God told

---

[200] Blue Letter Bible. "The Major Prophet Jeremiah 10 - (NASB - New American Standard Bible)." Blue Letter Bible. 1996-2018. 19 Jan 2018 http://www.blbclassic.org/Bible.cfm?b=Jer&c=10&v=10&t=NASB#vrsn/9

[201] BibleStudyTools.com. Septuagint w/ Apocrypha LXX, Old Testament, Jeremias 10. Accessed from the Internet https://www.biblestudytools.com/lxx/jeremias/10.html. However, BlueLetterBible.org shows a different version of the Septuagint, which *does* include verse nine, while also omitting the other verses [Blue Letter Bible. "The Major Prophet Jeremiah 10 - (NASB - New American Standard Bible)." Blue Letter Bible. 1996-2018. 19 Jan 2018. See http://www.blbclassic.org/Bible.cfm?b=Jer&c=10&v=1&t=NASB#conc/9]. This demonstrates there was more than one version of the Septuagint, which were not identical.

[202] Blue Letter Bible. "The Major Prophet Jeremiah 33 - (NASB - New American Standard Bible)." Blue Letter Bible. 1996-2018. 24 Jan 2018. Accessed from the Internet http://www.blbclassic.org/Bible.cfm?b=Jer&c=33&v=1&t=NASB#conc/14. This link only shows Jeremiah 33:14 omitted in the Septuagint. To see where verses fifteen through twenty-six are also omitted in the Septuagint, use the tools on the Web site for each individual verse. Once again, BibleStudyTools.com shows a version of the Septuagint, which only omits verses twenty-five and twenty-six from Jeremiah chapter thirty-three. Accessed from the Internet https://www.biblestudytools.com/lxx/jeremias/33.html

[203] Ibid. New American Bible. Jeremiah 33:14-20 footnotes, p.933.

Jeremiah, "Have you not observed what this people have spoken, saying, 'The two families which the LORD chose, He has rejected them'? Thus they despise My people, no longer are they as a nation in their sight." These "two families" refer to the divided kingdom of Israel and Judah.

When Paul wrote to the church in Rome, he alluded to Jeremiah 33:24, declaring "I say then, God has not rejected His people, has He? May it never be! For I too am an Israelite, a descendant of Abraham, of the tribe of Benjamin. God has not rejected His people whom He foreknew" (Romans 11:1-2a). Benjamin was one of the two tribes of the southern kingdom of Judah (1 Kings 12:23), which God gave to Solomon's son Rehoboam (1 Kings 11:36,43).

Paul was affirming this prophecy came true, by his own living example since he was from the tribe of Benjamin. Despite this passage from Jeremiah 33:14-26 not being in the Septuagint, these thirteen verses no doubt belong in the book of Jeremiah.

Since both of the above Catholic versions are under the Confraternity of Christian Doctrine, why does the Septuagint "omit" all of these verses, despite them being in the Vulgate,[204] as well as it being in the Douay-Rheims[205] which is believed to be "the safest, most traditional, and most trustworthy Catholic Bible"?[206]

Were *all* of these verses from Jeremiah chapter ten and chapter thirty-three part of the earliest Septuagint, but simply "removed" in later editions? If so, exactly *when* were they "removed", and *when* were they "added" back to use for the translation into the Vulgate? Why would the footnotes in the NAB state they were "lacking in the Greek" if they were in the Septuagint? Were these verses never part of the Septuagint, but simply "added" later to the Vulgate translation, and then to the Douay-Rheims? How can one claim the Douay-Rheims is "the safest, most traditional, and most trustworthy Catholic Bible" since none of these verses were ever in the Septuagint?

This is problematic since both the NAB and NCV claim to be a faithful translation of the Douay-Rheims, and the Douay-Rheims is professed to be "the literal (as word-for-word as possible) translation of the Latin Vulgate in English, so one might say it is on the same level at the Vulgate,"[207] and

[204] LatinVulgate.com: Helping You Understand Difficult Verses, The Prophecy of Jeremiah: Chapter 33. http://www.latinvulgate.com/lv/verse.aspx?t=0&b=28&c=33

[205] DRBO.ORG. Douay-Rheims + Challoner Notes. *Prophecy of Jeremias (Jeremiah) Chapter 33*. Accessed from the Internet http://drbo.org/chapter/28033.htm

[206] BestCatholicBible.com. *THE source for Douay-Rheims Bibles! Why is the Douay-Rheims Bible the best?* Accessed from the Internet http://www.bestcatholicbible.com/

[207] Ibid. BestCatholicBible.com. *Why is the Douay-Rheims Bible the best Bible?*

the Catholic Old Testament canon is supposed to be based on the Septuagint. Even if it can be argued the earliest version of Jeremiah in the Septuagint originally included all these verses, we still have two problems: one, the NAB commentators confess the verses in Jeremiah 33:14-26 were "lacking in the Greek"; and, two, there are versions of the Septuagint that do not agree with each other on exactly which verses were omitted. Therefore, the Old Testament of the Douay-Rheims cannot claim to be an accurate English translation.

The "omission" of these verses, as well as the "additions," are no different than the later Reformers "omitting" the uninspired Deuterocanonical writings, such as the "additions" to Daniel and Esther. The difference is the Reformers had *Scriptural* grounds from the New Testament for omitting them. This will be discussed in a later chapter.

As highlighted in this and previous chapters, the translation of the Old Testament was not as smooth of a transition into the Greek Septuagint and then into the Latin Vulgate as many might assume, nor was it as smooth of a transition from the Vulgate to the Douay-Rheims either. Just as not all versions and translations of the Old Testament accepted the exact same verses, not all Jews prior to, and contemporary with, the time of Christ accepted the same writings or Greek translations either. We saw this with the New Testament when the apostle John chose to abandon the Septuagint translation of Zechariah 12:10 and instead used his own Greek translation in both his gospel and in Revelation.

The Douay-Rheims, as well as later Catholic English translations like the NCV and the NAB, deviate from the Septuagint in *context* as well. One of these deviations is the ages of the pre-Flood ancestors of Noah. Another deviation is the "extra Cainan" found in the post-Flood genealogy from Noah to Abraham.

1. The pre-Flood genealogies from Adam to Noah.

Upon comparing the ages of the pre-Flood ancestors of Noah between the Douay-Rheims, the NCV, and the NAB, they are identical. The Douay-Rheims begins in Genesis 5:3 with Adam being one-hundred and thirty years old when he fathered Seth.[208] The NAB and the NCV are consistent with this age, as well as the rest of the ages throughout the genealogy up to Noah, concerning how old the particular father was when he had "begot" his son (Genesis 5:3-31). When you add all these ages up, it comes up to 1556 years after Creation when Noah gave birth to his son Shem at the age of five-hundred (v.31). The Douay-Rheims records Noah was six-

---

[208] Ibid. DRBO.org. *Book of Genesis Chapter 5*. Accessed from the Internet http://drbo.org/chapter/01005.htm

hundred years old when the Flood came (Genesis 7:6),[209] as does the NAB and the NCV. This would put the date of the Flood to 1656 years after Creation.

Incidentally, Methuselah – the longest living person documented in the entire Bible – is recorded to have lived nine-hundred and sixty-nine years (Genesis 5:25-27).[210] This means according to the Douay-Rheims, Methuselah died the year of the Flood. All of this is also confirmed in the NAB and the NCV, as well as in all the major Protestant translations.[211]

When we examine this same pre-Flood genealogy in the Septuagint, we find the age of Adam when he fathered Seth is *two-hundred and thirty*[212] – a deviation of one-hundred years from his age recorded in the Douay-Rheims, NAB, and NCV. We also find deviations between the Septuagint and the Douay-Rheims, NAB, and NCV for the rest of the genealogy, except for Jared and Noah.[213] These aberrant Septuagint genealogies changes the Flood date to 2242 years after Creation.[214] As a result, according to the Septuagint, Methuselah ends up dying 2256 years after Creation - *fourteen years after the Flood!*

Likewise, the Vulgate also affirms the "one-hundred and thirty year" age of Adam ("centum triginta" in Latin),[215] as well as the rest of the Pre-Flood genealogies, which matches the Douay-Rheims, NAB, and NCV, but *differs* from the Septuagint. How can this be if the Douay-Rheims is supposed to be "a very faithful translation of the Vulgate" and "the safest, most traditional, and most trustworthy Catholic Bible," when the Vulgate is supposed to be a faithful translation of the Septuagint Jesus and His disciples used, which conflicts with both the Vulgate and the Douay-Rheims?

One common view is while the pre-Flood people *themselves* were real, the ages are not *necessarily* literal. The footnotes of the NAB on Genesis 5:1-32 state, "The long lifespans attributed to these ten antediluvian

---

[209] Ibid. *Book of Genesis Chapter 7.* Accessed from the Internet http://drbo.org/chapter/01007.htm

[210] Ibid. *Book of Genesis Chapter 5.*

[211] Ibid. Blue Letter Bible. "Book of Beginnings - Genesis 5 - (NASB - New American Standard Bible)." Blue Letter Bible. 1996-2018. 24 Jan 2018. Accessed from the Internet http://www.blbclassic.org/Bible.cfm?b=Gen&c=5&v=1&t=NASB#vrsn/27

[212] Creation.com. *Biblical Chronogenealogies by Jonathan Sarfati, CMI-Australia: Date of creation, Table 1 Chronogenealogies of the Patriarchs according to different textual traditions.* Accessed from the Internet https://creation.com/biblical-chronogenealogies

[213] Ibid.

[214] Ibid.

[215] Ibid. LatinVulgate.com. *THE BOOK OF GENESIS: Chapter 5, The genealogy, age, and death of the Patriarchs, from Adam to Noe. The translation of Henoch.* Accessed from the Internet http://www.latinvulgate.com/lv/verse.aspx?t=0&b=1&c=5

patriarchs have a symbolic rather than a historical value."[216] However, the Catholic Church has always attributed the authorship of Genesis to Moses, who also wrote the rest of the Torah.

Moses recorded his brother Aaron's death at one-hundred and twenty-three (Numbers 33:39), which the Catholic Church has never had a problem with this advanced age being literal. They also do not have a problem with the High Priest, Jehoiada, living to the "ripe old age" of one-hundred thirty (2 Chronicles 24:15) – the same age Moses records Adam fathering Seth – despite the unusually "old age" he lived. Moses also recorded Abraham living to *one-hundred and seventy* (Genesis 25:7), despite no one in church history ever having reported living that long.

Another opinion is there were most likely generational "gaps" between the pre-Flood "father" and his "son" recorded in Genesis chapter five. This insinuation assumes the "father" was not actually the biological parent of the "son," but merely a biological ancestor. However, Moses recorded Adam and Eve were the biological parents of Seth (Genesis 4:25, cf. 5:3), and Seth was the biological father of his son Enosh (Genesis 4:26). In the New Testament, Jude records Enoch as "the seventh generation from Adam" (Jude v.14), which is the exact number of pre-Flood fathers from Adam to Enoch recorded in Genesis chapter five.

All this overlooks the point Moses is attempting to make – by adding up all these "ages": we can determine when the Flood came. Since the Septuagint (incorrectly) has Methuselah living fourteen years *after* the Flood, this is problematic. In proclaiming the Douay-Rheims is a faithful translation of the Vulgate, which is a faithful translation of the Septuagint, this cannot be so. The Septuagint not only deviates from both the Vulgate and the Douay-Rheims, but it also creates a contradiction with the rest of Scripture. Both the Old and New Testaments clearly state only <u>eight</u> people entered the ark before the Flood – Noah, his wife, their three sons, and their three wives (Genesis 7:7, cf. 1 Peter 3:20). This means Methuselah was not on the ark, so he could not have survived the Flood to live fourteen years after it, like the Septuagint erroneously teaches. In Protestant translations of the Old Testament, no such pre-Flood genealogical contradictions exist, because Protestant Old Testaments are not dependent on the Septuagint.

Even if one dismisses the "ages" of the fathers when they had their "sons" as being literal, the Septuagint "ages" are still different than the Douay-Rheims. Is the error in the Septuagint Jesus and the New Testament writers are claimed to have quoted from, or is it in the Douay-Rheims which conflicts with the Septuagint?

---

[216] Ibid. New American Bible. Genesis 5:1-32 footnotes, p.8.

Before we answer this, there is another problem with the Douay-Rheims being a faithful translation of the Vulgate, which is (allegedly) faithfully translated from the Septuagint: the "extra Cainan" in Luke's genealogy in the Septuagint.

2.   The post-Flood "extra Cainan" from Noah to Abraham.

When examining Luke's genealogy of Jesus, which goes all the way back to Adam, an "extra Cainan" is listed after the Flood in the Douay-Rheims (Luke 3:36).[217] This "extra Cainan" is not only missing from the genealogy in the Douay-Rheims in Genesis 10:24,[218] but he is also missing from the genealogies in the Douay-Rheims in Genesis 11:12[219] and 1 Chronicles 1:18 and verse 24.[220] He is not mentioned *anywhere* else in the entire Bible!

The Vulgate, likewise, includes this "extra Cainan" in its Latin translation of Luke's gospel,[221] as does the Douay-Rheims,[222] despite him being absent elsewhere in the Septuagint, the Vulgate, the Douay-Rheims, as well as later Catholic English translations. Who is this "extra Cainan," and if he really existed, why does he not show up anywhere else besides Luke's gospel?

Although the vast majority of later Greek manuscripts of Luke's gospel include this "extra Cainan," it is not found in the earliest Greek copies of Luke's gospel nor in the earliest copies of the Septuagint. Dr. Jonathan D. Sarfati, B.Sc. (Hon.), Ph.D., F.M., makes several historical arguments supporting this claim:

"The extra Cainan in Genesis 11 is found only in manuscripts of the LXX that were written long after Luke's Gospel. The oldest LXX manuscripts do not have this extra Cainan.

The earliest known extant copy of Luke omits the extra Cainan. This is the 102-page (originally 144) papyrus codex of the

---

[217] Ibid. DRBO.ORG. *Gospel According to Saint Luke Chapter 3*. Accessed from the Internet http://drbo.org/chapter/49003.htm

[218] Ibid. *Book of Genesis Chapter 10*. Accessed from the Internet http://drbo.org/chapter/01010.htm

[219] Ibid. *Book of Genesis Chapter 11*. Accessed from the Internet http://drbo.org/chapter/01011.htm

[220] Ibid. *1 Paralipomenon (1 Chronicles) Chapter 1*. Accessed from the Internet http://drbo.org/chapter/13001.htm

[221] Ibid. LatinVulgate.com. *THE HOLY GOSPEL OF JESUS CHRIST ACCORDING TO ST. LUKE: Chapter 3, John's mission and preaching. Christ is baptized by him.* Accessed from the Internet http://www.latinvulgate.com/lv/verse.aspx?t=1&b=3&c=3

[222] Ibid. DRBO.ORG. *Gospel According to Saint Luke Chapter 3*.

Bodmer Collection labeled P75 (dated between AD 175 and 225).

Josephus often used the LXX as his source but did not mention the second Cainan (see above).

Julius Africanus (c. AD 180–c. 250) was 'the first Christian historian known to have produced a universal chronology.' In his chronology, written in c. AD 220, he also followed the LXX ages but once again omitted this mysterious Cainan." [223]

Based on the historical evidence arguing against this "extra Cainan" being in the earliest manuscripts of either Luke's gospel as well as the Septuagint, how then did he get in the later Greek copies of Luke's gospel (as well as the Vulgate and the Douay-Rheims) while remaining absent from the earliest Septuagint?

Dr. Sarfati goes on to give a very reasonable explanation to what most likely happened to later copies of Luke's gospel:

"Note that the Greek New Testament was originally written without punctuation or spaces between words. So, Luke 3:35–38 would have been originally written as in Figure 1a. In this manuscript, TOYKAINAN (*the son* of Cainan) could have been on the end of the third line.

But suppose an early copyist of Luke's Gospel was copying the first line, but his eyes glanced at the end of the third line at TOYKAINAN. Then he would have written it on the first line as well (Figure 1b).

In English, keeping the same line formatting, and with italics indicating words added by the translators which were understood in the Greek, the passage makes sense (Figure 1c).

So, if a copyist of Luke's Gospel is responsible for the error, why is it in the LXX as well? As shown, it is not in the earlier copies, so [sic] must have been added later, by a copyist who wanted to bring it in line with Luke. And further supporting evidence comes from the fact that the ages of 'Cainan' at the birth of his son and at his death are identical to the dates of Shelah, the next one in line. This is not surprising—the copyist is confronted with the extra name in Luke, but this provides no ages. So all the

---

[223] Ibid. Creation.com. Sarfati: *Is Cainan a gap?*

copyist can do to maintain the pattern is to repeat the ages of the next patriarch."[224]

This would explain why the earliest Greek versions of Luke's gospel and the Septuagint omit this "extra Cainan" while the later versions include it. This also demonstrates the Vulgate translated from a *later* translation of Luke's gospel which included it, rather than the *earlier* versions which omitted it. Once the alleged copyist's error was made in Greek, this error was then translated into Latin in the Vulgate, and then into English in the Douay-Rheims and later English Catholic translations, like the NCV and NAB.

What this demonstrates is both the Latin translation of the Vulgate, as well as the English translation of the Douay-Rheims were <u>not</u> "faithful translations" based on the earliest copies of the Septuagint. Otherwise, the Vulgate and the Douay-Rheims would have based their translations from the *earliest*, and more accurate, Greek copies of Luke's gospel, rather than the *later* ones containing the error. The Douay-Rheims is not a faithful English translation since it contains this error, which produces a Biblical contradiction – which is impossible since the Bible is God-breathed (2 Timothy 3:16) and incapable of error.

This would not affect the inerrancy of the Bible, since Jesus promised "till heaven and earth pass away, one jot or one tittle will by no means pass from the law till all is fulfilled" (Matthew 5:18 NKJV). The original Inspired writings of both the Old and New Testaments contained no such errors, since they were penned by the original Inspired writers, "men moved by the Holy Spirit spoke from God" (2 Peter 1:21). Their copies and translations, on the other hand, are merely faithful representations of those inerrant written works. Since uninspired copyists and translators are prone to human error, it should not be surprising that an occasional "jot" or "tittle" might vary the text. Copyists were not under the Inspiration of the Holy Spirit, like the original writers were. However, none of these *few, minor* variations should affect our trust in the faithfulness of the transmission of God's Word, since <u>none</u> of these variations affect any major Christian doctrine.

As mentioned in Chapter Three, the Vulgate incorrectly translated the Greek word for "Repent" into Latin as "do penance," which was later mistranslated into English in the Douay-Rheims. In the twentieth century, English Catholic translations, like the NCV and the NAB, corrected this error echoing Luther's Latin translation of "Repent" in his *95 Theses*.

---

[224] Ibid. To view Figure 1 to see how the "extra Cainan" most likely was inadvertently copied from one line to another, refer to the article on Creation.com: https://creation.com/biblical-chronogenealogies

What is apparent from the Douay-Rheims, as well as from the NCV, NAB, the Vulgate, and the Septuagint, is they do not reflect *complete*, accurate translations and are not even completely consistent with each other in their translations. Some contain the "extra Cainan," while some do not. Some include Jeremiah 10:6-10 and 33:14-26, while some do not. Some have the same pre-Flood ages, while some do not. Some contained the Deuterocanonical book of Baruch and the epistle of Jeremiah, while some do not. Some correctly translate "Repent" from the Greek, while some do not.

As discussed in previous chapters, the *Prayer of Manasseh* appeared in early versions of both the Septuagint and the Vulgate. Yet, it was omitted from the Douay-Rheims, despite it (allegedly) being a faithful translation from the Vulgate. Obviously, this is not so.

Similarly, the same thing could be said about the early church fathers and church councils about their lack of consistency of including the books of Revelation, Baruch, the epistle of Jeremiah, and which books were attributed to Solomon versus which ones were not.

Admittedly, even Protestant translations have problems, such as including the "extra Cainan" in their translations. Some Protestant Bible commentaries have produced either footnotes or notes in the center reference column noting that the "extra Cainan" is not found in the earliest and most faithful Greek copies of Luke's gospel. It is not really an issue, since Protestants do not profess their translations are "faithful" translations from the Vulgate or the Septuagint. For Protestant Old Testaments, this is not a problem.

The best Protestant translations are taken from the earliest, most reliable Hebrew copies of the Old Testament, and the earliest, most reliable Greek copies of the New Testament. This reliance of the earliest known copies provides more assurance of a direct Hebrew-to-English and Greek-to-English translation, since this bypasses multiple translations which can lead to mistranslations of the text.

Furthermore, as mentioned in Chapter Three, the version of the Latin Vulgate the Douay-Rheims was based on was not the version Jerome produced under the authority of Pope Damasus I. Jerome's original version *excluded* the Deuterocanonical book of Baruch and the epistle of Jeremiah, which is *included* in the Douay-Rheims. Since not relying on the Septuagint, nor the Vulgate, nor the Douay-Rheims, nor the early church councils, nor even church leaders necessarily leads to the best translation or complete Old Testament canon, how can anyone be assured of the complete Old Testament canon?

Some Catholic apologists, like Trent Horn, have pointed to the canonical lists of early church fathers (ECFs) as "universal" acceptance in the early church for the Deuterocanon, including quoting some Protestant theologians for support: "For the great majority of the early church fathers, as Anglican scholar JND Kelly wrote, 'The Deuterocanonical writings ranked as Scripture in the fullest sense.'"[225] However, as Dr. James White stressed about JND Kelly, FBA:

> "Indeed, JND Kelly has said the view which now commended itself fairly generally in the Eastern Church is represented by Athanasius, Cyril of Jerusalem, Gregory Nazianzus, and Epiphanius, was that 'the Deuterocanonical books should be relegated to a *subordinate position outside the canon proper.*'"[226] (emphasis added)

As mentioned earlier, Old and New Testament canons – even among popes, bishops, and early church fathers – have produced different lists. Even Pope Siricius who reigned over the Council of Hippo in 393 and the Council of Carthage in 397 produced different lists of books. In the same way, Augustine, the bishop of Hippo, had a different list than the Council of Carthage of 397 where he was present. Even other Doctors of the Church, like Augustine, Jerome, Athanasius, Cyril of Jerusalem, Pope Gregory the Great, and others, disagreed on the canonical status of the Deuterocanon.

Some will attempt to demonstrate that as early as the second century the ECFs accepted the Deuterocanonical books as Scripture. However, many of these same ECFs accepted *non*-Deuterocanonical books too, which are not found in Catholic Bibles.

Enter Irenaeus.

IRENAEUS AND THE EARLY CHURCH FATHERS

Eusebius quoted the second century early church father (ECF), Irenaeus of Lyons (A.D. 130 to 203), from his *Against Heresies* 4:34 and 4:63, who not only "accepted" the Deuterocanonical book of Wisdom, but also *The Shepherd of Hermas*, which Irenaeus specifically called "Scripture":

> "And he [Irenaeus] not only knew, but also accepted *The Shepherd:* 'Well did *Scripture* say, "First of all believe that God is

---

[225] Horn, Trent. *Why Are Protestant Bibles Smaller?* "Catholic Answers." Published on YouTube, July 4, 2017. Accessed from the Internet https://www.youtube.com/watch?v=t_dsHmqRM1o (Begins around the 2:03 mark.)

[226] Ibid. White, James. *The Great Debate IX: Is The Apocrypha Scripture? (White vs Michuta).* (Begins around the 55:21 mark.)

one, who created and fit all things together, etc."' He quoted loosely, too, from Wisdom of Solomon: 'The vision of God confers incorruption, and incorruption brings us near to God.'"[227] (emphasis added)

Notice how Irenaeus merely "quoted loosely" from the book of Wisdom, while he more specifically referred to *The Shepherd* as "Scripture." This is significant since apologists for the Deuterocanon cite ECFs, such as Irenaeus, as historical evidence for including them as Scripture. Irenaeus did not actually refer to Wisdom as "Scripture" like he did with *The Shepherd*. He merely quoted it, much like Jude quoted *1 Enoch* in his Inspired New Testament epistle. Hence, an ECF simply quoting a writing does not necessarily equate with it being Inspired Scripture. Just because an ECF refers to a writing as "Scripture" (like *The Shepherd*) does not mean that it is, simply because it comes from the authority of an ECF from the second century.

Eusebius goes on to cite Irenaeus who wrote "...then at the time of Artaxerxes, king of Persia, he [God] inspired Ezra, the priest of the tribe of Levi, to restore *all the words of the prophets of old*, as well as *the Law given by Moses*"[228] (emphasis added). This "Ezra, the priest of the tribe of Levi" during the reign of King Artaxerxes who ruled Persia (465 to 425 B.C.), is the same Ezra mentioned in the book of Ezra (Ezra 7:11) who compiled the Old Testament, which came to be known later as the Hebrew Bible.

Irenaeus wrote God Inspired Ezra to restore "all" the words of "the prophets of old," as well as "the Law given by Moses." The use of the word "all" indicates Irenaeus recognized "all" of the prophets were limited to those prophets prior to the end of Artaxerxes' reign. As Pastor John MacArthur points out, historically, the last Old Testament prophet would have been Malachi in the Hebrew Bible:

"Over 400 years separated the final events (Nehemiah 13:4-30) and *final prophecy (Malachi 1:1-46)* recorded in the Old Testament (ca. 424 B.C.)"[229] (emphasis added)

Catholic author and apologist, Michael Voris, S.T.B., affirmed Malachi "as the last book of the Old Testament" on his YouTube channel "Church Militant":

---

[227] Ibid. Maier. *Eusebius: The Church History.* Book 5:8. *The Shepherd* was italicized in the original text by Maier, while the word "Scripture" was italicized by me for emphasis. Brackets inserted by me for clarity.

[228] Ibid. Brackets inserted by me for clarity.

[229] Ibid. The MacArthur Study Bible. *The Introduction to the Intertestamental Period*, p.1369.

"The official Bible of the [Catholic] Church has the book of Malachi as the last book of the Old Testament, and it was written probably about 400 B.C. That last book matters because the last book of the Old Testament is the first book before the New Testament, and the last book of the Old Testament talks about the coming prophet who will be the herald of the Messiah. ...you finish up with the book of Malachi, and the book of Malachi is sort of the final word on what happened in Jewish history, as far as predating the Messiah."[230]

Shortly before his conversion to Eastern Orthodoxy, Hank Hanegraaff, the President of the Christian Research Institute (CRI) and the host of the nationally syndicated "Bible Answer Man" radio broadcast, affirmed the Old Testament canon parameters ended with the prophet Malachi:

"before the four-hundred silent years, so I think we could say before or at the time of Malachi the prophet, you had the last of the Old Testament oracles and the establishment of the Old Testament Canon as complete."[231]

Ravi Zacharias reinforced Irenaeus', Mr. Voris', and Mr. Hanegraaff's understanding of the book of Malachi marking the end of the Old Testament canon:

"[Jesus] was the fulfillment of *the prophetic voices from Moses to Malachi*, who, over more than a thousand years, predicted his coming, his death, and his resurrection. From carpenters to fisherman to educators to theologians to civic leaders to a medical doctor – they all converge on the same truth. These don't sound like people who would make up a story and one by one go an early death to support it!"[232] (emphasis added)

So, by "all the prophets of old," Irenaeus was limiting those prophetic writings to the boundaries of the Hebrew Bible, ending with the last Old Testament prophet, Malachi, who had prophesized during the reign of Artaxerxes and then wrote it down later. Furthermore, Irenaeus seemed to include the Deuterocanonical book of Wisdom in his *New* Testament list

---

[230] Voris, Michael. *Once Saved Always Saved.* "Church Militant." Published on YouTube, Jul 24, 2013. Accessed from the Internet https://www.youtube.com/watch?v=00uUxWU9ADU (Begins around 05:13 in the YouTube video.) Brackets inserted by me for clarity.

[231] Hanegraaff, Hank. *The Old Testament Canon.* "Bible Answer Man." Published on YouTube, Jan 22, 2014. Accessed from the Internet https://www.youtube.com/watch?v=OeqlkH_mloY (Begins around the 0:32 second mark.)

[232] Zacharias, Ravi. *Why Jesus? Rediscovering His Truth in an Age of Mass Marketed Spirituality*, p.262. Published by FaithWords, a Hachette Book Group: New York, NY, 2012. Brackets inserted by me for clarity.

(see Appendix B. I will also discuss in more depth the role of Ezra compiling the Old Testament canon, as well as what qualified as Old Testament Scripture in a later chapter.)

Irenaeus was not the only ECF or early Christian writer to not accept all of the Deuterocanonical books, while embracing the books of the Hebrew Bible. As we read in Chapter Two, Cyril of Jerusalem – bishop and a "Doctor of the Church" – rejected all the Deuterocanonical books, except for Baruch and the epistle of Jeremiah, while embracing "all" of the books found in the Hebrew Bible.

Likewise, Eusebius quotes Julius Africanus (A.D. 160 to 240) who "suggests that the story of Susanna in the book of Daniel is spurious [apocrypha]."[233] This of course refers to the "additions" to Daniel, which were added later during the Intertestamental Period, and not from the original Inspired book of Daniel in the Hebrew Bible written centuries earlier.

Athanasius of Alexandria (A.D. 295 to 373) – another bishop and "Doctor of the Church," and known as the "champion of orthodoxy"[234] – affirmed in his *Festal Letter* 39:5-6 all the books of the Hebrew Bible except for Esther, while rejecting *all* of the Deuterocanonical books except for Baruch.[235] Among the "Two or three hundred bishops [that] were able to come"[236] to the First Ecumenical Council of Nicaea of A.D. 325, "Of course, Bishop Alexander was there, and so was the young Athanasius."[237]

Athanasius' influence was so profound in the early church, "In AD 381, Theodosius convened the second universal council of the church: the great Council of Constantinople. Here the 'Nicene Creed' assumed its final form – the form that is still used by Christians today."[238] This "great council" was the second ecumenical council of the church. The Nicene Creed was the predecessor of the Athanasian Creed attributed to Athanasius. "The statement of Christian doctrine known as the Athanasian Creed was

---

[233] Ibid. Maier. *Eusebius: The Church History*. Book 6:31, p.209. The word "apocrypha" was added by me, which means "spurious" – the word used by Africanus to refer to the writing of Susanna in the "additions" to Daniel.

[234] EWTN.com. *St. Athanasius: Bishop, Doctor of the Church*. Accessed from the Internet https://www.ewtn.com/saintsholy/saints/A/stathanasius.asp

[235] Slick, Matt. CARM.org. *Not all Church Fathers agree with the Catholic Church's view of the Canon. Athanasius (300?-375)*. Accessed from the Internet https://carm.org/early-church-fathers-canon

[236] Ibid. Litfin, *Getting to Know the Church Fathers: An Evangelical Introduction*, p.176. Brackets inserted by for clarity.

[237] Ibid.

[238] Ibid, p.181.

probably composed during his life, but not actually by him,"[239] despite Athanasius rejecting most of the Deuterocanonical books. I will discuss the implications of the Nicene Creed on the Old Testament canon in the next chapter.

Although not recognized by the Catholic Church as either an ECF nor a canonized saint, Origen of Alexandria (A.D. 185 to 232), rejected all of the Deuterocanonical books, except for Baruch and the epistle of Jeremiah. However, he too accepted "all" of the books in the Hebrew Bible.[240] Two centuries later, Jerome would reject and not include Baruch and the epistle of Jeremiah in his Latin Vulgate. Neither would the fourth and fifth century church councils mention them in their lists either.

It should be reiterated Jerome's Vulgate was *not* the same as the later version the Douay-Rheims was based on. A future version "added" the book of Baruch and the epistle of Jeremiah to it in the ninth century. The Douay-Rheims was neither a "faithful translation" of Jerome's Vulgate, nor is it the "the safest, most traditional, and most trustworthy Catholic Bible." Rather, this *much later* version of the Vulgate was a translation which "added" Baruch and the epistle of Jeremiah *FOUR CENTURIES after Jerome's original Latin translation!*

WHY WAS THE OLD TESTAMENT CANON NOT PRESERVED IN THE EARLY CHURCH?

Since the apostles and the New Testament writers, like Peter, Paul, and John, knew what the Old Testament canon included, why was it not preserved consistently into the second century and beyond? Unlike today, Scripture in the first century was not enclosed under a single cover. It was written on individual scrolls. This made copying and transporting all these scrolls nearly impossible to do, until the codex – an early form of a book – was later created as a more convenient replacement. As the death and resurrection of Jesus was spread throughout the Roman Empire, the gospel – rather than the Old Testament canon – was the essential message being preached based on the eyewitness accounts of the apostles (Luke 1:2; John 21:24; Jude v.3,17).

Until Constantine granted legal status to Christians in the Roman Empire at the Edict of Milan (A.D. 313), Christians faced intense persecution for the first three-hundred years of the church's history. Between spreading the gospel and evading persecution, defining and maintaining the Old Testament canon was not the top priority in the early church. Dr. John

---

[239] Ibid. EWTN.com. St. Athanasius.
[240] Ibid. Maier. *Eusebius: The Church History*. Book 6:25, p.206.

Barnett, B.S., B.A., M.A., M.Div. affirmed prior to this Edict, entire copies of the Bible were destroyed by the tyrannical Roman persecutor of Christians – Emperor Diocletian:

> "He [Diocletian] destroyed every Bible. There is not one complete copy of the Bible left that predates him. He destroyed every one of them.... We have pieces of all of them, because the people tore them up and distributed them. That's why we have twenty-five thousand manuscript portions. But he went through and systematically destroyed, there is not a complete copy of God's Word that predates Diocletian."[241]

This explains the lack of consistency of the Old Testament canon ECFs had in the first few centuries. Consequently, the further from Israel and the Middle East the gospel spread, the more writings were added to the Septuagint, as Gary Michuta mentioned in Chapter Two. With certain exceptions, such as Irenaeus, Jerome, and others who adopted (mostly) the Old Testament canon of the Pharisees, ECFs and Doctors of the Church in the West tended to accept later writings "added" to the Septuagint. Yet, NewAdvent.org acknowledges even ECFs from the West adopted the boundaries of the Hebrew Bible over those of the Septuagint:

> "The influence of Origen's and Athanasius's restricted canon naturally spread to the West. St. Hilary of Poitiers and Rufinus followed their footsteps, excluding the deuteros from canonical rank in theory, but admitting them in practice. The latter styles them 'ecclesiastical' books, but in authority unequal to the other Scriptures."[242]

Those in the East who rejected most of the Deuterocanon, like Cyril of Jerusalem and Athanasius of Alexandria in the fourth century, did so since they lived closer to where the Old Testament was originally written. Even Ignatius of Antioch most likely would have espoused to the Hebrew Bible embraced by the apostles Peter and Paul who frequented Antioch (Galatians 2:11), and where Peter's bishopric resided which Ignatius later succeeded.[243]

As a result, their Old Testament canons tended to be more reflective of the ancient Pharisees and later Protestants, with few exceptions. In the

---

[241] Barnett, John. *What is the Catholic Church?* "DTBM Online Video Training." Published on YouTube, Jan 17, 2017. Accessed from the Internet https://www.youtube.com/watch?v=blvtzXuayX8 (Begins at about the 38:15 mark.) Brackets inserted by me for clarity.

[242] NewAdvent.org. *Canon of the Old Testament, The canon of the Old Testament in the Catholic Church, The canon of the Old Testament during the fourth, and first half of the fifth, century.* Accessed from the Internet http://www.newadvent.org/cathen/03267a.htm

[243] Ibid. Maier. *Eusebius: The Church History.* Book 3:36, p.108.

cases where they accepted *some* books from the Deuterocanon, like Baruch and the epistle of Jeremiah, this was reflective of the early church erroneously assuming they were originally part of the canonical book of Jeremiah from the Hebrew Bible (see Chapter Four). If these ECFs and Doctors of the Church, including those in the West like Irenaeus and Augustine, had known these spurious writings were *not* part of the book of Jeremiah, they would have omitted them. Their lists would have been limited to the Hebrew Bible (see Appendix B regarding Augustine's relationship with the Hebrew Bible).

Of course, you can find ECFs and others who *did* accept the Deuterocanonical books (or at least some of them). However, this merely demonstrates the early church fathers, even in the West, were not "universal" in their acceptance of the Deuterocanon – *as a whole* – while they did acknowledge the authority of the books in the Hebrew Bible.

After the nation of Israel rejected Jesus as their promised Messiah, rabbinic Judaism continued to embrace the Hebrew Bible into the church age. Although the Roman Empire was responsible for Jesus' execution, the Jews demanded Pilate to "Crucify Him!" (Matthew 27:22-23) and accepted personal responsibility for His crucifixion, "His blood shall be on us and our children!" (v.25). As later ECFs, particularly in the West, began to embrace writings not found in the Hebrew Bible, they distanced themselves from non-messianic Jews as "Christ-killers," who espoused to the smaller canon adopted from the Pharisees.

As early as the second century, ECFs began to accept uninspired writings as Scripture (such as Irenaeus), including those being added to the Septuagint. As centuries elapsed, Catholicism adopted a larger canon, which included the so-called Deuterocanon, despite being rejected by Jesus, His disciples, and the apostle Paul in the first century (see Chapter One).

Although Jews contemporary with and after the time of Christ were wrong for rejecting His Messianic claims, it is inappropriate to conclude they also did not possess the complete Old Testament canon. Jesus acknowledged the Pharisees "have Moses and the Prophets" (Luke 16:14,16,19), referring to the complete Old Testament canon, which unbelieving Jews possess today. Their rejection was not because they were lacking any Inspired books. It was because they had added countless man-made "traditions" to their messianic expectations not found in their canon (Matthew 15:3-9). Because of this they rejected their Messiah, despite having possession of the entire Old Testament.

Before advancing to the next chapter, the implications from the noteworthy first century Jewish historian on the Old Testament canon should not be overlooked.

Enter Flavius Josephus.

FLAVIUS JOSEPHUS

Flavius Josephus (A.D. 37 to 100) is most known for his writings *Antiquities of the Jews* and *The Jewish War*. In two of his other books titled *Against Aprion*, "he enumerates the canonical Scriptures forming the Old Testament, so-called, showing which of them, rooted in ancient tradition, are undisputed among the Hebrews."[244]

In his list, Josephus records *all* of the books of the Hebrew Bible, either explicitly or implicitly, in an "only twenty-two" book format.[245] This involved blending individual books together in a single format, such as "*the prophets after Moses* recorded the events of their own times in thirteen books"[246] (emphasis added). Maier breaks these "thirteen prophets" down to be from Joshua to Nehemiah.[247] He also breaks down the "remaining four contain hymns to God and precepts for human conduct"[248] to be the Psalms, Proverbs, Ecclesiastes, and the Song of Solomon.[249]

Thus, Josephus affirmed the same thirty-nine Old Testament book canon of later Protestants, just in a condensed twenty-two-book format in his *Against Aprion* 1:8. The implication of this "twenty-two" book format is Jews prior to, and contemporary with, the time of Josephus would have been familiar with a third division of the Hebrew Bible, since they were able to number their canon "twenty-two" (or "twenty-four" – see Appendix A).

Josephus also agreed with the later ECF, Irenaeus, "From the time of Artaxerxes to our own history has been recorded, but *it does not merit equal credence with the rest because there has not been an unbroken succession of prophets*"[250] (emphasis added). No doubt "from the time of Artaxerxes" refers to the time period before the Deuterocanonical books, which were written long after the death of Artaxerxes – the Intertestamental Period.

---

244 Ibid, Book 3:9, p.90.
245 Ibid, Book 3:10, p.90-91.
246 Ibid, p.91.
247 Ibid, p.91, footnote #13 by Maier.
248 Ibid, p.91.
249 Ibid, p.91, footnote #14 by Maier.
250 Ibid, p.91.

Although Josephus was neither a Christian nor an early church father, NewAdvent.org notes many historians believed Josephus was a Pharisee.[251] As mentioned in previous chapters, while the Jews – as a whole – did not have a closed Old Testament canon, *the Pharisees did.* This Pharisaic canon was limited to the boundaries of the Hebrew Bible, which is reflected in the canon Josephus produced in *Against Aprion* 1:8, and later in Protestant Old Testaments.

Even early church fathers, like Irenaeus, Athanasius, Africanus, and others cannot be looked at as authorities to an early "universal" church belief in the Old Testament canon, let alone on doctrinal matters. Jimmy Akin from Catholic Answers exclaimed, "Boy, did they not always agree!"[252] They disagreed with not only the later church councils and later Catholic translations, but the ECFs even disagreed among themselves. Therefore, the only trustworthy authority to look towards to determine the canonicity of the *Old* Testament with confidence is the *New* Testament.

Before doing so, I must examine one other historic event that not only affected the structure of the church, but also the Old Testament canon itself – the Great Schism of 1054.

---

[251] NewAdvent.org. *Book of Daniel, Proto-canonical portions, Authorship and date of composition.* Accessed from the Internet http://www.newadvent.org/cathen/04621b.htm

[252] Akin, Jimmy. *Did the Fathers always agree with each other?* "Catholic Answers." Published on YouTube, Mar 25, 2011. Accessed from the Internet https://www.youtube.com/watch?v=2COKzO4Bd0U (Begins around the 0:18 mark.)

CHAPTER SIX: What about the Eastern Orthodox Bible?

"When the Helper comes, whom I will send to you from the Father, that is the Spirit of truth who proceeds from the Father, He will testify about Me" (John 15:26)

1054 was another historic year that completely changed the organization of the medieval church. Nearly half of a millennium before the Protestant Reformation was even a thought, another division in the church occurred, which later became known as "The Great Schism." The eastern Greek-speaking church in Constantinople had separated, or "schismed," from the western Latin-speaking church in Rome. Although the proverbial straw which broke the eastern church's back came to be known as the "Filioque Controversy," one of the effects of the Great Schism resulted in the change of the Old Testament canon in the East.

The issue of the *Filioque* (pronounced: "fill-ee-OH-quay") is paramount to understanding not only how it affected the unity of the eastern and western churches, but also the Old Testament canon itself. Before I discuss its implications on the canon, I must begin with how the issue of the *Filioque* split the church and ultimately affected the canon in the East.

THE FILIOQUE CONTROVERSY

The *Filioque*, or *Filioque Clause*, has its roots dated back to the First Ecumenical Council of Nicaea I in A.D. 325. This council formed what came to be known as the Nicene Creed. However, the form we have today is not the same as the one in this early fourth century council. The original Nicene Creed from A.D. 325, reproduced from the Christian Classics Ethereal Library, reads:

"We believe in one God, the Father Almighty, Maker of all things visible and invisible. And in one Lord Jesus Christ, the Son of God, begotten of the Father [the only-begotten; that is, of the essence of the Father, God of God], Light of Light, very God of very God, begotten, not made, being of one substance (ὁμοούσιον) with the Father; by whom all things were made [both in heaven and on earth]; who for us men, and for our salvation, came down and was incarnate and was made man; he suffered, and the third day he rose again, ascended into heaven;

113

from thence he shall come to judge the quick and the dead. And in the Holy Ghost."[253]

This text is not exactly the same Creed read in churches today. The words in brackets were added later to the Creed. To combat Arianism – the false belief of Jesus and the Holy Spirit being merely created beings, and not coequal and coeternal with the Father – a later ecumenical council was convened under the reign of Pope Damasus I, the same pope who commissioned Jerome to translate the Vulgate. The First Council of Constantinople of A.D. 381 (which was the second ecumenical council of the church) was assembled, which included additional wording to the Creed of A.D. 325 to clarify both the Deity of Christ and the Deity of the Holy Spirit:

> "We believe in one God, the Father Almighty, Maker of heaven and earth, and of all things visible and invisible. And in one Lord Jesus Christ, the only-begotten Son of God, begotten of the Father before all worlds (æons), Light of Light, very God of very God, begotten, not made, being of one substance with the Father; by whom all things were made; who for us men, and for our salvation, came down from heaven, and was incarnate by the Holy Ghost of the Virgin Mary, and was made man; he was crucified for us under Pontius Pilate, and suffered, and was buried, and the third day he rose again, according to the Scriptures, and ascended into heaven, and sitteth on the right hand of the Father; from thence he shall come again, with glory, to judge the quick and the dead; whose kingdom shall have no end. And in *the Holy Ghost*, the Lord and Giver of life, *who proceedeth from the Father*, who with the Father and the Son together is worshiped and glorified, who spake by the prophets. In one holy catholic and apostolic Church; we acknowledge one baptism for the remission of sins; we look for the resurrection of the dead, and the life of the world to come. Amen."[254] (emphasis added)

This extended version of the Creed expanded and clarified not only the Deity of Jesus, but also the Deity of the Holy Spirit, which we find in the New Testament (Matthew 28:19; 2 Corinthians 13:14; etc.) However, in this second ecumenical council the Creed states "the Holy

---

[253] Christian Classics Ethereal Library. Bringing classic Christian books to life. *Creeds of Christendom, with a History and Critical notes. Volume I. The History of Creeds by Philip Schaff: 8. The Nicene Creed.* Accessed from the Internet http://www.ccel.org/ccel/schaff/creeds1.iv.iii.html. English words in brackets and the Greek equivalent in parentheses were taken from the original text from the Web site.

[254] Ibid. The Latin term in parentheses was taken from the original text from the Web site.

Ghost...proceedeth from *the Father*," only. It does not say the Holy Spirit [Ghost] "proceedeth from *the Son*," also. This is the root of the *Filioque Controversy.*

The Latin term "filioque," which translated means "of the Son," was later "added to the creed recited in the Roman Mass (Latin Rite) by Pope Benedict VIII (1024)"[255] – the same year he died. However, Pope Benedict VIII did not "edit" the Creed in an ecumenical council, like the Council of Constantinople had. The Eastern Orthodox Church took issue with this, since they believed he did not have the ecclesiastical support of an ecumenical church council to make this decision on his own, like Pope Sylvester I had when he sent papal legates to the First Ecumenical Council of Nicaea in A.D. 325, which he later confirmed its decrees via their signatures.[256]

Furthermore, the church in the east believed Pope Benedict VIII violated Canon VII of the Third Ecumenical Council of A.D. 431 (the Council of Ephesus) since the words "of the Son" (filioque) were not included in either of the two previous Ecumenical Councils of Nicaea or Constantinople:

"When these things had been read, the holy Synod decreed that it is unlawful for any man to bring forward, or to write, or to compose a different (ἑτέραν) Faith as a rival to that *established by the holy Fathers assembled with the Holy Ghost in Nicæa.* But those who shall dare to compose a different faith, or to introduce or offer it to persons desiring to turn to the acknowledgment of the truth, whether from Heathenism or from Judaism, or from any heresy whatsoever, *shall be deposed, if they be bishops or clergymen; bishops from the episcopate and clergymen from the clergy;* and if they be laymen, they shall be anathematized."[257] (emphasis added)

The issue with the eastern church was not whether or not the eleventh century pope had *Scriptural* support for "adding" the *Filioque* to the Nicene Creed. Rather, they argued the pope could not – *on his own authority alone* – add anything to the Creed not found in either of the Ecumenical

---

[255] EWTN.com. *Straight Answers, Fr. William Sanders: The Wording of the Nicene Creed.* Accessed from the Internet
https://www.ewtn.com/library/ANSWERS/FILIOQUE.HTM

[256] NewAdvent.org. Pope Sylvester I (314-335). Accessed from the Internet
http://www.newadvent.org/cathen/14370a.htm

[257] Ibid. Christian Classics Ethereal Library. *NPNF2-14. The Seven Ecumenical Councils by Philip Schaff: Canon VII.* Accessed from the Internet
http://www.ccel.org/ccel/schaff/npnf214.x.xvi.x.html. The Greek term in parenthesis was taken from the original text from the Web site.

Councils of Nicaea or Constantinople, without another ecumenical council to back up his actions. They believed saying the Holy Spirit was "proceedeth" by the Son too could not be found in the original Creed from Nicaea, nor its update from Constantinople. They based this on Canon VII from the Ecumenical Council of Ephesus in A.D. 431.

The eastern church believed the *Filioque* was not explicit in either Creed from either council, and the later pope did not have the authority to add to it, since it "brought forward" something "different" by what was "established by the holy Fathers assembled with the Holy Ghost in Nicaea." Neither Nicaea nor Constantinople said anything about the Holy Spirit "proceeding from *the Son*." Constantinople <u>only</u> declared the Holy Spirit was: "proceeding by *the Father*."

It can be demonstrated from Scripture the *Filioque* is completely Biblical. Jesus began by saying, "But the Helper, the Holy Spirit, *whom the Father will send* in My name" (John 14:26). He continued, "When the Helper comes, *whom I will send* from the Father, that is the Spirit of truth, who proceeds from the Father, He will testify about Me" (John 15:26, emphasis added).

This "twofold-sending" of the Holy Spirit from *both* the Father <u>and</u> *"of the Son"* ("Filioque") is completely backed up by Scripture. Despite being Scripturally-supported, it is not supported by any of the first three ecumenical councils, nor is Pope Benedict VIII adding to it in the eleventh century.

The real dilemma is: "How can a pope 'change' a ruling of a previous ecumenical council, led by previous popes like Pope Sylvester I at Nicaea or Pope Damasus I at Constantinople, if he does not have an ecumenical council to back him up?" How can one pope "overrule" a previous pope, particularly one who reigned over an ecumenical council? Who has the higher authority: a pope heading an ecumenical council, or one who does not? This becomes an authority issue.

In his book, *Martin Luther: The Man Who Rediscovered God And Changed The World*, author Eric Metaxas declared "...it was at the Council of Nicaea that the Eastern Orthodox Church and the Western Roman Church had been declared equal."[258] As a result of Pope Benedict VIII taking it upon himself to "overrule" these previous ecumenical councils, despite having *Scriptural* support for doing so, this ultimate authority of the pope "ruling over" the other bishops of the east — including the bishop of

---

[258] Metaxas, Eric. *Martin Luther: The Man Who Rediscovered God and Changed the World*, p.167. Viking, an imprint of Penguin Random House LLC: New York, New York, 2017.

Constantinople – led to the Greek church in the east breaking away from the Latin church in the west.

It also led to the change in the Eastern Orthodox Old Testament Scriptures.

APOCRYPHAL BOOKS IN THE SEPTUAGINT AND THE NEW TESTAMENT

While including both the Hebrew Bible and the Deuterocanonical books in their canon, the Eastern Orthodox Church also included Apocryphal writings which are in neither Catholic nor Protestant Old Testaments. They argued these Apocryphal writings were *also* found in the Septuagint.

Some versions of the Septuagint contain the Apocryphal books of *3 Maccabees* and *4 Maccabees*, as well as the *Prayer of Manasseh* and *3 Esdras*.[259] Other versions, like those Apocryphal books included in the Old Testament canon of the Ethiopian Tewahedo Church, mentioned in Chapter Two, included additional writings. Some of these included: *4 Esdras*, *1 Enoch*, and *Jubilees*, which "The Ethiopic version of the Old and New Testament was made from the Septuagint."[260] Jude even quotes from *1 Enoch* in his Inspired epistle (Jude v.14).

In Chapter Two, Trent Horn, Catholic author and staff apologist for Catholic Answers, further admitted in an online audio episode: "Yes, Jesus and the apostles quote the Old Testament a lot, and, no, there's no direct quotation of the Deuterocanonical books in Scripture."[261] Yet, one of the criteria he used earlier in the episode to defend the Inspiration of the Deuterocanon was the New Testament "alluding" to the Deuterocanon.[262]

The argument for accepting the Deuterocanon, simply because these books are alluded to in the New Testament and because they were in the Septuagint, can *also* be used to justify the additional Apocryphal books found in Eastern Orthodox Old Testaments. The New Testament quotes or alludes to the Apocryphal books *more frequently* than most of the Deuterocanonical books.

---

[259] *Septuagint Bible w/ Apocrypha LXX. Old Testament.* Accessed from the Internet https://www.biblestudytools.com/lxx/. The Web site lists *3 Esdras* as "*1 Esdras*," which is how it is sometimes classified. "Esdras" is the Greek equivalent of Ezra but is listed as "*1 Esdras*" to differentiate it from the Old Testament book of Ezra.

[260] Ibid. *Ethiopian Orthodox Tewahedo Church Faith and Order: The Bible.*

[261] Ibid. Horn, Trent. *"Why Catholic Bibles Are Bigger."* Accessed from the Internet https://www.catholic.com/audio/cot/25 (Beginning at about the 19:47 mark.)

[262] Ibid.

In Appendix D of his book *"The Biblical Canon: Its Origin, Transmission, and Authority,"* Lee Martin McDonald gives a list of New Testament citations of, and allusions to, Apocryphal and Pseudepigraphal (false authorship) Writings:[263]

For example, the *Testament of Reuben* and the *Testament of Dan* are quoted or alluded to just as frequently in the New Testament as Susanna and Bel and the Dragon ("additions" to Daniel) – two times each. *Third Esdras*, the book of *Jubilees*, the *Assumption of Moses*,[264] the *Testament of Joseph*, and the *Testament of Levi* are all mentioned more frequently than both Susanna and Bel and the Dragon – three times, three times, four times, five times, six times, two times, and two times each, respectfully. *Second Baruch* and *3 Maccabees* are mentioned more times than Baruch – thirteen times, ten times, and eight times, respectfully. *Fourth Maccabees* and the *Psalms of Solomon* are mentioned more often than Judith, Tobit, and 1 Maccabees – thirty-two times, thirty-four times, fourteen times, twenty-nine times, and twenty times, respectfully. *First Enoch* is mentioned more frequently than 2 Maccabees – sixty-four times and thirty-seven times, respectfully.

In addition to these Apocryphal writings quoted or alluded to in the New Testament, there are several other Apocryphal writings referenced in the New Testament as well, such as: the *Testament of Zebulun*, the *Testament of Benjamin*, the *Testament of Naphtali*, the *Life of Adam and Eve*, the *Martyrdom and Ascension of Isaiah*, and the *Apocalypse of Baruch* – all of which are mentioned as frequently as the Deuterocanonical epistle of Jeremiah, all once each. As mentioned in Chapter Two, the apostle Paul quoted the Greek poet Epimenides (Acts 17:28; Titus 1:12), as well as from the play "Thais" by Menander (1 Corinthians 15:33).

Only the Deuterocanonical books of Sirach and Wisdom out-reference these Apocryphal books in the New Testament, one-hundred and thirteen times and one-hundred and nine times, respectively. However, their number of references pale in comparison to the New Testament quoting or alluding to some of the books from the Hebrew Bible, such as Isaiah, the Psalms, Exodus, Genesis, Deuteronomy, Ezekiel, Daniel, and Jeremiah – four-hundred and nineteen times, four-hundred and fourteen times, two-hundred and forty times, two-hundred and thirty-eight times, one-hundred

---

263 Ibid. McDonald, Lee Martin. *The Biblical Canon. Appendix D: New Testament Citations of and Allusions to Apocryphal and Pseudepigraphal Writings*, p.452-464. Source: Adapted from Novum Testamentum Graece (27th ed.; ed. B. Aland, K. Aland, J. Karavidopoulous, C. M. Martini, and B. M. Metzger; Stuttgart: Deutsche Bibelgesellschaft, 1993), 800-806.

264 McDonald does not list the reference to Jude v.9 as an allusion to the *Assumption of Moses*, and only lists three allusions. Yet, this fourth allusion is clearly from the *Assumption*.

and ninety-six times, one-hundred and forty-one times, one-hundred and thirty-three times, and one-hundred and twenty-five times, respectfully.[265]

Many would contend if a writing from the Old Testament *era* is alluded to in the New Testament then that should qualify for it being included in the Old Testament *canon*. Would this mean we would have to <u>also</u> include all of the above Apocryphal writings as well, since they too are quoted or alluded to in the New Testament and are from the Old Testament *era*?

Upon researching for the preparation of the five-hundred-year anniversary of the Protestant Reformation, I discovered most of these Apocryphal books were included in many Old Testaments, particularly in the Eastern Orthodox[266] and Oriental Orthodox traditions.[267] Many of them were found in either the Septuagint, the Vulgate, and/or alluded to in the New Testament.

So, using the "it-is-alluded-to-in-the-New Testament" argument causes more problems for *excluding* these Apocryphal books, than for including the Deuterocanonical books. The Great Schism of 1054 resulted in the Eastern Orthodox churches, and others, attempting to use the same criteria their Catholic forefathers used in determining the Old Testament canon — those being mentioned in either the New Testament, the Vulgate, the Septuagint, or all of the above.

Did Pope Benedict VIII have *Scriptural* justification for "adding" the *Filioque* to the Nicene Creed in the eleventh century? Yes, he did. But this creates a huge problem. If the justification for including the *Filioque* should be based on Scripture and not on ecumenical councils, then there is no justification for believing that *anything* in *any* ecumenical council is permanently binding in the church.

This would especially be true if someone discovered something later in Scripture to either "add to" or "take away" from a previous ecumenical council, such as "adding" the *Filioque* to the Nicene Creed. Therefore, the later Ecumenical Councils of Florence (1441) and Trent (1546) have no real validity, since a later pope could just as easily "add" books to the Old Testament, just as Pope Benedict VII "added" the *Filioque* to the Nicene Creed seven-hundred years later.

---

[265] Ibid, McDonald, p.244, reference #4 which he cites Andrew E. Hill, *Baker's Handbook of Bible Lists* (Grand Rapids: Baker, 1981), 102-3.

[266] Ibid. Bible Research. *The Old Testament Canon and Apocrypha.*

[267] Ibid. *Ethiopian Orthodox Tewahedo Church Faith and Order: The Bible.*

POPE JOHN PAUL II AND THE FILIOQUE / POPE GREGORY I AND THE DEUTEROCANON

Before concluding this chapter, the issue of the authority of including the *Filioque* in the Nicene Creed produced an interesting meeting in 2004. Dr. Ryan Reeves, Associate Professor of Historical Theology at Gordon-Conwell Theological Seminary, discussed a historical event he attended between the Patriarch of Constantinople and the late Pope John Paul II. At the Pallium Mass in Rome that year, they said the Nicene Creed together in Greek. However, Pope John Paul II did <u>not</u> say the *Filioque!*[268]

If Pope Benedict VIII had the authority to "add" the *Filioque* to the Nicene Creed, because he had Scriptural support, then by what authority did Pope John Paul II have for "removing" it during his prayer with the Patriarch? Can a pope simply "decide" for himself what is doctrinal, regardless if he has support or not for doing so, depending on the situation, and by what authority?

In the late sixth century, Pope Gregory I (Gregory the Great) and Doctor of the Church[269] rejected the canonicity of the Deuterocanonical books which were previously accepted by Pope Damasus I, Pope Siricius, and Pope Boniface I from the fourth and fifth century church councils:

> "We shall not act rashly, if we accept a testimony of books, which, although *not canonical*, have been published for the edification of the Church."[270] (emphasis added)

Can a book be Inspired Scripture, while not being "canonical" like Pope Gregory I appears to be implying? Are there different "levels" of canonicity of what classifies as God's Word? As mentioned in Chapter Four, although Sirach was considered a "sacred book" at the Council of Florence (1441), the canonicity of the Deuterocanonical book of Sirach was not officially "defined" until the next century at the Council of Trent (1546).[271]

In Chapter Five, Irenaeus referred to uninspired books as "Scripture." However, every book in the Protestant Bible is both "sacred," as well as

---

[268] Reeves, Ryan. "*Great Schism (1054).*" Published on YouTube Apr 4, 2015. Accessed from the Internet https://www.youtube.com/watch?v=Q_s9Rcsg5Ul (Begins about the 23:21 mark. The 24:29 mark is where Dr. Ryans states Pope John Paul II did not say the *Filioque.*)

[269] Ibid. NewAdvent.org. *Doctors of the Church.* Accessed from the Internet http://www.newadvent.org/cathen/05075a.htm

[270] EWTN.com. "*Catholic Q&A.*" Canon of Scripture Question from Gottscheer Turk on 10/31/2001: Answer by Fr. John Echert on 11/11/2001. Accessed from the Internet http://www.ewtn.com/v/experts/showmessage.asp?number=335152

[271] Ibid. ETWN.com. *Deuterocanonical Books in Canon of Scripture.* Accessed from the Internet http://www.ewtn.com/library/SCRIPTUR/DEUTEROS.TXT

"canonical" and Inspired, since "*All* Scripture is Inspired" (or "God-breathed" – 2 Timothy 3:16).

Even though Pope Gregory I was simply expressing his opinion, by what authority did he have to publicly reject the Deuterocanon as being "not canonical," after previous popes and church councils had accepted them? Again, can a pope simply "decide" what is and what is not canonical and doctrinal, regardless if he has support for it or not, and by what authority?

By the sixteenth century, the authority of the pope had usurped even the authority of ecumenical church councils to the point of contradicting them. Martin Luther asserted "the recent Lateran Council has reversed the claim of the councils of Constance and Basel that a council is above a pope."[272]

It was "Luther's contention – which he had made in his *Resolutions* – that it was not until the reign of Pope Sylvester in the early fourth century that the Roman church had put itself forward as above all other churches."[273] As Luther researched deeper into the issue of "papal primacy," he discovered "It was not possible from Scripture to find any evidence that it had been divinely ordained."[274] This included having "primacy above" the bishop of Constantinople in the eastern Greek church.

ERASMUS AND CARDINALS ON THE CANON

Even cardinals and other prominent Catholic leaders during the Reformation questioned the Old Testament canon of the Catholic Church. Dr. Ed Gallagher, who teaches Biblical studies at Heritage Christian University in Florence, Alabama, stated Cardinal Thomas Cajetan "did advocate a biblical canon more in keeping with the Reformers' views than what would become Catholic dogma a decade after his death at the Council of Trent (1546)."[275] On his commentary on the book of Esther, Cajetan wrote:

"And in this place we conclude the commentaries on the historical books of the Old Testament. For the rest (i.e., *Judith,*

---

[272] Ibid. Metaxas. *Martin Luther*, p.176. Metaxas quotes Luther citing him in Roland Bainton's *Here I Stand*. Nashville: Abingdon Press, 2013.

[273] Ibid, p.166.

[274] Ibid, p.168.

[275] Gallagher, Ed. *Our Beans: Biblical and Patristic Studies, especially dealing with the reception of the Hebrew Bible in Early Christianity*, "Cajetan on the OT Canon." Monday, February 27, 2017. Accessed from the Internet https://sanctushieronymus.blogspot.com/2017/02/according-to-wikipedia-thomas-cardinal.html

Tobit, and the books of the Maccabees) are reckoned by divine Jerome as *outside the canonical books* and he places them *among the apocrypha, with the book of Wisdom and Ecclesiasticus...*those books...are *not canonical.*"[276] (emphasis added)

Cardinal Ximénes and Erasmus "both excluded the deuterocanonical literature from the canon."[277] In his *Complutensian Polyglot* project, Ximénes identified "books outside the canon which the Church has received more for the edification of the people than for the authoritative confirmation of ecclesiastical dogmas," which he did not include in "the canonical OT [Old Testament] as Pentateuch, Prophets, Hagiographa [Writings]."[278] In Erasmus' 1525 edition of Jerome, Gallagher cites Erasmus:

> "By what spirit the Church approves certainly matters. For you would attribute equal authority to the volumes of the Hebrews and the four Gospels; she certainly does not want the same weight to belong to the books of Judith, Tobit, and Wisdom, as for the Pentateuch of Moses."[279]

In *The Explanation of the Apostle's Creed* (1533), Erasmus:

> "lists the OT [Old Testament] books thus: Pentateuch, Joshua, Judges, Ruth, four books of Kingdoms, Paralipomenon [the Chronicles], two books of Ezra (which the Hebrews count as one), Isaiah, Jeremiah, Ezekiel, Daniel, Twelve Minor Prophets (not individually named), Job, Psalms, Proverbs, Ecclesiastes, Song of Songs."[280]

These are further reasons why relying on church leaders and councils – including popes, cardinals, and ecumenical councils, which often contradict each other – can create confusion as to "what" is the ultimate authority on the Old Testament canon. While Catholic authors and apologists, like Gary Michuta and Catholic Answers attempt to defend why Catholic Bibles are "bigger" than Protestant Bibles, perhaps they should also attempt to address why Catholic Bibles are "smaller" than Eastern Orthodox and other Bibles.

---

[276] Ibid.

[277] Gallagher, Ed. *Our Beans: Biblical and Patristic Studies, especially dealing with the reception of the Hebrew Bible in Early Christianity,* "The Old Testament Canon in the Early Sixteenth Century." Wednesday, May 13, 2015. Accessed from the Internet http://sanctushieronymus.blogspot.com/2015/05/the-old-testament-canon-in-early.html

[278] Ibid. Brackets inserted by me for clarity.

[279] Ibid.

[280] Ibid. Parentheses included in the original text. Brackets inserted by me for clarity.

Upon studying a chart of the table of the canons of various Christian traditions, six out of seven include <u>all</u> twenty-seven books of the *New Testament*.[281] (I will cover the validity of the New Testament canon in Chapter Ten, as well as its dependability as a Christian's sole source for the canon of the Old Testament.)

This nearly universal agreement of the same twenty-seven-book New Testament canon is much more significant and harmonious, than the Old Testament canon of many of these same Christian traditions. The only agreements they all have on the Old Testament are the five books of Moses and the twelve "minor prophets." Where they disagree are the "major prophets" and the rest of the non-prophetic "writings." Since the New Testament has a lot to say about both the Old Testament era and writings, what can we discover from the New Testament about the Old Testament canon itself?

This will be the focus of the next chapter.

---

[281] Wikipedia.org. *Biblical canon, Christian biblical canons, Canons of various Christian traditions, New Testament, Table: 2.4.2.1.* Accessed from the Internet https://en.wikipedia.org/wiki/Biblical_canon#Table_2

CHAPTER SEVEN: The Law and the Prophets...*and the Psalms?*

"Now He said to them, 'These are My words which I spoke to you while I was still with you, that all things which are written about Me in the Law of Moses and the Prophets and the Psalms must be fulfilled. Then He opened their minds to understand the Scriptures" (Luke 24:44-45)

400 B.C. was a pivotal point in Jewish history. It marked the closing of the Hebrew Bible with its last book, Nehemiah, which was originally one book with Ezra (Ezra-Nehemiah, or 1 and 2 Esdras in Greek). Although there would be other Jewish texts written later, like the Deuterocanonical and Apocryphal writings mentioned in the previous chapter, they would not *all* be accepted by every Jew as Inspired Scripture, particularly the Pharisees. They would also be rejected by Jesus, His disciples, the New Testament writers, and the first century Christian Church as part of the Old Testament canon.

Some may insist there is no historical nor Scriptural evidence for the Hebrew Bible "closing" at the conclusion of the fifth century B.C. Others may argue the lack of evidence the Pharisees only accepted the books found in the boundaries of the Hebrew Bible. As Catholic author, apologist, and church historian Jimmy Akin mentioned in Chapter One, the Pharisees shared the exact same books found in Protestant Old Testaments today.

Still, some may contend there was no fixed Pharisaic canon in the early first century A.D. during Jesus' earthly ministry. In his Revised Second Edition of *Why Catholic Bibles Are Bigger* (referenced from Mishnah, *Yadayim* 3:5 et al), Gary Michuta states: "Even the Pharisees were not unified on this point. The Pharisaic schools of Shammai and Hillel were divided on Ecclesiastes, Song of Solomon, Esther, and possibly other books as well."[282] Commenting on the Pharisaic school of Shammai on the book of Proverbs from "the Writings," NewAdvent.org states:

"It is true that certain doubts as to the inspiration of the Book of Proverbs, which had been entertained by ancient rabbis who belonged to the School of Shammai...but these were only

---

[282] Michuta, Gary G. *Why Catholic Bibles Are Bigger*, Revised Second Edition., Chapter One *"Was the Old Testament Canon Closed Before Christ?: Romans 3:1-2 – Jewish Province Argument."* Published by Catholic Answers, Inc: El Cajon, California, 2017. Referenced from Mishnah, *Yadayim* 3:5 et al. See William Osterley's *The Books of the Apocrypha: Their Origin, Teaching, and Contents* (New York: Fleming Revell Company, 1914), 170-171.

theoretical difficulties which could not induce the Jewish leaders of the time to count this book out of the Canon."[283]

"Marcel" serves as a pastoral counselor at St. Mary's Catholic Center at Texas A&M and is the founder of and Executive Director of Catholic Missionary Disciples.[284] He affirms, "The Samaritans and Sadducees accepted the law but rejected the prophets and writings. The Pharisees accepted all three."[285]

NewAdvent.org further acknowledges, "It was the method of the school of Shammai rather than that of Hillel which Christ condemned."[286] A few Catholic scholars "make Him [Christ] out to have belonged to the school of Hillel... (Gigot, "General Introduction to the Study of the Holy Scripture", New York, 1900, p. 422)."[287] However, there is no Scriptural evidence "Christ belonged to any of the fallible Jewish schools of interpretation."[288]

Early Pharisees from the school of Hillel espoused to the Hebrew Bible as I will demonstrate in this chapter. NewAdvent.org describes Hillel as "perhaps the cleverest and best of the rabbis of his day."[289] It was from the Pharisaic school of Hillel which the apostle Paul was a student (see below).

Albert C. Sundberg was a Professor of the New Testament, and an ordained minister in the Reformed United Church. In his work, "The Old Testament of the Early Church" Revisited, he wrote:

> "We cannot press the date of the fixation of the Pharisaic canon earlier than the time of Hillel, as an occasional scholar has attempted to do."[290]

---

[283] NewAdvent.org. *Book of Proverbs, Names and general object.* Accessed from the Internet http://www.newadvent.org/cathen/12505b.htm

[284] Marcel. St. Mary's Aggie Catholic Blog, *A New 'Marcel the Shell,'* November 16, 2011. Accessed from the Internet http://www.aggiecatholicblog.org/2011/11/a-new-marcel-the-shell/

[285] Ibid. *Why Catholic Bibles Have More Books Than Protestant Bibles,* April 25, 2015. Accessed from the Internet http://www.aggiecatholicblog.org/2016/04/why-catholic-bibles-have-more-books-than-protestant-bibles/

[286] NewAdvent.org. *Shammai.* Accessed from the Internet http://www.newadvent.org/cathen/13751a.htm

[287] Ibid. Brackets inserted by me for clarity. Parentheses in the original text.

[288] Ibid.

[289] NewAdvent.org. *Hillel.* Accessed from the Internet http://www.newadvent.org/cathen/07354c.htm

[290] Sundberg, Jr., Albert C. "The Old Testament of the Early Church" Revisited. Published by Monmouth College: Monmouth, Illinois. 1997. Accessed from the Internet https://department.monm.edu/classics/speel_festschrift/sundbergjr.htm

McDonald points out Sundberg also "argues that the Christians simply adopted the sacred writings in use within Pharisaic Judaism prior to the separation of Christians from Jews" and "what literature was held to be sacred and authoritative by the early Christians was the same as that which existed in pre-70 C.E. Pharisaic Judaism in Palestine."[291] McDonald stressed Sundberg "essentially dismantled the familiar old Alexandrian canon hypothesis that tried to account for the larger Christian canon of the OT [Old Testament] books adopted and used by the early Christians."[292] The Alexandrian canon was comprised of the Hebrew Bible and the Deuterocanon, while the Palestinian canon was limited to the Hebrew Bible.

As demonstrated in this book from both a historical and Biblical standpoint, Pharisaic Judaism from the school of Hillel espoused to the boundaries of the Hebrew Bible for their Old Testament canon excluding the Deuterocanon, which Sundberg even concedes. McDonald confirms this:

> "…Hillel, who came from Babylon, heavily influenced the scope of the biblical canon for Pharisaic Judaism. …it reflects the views that eventually obtained acceptance in rabbinic Judaism."[293]

> "…Hillel's interpretation prevailed and became foundational for surviving Judaism of the late first and second centuries C.E. Many of the teachings of Hillel were passed on to his best-known pupil in the first century C.E., Rabban Gamaliel, who was the teacher of the Apostle Paul (Acts 22:3; cf. 5:34-35)."[294]

> "The Jews were probably influenced to adopt a more conservative collection of sacred Scriptures by Hillel, who came from Babylon and accepted only those writings that dated from roughly the time of Ezra and Nehemiah and earlier….the earliest list of sacred books among the Jews…comes from Babylon…. As a result, the current canon of the HB [Hebrew Bible] and the Protestant OT [Old Testament] reflects a Babylonian flavor."[295]

---

[291] Ibid. McDonald, Lee Martin. *The Biblical Canon*, pp.76-77. Referenced from Sundberg, A. C., Jr. "The Bible Canon and the Christian Doctrine of Inspiration." *Interpretation* 29 (1975): 352-71.

[292] Ibid, Preface to the Third Edition, p. xviii. Brackets inserted by me for clarity.

[293] Ibid, p.165

[294] Ibid, p.181.

[295] Ibid, p.223. Brackets inserted by me for clarity.

Hillel the Elder lived from about 70 B.C. to 10 A.D.,[296] and was (allegedly) the head of the Sanhedrin in his day and a descendant of the family of King David.[297] He was also the grandfather of Gamaliel[298] (although Pope Benedict XVI wrote Gamaliel was his nephew "in accordance with the strictest Pharisaic norms"[299]). The New Testament records Gamaliel was also a Pharisee and a respected member of the Sanhedrin (i.e.: "the Council" – Acts 5:34), who the apostle Paul was "educated under" (Acts 22:3).

Enter the apostle – and Pharisee – Paul.

THE APOSTLE (AND PHARISEE) PAUL

"I am a Pharisee, a son of Pharisees.... I lived as a Pharisee according to the strictest sect of our religion." (Acts 23:6; 26:5)

The apostle Paul was born roughly between A.D. 5 to 15,[300] sometime shortly before or after the death of Hillel. This was long before Jesus began His earthly ministry, roughly around A.D. 30, when He used the term "the Law and the Prophets" before the Pharisees (Luke 16:14-16). This would put the apostle Paul, at the oldest, at five years old at the death of Hillel.

"Pressing" the date of the fixation of the Pharisaic canon to Hillel, or even to Gamaliel, poses no problems, since they both lived and were active Jewish leaders in the Sanhedrin prior to the ministry of Jesus. It was also long before Paul's conversion to Christianity, when he later referred to the Old Testament canon as "the Law and the Prophets" (Romans 3:21). It would be long after Hillel died before Paul would even become a Pharisee.

Jesus' use of this Old Testament metonym before the Pharisees, and Paul's use of it as a Pharisee, illustrates they both understood it to refer to the same canon of Scripture. As mentioned in Chapter One, Jesus told the Pharisees "the Law and the Prophets were proclaimed until John [the Baptist]" (Luke 16:16). To a Pharisee, "the Law and the Prophets" would have been limited to only those writings found in the boundaries of the Hebrew Bible. They would have understood "until John" to mean only

---

[296] Ibid. NewAdvent.org. *Hillel.*

[297] Ibid.

[298] NewAdvent.org. *Gamaliel.* Access from the Internet http://www.newadvent.org/cathen/06374b.htm

[299] EWTN.com. *Paul: Non-Stop Venture for the Sake of the Gospel,* Pope Benedict XVI. Accessed from the Internet http://www.ewtn.com/library/PAPALDOC/b16stpaul2.HTM

[300] PBS.org. "In the Footsteps of Paul: Tarsus (Birth – 30CE)." Accessed from the Internet https://www.pbs.org/empires/peterandpaul/footsteps/footsteps_1_1.html

those writings were proclaimed as Inspired Old Testament Scripture, until the ministry of the Baptist.

JOHN THE BAPTIST AND THE PHARISEES

John the Baptist was the first prophet since the completion of the prophetic books in the Hebrew Bible to proclaim the Messiah's arrival to the Jewish leaders, who the prophet Isaiah prophesied about:

> "Then they said to him [John the Baptist], 'Who are you, so that we may give an answer to *those who sent us*? What do you say about yourself?' He said, 'I am A VOICE OF ONE CRYING IN THE WILDERNESS, "MAKE STRAIGHT THE WAY OF THE LORD," as Isaiah the prophet said.' Now *they had been sent from the Pharisees.*" (John 1:22-24, emphasis added)

The fact they were sent by Pharisees, John's reply of quoting Isaiah 40:3 demonstrates he knew the Pharisees would have accepted that prophecy from that prophetic book from their own canon. They would have also understood John was proclaiming Jesus was the fulfillment of their long-awaited Messiah *based on their Old Testament canon*, which included the book of Isaiah.

By Jesus saying the Pharisees "*have* Moses and the Prophets" (Luke 16:14,29, emphasis added), this means the Pharisees "had" possession of <u>all</u> of the Old Testament canon (not just "part" or "most" of it), which both Jesus and Paul referred to as "the Law and the Prophets." In other words, the Pharisees, Jesus, and Paul *all* understood this metonym for the Old Testament canon to refer to the same canon of Scripture the Pharisees "had" – the Hebrew Bible.

Both historically and Scripturally, the Pharisaic canon was limited to <u>only</u> those books found in Protestant Old Testaments today, as attested to by Jimmy Akin from Catholic Answers.

What about when Jesus referred to "the Law of Moses and the Prophets and the Psalms" (Luke 24:44)? Does this mean elsewhere in the New Testament when Jesus referred to "the Law and the Prophets" (Matthew 7:12; Luke 16:16; etc.) He was simply referring to the first two divisions of the Old Testament, but not "the Psalms" or the other later third division of the "Writings"?

THE LAW AND THE PROPHETS AND THE PSALMS

Although this is a common assumption, Luke dispels this just a few verses earlier when he wrote, "Then beginning with Moses and with *all the prophets*, He explained to them the things concerning Himself in *all the Scriptures*" (Luke 24:27). By Luke saying "all" the Scriptures, this consists of Moses and "all" the prophets. Does this exclude "the Psalms" which Luke also referred to as "the Scriptures" (v.45)? Hardly. In verse twenty-seven, Luke is including "the Psalms" as being part of "*all* the prophets." But in verse forty-four, Luke separated "the Psalms" *from* "the Prophets" as a separate third division of the Old Testament. How can this be explained?

Luke is using the term "the Prophets" in two different ways in these two verses in the same chapter: first, as the part of the Old Testament which includes everything apart from the five books of "Moses" (v.27); then later, as the second division of the Old Testament apart from "the Law of Moses" and "the Psalms" (v.44).

This is not unusual in the New Testament to use the same term in different ways to describe different divisions of the Old Testament. For example, "the Law" generally refers to the five books of Moses ("the Law *or* the Prophets" [Matthew 5:17, emphasis added], see also Matthew 12:5, cf. Numbers 28:9). Other times, "the Law" refers to one of the books of "the Prophets" like Isaiah, "In *the Law* it is written, 'BY MEN OF STRANGE TONGUES AND BY THE LIPS OF STRANGERS I WILL SPEAK TO THIS PEOPLE, AND EVEN SO THEY WILL NOT LISTEN TO ME,' says the Lord" (1 Corinthians 14:21, cf. Isaiah 28:11-12). In other ways, "the Law" can refer to the Psalms: "Jesus answered them, 'Has it not been written in your *Law*, "I SAID, YOU ARE GODS"?'" (John 10:34, cf. Psalm 82:6).

Is Jesus contradicting Himself in John 10:34 when He refers to "the Psalms" *as* "the Law," but then in Luke 24:44 he separates "the Psalms" *from* "the Law"? Not at all! Jesus is simply using the term "the Law" in two different ways. In John 10:34, He uses it as a general term to describe the Old Testament as a whole, which *includes* "the Psalms." In Luke 24:44, He uses it as the first division of the Old Testament *separate from* "the Psalms" and "the Prophets" – the third and second divisions of the Old Testament, respectfully. So, "the Psalms" is a metonym to describe the third division of the Old Testament in Luke 24:44, just as "the Law" and "the Prophets" in the same verse describe the first and second divisions of the Old Testament, respectfully.

Likewise, the New Testament also uses the term "the Prophets" to refer to something other than the second division of the Old Testament, like the Psalms: "This was to fulfill what was spoken through *the prophet*: 'I WILL OPEN MY MOUTH IN PARABLES; I WILL UTTER THINGS HIDDEN SINCE THE FOUNDATION OF THE WORLD'" (Matthew 13:35, cf. Psalm 78:2).

This "prophet" was the psalmist Asaph, who is referred to as "the son of Berechiah" in the third division of "the Writings" (1 Chronicles 6:39).

He is referred to elsewhere in the Old Testament as "Asaph the seer" with King David (2 Chronicles 29:30). The Hebrew word for "seer" (*"chozeh"*) is also translated "prophet" in the Old Testament (Isaiah 30:10). By the Old and New Testaments referencing Asaph the psalmist as a "prophet," the New Testament is including the Psalms as being part *of* "the Prophets," even though Jesus separated the Psalms *from* "the Prophets" (Luke 24:44). Likewise, by Asaph being mentioned in the Old Testament (1 Chronicles 6:39) as a "seer (prophet)" (2 Chronicles 29:30), the New Testament – indirectly – affirms the books of the Chronicles as part *of* "the Prophets," even though they are part of the "third division" ("the Writings") of the Old Testament, *separate from* "the Prophets."

Catholic apologists, like Trent Horn, believe when Jesus and the New Testament writers used the term "the Law and the Prophets" (Luke 16:16) they limited it to <u>only</u> the *first and second divisions* of the Old Testament, which excludes the *third division* of "the Writings":

> "The fact that the term 'Law and the Prophets' is used in Scripture, it doesn't follow from that that the Deuterocanonical books were not considered Inspired, or canonical, because there's *other aspects of 'the Writings'* like Job, the Psalms, Song of Solomon, and Esther that were considered Inspired and *were part of 'the Writings.'"* [301] (emphasis added)

> "So, in [sic] the Old Testament is divided into *three parts*: 'the Law' (the first five books), 'the Prophets,' and *'the Writings.'"* [302] (emphasis added)

Even though Jesus affirmed the threefold division of the Old Testament in Luke 24:44-45, when Jesus and Paul used the *specific* metonym "the Law and the Prophets" (Luke 16:16; Romans 3:21) they used it to describe the Old Testament canon – as a whole – which *included* the books in "the Writings."

When the apostle Paul spoke before Felix, the governor of Judea, he defended the false accusations against him proclaiming "I do serve the God of our fathers, believing everything that is in accordance with *the Law and that is written in the Prophets*; having a hope in God, which these men cherish themselves, that there shall certainly be *a resurrection of both the righteous and the wicked*" (Acts 24:14-15, emphasis added).

---

[301] Ibid. Horn, Trent. *Catholic Answers Live – 06/26/17*. YouTube.com. (Begins around the 46:16 mark.)
[302] Ibid. Horn, Trent. *Why Catholic Bibles Are Bigger. August 16, 2018. Counsel of Trent*. (Audio podcast). Catholic.com. (Begins around the 15:50 mark.)

Although Jesus defended the bodily resurrection of the dead from the *first half* of the Old Testament: "the Law" (Matthew 22:31-32, cf. Exodus 3:6), the *earliest* written witness comes from the *second half*: "the Prophets," which includes books like Job and Daniel from "the Writings." The book of Job records the bodily resurrection of the righteous, and the book of Daniel records the bodily resurrection of the wicked, which are both part of the *third division* of the Old Testament: "the Writings":

> "Even after my skin is destroyed, Yet from my flesh I shall see God; Whom I myself shall behold, And whom my eyes will see and not another. My heart faints within me!" (Job 19:26-27)

"Many of those who sleep in the dust of the ground will awake, these to everlasting life, but the others to disgrace and everlasting contempt." (Daniel 12:2)

When Paul uses the metonym "the Law and the Prophets" before Felix, he is not limiting it to describe the *first and second divisions* of the Old Testament. Instead, he is using it as a term to include the *third division* of "the Writings" by referencing the books of Job and Daniel. These books are not part of the *second division* of "the Prophets," but the *second half* of the Old Testament. This is also how Jesus used it (Luke 16:16), except when He was describing the threefold division of the Hebrew Bible (Luke 24:44-45). Jesus *may* have been referencing these two books when He warned about the "resurrection of life" and the "resurrection of judgment" (John 5:28-29, cf. Matthew 25:31-46).

MATTHEW AND JEREMIAH

One of the most curious Old Testament quotes in the New Testament is when Matthew quotes the prophet Jeremiah:

> "Then that which was spoken through *Jeremiah the prophet* was fulfilled: 'AND THEY TOOK THE THIRTY PIECES OF SILVER, THE PRICE OF THE ONE WHOSE PRICE HAD BEEN SET by the sons of Israel; AND THEY GAVE THEM FOR THE POTTER'S FIELD, AS THE LORD DIRECTED ME.'" (Matthew 27:9-10, emphasis added)

This quote is not from the prophet *Jeremiah*, but from the prophet *Zechariah* (Zechariah 11:12-13). At first, this appears to be an error. However, this is easily reconciled when we grasp the historical Jewish understanding of this passage, and how it relates to the Hebrew Bible. MacArthur in the footnotes of his Study Bible reveals:

"Jeremiah came first in the order of prophetic books, so the Prophets were sometimes collectively referred to by his name."[303]

The Sadducees rejected the prophetic books, including Jeremiah and Zechariah. *Only the Pharisees* accepted these writings as Inspired Scripture. The Pharisaic canon would have had Jeremiah "in the order" as their "first book," because it was the longest prophetic book in the Old Testament. Although Isaiah has more chapters, many of them are relatively short (Isaiah 6; 20; etc.). Jeremiah is actually longer than Isaiah in terms of words. So, despite Isaiah being the first "major prophet" *listed* in Christian Old Testaments, Jeremiah would have been first in the *order* of the Pharisaic canon.

Not only was Matthew part of "the Twelve" original disciples of Jesus (Matthew 10:2-4), he was also the only New Testament writer to mention Jeremiah *by name* (Matthew 2:17; 16:14; 27:9). Just as the other disciples espoused to the Hebrew Bible, like Peter, Andrew, Philip, Nathanael, as well as the evangelist Luke and the apostle Paul (see Chapter One), Matthew's high regard for Jeremiah's prophetic authority demonstrates he embraced the Hebrew Bible as well when He heard Jesus refer to it as "the Law and the Prophets" (Matthew 7:12).

THE DISCIPLES, THE JEWS, JEREMIAH, AND DAVID

The authority of Jeremiah over Isaiah and the rest of the prophets can be seen when Jesus questioned His disciples about who people said He was:

"Now when Jesus came into the district of Caesarea Philippi, He was asking His disciples, 'Who do people say that the Son of Man is?' And they said, 'Some say John the Baptist; and others, Elijah; but still others, *Jeremiah*, or one of the prophets.'" (Matthew 16:13-14, emphasis added)

Believing Jesus was Elijah is understandable since Elijah was prophesied to return (Malachi 4:5). Elijah later appeared along with Moses at the Transfiguration of Jesus (Matthew 17:2-3). Still, what about Jeremiah? Nothing in the Old Testament says anything about Jeremiah returning.

Again, Jeremiah was the first prophetic book listed in the Pharisaic canon. This explains why Jesus' disciples specifically mentioned Jeremiah along with Elijah. Incidentally, Malachi, who prophesied about Elijah, is

[303] Ibid. The MacArthur Study Bible: *The Gospel According to Matthew*, footnote Matthew 27:9, p.1447.

the *last* book listed in the "twelve Minor Prophets,"[304] as well as the last prophetic book written in the Hebrew Bible. Likewise, Jeremiah is the *first* book listed in the prophetic section of the Old Testament.

In Jewish rabbinic literature, Moses and Jeremiah are frequently mentioned together and their lives viewed in parallel manner:

> "As Moses was a prophet for forty years, so was Jeremiah; as Moses prophesied concerning Judah and Benjamin, so did Jeremiah; as Moses' own tribe [the Levites under Korah] rose up against him, so did Jeremiah's tribe revolt against him; Moses was cast into the water, Jeremiah into a pit; as Moses was saved by a female slave (the slave of Pharaoh's daughter), so Jeremiah was rescued by a male slave [Ebed-melech]; Moses reprimanded the people in discourses, so did Jeremiah (Pesiḳ., ed. Buber, xiii. 112a; comp. Matt. xvi. 14)."[305]

This high regard for Jeremiah by comparing him to Moses in Jewish literature further explains why Jeremiah was the first of the prophetic books in the Pharisaic canon. It also explains why the disciples mentioned some of the people believed Jesus was Jeremiah. Just as Genesis written by Moses was the first book of "the Law," likewise, Jeremiah, written by the prophet of the same name, was the first book of "the Prophets." "David" is also used as a metonym in the New Testament for "the Psalms," even when King David was not explicitly mentioned as the author of the particular psalm referenced (Acts 4:25, cf. Psalm 1:2; Hebrews 4:7, cf. Psalm 95:7-8).

When Jesus referred to the threefold division of the Old Testament, as "the Law of Moses and the Prophets and the Psalms" (Luke 24:44), He was using the metonym "the Psalms" as the third division of the Hebrew Bible. In much the same way, Jesus used "Moses" to refer to the first five books of the Old Testament (John 5:45), Matthew used "Jeremiah" to refer to the first book of "the Prophets" (Matthew 27:9), and Peter, John, and the writer of Hebrews used "David" to refer to "the Psalms" (Acts 4:25; Hebrews 4:7). Jesus used "the Psalms" (Luke 24:44) as a metonym for the first book of the third division of the Pharisaic Old Testament – the Hebrew Bible – just as He used the metonym "Moses" earlier to refer to "the Law" (Luke 16:29).

---

[304] NewAdvent.org. *Prophecy, Prophet, and Prophetess. In the Old Testament, Brief sketch of the history of prophecy, (2) Prophetic Writers.* Accessed from the Internet http://www.newadvent.org/cathen/12477a.htm

[305] JewishEncyclopedia.com. *Jeremiah – Rabbinic Literature.* By: Emil G. Hirsch, Victor Ryssel, Solomon Schechter, Louis Ginzberg. Accessed from the Internet http://jewishencyclopedia.com/articles/8586-jeremiah

JESUS AND THE PHARISEES

Jesus had more interaction with the Pharisees than any other Jewish sect including the Sadducees (the Pharisees are mentioned twenty times more frequently in the New Testament than the Sadducees). Unlike the Sadducees, some of the Pharisees actually became followers of Jesus.

Nicodemus is identified as a Pharisee (John 3:1), who later defended Jesus among the other Pharisees (John 7:47-50). He is later seen with Joseph of Arimathea taking Jesus' body for burial (John 19:38-42), something an unbelieving Pharisee would not have done.

When Jesus told Nicodemus unless he is "born again" (John 3:3), or "born of water and the Spirit he cannot enter into the kingdom of God" (v.5), Nicodemus' response is "How can these things be?" (v.9). Jesus gives him the answer by asking, "Are you the *teacher of Israel* and do not understand these things?" (v.10, emphasis added). As a Pharisee, Nicodemus would have been a "teacher" of Israel by teaching them from the Old Testament. As MacArthur illustrates:

> "When water is used figuratively in the OT [Old Testament], it habitually refers to renewal or spiritual cleansing, especially when used in conjunction with 'spirit' (Num. 19:17-19; Psalms 51:9,10; Is. 32:15; 44:3-5; 55:1-3; Jer. 2:13; Joel 2:28,29)."[306]

All these Old Testament books (Numbers, Psalms, Isaiah, Jeremiah, Joel) were part of Nicodemus' Pharisaic canon which he would have "taught Israel" from. Jesus' question would have been irrelevant to Nicodemus if the answer to it was found in books not in Nicodemus' canon. Jesus asked this question knowing Nicodemus would have understood Jesus was referring to Nicodemus' own canon he would have "taught Israel" from.

As previously mentioned, Joseph of Arimathea was described as a "secret" follower of Jesus (John 19:38), who along with Nicodemus, buried Jesus in his own new tomb (v.39-42). Joseph was no doubt a Pharisee too. He was a member of the Sanhedrin (Mark 15:43), he was rich (Matthew 27:57) – Luke describes Pharisees as "lovers of money" (Luke 16:14) – and he was waiting for the kingdom of God (Luke 23:50-51).

Pharisees even dined with Jesus (Luke 11:37), such as Simon the Pharisee (Luke 7:36-40). This demonstrates the Pharisees were curious about whether or not Jesus was the promised Messiah. Not only was He

---

[306] Ibid. The MacArthur Study Bible: The *Gospel According to John*, footnote John 3:5, p.1581. Brackets inserted by me for clarity.

fulfilling "the Law," but also "the Prophets" (Matthew 5:17), which the Pharisees accepted. The Sadducees did not accept "the Prophets."

Later, at the Council of Jerusalem (~A.D. 50) "some of the sect of the Pharisees who had believed stood up, saying, 'It is necessary to circumcise them and to direct them to observe the Law of Moses'" (Acts 15:5). Despite their legalism, it was *Pharisees* – not any other religious sect – who became believers in the early church, because they shared the same Old Testament canon of Scripture the rest of the church believed in.

In Matthew 23:13-29, Jesus rebuked the Pharisees and scribes (who were also Pharisees – Acts 23:9) seven times with the expression of deep sorrow of their eternal fate: "Woe!" The seventh "Woe!" (v.29) was directed towards the Pharisees, who mimicked their forefathers who had plotted to murder the Old Testament prophets (v.31,35). The Pharisees were plotting to murder Jesus and the New Testament prophets He was sending them (v.34).

Jesus limited His rebuke to the Pharisees, who He described as having "seated themselves in the chair of Moses" (v.2), not any other Jewish sect including the Sadducees. Unlike the Sadducees and other sects, the Pharisees had the complete Old Testament canon. Jesus held them responsible for knowing He was the prophesied Old Testament Messiah, Who they were plotting to crucify. Jesus based this on the Pharisees having possession of "the Law and the Prophets" (Luke 16:14,16,29).

How does all this support a closed canon of the Hebrew Bible at the time of the Old Testament scribe Ezra? Jewish history provides some convincing evidence.

Enter Ezra.

EZRA AND THE GREAT SYNAGOGUE

In their book, *The Bible for Dummies*, coauthors Jeffrey Geoghegan, PhD, Assistant Professor of Biblical Theology at Boston College, and Michael Homan, PhD, Assistant Professor of Biblical Studies at Xavier University of Louisiana wrote about the fixation of the Jewish Old Testament:

"In Babylon, these documents were edited and compiled. Although this process involved many people, the person credited with heading up the project was the scribe and priest Ezra. Not long afterwards, Ezra brought these scrolls back to the now rebuilt Jerusalem, where he instigated a religious reform based on those Scriptures (around 450 B.C.E.). During this period, additional works were penned and included in the library

135

eventually resulting in a relatively complete edition of the Jewish Bible."[307]

"These books making up the Jewish Scriptures are often called the *Hebrew Bible*, because, with few exceptions, this material was originally written in Hebrew. In Christian tradition, these same books are referred to as the *Old Testament*."[308]

These "documents" which were "edited and compiled" were, no doubt, those specific writings written prior to 450 B.C., such as the five books of Moses referred as "the Law." They also included "the Prophets" who wrote prior to the time of Ezra and the Babylonian exile. The prophet Zechariah referred to them as the "former prophets" (Zechariah 1:4).

For instance, God commanded defective Israel to "return to Him" through the "former prophet" Isaiah (Isaiah 31:6, cf. Zechariah 1:3). He commanded Judah and Jerusalem through the "former prophet" Jeremiah, "Oh turn back, each of you from his evil way, and reform your ways and your deeds" (Jeremiah 18:11, cf. Zechariah 1:4). Through the "former prophets" Ezekiel and Hosea, God pleaded with Israel to "Repent and turn away from all your transgressions, so that iniquity may not become a stumbling block to you" (Ezekiel 18:30, cf. Hosea 14:1). Jeremiah later lamented Israel's transgressions against God, "The LORD has done what He purposed; He has accomplished His word which He commanded from days of old" (Lamentations 2:17, cf. Zechariah 1:6).

When Israel asked when they should ritualistically fast and mourn (Zechariah 7:3), God responded again through the prophet Zechariah, "When you fasted and mourned...was it for Me that you fasted?" (v.5). God then admonished them by asking, "When you eat and drink, do you not eat for yourselves and do you not drink for yourselves? Are not these the words which the LORD proclaimed by the former prophets?" (v.6-7). Through the "former prophet" Isaiah, God rebuked Israel for fasting hypocritically, "Behold, you fast for contention and strife and to strike with a wicked fist. You do not fast like you do today to make your voice heard on high" (Isaiah 58:4).

God reminded Israel through the prophet Zechariah, "Dispense true justice and practice kindness and compassion each to his brother; and do not oppress the widow or the orphan, the stranger or the poor; and do not devise evil in your hearts against one another" (Zechariah 7:9-10). This was a reminder when God had commanded Israel through the "former prophet" Jeremiah: "Do justice and righteousness and deliver the one who

---

[307] Geoghegan, Jeffrey, and Homan, Michael. *The Bible For Dummies*, Chapter 1, p. 11. Published by Wiley Publishing, Inc.: Indianapolis, Indiana, 2003.

[308] Ibid, p.10. Italics in original text.

has been robbed from the power of his oppressor. Also do not mistreat or do violence to the stranger, the orphan, or the widow; and do not shed innocent blood in this place" (Jeremiah 22:3, cf. Zechariah 7:12). A similar command and rebuke was made by God to Israel through the "former prophet" Amos (Amos 5:11-15).

The "additional works" Geoghegan and Homan mentioned, which resulted in a "relatively complete edition of the Jewish Bible," no doubt refer to the rest of the "works" which "were penned and included in the library," such as Ezra-Nehemiah and 1 and 2 Chronicles. Other post-Exilic writings, such as the "latter prophets" like Haggai, Zechariah, and Malachi, would have also been included in these "additional works." The poetic writings, the Psalms, Proverbs, Ecclesiastes, and the Song of Solomon, would have also been included in this "Jewish Bible," which were also written before 450 B.C. This "process" by Ezra and others – such as Nehemiah and the "latter prophets" Haggai, Zechariah, and Malachi – resulted in what came to be known as the Hebrew Bible at the Great Synagogue. Again, from *The MacArthur Study Bible*:

> "Tradition says he [Ezra] was the founder of the Great Synagogue, where the complete OT [Old Testament] canon was first formally recognized."[309]

> "According to tradition, he [Zechariah] was a member of the Great Synagogue, a council of 120 originated by Nehemiah and presided over by Ezra. This council later developed into the ruling elders of the nation, called the Sanhedrin."[310]

> "Jewish tradition identifies him [Malachi] as a member of the Great Synagogue that collected and preserved the Scriptures."[311]

The birth of the church began with "about one hundred and twenty persons" (Acts 1:15) in the upper room at Pentecost at the beginning of the New Testament era. In similar fashion, the Great Synagogue witnessed the completion of the Old Testament with "a council of 120."

Wilhelm Bacher, Ph.D., professor at the Jewish Theological Seminary in Budapest, Hungary, also wrote concerning Ezra and the fixation of the

---

[309] Ibid. The MacArthur Study Bible. *The Book of Ezra, Author and Date*, p.638. Brackets inserted by me for clarity.

[310] Ibid. *The Book of Zechariah, Author and Date*, p.1337. Brackets inserted by me for clarity.

[311] Ibid. *The Book of Malachi, Author and Date*, p.1359. Brackets inserted by me for clarity.

Hebrew Bible, which took place at "The Great Synagogue" (sometimes called "The Great Assembly"):

> "The Prophets transmitted the Torah to the men of the Great Synagogue.... Haggai, Zechariah, and Malachi received from the Prophets; and the men of the Great Synagogue received from Haggai, Zechariah, and Malachi..... These one hundred and twenty elders are undoubtedly identical with the men of the Great Synagogue.... These passages indicate that this assembly was believed to be the one described in Neh. ix.-x.... They included the books of Ezekiel, Daniel, Esther, and the Twelve Minor Prophets in the Biblical canon...the division of the Minor Prophets was completed by the works of the three post-exilic prophets, who were themselves members of that council. The same activity in regard to these books is ascribed to the men of the Great Synagogue as had been attributed to King Hezekiah and his council, including the prophet Isaiah, with regard to the three books ascribed to Solomon (see also Ab. R. N. i.) and the Book of Isaiah. It should be noted that in this baraita, as well as in the gloss upon it, *Ezra and Nehemiah, 'men of the Great Synagogue,' are mentioned as the last Biblical writers. The men of the Great Synagogue,* therefore, not only *completed the canon,* but introduced the scientific treatment of tradition."[312] (emphasis added)

Bacher goes on to detail how the "spirit of Ezra's teaching" was later carried out by the Pharisees:

> "These three clauses indicate the program of the scholars of the Persian period, who were regarded as one generation, and evidence their harmony with *the spirit of Ezra's teaching.* Their program was *carried out by the Pharisees.*"[313] (emphasis added)

This demonstrates the Old Testament canon of Ezra compiled at the "Great Synagogue" was adopted later by the Pharisees, which was identical to that of later Protestant Old Testaments. Bacher also points out, "while according to the introduction to the Second Book of the Maccabees (ii. 13) Nehemiah also collected a number of the books of the Bible"[314]:

> "Besides these things, it is also told in the records and in Nehemiah's Memoirs how he collected the books about the

---

312 JewishEncyclopedia.com. *The unedited full-text of the 1906 Jewish Encyclopedia.*
SYNAGOGUE, THE GREAT (כנסת הגדולה): By Wilhelm Bacher. Accessed from the Internet
http://www.jewishencyclopedia.com/articles/14162-synagogue-the-great
313 Ibid.
314 Ibid.

kings, the writings of the prophets and of David, and the royal letters about sacred offerings." (2 Maccabees 2:13 NAB)

None of these "writings," including "the Prophets," were comprised of any of the Deuterocanonical books, since the Deuterocanon would not begin to be written until a few hundred years *after* the "Great Synagogue." Therefore, the book of Baruch would not have been considered one of "the Prophets" by the Jews during Ezra's time, since it had not been written yet. It was not part of the canon of Ezra and the "Great Synagogue," nor that of the later Pharisees who adopted their canon nor the early church.

Regardless if the canon of Ezra and the Pharisees did not have the exact same threefold divisional *format* of the Old Testament which later Judaism produced, they undoubtedly embraced the exact same *writings* you find in today's Protestant Old Testaments. So, even if some of "the Writings" (like Daniel) were originally in "the Prophets," nonetheless, *every writing* in the Hebrew Bible was contained in one of these three divisions.

Hence, Jesus' later use of the metonym "the Law of Moses and the Prophets and the Psalms" (Luke 24:44) simply reflects this threefold division of the Old Testament, which mirrored this earlier canon of Ezra and the "Great Synagogue." McDonald cites F.F. Bruce who wrote Jerome's Old Testament canon would reflect Ezra's earlier threefold Jewish division:

> "Jerome put the Jewish biblical canon, consisting of twenty-four books...and he numbered them in the three Hebrew categories: Law (5), Prophets (8), and Writings (11)."[315]

During a lecture in May 2018, Dr. John Barnett, discussed the influence Ezra had on not only the modern Hebrew language, but also the compilation of the Hebrew Bible which Ezra had divided into "seventeen books of History, five books of Wisdom, and seventeen books of Prophecy":

> "He [Ezra] not only invented the modern Hebrew language, he invented the scribes. You know in the New Testament when you see the scribes and the Pharisees bothering Jesus all the time? Ezra was the one who started those, and they copied the Bible that no one could read into modern Hebrew that every Jew in the world can still read.... By the time of Jesus, everybody was going to synagogue reading the Scriptures that Ezra copied from all the Pentateuch, through the history books, through the writing prophets, into a Hebrew that they could understand. And when he [Ezra] did it, he followed this pattern. He made books of

---

[315] Ibid. McDonald, *The Biblical Canon*, p.205 cites Bruce, F.F., *The Canon of Scripture*, p.90. Downers Grove Ill.: InterVarsity, 1988.

history – or Torah, 'the teaching of the teacher' – and the books of Wisdom, and the books of Prophecy, and Jesus said 'These are the words which I spoke to you that all must be fulfilled which is written in the Law of Moses (the Torah, the seventeen books of history); the Prophets (the seventeen books of prophecy); and the Psalms' or the Writings (the Ketuvim, the Hebrew literature). So, these three divisions that Jesus referred to, Jesus actually cited the three are what Ezra designed."[316]

Ezra established a symmetrical pattern of five Wisdom books, as well as five major History books, and five major Prophetic books. He also formulated a symmetry of nine pre-Exilic History books and nine pre-Exilic Prophetic books, as well as three post-Exilic History books and three post-Exilic Prophetic books.[317] These three divisions of Ezra contained the exact same books, which were later adopted by the Pharisees and scribes in Jesus' day and afterwards by rabbinic Judaism, and rediscovered by Protestants in the sixteenth century.

WHAT ABOUT THE "PROPHECIES" IN WISDOM?

One of the arguments for including the Deuterocanon is the alleged prophecies in the book of Wisdom regarding the future Messiah, particularly Wisdom 2:13-20:

"[13] He boasteth that he hath the knowledge of God, and calleth himself the son of God. [16] We are esteemed by him as triflers, and he abstaineth from our ways as from filthiness, and he preferreth the latter end of the just, and glorieth that he hath God for his father. [18] For if he be the true son of God, he will defend him, and will deliver him from the hands of his enemies. [20] Let us condemn him to a most shameful death: for there shall be respect had unto him by his words." (Wisdom 2:13,16,18,20 Douay-Rheims)[318]

In the footnotes of the New American Bible (NAB) it states "many have understood these verses as a direct prophecy. Cf Mt 27, 41-44."[319] Although these verses "appear" to be new prophecies about Jesus found

---

[316] Barnett, John. *The Minor Prophets – Part 2 – The Bible – Structure & History.* "DTBM Online Video Training." Published on YouTube, May 11, 2018. Accessed from the Internet https://www.youtube.com/watch?v=oLYz8T1m0iM (Begins at about the 34:58 mark.) Brackets inserted by me for clarity.

[317] Ibid.

[318] Ibid. DRBO.org. *Book of Wisdom Chapter 2.* Accessed from the Internet http://drbo.org/chapter/25002.htm. Brackets with verse numbers in the original text.

[319] Ibid. New American Bible, footnotes to Wisdom 2:12-20, p.751.

only in the Deuterocanon and independent of the Hebrew Bible, this assumption fails to take a few Scriptural factors into consideration.

While the New Catholic Version (NCV) also translates verse thirteen as "the son of God," the New American Bible translates it simply as "a child of God." Regarding Wisdom 2:16, the NAB references Jeremiah 6:30 which reads "'Silver rejected' they shall be called, for the LORD has rejected them" (NAB). The NCV references Wisdom 2:18 to Psalm 21:9: "He hoped in the Lord, let him deliver him: let him save him, seeing he delighteth in him" (NCV) (which is Psalm 22:9 in the New American Bible – one of the most significant prophetic chapters in the Old Testament about the Messiah [see also Isaiah 53]).

The NAB also references Jeremiah 42:1: "Here is my servant whom I uphold, my chosen one with whom I am pleased, Upon whom I have put my spirit; he shall bring forth justice to the nations" (NAB). Lastly, regarding Wisdom 2:20, the NCV references Jeremiah 11:19: "And I was a meek lamb, that is carried to be a victim: and I knew not that they had devised councils against me, saying: Let us put wood on his bread, and cut him off from the land of the living, and let his name be remembered no more" (NCV). Oddly enough, the NAB *omits* verses nineteen through twenty-three of Jeremiah chapter eleven, despite them being in the Douay-Rheims, the NCV, and virtually all Protestant translations. In other words, the translators of the NAB "removed" these verses from the Douay-Rheims.

Additionally, Psalm 2:7 reads, "I will surely tell of the decree of the LORD: He said to Me, 'You are My Son, Today I have begotten You.'" This is a clear reference to 2 Samuel 7:14, when God instructed the prophet Nathan to tell David an eternal kingdom will be established on his throne after his death, and "I will be a father to him and he will be a son to Me."

Although the immediate context of this passage applied to King David's son, Solomon, who would build the Temple after King David died, these words had a more profound and prophetic application to the future Messiah, Who would refer to Himself as "the Son of God" (Matthew 27:40,43). Later, the writer of Hebrews quoted Psalm 2:7 and 2 Samuel 7:14 to refer specifically to Jesus (Hebrews 1:5), and the apostle Paul even mentioned this quote about Jesus came from "the second Psalm" (Acts 13:33).

Proverbs 30:4 reads, "Who has ascended into heaven and descended? Who has gathered the wind in His fists? Who has wrapped the waters in His garment? Who has established all the ends of the earth? What is His name or His son's name? Surely you know!" (Proverb 30:4, cf. John 3:13). When the chief priests, scribes, elders, and rulers of Israel, along with those who looked on, who "sneered" at Jesus on the cross and mockingly referred to Him as the "Son of God" or the "chosen of God" (Matthew 27:41-43; Luke 23:35), they were referencing back to 2 Samuel 7:14 and Psalm 2:7.

Therefore, they were not citing Wisdom 2:12-20. Rather, they were referencing these *earlier* verses from the Hebrew Bible, which talk about the Messiah being God's "Son." In Psalm 22:7, when the Hebrew word for "sneer" (*"la`ag"*) is translated into Greek, it is the same Greek word used in Luke 23:35, where it says, "even the rulers *sneered.*" This is how we know the passage in Luke 23:35 (and its cross-reference from Matthew 27:40-41) is referring back to these *earlier* passages in the Psalms and 2 Samuel in the Hebrew Bible, rather than to the *later* passages in the Deuterocanonical book of Wisdom.

Psalm 110:1 is an explicit prophecy about Jesus, which reads: "A Psalm of David. The LORD says to my Lord: 'Sit at My right hand Until I make Your enemies a footstool for Your feet.'" Jesus quoted this prophecy in Matthew 22:55 (see also Mark 12:36; Luke 20:42-43), as does the apostle Peter at Pentecost (Acts 2:34-35) and the writer of Hebrews (Hebrews 1:13).

The verses in Wisdom 2:13-20 are clearly <u>not</u> new prophetic passages about the *future* Messiah in Matthew 27:42-43 independent of the Hebrew Bible. They are referring *back* to the prophetic passages from "the Prophets" (2 Samuel, Isaiah, and Jeremiah) and "the Writings" (the Psalms and Proverbs) from the Hebrew Bible. If Wisdom would have to be included in the Old Testament canon simply because it uses the term "son of God," then the Dead Sea Scrolls would also have to be included. Cale Clarke from Catholic.com illustrates:

> "One example comes from an Aramaic scroll found in Cave 4 (which was the motherlode, the cave containing the most scrolls), which speaks of a coming 'Son of God,' a 'Son of the Most High' who will be "great" and reign forever. Notice how this closely echoes the Annunciation narrative found in Luke 1."[320]

In the Gospel of Luke, the angel Gabriel used the terms "Son of God" (Luke 1:35) and "Son of the Most High" and "great" (v.32) to describe Jesus Who would be conceived in the virgin's womb. These are the same terms used in the Dead Sea Scrolls. Does this mean we need to include <u>all</u> of them – or at least this single Aramaic scroll – into the Christian Old Testament canon, since it used these terms utilized in the New Testament? Certainly

---

[320] Ibid. Clarke, Cale. Catholic.com. *The Ever-Deepening Mystery of the Dead Sea Scrolls.*

142

not! This is why we have to reference the *earliest* use of these terms, which are found in the Hebrew Bible, not the Deuterocanon.

Even *if* these "alleged" prophecies were only found in the Deuterocanon, we would also have to include other writings from the Old Testament era as well which also "appear" to be prophesying about Jesus, such as the *Sibylline Oracles*.

THE SIBYLLINE ORACLES

The *Sibylline Oracles* was "The name given to certain collections of supposed prophecies, emanating from the sibyls or divinely inspired seeresses ["a woman who predicts events or developments"[321]], which were widely circulated in antiquity."[322] Rich Deem, founder of Godandscience.org, wrote regarding the *Sibylline Oracles*:

> "that even the rabbinical writers recognized the messianic nature of these prophecies. Some of these writings are, of themselves prophetic, and contain prophecies not even found in the Old Testament scriptures. One stunning example is from the Sibylline Oracles, which were written during the period of 184-117 B.C.:

> 'And being beaten He shall be silent lest any one [sic] should know what the word is, or whence it came, that it may speak with mortals; and HE SHALL WEAR THE CROWN OF THORNS.' Sibylline Oracles (B.C. 184-117)"[323]

This is a clear reference to when Jesus stood before the Sanhedrin at His mock trial prior to His crucifixion, where He was questioned "But Jesus kept silent" (Matthew 26:63). Later, "after having Jesus scourged, he [Pilate] handed Him over to be crucified" (Mark 15:15). Then, "They [the Roman soldiers] dressed Him up in purple, and after twisting a crown of thorns, they put it on Him" (v.17). Since the *Sibylline Oracles* appear to be prophesying about these then-future Messianic events, does that justify them being included in the Old Testament canon as well? If so, why are they not in Catholic, Protestant, or Eastern Orthodox Bibles?

---

[321] Merriam-Webster.com. Accessed from the Internet https://www.merriam-webster.com/dictionary/seeress. Brackets inserted by me for clarity.

[322] NewAdvent.org. *Sibylline Oracles*. Accessed from the Internet http://www.newadvent.org/cathen/13770a.htm

[323] Deem, Rich. Godandscience.org. *Evidence for God from Science Newsletter November, 1999, Apologetics*. Accessed from the Internet http://www.godandscience.org/newsletters/1999-11.html. Capital letters in the original text from the Web site.

Just as the passages from Wisdom chapter two were referring *back* to prophecies from the Hebrew Bible and not actually new prophecies about future events, likewise, the *Sibylline Oracles* were also referring *back* to prophecies in the Hebrew Bible, such as Psalm 22:16; 38:13-14; Isaiah 50:6; 53:7; Zechariah 12:10, etc.

Simply because a particular writing from the Old Testament *era* "appears" to be prophesying about an event in the New Testament, this does not automatically mean it belongs in the Old Testament *canon*, or it is a new prophecy. It may simply be referring to a previous prophecy in the Hebrew Bible, rather than about a later fulfilled one in the New Testament. This, among other reasons, is why Wisdom and the *Sibylline Oracles* are not in the Protestant Old Testament.

In the next chapter, I will critique some of the other common New Testament verses, which "appear" to support the Deuterocanon, like Hebrews 11:35. I will also reexamine some of the verses which support the canon of the Hebrew Bible, like Luke 11:50-51, from a fresh perspective.

CHAPTER EIGHT: The New Testament Case against the Deuterocanon

"So that the blood of all the prophets, shed since the foundation of the world, may be charged against this generation, from the blood of Abel to the blood of Zechariah, who was killed between the altar and the house of God; yes, I tell you, it shall be charged against this generation." (Luke 11:50-51)

32 A.D. is the approximate year which marked the two most significant and important moments in all of human history – the crucifixion and resurrection of Jesus Christ. The sinless God Who created the universe became a human being in the form of the Father's only begotten Son (John 1:1,14,18). He was sent to die for the sins of all those who would ever believe in Him as their sole Savior from the eternal penalty of Hell (John 3:16-18). This was the self-sacrificing love message He spread during His three-year ministry on earth in the early first century. It was also the legacy He left and offered to us as well. So, as you are reading this, if you have not already trusted in the sufficiency of the Atonement of Christ alone for your salvation and *genuinely* repented of your sins against God, I seriously encourage you to accept His free gift of salvation of being justified by His grace alone through faith alone (Romans 3:23-25; 4:4-5,9-11; Romans 5:1-2; Ephesians 2:4,8-9).

In the Parable of the Good Samaritan, a lawyer (an expert in the Mosaic Law) asked Jesus, "Teacher, what shall I do to inherit eternal life?" (Luke 10:25). Jesus replied to him, "What is written in the Law? How does it read to you?" (v.26). The lawyer responded by quoting Deuteronomy 6:5 and Leviticus 19:18 in "the Law" (v.27). Jesus then gave him a command from the Law, "Do this and you will live" (v.28, cf. Leviticus 18:35), which God had reiterated in the Old Testament to the elders in Israel through the prophet Ezekiel from the Hebrew Bible (Ezekiel 20:11).

Jesus frequently referred back to the Old Testament when He spoke about the Kingdom of God. He also did so when He addressed the Old Testament canon as well.

Enter Jesus Christ.

"FROM THE BLOOD OF ABEL TO THE BLOOD OF ZECHARIAH"

One of the most disputed passages in the New Testament is when Jesus addressed the hypocrisy of the Pharisees and lawyers. Jesus pointed out to them they were not any different than their spiritual forefathers who had murdered the Old Testament prophets:

> "Woe to you! For you build the tombs of the prophets, and it was your fathers who killed them. So you are witnesses and approve the deeds of your fathers; because it was they who killed them, and you build their tombs. For this reason also the wisdom of God said, 'I will send to them prophets and apostles, and some of them they will kill and some they will persecute, so that *the blood of all the prophets, shed since the foundation of the world*, may be charged against this generation, *from the blood of Abel to the blood of Zechariah*, who was killed between the altar and the house of God; yes, I tell you, it shall be charged against this generation.'" (Luke 11:47-51, emphasis added)

In the middle of this passage, Jesus said the blood of "<u>all</u>" of the prophets from the Old Testament era had been shed – not just "some" or "most" of the prophets, but "<u>all</u>" of them. Jesus then designated the time frame, "since the *foundation of the world*" with the first murdered prophet, Abel. It was also the first fratricide committed by Abel's older brother Cain (Genesis 4:8). By Jesus saying "from" the blood of Abel, He is indicating Abel was the <u>first</u> murdered prophet in human history, "*since the foundation* of the world," which occurred in the first book of the Bible which records when the "foundation of the world" took place (Genesis 1:1-31).

Jesus continued by saying "*to* the blood of Zechariah." By saying "to," Jesus was specifying when the <u>last</u> murdered prophet, Zechariah, took place. There were no other prophets murdered *after* Zechariah. "All" of the Old Testament prophets who were murdered began "from" Abel and ended "to" Zechariah. *Who* was this "Zechariah" Jesus is talking about?

Jesus described Zechariah's fate as "who was killed between the altar and the house of God" (Luke 11:51). The identity of this "Zechariah" is debatable. Many Protestants believe he was "Zechariah the son of Jehoiada" (2 Chronicles 24:20), who the leaders of Judah "conspired against him and at the command of the king they stoned him to death in the court of the house of the LORD" (v.21). He is later inferred to by Stephen in Acts 7:52, after he gives a detailed review of the Old Testament period to the Jewish leaders. The writer of the book of Hebrews also alluded to him when mentioning the great people of faith in the Old

Testament era (Hebrews 11:37). In Jewish Bibles, Genesis and 2 Chronicles are the <u>first</u> and <u>last</u> books in their canon, making Abel and Zechariah the first and last murdered Old Testament prophets in the canon of the Hebrew Bible of the Pharisees.

However, some will be quick to point out in Matthew's gospel, Jesus referred to him as "Zechariah, the son of *Berechiah*" (Matthew 23:35) mentioned in the book of Zechariah (Zechariah 1:1), rather than the son of Jehoiada (2 Chronicles 24:20). Therefore, he would not have been the <u>last</u> murdered Old Testament prophet in the Jewish Bible. Hence, Jesus was not affirming the canon of the Hebrew Bible. So, which "Zechariah" was Jesus actually referring to?

There are a couple of different ways to address this – both of which can still support Zechariah being the last murdered Old Testament prophet of the Hebrew Bible. The footnotes of Matthew 23:35 in *The MacArthur Study Bible* point out:

> "The OT [Old Testament] does not record how he [Zechariah, the son of Berechiah] died. However, the death of another Zechariah, son of Jehoiada, is recorded in 2 Chr. 24:20,21. He was stoned in the court of the temple, exactly as Jesus describes here.... Some have suggested that the Zechariah in 2 Chr. 24 was actually a grandson of Jehoiada, and that his father's name was also Berechiah."[324]

In the center reference column in the New King James Version of the Bible, it indicates "father" in 2 Chronicles 24:22 means "Foster father."[325] Likewise, in the endnotes of 2 Chronicles 24 in the *Believer's Bible Commentary* by William MacDonald, it states, "in Hebrew usage, *son* can also mean *grandson*. The Zechariah who wrote the book that bears his name was also the son of Berechiah, but a different Berechiah, of course."[326] Therefore, when Jesus said "Zechariah, the *son* of Berechiah," He *may* have been referring to Berechiah's *grandson*. This would mean <u>both</u> Zechariah the murdered prophet (2 Chronicles 24:20-21) *and* the author of the book of Zechariah (Zechariah 1:1) would have had a father (or grandfather) named Berechiah.

This would not have been the first time Matthew used the word "son" to mean something other than a biological male child. Matthew begins his gospel by referring to "Jesus the Messiah, the *son of David*" (Matthew 1:1,

---

[324] Ibid. The MacArthur Study Bible. Footnotes to Matthew 23:35, p.1437. Brackets inserted by me for clarity.

[325] Ibid, 2 Chronicles 24:22, center reference column, p.622.

[326] MacDonald, William. *Believer's Bible Commentary, 2 Chronicles, Endnote #24,* p.470. Edited by Art Farstad. Thomas Nelson Publishers, Inc.: Nashville, Tennessee, 1995.

emphasis added). King David was not Jesus' biological father, since Jesus was virgin-born (v.23,25), and King David died several hundred years before Jesus was even conceived. Jesus being called the "son" of David simply means He was a physical descendant of King David through Mary (v.18, cf. Romans 1:1-3).

Similarly, Ezra referred to Zechariah, the son of Berechiah, as "the son of *Iddo*" (Ezra 5:1; 6:14), even though Zechariah identified himself as "the son of *Berechiah*" (Zechariah 1:1). Zechariah was Iddo's *grandson*, despite being referred to as "*the son* of Iddo." When 2 Chronicles 24:20 refers to Zechariah as "*the son* of Jehoiada," he *may* have been the *grandson* of Jehoiada, and the biological son of Berechiah. This is who Jesus *may* have meant when He referred to Zechariah as "the *son* of Berechiah." Plus, 2 Chronicles 24:21 records the same manner of death of Zechariah which Jesus mentioned in Matthew 23:35. The use of the word "son" in the Bible does not automatically assume immediate biological offspring.

However, there is a simpler and more accepted view, having more Scriptural support: when Jesus said, "the son of Berechiah," He *was* referring to the writer of the book of Zechariah, who is last mentioned in the book of Nehemiah (Nehemiah 12:16). Even though 2 Chronicles is the last book in the *canon* of the Jewish Bible, the book of Nehemiah is the last book written *chronologically* in the Hebrew Bible.

Zechariah the *son of Jehoiada* died sometime prior to 430 B.C. before 2 Chronicles was written,[327] which records his death. In both the books of Ezra and Nehemiah, Zechariah the *son of Berechiah* ("the son of Iddo") was still alive (Ezra 5:1; Nehemiah 12:16), which were written sometime before 400 B.C.,[328] but after the other Zechariah had died. Again, from the footnotes of *The MacArthur Study Bible*:

> "Over 400 years separated the *final events (Neh.13:4-30)* and final prophecy (Mal. 1:1-4:6) recorded in the Old Testament (ca. 424 B.C.)"[329] (emphasis added)

While the book of Malachi was the last Inspired *prophetic* book written in the Old Testament, the book of Nehemiah was the last Inspired *historical* book written before the events of the New Testament. When the Pharisees heard Jesus say, "The Law and the Prophets were proclaimed until John" (Luke 16:14,16), they would have understood this to refer to their

---

[327] Ibid. The MacArthur Study Bible. *The First and Second Books of Chronicles, Author and Date*, p.563.
[328] Ibid. *The Book of Nehemiah, Author and Date*, p.656.
[329] Ibid. *Introduction to the Intertestamental Period*, p.1369.

canon, the Hebrew Bible which ended with Nehemiah, but not the Deuterocanonical books written centuries later.

Therefore, when Jesus said, "*from* the blood of the righteous Abel *to* the blood of Zechariah the son of Berechiah," Jesus was beginning with the first Old Testament martyred prophet written *chronologically* in the first Old Testament book (Genesis) of the canon of the Pharisees. Likewise, Zechariah was the last Old Testament martyred prophet written *chronologically* in the last Old Testament book (Nehemiah) of the canon of the Pharisees. Hence, Jesus did not end with a later prophet martyred *after* the completion of the canon of the Hebrew Bible when He said "*from* Abel *to* Zechariah."

Regardless of whether Jesus was referring to the prophet who was *the writer of the book of Zechariah*, or Zechariah the prophet *recorded martyred in the Old Testament*, Jesus was addressing the boundaries of the Old Testament canon. Whether *chronologically* beginning with Genesis and ending with Nehemiah, or in the *canon order* beginning with Genesis and ending with 2 Chronicles, Jesus was limiting the Old Testament canon to the boundaries of the Hebrew Bible of the Pharisees.

Some might argue Jesus was not addressing the canon *itself*, but merely the prophets who died. But again, Jesus said, "the blood of ALL the prophets, shed since the foundation of the world...*FROM* the blood of Abel *TO* the blood of Zechariah who was killed between the altar and the house of God" (Luke 11:50-51, emphasis added). The "foundation" refers to the time period of Abel, the FIRST martyred Old Testament prophet recorded in the FIRST book of the Old Testament. "Between the altar and the house of God" refers to the events surrounding Zechariah, the LAST martyred Old Testament prophet recorded in the LAST book of the Old Testament. Both of these books begin and end within the boundaries of the Hebrew Bible – the canon of the Pharisees, centuries before the Deuterocanonical books began to be penned.

This would exclude the book of Baruch as well, since it was written long after the last of "ALL the prophets" (Zechariah) from the Hebrew Bible died. Therefore, the book of Baruch was not part of "the Prophets" which Jesus, Paul, and the New Testament writers were referring to, because there were no prophets of God during the Intertestamental Period to martyr. Even if the books in the Deuterocanon "claimed" prophets were martyred during the Intertestamental Period, the words of Jesus conflict with this, since He said the last prophet who was murdered was "Zechariah the son of Berechiah" mentioned in the last book of the Hebrew Bible. Therefore, none of the Deuterocanonical books were Inspired Scripture.

Jesus addressed and rebuked the hypocrisy of the Pharisees and lawyers (who were also Pharisees – Matthew 22:34) for this. Matthew described them as "*scribes* and Pharisees" (Matthew 23:29). Again, the *Pharisees* would have understood "ALL the prophets...from Abel to Zechariah" to refer to the prophets prior to 400 B.C., based on the boundaries of their canon, the Hebrew Bible.

Prior to this rebuke, Jesus commanded His disciples, "The scribes and the *Pharisees have seated themselves in the chair of Moses; therefore all that they tell you, do and observe,* but do not do according to their deeds; for they say things and do not do them" (Matthew 23:2-3). The "chair of Moses" was a synonym for someone usurping the highest authority to teach people based on the Law of Moses.

Notice, this privilege was not given to the Sadducees or any other Jewish sect. Jesus <u>only</u> bestowed this on the Pharisees, because they had embraced the complete Old Testament canon ("from the blood of righteous Abel to the blood of Zechariah"). However, Jesus only commanded His disciples to "do and observe" what they "tell you" based on their Scriptures, but not based on their extra-scriptural man-made traditions which conflicted with and added to them.

ABEL TO ZECHARIAH: OLD TESTAMENT BOOKENDS?

In Matthew chapter twenty-one, Jesus told the parable of the wicked vine-growers to the chief priests and the Pharisees (v.45). Jesus described how the landowner (representing God) "sent his slaves to the vine-growers" who "took his slaves and beat one, and killed another, and stoned another" (vv.33-35). This correlates to how the Jewish leaders treated the Old Testament prophets (1 Kings 22:24; 2 Chronicles 24:20-21; 36:15-16; Nehemiah 9:26; Jeremiah 2:30).

The landowner then "sent his son" (v.37) to the vine-growers (Mark 12:6 records "a *beloved* son" which is how God described Jesus – Mark 1:11), who they also killed (v.39). Upon hearing this parable, the chief priests and the Pharisees "understood that He was speaking about them" (v.45).

Jesus then told them the parable of the wedding feast (Matthew 22:1-14). After the king (representing God) sent his slaves (representing the Old Testament prophets) to invite those to the wedding feast (v.3), some of those who were invited "seized his slaves and mistreated them and killed them" (v.6).

In Matthew 23:29-31, Jesus condemned the spiritual forefathers of the scribes and Pharisees "who murdered the prophets." The "slaves" of the landowner and the king who were murdered (Matthew 21:35; 22:6) were these same Old Testament prophets. Jesus accused the chief priests and Pharisees if they "had been living in the days of our fathers," they too would have been guilty of "shedding the blood of the prophets" (v.30), because they were "sons of those who murdered the prophets" (v.31), who "approve the deeds of your fathers" (Luke 11:48).

Jesus concluded by rebuking their spiritual forefathers, "Jerusalem, Jerusalem, who kills the prophets and stones those who are sent to her!" (Matthew 23:37, cf. 21:35), as well as the Pharisees who would kill the New Testament prophets Jesus would send (v.34). To a Pharisee, the Old Testament "prophets" whose blood was shed "from Abel to Zechariah" (Matthew 23:34-35; Luke 11:49-51) was limited to the "bookends" of the Hebrew Bible beginning with Genesis and ending with either 2 Chronicles or Nehemiah (see above). This would exclude the Deuterocanonical books the Pharisees rejected, which were written centuries later.

"WOMEN RECEIVED BACK THEIR DEAD BY RESURRECTION; AND OTHERS WERE TORTURED, NOT ACCEPTING THEIR RELEASE, SO THAT THEY MIGHT OBTAIN A BETTER RESURRECTION"

The book of Hebrews chapter eleven is sometimes called the "Hall of Faith." It details believers in the Old Testament era who exercised their faith in God. They either trusted in what God said, commanded, or promised, or they demonstrated that faith by their deeds. One of the "silver bullets" used to defend the Deuterocanonical books as Inspired Scripture is in Hebrews 11:35, which states:

> "Women received back their dead by resurrection; and others were tortured, not accepting their release, so that they might obtain a better resurrection."

Examples of the first part ("Women received back their dead by resurrection") can be found in the Hebrew Bible. For example, Elisha resurrected the son of a widow from Zarephath (1 Kings 17:21-22), and later he raised the son of a Shunammite woman from the dead (2 Kings 4:32-34).

The second part ("and others were tortured, not accepting their release, so that they might obtain a better resurrection") appears to be alluding to stories in the Deuterocanonical book of 2 Maccabees. In chapter six, the author describes the martyrdom of Eleazar, who refused to eat pork, but rather "preferring a glorious death to a life of defilement" (2 Maccabees 6:19 NAB). Chapter seven records the torture and death of a Jewish woman and her seven sons, who also refused to eat pork (2 Maccabees 7:1-42 NAB).

Since the writer of Hebrews appears to be referencing these events in the Old Testament *era*, the assumption is he is affirming 2 Maccabees as part of the Old Testament *canon*. Just because a writing from the Old Testament *era* is referenced in the New Testament, we should not automatically assume it belongs in the Old Testament *canon*. Otherwise, we would also have to include *1 Enoch* and *the Assumption of Moses* in the Old Testament canon, since the epistle of Jude references them too. We would also have to include all the other Apocryphal and Pseudoepigraphical writings alluded to in the New Testament (see Chapter Six), many of which were also in early versions of the Septuagint (see Chapter Two).

One argument in favor of including it is the writer of Hebrews is beginning with the faith of Abel (Hebrews 11:4) and progressing through the rest of the Old Testament heroes. In his book *The Case For The Deuterocanon*, Gary Michuta comments on Hebrews 11:35: "The Letter to the Hebrews is not laying out a *secular* history, but expounding on the *sacred* history of the Jews."[330] He goes on to say "Hebrews 11 presents examples of men and women who lived out their supernatural faith in Sacred Scripture.... Therefore, the inspired author's Bible included the book of Second Maccabees, which he considered an authentic part of sacred Scripture."[331]

Just two verses later, Hebrews 11:37 states, "they were sawn in two, they were tempted, they were put to death with the sword." This describes the alleged events of the death of the prophet Isaiah recorded in the Pseudoepigraphical text of the *Ascension of Isaiah* written around A.D. 70[332]:

> "In the presence of Balkira and of other false prophets, Isaiah, refusing to recant, is sawn asunder by means of a wooden saw."[333]

---

[330] Michuta, Gary G. *The Case For The Deuterocanon: Evidence And Arguments*, Second Edition., Chapter One *"New Testament Use: Hebrews 11:35."* Published by Nikaria Press: Livonia, Michigan, 2015, 2017.

[331] Ibid.

[332] Catholic.com. "Mary, Full of Grace." September 01, 2003. Accessed from the Internet https://www.catholic.com/magazine/print-edition/mary-full-of-grace

[333] JewishEncyclopedia.com. ISAIAH, ASCENSION OF: By: Crawford Howell Toy, Enno Littmann. Ch. v. 1b-14. —Conclusion of the Martyrdom of Isaiah. Accessed from the Internet http://jewishencyclopedia.com/articles/8237-isaiah-ascension-of#anchor4

Mr. Michuta even cross-referenced Hebrews 11:37 to the *Ascension of Isaiah* in his own book![334] If the epistle to the Hebrews is "expounding on *sacred* history...in Sacred Scripture" does this mean "the inspired author's Bible included" the *Ascension of Isaiah*? Mr. Michuta anticipates this question by stating:

> "The point is not that Hebrews 11 uses only biblical *sources*, but that is uses only biblical *characters*...the fact remains that the prophet Isaiah is a biblical *character*...Hebrews considered the Maccabean martyrs to be biblical characters."[335]

Although this is a compelling argument, it fails on a number of points. First, nowhere in either the Hebrew Bible or the Deuterocanon is Isaiah's *method* of death recorded. It is only found in the *Ascension of Isaiah*, which is what the writer of Hebrews is addressing.

Second, the argument being made by Catholic apologists is the writer of Hebrews is referencing the *events* ("sacred *history*") of the martyrs in 2 Maccabees. It is the *event*, or "history," of Isaiah's death the writer of Hebrews is also addressing, which is not recorded in the book of Isaiah. As early as the second century, the early church father, Justin Martyr, acknowledged the historical *event* "about the death of Isaiah, whom you sawed asunder with a wooden saw."[336] Justin was clearly referencing Hebrews 11:37 as "sacred *history*" of this "biblical character," which can only be found in the *Ascension of Isaiah*, not the book of Isaiah.

Third, equating an event in the Old Testament *era* with that same writing being justified as being part of the Old Testament *canon* is problematic for numerous reasons. For one, the Old Testament would be a LOT larger than current Catholic Old Testaments.

Fourth, Mr. Michuta *assumes* the Jews martyred in 2 Maccabees are Biblical characters, and he *assumes* the writer of Hebrews believes this too, but these are just his assumptions. He is also assuming the writer of Hebrews is referencing the martyrs *in* 2 Maccabees, even though the writer only describes nonspecific examples of torture, but he does not name anyone *specifically*, like he does with Abel and others. Countless Jews throughout the Old Testament era were also tortured, not just during the events of 2 Maccabees.

---

[334] Ibid. Michuta. *The Case For The Deuterocanon.*

[335] Ibid. Italics in original text.

[336] NewAdvent.org. *Dialogue with Trypho (Chapters 109-124), Chapter 120. Christians were promised to Isaac, Jacob, and Judah.* Accessed from the Internet http://www.newadvent.org/fathers/01288.htm

Fifth, the writer of Hebrews never once uses one of the New Testament metonyms, such as "it is written," to qualify 2 Maccabees or the rest of the Deuterocanon as Inspired Scripture, nor does any other New Testament book like they do with the Hebrew Bible.

Sixth, Stephen also progresses through the Old Testament *era* in the book of Acts. He begins with the events of Abraham, Isaac, and Jacob (Acts 7:2-8), proceeds through the events of Joseph (v.9-16), and then details a historical narrative of Moses' deliverance of Israel from Egypt into the wilderness (v.17-41). He then quotes the prophets of the Hebrew Bible like Amos (v.42-43) and Isaiah (v.49-50), but he completely omits any reference to any of the Deuterocanonical books, as well as most of the "Writings" in the Hebrew Bible.

Does this mean these writings should be omitted from the Old Testament, if the "rule" is: "*only* if a writing or 'biblical character' is referenced in a narrative of the history of the Old Testament era then that book is part of the canon"? If so, then Catholic Old Testaments should omit all of the Deuterocanonical writings, including 2 Maccabees, since Stephen never even alludes to them. A considerable part of the Hebrew Bible would have to be omitted as well, since Stephen does not reference much of those writings either. The writer of Hebrews also does not include many of the books from either the Hebrew Bible nor the Deuterocanon.

Seventh, Mr. Michuta attempts to create his own Old Testament "bookends" beginning with Abel in Genesis and ending with the Maccabean martyrs in 2 Maccabees. However, 2 Maccabees was not the last Deuterocanonical book written. "The Book of Wisdom was written about a hundred years before the coming of Christ,"[337] and some of the "additions" to Daniel, like The Story of Bel and the Dragon and The Story of Susanna were written between 100 B.C. to the first century B.C. (see Appendix B). The "additions" to Esther were also written somewhere between 114 B.C. to the first century B.C.[338] "First Maccabees was written around 100 B.C.,"[339] while 2 Maccabees was most likely written "some time [sic] after 124 B.C."[340] or "probably not have been produced much before the end of the second century B.C."[341]

If the writer of Hebrews was attempting to create these same "bookends" ending with 2 Maccabees, then Catholic Old Testaments

---

[337] Ibid. New American Bible. Introduction to *The Book of Wisdom*, p.750.

[338] Ibid. Goodspeed, & Hadas. The Apocrypha: an American translation, p.165 and p.xxi.

[339] Ibid. New American Bible. Introduction to *The First Book of Maccabees*, p.513.

[340] Ibid. Introduction to *The Second Book of Maccabees*, p.546.

[341] Ibid.

would have to remove the Deuterocanonical books of Wisdom, some of the "additions" to Daniel, the "additions" to Esther, and even 1 Maccabees *since they were written later than 2 Maccabees.*

Eighth, "The Ethiopic version of the Old and New Testament was made from the Septuagint.... The preservation of yet one more book in its entity, namely, the Ascension of Isaiah, is to be remembered to the credit of the Ethiopic Church."[342]

Lastly, if "The point is not that Hebrews 11 uses only biblical *sources*, but that is uses only biblical *characters*" for including the martyrs from 2 Maccabees, then the writer of Hebrews would need to include the gospel of Matthew since it "uses the biblical *character*" of John the Baptist. Hebrews 11:37-38 concludes the writer's narrative by describing men being "put to death with the sword... (men of whom the world was not worthy), wandering in deserts and mountains and caves and holes in the ground." EWTN.com recognizes John the Baptist as an *Old Testament* prophet and martyr:

> "And *John the Baptist, beheaded by Herod* for publicly accusing him of adultery, is often considered to be *the last of the Old Testament prophets* (Mtt [Matthew] 14:1-12)."[343] (emphasis added)

Matthew chapter fourteen records the death of John the Baptist who was beheaded by King Herod. Matthew 3:1-4 records John "preaching in the wilderness of Judea" and "had a garment of camel's hair and a leather belt around his waist; and his food was locusts and wild honey." Based on Mr. Michuta's "bookends" argument, the Old Testament should end with the gospel of Matthew since the "biblical *character*" of John the Baptist, who was martyred, is <u>only</u> recorded in the gospels, not the Deuterocanon.

The writer of Hebrews was simply addressing the *faith* of genuine believers throughout the Old Testament *era* (Hebrews 11:2), but not the Old Testament *canon of Scripture itself* beginning with Genesis and ending with 2 Maccabees.

JESUS AND HANNUKAH

One of the events of the New Testament used to support the canonicity of 1 Maccabees is when "Jesus was walking in the temple in the

---

[342] Ibid. *Ethiopian Orthodox Tewahedo Church Faith and Order: The Bible.*

[343] EWTN.com. "Catholic Q & A." *Old Testament prophets, Question from anonymous on 10/16/2008: Answer by David Gregson on 12/10/2008.* Accessed from the Internet http://www.ewtn.com/v/experts/showmessage.asp?number=560445. Brackets inserted by me for clarity.

portico of Solomon" (John 10:23), during the "Feast of Dedication" (v.22). This "feast" is translated from the Hebrew (*"chanukkah"*), which is sometimes called the "Festival of Lights." BlueLetterBible.org defines the origin of Hanukkah:

> "in particular the annual feast celebrated eight days beginning in the 25th of Chislev (middle of our December), instituted by Judas Maccabaeus [164 BC] in memory of the cleansing of the temple from the pollution of Antiochus Epiphanes."[344]

The origin of this "Dedication" is detailed in 1 Maccabees 4:36-59 (NAB), which the Jewish celebration of Hanukkah is based on. Since Jesus was present at the Temple during "Hanukkah," did He accept 1 Maccabees as an Inspired book?

NewAdvent.org points out it was "*Unlike the great Hebrew annual feasts,*" so "it could be celebrated not only in the temple at Jerusalem, but also in the synagogues of all places" (emphasis added).[345] Unlike the "great Hebrew annual feasts" commanded by God to be observed in the Hebrew Bible (such as the Feast of Unleavened Bread, the Feast of Tabernacles, etc.), the Feast of Dedication was not. It was considered a "lesser" Hebrew annual feast. MacDonald and GotQuestions.org echo this fact:

> "It was a yearly feast, instituted by the Jewish people, and not one of the feasts of the Lord." (emphasis added)[346]

> "Hanukkah, or the Feast of Dedication, is *not one of the festivals instituted by God* through Moses as part of the Law."[347] (emphasis added)

Neuroscientist Mayim Bialik, who is probably best known as the actress who played the lead role of "Blossom" in the television series and Amy Fowler in "The Big Bang Theory," identifies herself as an "aspiring modern Orthodox" Jew.[348] In a video on her Facebook page, she explained

---

[344] Blue Letter Bible. "Dictionary and Word Search for *egkainia (Strong's 1456)*". Blue Letter Bible. 1996-2018. 2 Feb 2018.
<http://www.blbclassic.org/lang/lexicon/lexicon.cfm?Strongs=G1456&t=NASB >

[345] NewAdvent.org. *Feast of the Dedication (Scriptural)*. Accessed from the Internet http://www.newadvent.org/cathen/04673b.htm

[346] Ibid. MacDonald. Believer's Bible Commentary, *The Gospel According to John*, p.1527.

[347] GotQuestions.org. *"What is the Feast of Dedication?"* Accessed from the Internet https://www.gotquestions.org/Feast-of-Dedication.html

[348] Cohen, Marla. *"Geek love, parenting, and Judaism: Mayim Bialik proves you can do it all, if what you do is different."* Jewish Federation of Rockland County. Copyright 2012. The Jewish Federation of North America, Inc. All Rights Reserved. Accessed from the

"Jewish holidays are divided up into major holidays and minor holidays. Major holidays are things like Passover, Rosh HaShanah, Yom Kippur, and some other really awesome holidays that you may have never heard of like Sukkos and Shavuos. Hanukkah...it's still minor."[349] Sukkos (or Sukkot) is the Feast of Tabernacles (or Feast of Booths). Shavuos (or Shavuot) is the Feast of Weeks. She also affirmed "it's [Hanukkah is] detailed in the Apocrypha, not the Old Testament,"[350] thus, avowing 1 Maccabees was never part of the Jewish canon.

Jews distinguishing the level of importance between "major and minor holidays" is similar to a Christian today obeying Jesus' command during communion to "do this in remembrance of Me" (Luke 22:19). While annual church holidays and events, such as Ash Wednesday, Lent, and Advent, are observed among various denominations within the *church*, they were never commanded by our *Lord* to observe them, like He did when He commanded the church to observe communion.

Although most Christians do not observe the "minor holiday" of the Hanukkah, Jesus used this "Festival of Lights" (John 10:22) to point towards Him being "the Light of the world" (John 9:5). Although Christmas was not commanded by our Lord to be observed specifically on December 25th, Christians point to Christ coming into the world to save sinners (1 Timothy 1:25), nine months after the Annunciation of the angel Gabriel to Mary[351]: "you will conceive in your womb and bear a son, and you shall name Him Jesus. He will be great and will be called the Son of the Most High...for that reason the holy Child shall be called the Son of God" (Luke 1:31-32,35).

Likewise, the Jews in the Old Testament were "commanded" to observe <u>all</u> of the "major feasts" in the Old Testament Ms. Bialik mentioned, which were then written down in the Hebrew Bible. No command was given by God for the Jews to observe Hanukkah (the Feast of Dedication), because it was a "minor holiday" *instituted by the Jews* recorded in the Deuterocanon, but *not by God Himself.* Despite Jesus walking in the Temple during Hanukkah, this is not validation for including

---

Internet
https://web.archive.org/web/20120512212859/http://www.jewishrockland.org/Mayim-Bialik.aspx

[349] Accessed from an uploaded video from Mayim Bialik's Facebook page, posted December 7, 2017
https://www.facebook.com/MissMayim/videos/10159765181265008/?hc_ref=ARRoyOYLbl hyVX8cV0WvVNS_HDniF1XpQbU06t5Ckh5-lQm1-TGKW4HWGcE6kC0c7j0

[350] Ibid. Brackets inserted by me for clarity.

[351] EWTN.com. *The Annunciation. Feast: March 25.* Accessed from Internet https://www.ewtn.com/saintsHoly/saints/A/theannunciation.asp

1 Maccabees as a canonical book since it is a "minor" holiday and not a "major" holiday instituted by God.

As Michelle Arnold from Catholic.com points out: "If Christians learn nothing else about Hanukkah, they should learn that it is a holiday that commemorates a rejection of false worship and an affirmation of worship of the one true God."[352] GotQuestions.org adds: "The Feast of Dedication is about the darkness of persecution and the light of God that leads His people through the darkness of those figurative nights with a promise of joy in the morning (Psalm 30:5)."[353]

It was during this "minor" holiday when Jesus used the time and "pointed out to His listeners that the miracles He had done authenticated His claim that He was, indeed, the long-awaited Jewish Messiah (see John 10:37-38). His works and His true character clearly demonstrated who He was."[354] In light of all this, the apostle John simply mentioning Jesus walking in the Temple during this time in no way justifies including 1 Maccabees in the canon of Scripture.

A WIDOW MARRIED TO SEVEN BROTHERS, THE RESURRECTION, AND HEAVEN

One final passage worth mentioning is when the Sadducees confronted Jesus about the resurrection of the dead and how it would affect marriage in Heaven:

> "On that day some Sadducees (who say there is no resurrection) came to Jesus and questioned Him, asking, 'Teacher, Moses said, "IF A MAN DIES HAVING NO CHILDREN, HIS BROTHER AS NEXT OF KIN SHALL MARRY HIS WIFE, AND RAISE UP CHILDREN FOR HIS BROTHER." Now there were seven brothers with us; and the first married and died, and having no children left his wife to his brother; so also the second, and the third, down to the seventh. Last of all, the woman died. In the resurrection, therefore, whose wife of the seven will she be? For they all had married her.'" (Matthew 22:23-28)

---

[352] Arnold, Michelle. *Catholic Answers: Myths About Hanukkah*. December 2, 2013. Accessed from the Internet https://www.catholic.com/magazine/online-edition/myths-about-hanukkah

[353] Ibid. GotQuestions.org. "What is the Feast of Dedication?"

[354] GotQuestions.org. "What is Hanukkah? Should a Christian celebrate Hanukkah (Christmaskah)?" Accessed from the Internet https://www.gotquestions.org/Hanukkah-Christian.html

There is a similar story in the Deuterocanonical book of Tobit where a woman named Sarah had been married seven times, but she bore no children to any of them (Tobit 3:7-9 NAB). Some have assumed the Sadducees borrowed this story from the book of Tobit in an attempt to trick Jesus, since Sadducees did not believe in a literal bodily resurrection of the dead (Matthew 22:23). It is assumed Matthew is affirming the canonicity of the book of Tobit. There are several textual problems with this assumption the Sadducees took this from Tobit.

First, the religious sect who asked this question to Jesus were *Sadducees*, who only believed the first five writings of the Bible written by Moses ("the Pentateuch") were Inspired. In the footnote to Matthew 3:7 in the New American Bible:

> "The Sadducees were the priestly aristocratic party, centered in Jerusalem. They accepted as scripture only the first five books of the Old Testament...and were opposed to teachings not found in the Pentateuch." (emphasis added)[355]

Why would they choose a story from a book (Tobit) they did not believe was Inspired nor part of their canon? When Jesus responded to them, He referred back to "the Law" as "the *book* of Moses" (Mark 12:26) instead of referencing the Deuterocanon. Since the Sadducees rejected the second half of the Old Testament – "the Prophets" – Jesus responded by quoting Exodus 3:6: "But regarding the resurrection of the dead, have you not read what was spoken to you by God: 'I AM THE GOD OF ABRAHAM, AND THE GOD OF ISAAC, AND THE GOD OF JACOB'? He is not the God of the dead but of the living" (Matthew 22:31-32). Just as the Sadducees *inquired* from "the Law" from the Hebrew Bible (not the Deuterocanon), likewise, Jesus *responded* from "the Law" from the Hebrew Bible instead of the Deuterocanon.

Second, the story of Tobit does not say the woman, Sarah, had been married to seven *brothers*, but simply seven *husbands* (Tobit 3:8 NAB). Plus, in the tale, Sarah ends up getting married an <u>eighth</u> time to Tobit's son Tobiah (Tobit 7:9-17 NAB), and they end up having *seven sons* together (Tobit 14:3 NAB, emphasis added). The example given by the Sadducees does not say anything about the woman having any children, let alone an eighth husband.

Although Tobiah was Sarah's closest relative ("kinsmen") and had the right to marry her (Tobit 3:17; 6:12; 7:9-10 NAB) based on "levirate marriage" (see below), the text does not specify her previous husbands were actually brothers, let alone related. Although the stories are similar,

---

[355] Ibid. New American Bible, footnote to Matthew 3:7, p.14.

they are not the same. The Sadducees would not have been referencing this story from a text they did not believe was Inspired.

If these "husbands" were all brothers and since Tobiah was next of kin, then why was he not the *second* husband to marry her instead of the *eighth*? Sarah's father told Tobiah "you are my *closest* relative" (Tobit 7:10 NAB, emphasis added). Nothing in the text indicates these seven "husbands" were also "brothers," only that she had seven husbands before she married Tobiah.

Third, the actual text the Sadducees quoted (Matthew 22:24) was from Moses in Deuteronomy 25:5 ("the Law"), which discusses "levirate marriage." The Sadducees' point of bringing up this command from God was to demonstrate all seven brothers were legally married to the same woman after the previous brother died. Since the Sadducees did not believe in a bodily resurrection (Matthew 22:23), and because all seven brothers in *their* hypothetical story had been married to the widow, they were simply asking which of them were married to her if indeed there was a resurrection of the dead (v.28).

Jesus answered them by stating although there is a bodily resurrection, God commanded marriage to be an <u>earthly</u> institution, rather than a heavenly one (v.30). Earlier, Jesus quoted from Genesis 2:24 on God's command of marriage: "FOR THIS REASON A MAN SHALL LEAVE HIS FATHER AND MOTHER AND BE JOINED TO HIS WIFE, AND THE TWO SHALL BECOME ONE FLESH" (Matthew 19:5). Husbands and wives who were previously married on earth will not be married in Heaven, just as heavenly angels are not married either (Matthew 22:30).

Fourth, the use of the number "seven" is an indivisible number used in the Old Testament to symbolize completion or perfection. A woman who bears seven children was seen as receiving a blessing from God (1 Samuel 2:5). Ruth was seen by the women as being "better to you [Naomi] than seven sons" (Ruth 4:15). A person who had seven sons was considered to have the ideal family (Job 1:2; 42:13; Jeremiah 15:9). The number "seven" is also used extensively in the New Testament to signify the spiritual realm (Luke 8:2; 11:26), including referring to the fullness of the Holy Spirit as the "seven Spirits of God" (Revelation 1:4; 3:1; 4:5; 5:6).

Lastly, in a personal email I received from EWTN.com, I asked them if the story of the widow of Matthew 22 was taken from the Deuterocanonical book of Tobit. Their response affirmed it was not:

> "Thank you for your email. *When the Sadducees are speaking to Jesus in Matthew 22, they cite Moses' law*, 'If a man dies, having no children, his brother must marry the widow, and raise up children for his brother.' *We find that law in*

Deuteronomy 25:5-10, referring to what was called a Levirate Marriage. However, *the scenario the Sadducees present to Jesus about the 7 brothers is only a hypothetical situation in which that law would have been applied; the 7 brothers scenario is not taken from any story in the Deuterocanonical books,* or any story in the Old Testament."[356] (emphasis added)

All the Sadducees were doing was using a hypothetical example of a woman being married seven times to show she had completed her final marriage and then died (Matthew 22:26-27). It had nothing to do with them borrowing a similar – but completely different – story from the book of Tobit, which they did not believe was Inspired Scripture, nor part of their canon.

There are no verses in the New Testament which support any of the Deuterocanonical books as being Inspired Scripture by Jesus, the apostles, the Pharisees or Sadducees, nor any of the New Testament writers.

How can anyone be certain the books in the Hebrew Bible are all Inspired and belong in the Old Testament canon, if readers cannot rely on the New Testament simply *quoting* from or *alluding* to them? If Christians cannot rely solely on the testimony of early church fathers, early church councils, popes, or even the various Old Testament translations covered in previous chapters, which conflict even with each other, what reliable assurance *do* they have?

What about writings like Esther and Song of Solomon that are not quoted or even alluded to in the New Testament, which *are* included in Catholic, Protestant, Eastern Orthodox, and other Old Testaments? What about the Inspiration of the New Testament *itself?* Why should the New Testament be used as a reliable source solely for the Inspiration of the Hebrew Bible? I will be answering all these questions and more in the final two chapters.

---

[356] From my personal email server. Response sent by EWTN Global Catholic Network | Global Catholic Network, Irondale, Alabama. Received Feb 5, 2018 at 5:37 PM.

CHAPTER NINE: The New Testament Support for the Hebrew Bible

"For in it the righteousness of God is revealed from faith to faith; as it is written, 'BUT THE RIGHTEOUS man SHALL LIVE BY FAITH.'" (Roman 1:17)

1521 was another pivotal year to the growth of Protestantism. One could say it was a vital time to its survival. The Protestant Church was still very much in its infancy. Martin Luther's posting of his *95 Theses* in 1517 arguably marked the "birth" of the Reformation. However, 1521 was the turning point in what direction the Reformation was going to go, including if it was to survive at all. It also resulted in the recovery of the complete Christian Old Testament.

Enter Martin Luther.

MARTIN LUTHER AND "THE DIET OF WORMS"

Martin Luther was summoned to appear before the Holy Roman Empire at the Diet (Assembly) of Worms, Germany to recant his faith in: 1) the sole sufficiency of Scripture for Christian doctrine (*sola scriptura*); 2) salvation by justification by faith alone (*sola fide*); and 3) his rejection of the Pope's absolute authority over doctrinal issues such as *his* teaching on indulgences. The assembly met from April 16th to the 18th, 1521 at which time Luther had to decide whether or not to recant as he was ordered.

Luther knew what was at stake. He had been excommunicated earlier that year by Pope Leo X in a Papal Bull (Edict). Now, he was facing public declaration of being a heretic, and then turned over to the State. This meant certain death as was the fate of the "proto-Protestant" Jan Hus from Bohemia (modern-day Prague) a century before, who was brought up on similar "charges." Hus, likewise, was publicly declared a heretic at the Ecumenical Council of Constance in 1415. Hus was then "handed over to the secular arm, which in turn condemned him to perish at the stake, at that time the usual legal punishment of convicted heretics."[357] Despite Luther's awareness that his very life was on the line, he delivered his heroic response before the Holy Roman Empire on April 18th, 1521:

---

[357] NewAdvent.org. *Council of Carthage. The repression of heresy: Condemnation and execution of John Hus.* Accessed from the Internet
http://www.newadvent.org/cathen/04288a.htm

"Unless I am refuted and convicted by testimonies of the Scriptures or by clear arguments (since I believe neither the Pope nor the Councils alone; it being evident that they have often erred and contradicted themselves), I am conquered by the Holy Scriptures quoted by me, and my conscience is bound in the word of God: I can not and will not recant any thing [sic], since it is unsafe and dangerous to do any thing [sic] against the conscience. Here I stand. [I can not do otherwise.] God help me! Amen."[358]

By God's providence – and a little help from Frederick III (aka: "Frederick, the Wise"), Elector of Saxony – Luther escaped persecution and death and the Reformation continued. It also led to the recovery of the true gospel of Jesus Christ, and the rediscovery of the complete Christian Old Testament canon.

Although Luther was highly educated (he had earned his Doctorate in Theology, long before the posting of his *95 Theses* and the Diet of Worms), his true conviction of the gospel did not take place until sometime after the completion of his education. Luther had read through the entire New Testament and even lectured on some of the books, such as Romans, Galatians, and Hebrews. However, it would not be until *after* this time when he was convicted of the gospel the apostle Paul had written to the church of Rome:

"For in it the righteousness of God is revealed from faith to faith; as it is written, 'BUT THE RIGHTEOUS man SHALL LIVE BY FAITH'" (Roman 1:17).

This quote from Paul is taken from Habakkuk 2:4 from the Hebrew Bible. It is also reiterated in Paul's epistle to the churches of Galatia (Galatians 3:11), as well as in the epistle to the Hebrews (Hebrews 10:38) – all New Testament books Luther had previously lectured on. One of the reasons this verse was significant to Luther was because of Paul's use of the phrase "it is written."

In Chapter One, Pastor John MacArthur wrote when the New Testament writers used this idiom, it "stands written as an eternal truth" which "serves to underscore the finality and continuing authority of Scripture."[359] Whenever the New Testament writers use this expression, and

---

[358] Ibid. Christian Classics Ethereal Library. *History of the Christian Church, Volume VII. Modern Christianity. The German Reformation: § 55. Luther's Testimony before the Diet, April 17 and 18, 1521,* by Philip Schaff. (Note: the article questions the historicity of the words in brackets ["I can not do otherwise"] as being part of Luther's original response.) Accessed from the Internet http://www.ccel.org/ccel/schaff/hcc7.ii.iii.xxv.html

[359] Ibid. MacArthur, John. *The Gospel According to Paul,* p.34.

others like it (see below), they *always* refer to books found in the boundaries of the Hebrew Bible (see Appendix A for a detailed list).

By using this phrase, Paul was declaring the book of Habakkuk was Inspired Scripture. All five books of Moses ("the Law") are quoted by the gospel writers using this same phrase, "it is written": Luke 11:49 (Genesis 4:8); Luke 2:23 (Exodus 13:12); Matthew 22:39 (Leviticus 19:18); Matthew 12:5 (Numbers 28:9); Matthew 22:37 (Deuteronomy 6:5). In contrast, neither the gospel writers, nor the other New Testament writers, use "it is written" or any other idiom to refer to *any* of the Deuterocanonical books independent of the Hebrew Bible.

This is not the same argument as: "If it is quoted in the New Testament, then it is Scripture." Rather, when the New Testament uses a specific *metonym*, such as "it is written" or "the Law and the Prophets," then it is defining that book as being part of the Old Testament Scriptures, and what Paul described as being Inspired, or God-breathed (2 Timothy 3:16).

When it comes to the second and third divisions of "the Prophets" and "the Writings" from the Hebrew Bible, the New Testament also uses these metonyms, and others like it, when quoting books from every section, as well as every subsection, from the Hebrew Bible. Some of these metonyms include: the "Scripture(s)," "Have you not read...?", "the Law and the Prophets," "It is written," "He has spoken," "Moses and the Prophets," "Moses," "written by the Prophets," "the Prophet(s)," "the Psalm(s)," "the true Proverb," and others (see Appendix A).

For example, the apostle Peter quoted the "true Proverb" from Proverbs 26:11 in the Hebrew Bible: "A DOG RETURNS TO ITS OWN VOMIT" (2 Peter 2:22). The Greek word Peter uses for "true" (*"alēthēs"*) is used elsewhere by Jesus in the New Testament to describe "the Law" of Moses: "It is also written in your law that the testimony of two men is *true*." (John 8:17 NKJV, cf. Deuteronomy 17:6; 19:15, emphasis added).

When Jesus said, "For everyone who asks receives, and he who seeks finds, and to him who knocks it will be opened" (Matthew 7:8), He was also referencing Proverbs 8:17: "I love those who love me; And those who diligently seek me will find me." Incidentally, Jesus was declaring the book of Proverbs to be Inspired Scripture, since He went on to say, "In everything, therefore, treat people the same way you want them to treat you, for this is *the Law and the Prophets*" (Matthew 7:12, emphasis added).

When Jesus overturned the tables in the Temple during Passover, His disciples remembered and believed the Old Testament "Scripture" (John 2:20) from the book of Psalms "that *it was written*, 'ZEAL FOR YOUR HOUSE WILL CONSUME ME'" (v.17, cf. Psalms 69:9, emphasis added). Later, the apostle Paul used this metonym "it is written" when quoting both the book of Job and the Psalms: "For the wisdom of this world is foolishness before God. For *it is written*, 'He is THE ONE WHO CATCHES THE WISE IN THEIR CRAFTINESS'; and again, 'THE LORD KNOWS THE REASONINGS of the wise, THAT THEY ARE USELESS' (1 Corinthians 3:19-20, cf. Job 5:13; Psalm 94:11, emphasis added). These Inspired Old Testament books (the Psalms, Proverbs, and Job) are <u>all</u> from the third section of "the Writings" from the Hebrew Bible.

As mentioned in Chapter Seven, sometimes the New Testament writers used the term "the Prophet" or "the Prophets" to refer to writings other than those found in the second division of the Old Testament. When Matthew referred to "the Prophet" (Matthew 11:35), he was referencing the prophet Asaph in the Psalms (Psalm 78:2), who is mentioned in the third division of "the Writings" (1 Chronicles 6:39). He is referred to elsewhere in "the Writings" as: "Asaph the seer [prophet]" (2 Chronicles 29:30).

Another example alluded to in Matthew's gospel is when Joseph returned with Jesus and Mary to Galilee, "and came and lived in a city called Nazareth. This was to fulfill what was spoken through *the prophets*: 'He shall be called a Nazarene'" (Matthew 2:22-23, emphasis added). The "prophets" most likely refers to Isaiah (Isaiah 49:7; 53:3), but would also include Psalm 22:6-8 written by King David. They both wrote the Messiah ("the Redeemer") would be despised, rejected, and reproached by men, who would "sneer" at Him.

As mentioned in Chapter One, even the apostle Nathanael understood this significance of being from Nazareth. When Philip declared, "We have found Him of whom Moses in *the Law and also the Prophets wrote*—Jesus of Nazareth, the son of Joseph", Nathanael's response was "*Can any good thing come out of Nazareth?*" (John 1:45-46, emphasis added).

When Jesus corrected the Sadducees' false religious belief of their denial of a bodily resurrection, He corrected them by using the idiom "Have you not read?" He used it when He quoted the book of Exodus in "the Law" stating, "But regarding the resurrection of the dead, *have you not read* what was spoken to you by God: 'I AM THE GOD OF ABRAHAM, AND THE GOD OF ISAAC, AND THE GOD OF JACOB'? He is not the God of the dead but of the living" (Matthew 22:31-32, cf. Exodus 3:6, emphasis added).

Several other examples could be given. Out of the nearly three-hundred times one of these specific metonyms are used in the New Testament to reference the Old Testament Scriptures, *one-hundred percent of the time they are used to describe one of the books found in the boundaries of the Hebrew Bible.* <u>None</u> of them are used to describe even *one verse* in the Deuterocanon independent of the Hebrew Bible.

Even though not *every* book in the Hebrew canon uses one of the metonyms above, twenty-eight out of the thirty-nine books from the Hebrew canon use at least one of them.[360] The significance is every section, as well as every subsection, of the Hebrew Bible uses one of these terms. When a book in a section or subsection uses one, that validates the rest of the section or subsection as being Inspired Old Testament Scripture as well.

I already covered even the "latter prophet" Zechariah made reference to the "former prophets" (Zechariah 1:4; 7:7,12), which is a subsection of "the Prophets" in the Hebrew Bible. When Matthew referred to "Jeremiah the prophet" (Matthew 27:9), he was actually referencing *Zechariah* the prophet (Zechariah 11:12-13). Matthew did this because Jeremiah was listed first in order of "the Prophets" in the canon of the Pharisees. Essentially, Matthew was using "Jeremiah" as a metonym for "the Prophets" as a whole. By referring to Jeremiah, he was covering the entire second division and Inspiration of the Hebrew Bible, which includes Zechariah.

The twelve "minor prophets" were "collected in one scroll."[361] The writer of the Deuterocanonical book of Sirach affirmed this when he acknowledged some of the prophets from the second half of the Hebrew Bible, as well as Job from the third division of "the Writings":

> "Who burned the holy city and left its streets desolate, As *JEREMIAH* had foretold; for they had treated him badly who even in the womb had been made *a prophet,* To root out, pull down, and destroy, and then to build and to plant. *EZEKIEL beheld the vision* and described the different creatures of the chariot; He also referred to *JOB, who always persevered in the right path.* Then too, the *TWELVE PROPHETS* – may their bones return to life from their resting place! – Gave new strength to Jacob and saved him by their faith and hope." (Sirach 49:6-10 NAB, emphasis added, capital letters in original text)

Just as Matthew used the metonym "Jeremiah" to refer to the second division of "the Prophets" as a whole, likewise, Sirach used the "Twelve Prophets" as a separate subdivision of "the Prophets." This demonstrates as early as the Intertestamental Period (after the completion of Hebrew Bible, but before the New Testament era), Jews like Sirach recognized there

---

360 Ibid. Christie, Steve. *The Protestant Reformation - 500 Year Anniversary (Part 1 of 3).* "BornAgainRN." (YouTube.com). At the making of this video, I only found two-hundred and nine verses, but when I began to write this book, I discovered nearly three-hundred verses. (Begins around the 21:41 mark.)

361 Ibid. McDonald, Lee Martin. *The Biblical Canon,* p.82.

were subdivisions, or "groupings," within "the Prophets" in the second division of the Old Testament canon, such as the "Twelve Prophets" and the "Former Prophets."

By Sirach including Job in with the prophets Jeremiah, Ezekiel, and the Twelve Prophets, he recognized the book of Job to be just as authoritative Old Testament Scripture as the others, despite Job being part of the third division of "the Writings." The "latter prophet" Ezekiel likewise acknowledged Job as authoritative, by listing him along with Daniel and Noah (Ezekiel 14:14,20).

DANIEL...OR DANIEL *"THE PROPHET"*?

Daniel is no doubt an Old Testament prophet and writer of Inspired Scripture. Jesus referred to him as "Daniel *the prophet*" when He quoted from the book of Daniel in the Hebrew Bible (Matthew 24:15, cf. Daniel 11:31; 12:11). In some Catholic Old Testaments, like the NAB, the book of Daniel is listed under "The Prophetic Books." Even in Protestant and Catholic Old Testaments, Daniel falls in-between the book of Ezekiel (the last "Major Prophet") and the book of Hosea (the first "Minor Prophet").

However, in the Hebrew Bible, he is listed in the third division of "the Writings," rather than in the second division of "the Prophets." This *may* be because of the specific type of prophetic ministry God designated Daniel to. MacDonald explains:

> "...Daniel was a prophet not by *calling*, but *by ministry*. By vocation he was a statesman. Hence, he was not put with the professional prophets – Isaiah, Jeremiah, etc.... As noted this is probably why the Hebrew OT [Old Testament] has Daniel in the section known as 'The Writings,' and not with 'The Prophets,' as in English."[362] (emphasis added)

This would explain its place in-between the "Major Prophets" and "Minor Prophets." Daniel was no doubt an Old Testament prophet, but his writing was not classified in either of the aforementioned subdivisions of "the Prophets." It was not unusual for a writer of an Old Testament book, like the Psalms, to be referred to as "the Prophet" (Matthew 11:35). McDonald quotes James Barr (*"Holy Scripture: Canon, Authority,*

---

[362] Ibid. MacDonald, William. Believer's Bible Commentary, *Daniel: Introduction, II. Authorship*, pp.1076-1077. Brackets inserted by me for clarity.

Criticism"): "...any non-Torah book that was holy Scripture was a Prophet."[363]

This is why in the New Testament, Jesus, Paul, and others simply referred to the Old Testament as a whole as "the Law and *the Prophets.*" They were not simply addressing the first two divisions of the three-tiered Old Testament canon. They were using it as a metonym for the Old Testament *as a whole* – "the Law" to refer to the five books of Moses, and "the Prophets" to everything else.

MELITO OF SARDIS (A.D. SECOND CENTURY)

Melito of Sardis was a second century Catholic bishop[364] and a canonized saint in the Catholic Church[365], who gave a list of Old Testament books which he referred to as "the Law and the Prophets."[366] In his list, he records several books, such as the Psalms, Proverbs, Song of Solomon, and Daniel, as well as others, which are not classified under "The Prophetic Books" in Catholic Old Testaments (nor in the second division of "the Prophets" in the Hebrew Bible).[367] Moreover, Melito did not include *any* of the Deuterocanonical books in his Old Testament list,[368] but only the books from the Hebrew Bible (except for Esther). He too categorized the subsection of "the Twelve in a single book."[369] This demonstrates the recognition of subsections within "the Prophets" in the early church.

This reinforces Daniel's place in the third division of "the Writings" in the Hebrew Bible, instead of the second section of "the Prophets," despite Jesus referring to him as "Daniel *the prophet.*" Just as Melito listed books from "the Writings" under the metonym "the Law and the Prophets," like the Psalms, Proverbs, and Job, he also included the book of Daniel under

---

363 Ibid. McDonald, Lee Martin. *The Biblical Canon*, p.99. Martin quotes James Barr from his book, *Holy Scripture: Canon, Authority, Criticism*, p.55, Philadelphia: Westminster, 1983.

364 EWTN.com. "Who is Melito of Sardis?" Copyright 2018. Accessed from the Internet
http://www.ewtn.com/v/experts/showmessage.asp?number=347312&Pg=&Pgnu=&recnu=

365 Catholic.com. Macerlean, A. A. *Melito, Saint.* Accessed from the Internet
https://www.catholic.com/encyclopedia/melito-saint

366 Ibid. Maier. *Eusebius: The Church History*, Book 4:26, p.144.

367 Ibid, p.145.

368 Ibid. Melito does not specifically list the books of Lamentations and Nehemiah by name. As we mentioned elsewhere in this book, Jeremiah and Lamentations were considered one book, as were Ezra and Nehemiah. This was the testimony of several early church fathers and church councils as well. EWTN.com also acknowledges the Deuterocanonical book of Sirach "is not in the canonical list of Melito of Sardes (c.280AD)" (see http://www.ewtn.com/library/SCRIPTUR/DEUTEROS.TXT).

369 Ibid.

this same metonym as well, which they were all later classified under the third division of "the Writings."

One final observation about Daniel: despite Jesus referring to him as "Daniel the prophet," in the Old Testament, McDonald cites C.A. Evans ("The Scriptures of Jesus and His Earliest Followers") showing prophets were generally introduced in their books by being identified with their father:

> "...for Jesus more typically refers to the given name, e.g., 'Jonah' not 'Jonah son of Amittai,' or 'Isaiah' not 'Isaiah the son of Amor.'"[370]

In the book of Jonah, Jonah is introduced as "Jonah *the son of Amittai*" (Jonah 1:1), rather than "Jonah *the prophet*." Isaiah is introduced in his book as "Isaiah *the son of Amoz*" (Isaiah 1:1), rather than "Isaiah *the prophet*." However, when Daniel is introduced in the book which bears his name, he is simply referred to as "Daniel" (Daniel 1:6) and is identified with *his tribe* "Judah," rather than his father. Aside from Jesus referring to him as a "prophet," Daniel is never referred to as a prophet in either the Old or New Testament, including in his own book. Yet, Daniel refers to Jeremiah as "Jeremiah *the prophet*" (Daniel 9:2). Likewise, in the book of Jeremiah, he is introduced as "Jeremiah *the son of Hilkiah*" (Jeremiah 1:1), rather than "Jeremiah *the prophet*."

Hence, Daniel was a "prophet" of God in the same way Moses was a prophet (Deuteronomy 18:18). Similarly, Joseph was a prophet for Pharaoh who interpreted his dreams (Genesis 41:1-36), just as Daniel had interpreted Nebuchadnezzar's dreams (Daniel 2:24-45). Job was a prophet who God declared he "had spoken of Me what is right" (Job 42:7). Yet, neither the book of Deuteronomy nor the book of Job is in the second division of "the Prophets," but rather in the first and third division of "the Law" and "the Writings," respectfully. In the same manner, the book of Daniel is also placed in the third division of "the Writings" in the Hebrew Bible, instead of the second division of "the Prophets" despite being a prophet of God like Moses and Joseph.

By Jesus using the metonym, "the prophet," to refer to Daniel when quoting from this Old Testament book, the New Testament is acknowledging another one of "the Writings" from the third division of the Hebrew Bible – the book of Daniel. McDonald references R.T. Beckwith's assertion of this:

---

[370] Ibid. McDonald, *The Biblical Canon*, p.98 cites C. A. Evans, "The Scriptures of Jesus and His Earliest Followers," 90 n.17 in *The Canon Debate*, edited by L. M. McDonald and J. A. Sanders. Peabody, Mass: Hendrickson, 2002.

"Beckwith...reasons that since Jesus also cites the book of Daniel (e.g., Dan 4:26 in Matt 4:17 and 9:27; 11:31; 12:11 in Matt 14:15 and Dan 7:13 in Mark 14:62), which was part of the Writings, he surely must have intended the whole of the Writings when he mentioned the 'psalms' in Luke 24:44."[371]

When Jesus was rebuking the apostle Peter by asking him three times if he loved Him (John 21:15-17), Peter answered by acknowledging Jesus' Omniscience, "Lord, *You know all things*" (v.17, emphasis added). Even though the *specific* books from the third division of "the Writings" are not explicitly listed in the text of Luke 22:44, since Jesus is all-knowing He was fully aware of the three-tiered Old Testament canon. Otherwise, He would not have separated "the Psalms" from "the Prophets." He would have simply said "the Law (of Moses) and the Prophets" like He did elsewhere and how Luke had earlier in verse twenty-seven. Jesus would have been aware of which books fell under "the Prophets" and which fell under "the Writings."

Several other examples could be given from the New Testament, as well as from both early Jewish and Christian history, for a recognized third division of "the Writings" encompassed in the Hebrew Bible. For example, "Rabban" (the Elder) Gamaliel, mentioned in Chapter Seven,[372] was a Pharisee and teacher of the Law (Acts 5:34) and had educated the apostle Paul (Acts 22:3). He, too, acknowledged a three-tiered Old Testament canon consisting of "the Law" and "the Prophets" and "the Hagiographa (i.e.: "the Writings"):

"Sectarians asked Rabban Gamaliel: Whence do we know that the Holy One, blessed be He, will resurrect the dead? He answered them from *the Torah, Prophets, and Hagiographa* [Holy Writings], yet they were not convinced" (*b. Sanhedrin* 90b, Leiman, *Canonization of the Hebrew Scripture,* 67)."[373] (emphasis added)

Catholic author Gary Michuta (mentioned in Chapter Two) stated after the destruction of the Temple in A.D. 70, "there were two sects that really survived intact. One was the Pharisees; the other were Christians."[374]

---

371 Ibid. McDonald, p.95. McDonald cites R.T. Beckwith, *The Old Testament Canon of the New Testament Church and Its Background in Early Judaism*, p.438 (citing *Sepher Torah* 2:3-4 and *Sopherim* 2:4); see also 111-14. Grand Rapids: Eerdmans, 1985.

372 Ibid. NewAdvent.org. *Gamaliel.*

373 Ibid. McDonald, *The Biblical Canon*, p.94. McDonald cites S. Z. Leiman. *The Canonization of the Hebrew Scripture: The Talmudic and Midrashic Evidence.* Brackets inserted by me for clarity.

374 Ibid. Michuta, Gary. *Gary Michuta & Fr. Hugh Barbour - Catholic Answers Live - 10/23/17.* YouTube.com. (Begins around the 50:58 mark.)

Michuta stated other Jewish sects like the Sadducees and the Essenes were "disenfranchised"[375] – meaning they did not survive as a Jewish authoritative entity shortly after the destruction of the Temple. McDonald also affirmed the sole survival of these "two sects" of Judaism: "of the various Judaisms of the first century, of which two – Pharisaic Judaism and Christianity – are the primary survivors."[376]

Unlike the Sadducees and the other Jewish sects, the Pharisees *did* survive along with their Jewish canon well into the church age, such as the apostle Paul who wrote nearly one-third of the Inspired New Testament. It was the spiritual descendants of the Pharisees in the church age which transformed into modern-day Judaism, just as the Judaism of Ezra had transformed into the Pharisees, which included the same Old Testament canon – the Hebrew Bible (see Chapter Seven).

This explains why their Old Testament canons are identical in terms of sharing the exact same books. The Old Testament canon shared by Ezra, Sirach, Hillel, Gamaliel, the Pharisees, Jesus, His disciples, the apostle Paul, the New Testament writers, and the early first century church, and then by later Judaism is what was rediscovered centuries later by Protestants in the sixteenth century.

THE ORACLES OF GOD

The New Testament writers refer to this passing on of divine revelation of the "utterances of God" (1 Peter 4:11) as the "oracles of God" (Acts 7:38; Romans 3:2; Hebrews 5:12). These "oracles" were entrusted by the Jews (Romans 3:1-2), but "which" Jews? Which sect of Judaism were entrusted?

These "oracles" referred to the Old Testament Scriptures, which began with Moses prophesying about the Messiah (Acts 7:37) "together with the angels" (v.38). These "oracles" also included the rest of the Old Testament Scriptures, such as "the Prophets" like Malachi who referred to his book as "The *oracle of the word of the LORD* to Israel through Malachi" (Malachi 1:1, emphasis added). (See also Nahum 1:1; Habakkuk 1:1; etc.) While the Sadducees rejected angels (Acts 23:8), the Pharisees believed in them. The Old Testament "oracles" of Scripture faithfully passed on to the time of Jesus was the canon of the Pharisees who believed in angels, as well as the "oracles" of Moses, Nahum, Habakkuk, Malachi, the Psalms, etc., from the Hebrew Bible.

---

[375] Ibid. Michuta. YouTube.com. (Begins around the 50:48 mark.)

[376] Ibid. McDonald, Lee Martin. *The Biblical Canon*, Preface to the Third Edition, p. xvii.

When the apostle Paul wrote "they [the Jews] were entrusted with the oracles of God" (Romans 3:2), he used the Greek word "*pisteuō*" for "entrusted." Elsewhere, he used this same Greek word when he wrote "we have been approved by God to be entrusted ("*pisteuō*") with the gospel" (1 Thessalonians 2:4). Paul and the rest of the apostles understood what the gospel was which was "entrusted" to them. Likewise, the Jews – specifically, the Pharisees, which included Paul – would have understood the "oracles of God" which were "entrusted" to them.

Before I conclude this chapter, I would like to share one other defense from the late Old Testament and early New Testament eras for a reliable defense for the canon of the Hebrew Bible which Luther himself utilized: the Targums.

LUTHER AND THE TARGUMS

Martin Luther is often criticized for "removing" the Deuterocanonical books from the Vulgate, because they conflicted with "his theology." It is assumed his decision for doing this was because he was convinced by the Jewish leaders of his day that they were not found in the *TaNaKh* (the modern Jewish Bible). The *TaNaKh* is an acronym for *"the Torah"* ("the Law"), *"the Nevi'im"* ("the Prophets"), and *"the Ketuvim"* ("the Writings") – the same threefold canon of the Pharisees and later Judaism.

Contrary to popular belief, Luther never actually "removed" *any* of the Deuterocanonical books from his German translation of the Bible. He placed them in a separate uninspired section in-between the Old and New Testaments labeled the "Apocrypha" – the same term Jerome and other early Catholics used to describe these questionable writings. In fact, Luther *included* the Deuterocanonical book of Baruch which Jerome omitted in his original Latin Vulgate. If anything, Luther **added** a book to his German translation, rather than "removing" any!

Luther did not reject them based simply on the Jewish leaders of his day. He learned from Jewish sources, centuries earlier, that the Deuterocanonical books were not translated into the Targums, while the books from the Hebrew Bible were:

"The forerunners and leaders of the Renaissance and the Reformation (14th-15th Centuries), and especially Martin Luther and William Tyndale (16th Century), made use of Latin translations of the classic Jewish commentators Rashi, Ibn Ezra, and Kimhi (11th-13th Centuries), whose works were imbued with the direct knowledge of the Targums."[377]

"In the last few centuries B.C., the Jews who lived to the north and east of Judea also found the Hebrew Bible difficult to understand, for their spoken language had become largely Aramaic. Translations into the Aramaic, *first of the Torah and then of the rest of the Bible, became known as the Targums*."[378] (emphasis added)

WHAT ARE THE TARGUMS?

The Targums were early Aramaic translations, or more specifically paraphrases, of the Hebrew Bible. McDonald comments on the Targums:

"These writings are translations or extended paraphrases of the Hebrew Scriptures into Aramaic, the language of the Jewish people following their return from exile in Babylon."[379]

They would be comparable to a modern-day "word-for-thought" version of the Bible, such as *The Message* or *The New Living Translation*, rather than a literal "word-for-word" translation, like the KJV or the NASB. The significance is, "There are Targums on all of the books of the HB [Hebrew Bible] except Daniel, Ezra, and Nehemiah. *There are no Targums on noncanonical books*"[380] (emphasis added).

This is understandable since McDonald points out, "These three books may have no Targum because all of them are written partially in Aramaic."[381] Every book of the Hebrew Bible was either translated into the Aramaic Targums in its entirety, or they were originally written, at least partially, in Aramaic. *None* of the Deuterocanonical books were translated into the Targums.

Although the dating of the Targums – as a whole – is debated, "three or four of them were found in Qumran and date to the first century B.C.E. or early first century C.E."[382] This would have been around the time of the completion of the Deuterocanon or afterwards. Not a single Deuterocanonical book was translated into the Targums during this time.

---

[377] "*The TaNaKh: the Holy Scriptures* – The New JPS Translation according to the Traditional Hebrew Text" (1985), Jewish Publication Society, p. xvii, Preface.

[378] Ibid, p.xv, Preface.

[379] Ibid. McDonald, Lee Martin, *The Biblical Canon*, p.185.

[380] Ibid. p.186. Brackets inserted by me for clarity.

[381] Ibid.

[382] Ibid.

McDonald notes the ones which were found "preserves Lev[iticus] 16:12-15, 18-21; Job 3:5-9(?); 4:16-5:4; Job 17:14-42:11. A fourth possible Targum preserves Gen[esis] 10:20)."[383] The significance of the two middle groupings is they are from the book of Job, which is from the third division of "the Writings" from the Hebrew Bible.

Since they were found with the Targums of Genesis and Leviticus, this demonstrates the Jewish translators even back then considered "the Writings" to be just as significant, authoritative, and Inspired as "the Law." Their high view of these Inspired writings justified translating them into Aramaic, so the Jewish people could read them in their own language. This same desire was shared by later Catholics, like Jerome, to translate them into Latin, as well as later Protestants, like Luther and Tyndale, to translate them into German and English, respectfully. Yet, there was no desire to translate *any* of the Deuterocanon into the Targums.

This desire goes all the way back to the last canonical book of the Hebrew Bible (Nehemiah), when Ezra brought "the book of the Law of Moses which the LORD had given to Israel" (Nehemiah 8:1) and "They read from the book, from the law of God, *translating to give the sense so that they understood the reading*" (v.8, emphasis added). McDonald states "Jewish tradition claims that they [the Targums] go back to the time of the Jews' return from Babylon under the leadership of Ezra (Neh[emiah] 8:8, see *b. Megillah* 18b and *Genesis Rabbah* 36:8)"[384] (emphasis added).

This is likely since the Hebrew term *tirgum* (*targuma* in Aramaic[385]) means "to interpret, or translate from one language to another." This Aramaic word is used in the book of Ezra when "the text of the letter was written in Aramaic and *translated* [*tirgum*] from Aramaic" (Ezra 4:7). Moreover, McDonald points out the similarities in context between "the Targums and the Gospels.... They share similar views about the world.... They frequently offer similar interpretations of the Hebrew Scriptures. As a result, scholars often use both to interpret each other."[386] Allen Myers recognizes, "Despite this uncertainty with regard to dating, the Targums have been drawn on extensively in recent New Testament studies to illuminate themes, exegetical traditions, and particular linguistic features."[387]

---

383 Ibid, footnote #51. Brackets inserted by me for clarity.

384 Ibid, p.185. Italics in the original text. Brackets inserted by me for clarity.

385 Ibid.

386 Ibid, footnote #49.

387 Myers, Allen C. The Eerdmans Bible Dictionary. Grand Rapids, MI: Eerdmans, 1987. Accessed from the Christian Apologetics and Research Ministry, *What are the Targums? Where did Aramaic come from in the Old Testament?* by Matt Slick. 2/17/2017 https://carm.org/what-are-the-targums

Since the Hebrew Scriptures were translated into Aramaic during the late Intertestamental Period, and even up to the time of Jesus, WHY were not any of the Deuterocanonical books translated into the Targums? At the very least, why were those originally written in Hebrew, such as Tobit and Sirach discovered among the Dead Sea Scrolls (and possibly 1 Maccabees, Judith, Baruch, and parts of Wisdom), not translated?[388] Why is there not even a *single Deuterocanonical book* translated into the Targums during this time – or after – like there is with virtually every book from the Hebrew Bible (besides the three originally written partially in Aramaic)?

It is still difficult for many people to grasp the idea prophecy from God remained silent for four-hundred years from the book of Nehemiah to the revelation of the conception of John the Baptist (Luke 1:11-13). This would not be the first time God's prolonged prophetic silence occurred in Israel's history.

The events between the books of Genesis to Exodus also spanned four-hundred years of prophetic silence (Genesis 15:13, cf. Acts 7:6). More specifically, both the Old and New Testaments state the exact time frame Israel was enslaved before the Law was given to Moses by God: *four-hundred thirty years* (Exodus 12:40-41; Galatians 3:17), which is a silence of thirty years *longer* than the time between Nehemiah and John the Baptist.

In lieu of the overwhelming mountain of evidence from the New Testament, as well as from both early Jewish and Christian history, as McDonald concedes: "There is little doubt that the core of the biblical collection of authoritative books is essentially the same collection that we now have in the Protestant OT [Old Testament] collection."[389]

What about the reliability of the *New* Testament as an Inspired source to trust in the canonicity of the *Old* Testament? Even though the New Testament supports the canon of the Hebrew Bible, what objective godly criteria do we have to believe the twenty-seven-book canon Catholics, Protestants, and virtually all Christians share and believe in is reliable? Why trust in only those twenty-seven books? What about books like the *Didache*, *1 Clement*, and the *epistle of Barnabas* written around the same time as the New Testament canon, including some of the alleged "disciples of the disciples" like Papias and Ignatius?

These and other questions will be addressed in the final chapter.

---

[388] EWTN.com. Catholic Q&A. *The 7 books removed by Martin Luther. Question from Rhonda Kaiser on 5/1/2005: Answer by Rev. Mark J. Gantley, JCL on 5/1/2005.* Accessed from the Internet
http://www.ewtn.com/v/experts/showmessage.asp?number=438095
[389] Ibid. McDonald, Lee Martin. *The Biblical Canon*, p.216. Brackets inserted by me for clarity.

CHAPTER TEN: Why Should I Trust the New Testament?

"I felt the necessity to write to you appealing that you contend earnestly for the faith which was once for all handed down to the saints." (Jude v.4)

95 A.D. marked the closing of the New Testament with the completion of the book of Revelation, written by the apostle John (Revelation 1:1; 22:8,18-21). It was also the conclusion of the Biblical canon as well. No further Inspired revelation was to be penned after the last "jot and tittle" of John was written down. There would be other writings during this time (and afterwards) written by contemporaries and "disciples" of the apostles. It will be shown in this final chapter they did not have the godly criteria the thirty-nine books of the Hebrew Bible and the twenty-seven books of the New Testament possessed.

Before discussing how a Christian can objectively discern what does and does not qualify as Scripture, the subject of the New Testament canon is really not in dispute. Unlike the Old Testament canon, Catholics and Protestants actually *agree with each other* on the exact same twenty-seven-book canon. The seven major historical groups classified under "Christendom," including Eastern Orthodoxy, all embrace these same twenty-seven books (with a few specific exceptions within the Syriac traditions).[390] So, this really is not even a defense Protestants have to make. It would only be required if they *disagreed* on the New Testament canon.

One might ask why Protestants would embrace only the New Testament of the "Catholic Bible," but not the Old Testament as well? As discussed in previous chapters, the Old Testament canon was *already established* by the time of Jesus, while the New Testament was not yet written. Rather than simply "depend" on the early church fathers and early church councils who did not all agree with each other – even on the New Testament – I will be discussing the godly criteria which was used by the Reformers to discern the Biblical canon.

The apostle Paul stated, "<u>All</u> Scripture is Inspired" (2 Timothy 3:16), or God-breathed. This means in order to classify as Scripture, a particular piece of writing would have to reflect the attributes of God. For example, God would have to be incapable of changing (Malachi 3:6) in order to be consistent with His nature. Even a single passage of His Scriptures could

---

Ibid, Wikipedia.org. *Biblical canon, Christian biblical canons, Canons of various Christian traditions, New Testament, Table: 2.4.2.1*

not "change" what a previous one declared. God would also have to be incapable of lying (Numbers 23:19; Titus 1:2). His Scriptures could not say something that is not true, either prophetically, logically, scientifically, or anything else. Otherwise, readers could not trust anything written in it.

Over the past two millennia, Christians have used some of these godly criteria to test various pieces of writings to determine its Inspiration, and whether it originated from the mind of God or from man. In *The MacArthur Study Bible*, MacArthur lists three of them in the section in "How We Got The Bible":

> "First, the writing had to have a recognized prophet or apostle as its author (or one associated with them, as in the case of Mark, Luke, Hebrews, James, and Jude). Second, the writing could not disagree with or contradict previous Scripture. Third, the writing had to have general consensus by the church as an inspired book. Thus, when various councils met in church history to consider the canon, they did not vote for the canonicity of a book but rather recognized after the fact, what God had already written."[391]

Unfortunately, the early church councils did not do this consistently with the already established *Old* Testament canon (they all affirmed the Deuterocanonical books, except for Baruch, instead of limiting it to the Hebrew Bible). They were also not all consistent with the *New* Testament canon either (Revelation was not included in the Council of Carthage of 397). Since the New Testament was yet to be canonized, God revealed the canon to the early church *in spite* of their rejection of the complete Old Testament canon, which God had already revealed through Pharisaic Judaism.

One of the key measures for discerning if a piece of literature was Inspired or not was authorship. The apostle Paul wrote about God's household "having been built on the foundation of the apostles and prophets, Christ Jesus Himself being the corner stone" (Ephesians 2:20). By "prophets" this refers to the *New* Testament prophets (Ephesians 3:5), such as Silas, Judas Barsabbas, and Agabus (Acts 15:22,32; 21:10), not the *Old* Testament prophets. Some of the apostles were writers of the New Testament, such as Matthew, John, Peter, and Paul.

When Paul wrote the apostles and prophets were the "foundation" of the church, he was indicating their existence was limited to the time period of the first century. Prophets received direct revelation from God, while apostles were "sent out" either by Jesus or the first century church to spread

---

[391] Ibid. The MacArthur Study Bible. *How We Got The Bible, The Publishing Process, Canonicity*, pp.xiv-xv.

His gospel. Once the last apostle, John, died, there would be no forthcoming "apostles" nor "prophets." While the *church* would be "built on" them, future *apostles and prophets* would not since they were limited to the first century "foundation." Since Scripture is a revelation from God to the apostles, like John (Revelation 1:1), as well as to their contemporaries, like Mark and Luke, no further New Testament authorship was possible after the close of the first century.

If divine prophetic and apostolic revelation did continue into the second century, then the New Testament canon would still be open and further Inspired writings could potentially be added to it. However, the apostle John commanded in the book of Revelation – the last book of the New Testament and Biblical canon – not to "add to" nor "take away from" it (Revelation 22:19-20).

Although this immediate command is about not adding to or removing from the *book of Revelation*, Jesus started off by commanding John to "write the things which you have seen, and the things which are, and the things which will take place after these things" (Revelation 1:19). John was commanded to write about what had taken place (his past), as well as what was occurring (his present), and what will take place (his future). In context, John's command was to not "add to" nor "take away" from that entire time period, which includes not "adding" any further written Inspired text to the New Testament *itself*, because it – and the Biblical canon as a whole – was closed.

The same godly criteria which Pharisaic Judaism used to recognize the Old Testament Scriptures (i.e.: lack of errors and contradictions, *prophetic* authorship, written during the prophetic era, etc.) was used later by the church to discern the New Testament Scriptures, but based on *apostolic* authority. One such criterion was the presence of miracles during the various time periods Scripture was being written. MacArthur observed:

> "*Miracles introduced new eras of revelation.* All three periods of miracles were times when God gave His written revelation – Scripture – in substantial quantities. Those doing the miracles were essentially the same ones heralding an era of revelation. Moses wrote the first five books of Scripture. Elijah and Elisha introduced the prophetic age. The apostles wrote nearly all of the New Testament."[392]

MacArthur then goes on to give further examples when divine miracles were performed by people in other eras, followed by written revelation recording these events, such as Joshua and Daniel, Hezekiah in the book of

---

[392] MacArthur, Jr., John F. *Charismatic Chaos*, p.136-137. Zondervan Publishing House: Grand Rapids, Michigan. 1992. Italics in original text.

Isaiah, King David and King Solomon penning wisdom literature, etc.[393] He then stressed not every believer was given the ability to perform miracles:

> "Moses and Joshua, Elijah and Elisha, and Christ and the apostles all had the ability to do frequent signs and wonders. These were designed to convince people that God was with these men and that he was speaking through them.... *Not every believer had the power to do miracles*."[394] (emphasis added)

Clearly, this was the primary purpose God had for allowing certain individuals to perform miracles but not others. As MacArthur points out, it was also the reason Jesus had for allowing the apostles to perform them: "His major purpose was to authenticate his messianic claims (cf. John 20:30-31). Similarly, while the apostles also healed people, *their primary purpose was to authenticate new revelation*"[395]; "God's *intended purpose for miracles: to confirm new scriptural revelation*,"[396] (emphasis added).

The apostle Peter realized this even when he wrote his own epistles. Despite performing miracles himself and being an eyewitness to supernatural acts, like the Transfiguration, Peter recognized this was all done to legitimize the Inspiration of Scripture:

> "So we have *the prophetic word made more sure*, to which you do well to pay attention as to a lamp shining in a dark place, until the day dawns and the morning star arises in your hearts. But know this first of all, that *no prophecy of Scripture is a matter of one's own interpretation*, for *no prophecy was ever made by an act of human will*, but men *moved by the Holy Spirit spoke from God*." (2 Peter 1:19-21, emphasis added).

As discussed in Chapter One, by the mid-first century A.D. most of the New Testament had been written by miracle-performing apostles. Peter, who miraculously healed a crippled man (Acts 3:1-7), had the authority to declare not only his epistles were Scripture, but also all of Paul's (2 Peter 3:15-16).

In his first epistle, Peter refers to the writer of the gospel of Mark as "my son, Mark" (1 Peter 5:13). According to Papias, an alleged disciple of the apostle John, Papias affirms Mark's gospel was a faithful recollection of the words of Peter:

> "Regarding Mark, the writer of the Gospel, he [Papias] states: 'The Presbyter used to say this also: "Mark became Peter's

---

[393] Ibid, p.137-138.
[394] Ibid, p.138-139.
[395] Ibid, p.143.
[396] Ibid, p.246.

interpreter and wrote down accurately, but not in order, all that he remembered of the things said and done by the Lord.... So that Mark did not err in writing down some things just as he recalled them. For he had one overriding purpose: to omit nothing that he had heard and to make no false statements to his account."""[397]

On the apostolicity of Peter, as well as his ability to perform miracles, Peter had the authority to declare Mark's gospel was Inspired, since it was based on the words of the miracle-performing apostle. The apostle Paul who miraculously brought Eutychus back from the dead (Acts 20:9-12), also had the authority to proclaim Luke's writings as Scripture (1 Timothy 5:18, cf. Luke 10:7).

As the New Testament was coming to a close, these miracle-working apostles and some of their close contemporaries wrote to communicate "the faith which was *once for all handed down to the saints*" (Jude v.3, emphasis added), which "were spoken beforehand by the apostles of our Lord Jesus Christ" (v.17). Here, Jude, is communicating the Christian faith was handed down by Jesus' apostles, such as Peter who Jude quoted (Jude v.18, cf. 2 Peter 3:3) validating Peter's epistles as Scripture. These Inspired works were then written down for the church, "once for all." Once there were no more apostles after the death of John, there would be no further written revelation to add to the New Testament canon.

What about some of the letters written during this time, including those attributed to the apostles and their contemporaries, which were not included in the New Testament? Why are they not Scripture and not included in the New Testament canon?

PAPIAS, THE EPISTLE OF BARNABAS, FIRST CLEMENT, AND THE DIDACHE

There were countless letters and other pieces of literature written during the first few centuries of the church, including "the disciples of the disciples," like Ignatius of Antioch, Papias, Polycarp, etc. who wrote in the early- to mid-second century. One of the godly criteria used by the early church and later Protestants to discern an Inspired New Testament book was *first* century authorship ending with the death of the apostle John. Many later works were written in the _second_ century or long afterwards – years, decades, and even centuries after the apostolic and prophetic "foundation" of the church was over.

---

[397] Ibid. Maier. *Eusebius: The Church History*. Book 3:39, p.113-114. Brackets inserted by me for clarity.

Another criterion previously mentioned was Scripture could not contradict previous Scripture or contain errors. Papias, the second century bishop of Hierapolis, was believed by Irenaeus to be "a hearer of John, and companion of Polycarp, a man of old time"[398] (although Papias himself seems to testify he only *heard* about John and the other apostles from the "Presbyters"[399]). In some of the fragments attributed to him, Papias professes some beliefs which appear to run counter to previous New Testament Scriptures.

THE FRAGMENTS OF PAPIAS

NewAdvent.org describes "A wild and extraordinary legend about Judas Iscariot is attributed to Papias by a catena":[400]

> "Judas walked about in this world a sad example of impiety; for his body having swollen to such an extent that he could not pass where a chariot could pass easily, he was crushed by the chariot, so that his bowels gushed out."[401]

This seems to contradict what we know about the fate of Judas Iscariot from the gospels, which records he died after hanging himself (Matthew 27:5). Papias implies Judas survived his hanging. Yet, when the apostle Peter recollects Judas' demise: "Now this man acquired a field with the price of his wickedness, and *falling headlong, he burst open* in the middle and all *his intestines gushed out*" (Acts 1:18, emphasis added). Peter records Judas' "intestines gushed out" after falling from the tree he hung himself on, not from being "crushed by a chariot." Papias seems to have either heard the story incorrectly from "the presbyters" who told him, or he had a wrong recollection of it. In the unlikely event Judas survived his hanging, it is odd Peter would not have mentioned this in the book of Acts, but instead reported his death resulted from the fall itself.

Papias believed there are three eternal destinations after death for believers based on the amount of spiritual crop they produce: "for the first will be taken up into the heavens, the second class will dwell in Paradise, and the last will inhabit the city."[402] This is akin to Mormonism, which teaches a similar kind of three-tiered eternal destination – celestial,

---

[398] NewAdvent.org. *St. Papias*. Accessed from the Internet http://www.newadvent.org/cathen/11457c.htm

[399] Ibid.

[400] Ibid. A "catena" is a patristic Biblical commentary.

[401] NewAdvent.org. *Fragments of Papias, III*. Accessed from the Internet http://www.newadvent.org/fathers/0125.htm

[402] Ibid. *Fragments of Papias, V.*

terrestrial, telestial.[403] Papias makes a distinction between "the heavens" versus "Paradise," which conflicts with the apostle Paul who wrote they are synonymous (2 Corinthians 12:2,4, cf. Luke 23:43). Papias' confusion comes from Paul's use of the term "third heaven," which Paul simply used to distinguish between the *heavenly* Paradise where all believers go after death versus the first and second *physical* "heavens": earth's atmosphere and outer space, respectively (Genesis 1:6-8,14-15,17,20, cf. Psalm 19:1).

In Eusebius' *The Church History*, Papias relies on a false gospel, alongside New Testament writings, for his information about the New Testament era: "Papias also used evidence from 1 John and 1 Peter and provides another story about a woman falsely accused before the Lord of many sins, which is contained in the *Gospel of the Hebrews*"[404] (emphasis added). NewAdvent.org describes this "*gospel* according to the Hebrews" as being "apocryphal"[405] (emphasis added), to distinguish it from the Inspired New Testament *epistle* to the Hebrews.

Despite Papias being an early church father and allegedly "the illustrious, a disciple of the apostle who leaned on the bosom of Christ,"[406] the fragments of his writings do not qualify as Inspired New Testament Scripture. They were clearly written too late after the canon was closed, and they contain several errors and contradict previous Inspired Scripture.

THE EPISTLE OF BARNABAS

The epistle of Barnabas (attributed to the apostle and traveling companion of Paul from Acts 14:14; 15:2), was also written in the second century (~A.D. 130-131).[407] This was written far too long after the death of the apostle Barnabas around A.D. 61,[408] and decades after the apostle John died, who closed the Biblical canon near the end of the first century. Eusebius referred to it as the "alleged epistle of Barnabas" among the "spurious books."[409] Like Papias, this epistle contains some theological and

---

403 GotQuestions.org. *"What is Mormonism? What do Mormons believe?"* Accessed from the Internet https://www.gotquestions.org/Mormons.html

404 Ibid. Maier. *Eusebius: The Church History.* Book 3:39, p.114. Italics inserted by me for emphasis.

405 NewAdvent.org. *Gospel and Gospels, Number of the gospels.* Accessed from the Internet http://www.newadvent.org/cathen/06655b.htm

406 Ibid. NewAdvent.org. *Fragments of Papias, IX.*

407 NewAdvent.org. *Epistle of Barnabas, Date.* Accessed from the Internet http://www.newadvent.org/cathen/02299a.htm

408 EWTN.com. *St. Barnabas, Apostle.* Accessed from the Internet https://www.ewtn.com/saintsholy/saints/B/stbarnabas.asp

409 Ibid. Maier. *Eusebius: The Church History.* Book 3:25, p.101.

doctrinal beliefs, which are not in-line with previous Scripture, as well as other errors.

Its tenth chapter begins by quoting Moses from the Old Testament. However, it misrepresents what Moses wrote about the weasel: "These also shall be unclean unto you among the creeping things that creep upon the earth; the weasel.... These are to you the unclean among all the swarming things; *whoever touches them when they are dead becomes unclean until evening*" (Leviticus 11:29,31 KJV, emphasis added). However, the *epistle of Barnabas* states:

> "But forasmuch as Moses said... 'Moreover He hath hated the *weasel* also and with good reason. Thou shalt not, saith He, become such as those men of whom we hear as working iniquity with their mouth for uncleanness, neither shalt thou cleave unto impure women who work iniquity with their mouth. *For this animal conceiveth with its mouth.*'"[410] – *the epistle of Barnabas* (Chapter 10:1a,8, emphasis added)

Undoubtedly, Moses did not teach a weasel "conceives with its mouth." Neither Scripture nor science teaches this. Rather, Moses commanded Israel *against touching them when they are dead*; otherwise, they would become ceremonially unclean. The *epistle of Barnabas* is clearly in error for teaching Moses taught this.

Another obvious error, just one verse earlier, is its false claim regarding what Moses taught about the hyena:

> "Again, 'neither shalt thou eat *the hyena;*' thou shalt not, saith He, become an adulterer or a fornicator, neither shalt thou resemble such persons. Why so? Because *this animal changeth its nature year by year, and becometh at one time male and at another female.*"[411] – the *epistle of Barnabas* (Chapter 10:7, emphasis added)

Although the prophets Isaiah and Jeremiah talk about hyenas (Isaiah 13:22), sometimes referring to them as "wolves" (Isaiah 34:14) or "jackals" (Jeremiah 50:39), they never state hyenas can change sex between male and female. Moses never even used the Hebrew term (*"iy"*) to refer to hyenas, let alone they can change sex. Even the Deuterocanonical book of

---

[410] EWTN.com. THE EPISTLE OF BARNABAS. Translated by J.B. Lightfoot. Adapt. and mod. (c) 1990. ATHENA DATA PRODUCTS. Accessed from the Internet
https://www.ewtn.com/library/SOURCES/BARNABAS.TXT

[411] Ibid. For a more detailed list of the errors in the epistle of Barnabas, I highly recommend viewing "Introduction to the Letter of Barnabas" on the YouTube channel "Post-Apostolic Church," published on May 16, 2014:
https://www.youtube.com/watch?v=I9pdxXQcNPg

Sirach mentions them (Sirach 13:17 NAB), but it too does not state anything about their ability to change from one sex to another. Neither are they capable of doing this in nature. The *epistle of Barnabas* is clearly in error here as well.

NewAdvent.org points out, "The author regards several apocryphal books as belonging to the Old Testament--probably IV Esdras (ch. xii, I) and without doubt Henoch (ch. iv, 3; xvi, 5)."[412] McDonald agrees: "In the Christian era, the author of *Barnabas* cites *1 Enoch* three times, twice referring to it as Scripture: 'It has been written, just as Enoch says' (*Barn[abas]*. 16:5, referring to *1 En[och]*. 89:61-64; 90:17) and 'For the Scripture says' (*Barn[abas]*. 16:5, citing *1 En[och]*. 89:55, 66-67)."[413] I will be covering why *1 Enoch* does not qualify as Inspired Scripture later in this chapter.

Based on these multiple theological and scientific errors and contradictions with previous Inspired Scripture, as well as the late date (second century), the alleged *epistle of Barnabas* was clearly not written by the apostle Barnabas from the New Testament and is not Inspired Scripture.

THE FIRST EPISTLE OF CLEMENT

The author of this epistle is believed to have been written by the "Clement" mentioned by the apostle Paul in his epistle to the church of Philippi (Philippians 4:3). Eusebius identifies him as "the third bishop of Rome"[414], who "succeeded Anencletus,"[415] "the third in the list of bishops of Rome who followed Paul and Peter: Linus the first and Anencletus the second."[416] NewAdvent.org writes, "It is now universally acknowledged, after Lightfoot, that it was written about the last year of Domitian (Harnack) or immediately after his death in 96 (Funk)."[417]

This is the first epistle in this chapter, allegedly written by a contemporary of an apostle, during the apostolic age – at the very latest, the same year the apostle John wrote the book of Revelation (or possibly

---

[412] Ibid. NewAdvent.org. *Epistle of Barnabas, General characteristics.* "Henoch" is the same as *1 Enoch*.

[413] Ibid. McDonald, Lee Martin, *The Biblical Canon*, p.398. Italics in the original text. Brackets inserted by me for clarity.

[414] Ibid. Maier. Eusebius' *The Church History*. Book 3:4, p.82.

[415] Ibid, Book 3:15, p.93.

[416] Ibid, Book 3:21, p.96.

[417] NewAdvent.org. *Pope St. Clement I, The Epistle to the Corinthians, Date and authenticity.* Accessed from the Internet http://www.newadvent.org/cathen/04012c.htm

a year before it[418]). Bishop Dionysius of Corinth reported in a letter to Bishop Soter and the Roman Church "it had been customary to read it in the church from the beginning: 'We read your letter today, the Lord's Day, and shall continue to read it frequently for our admonition, as we do with *the earlier letter Clement wrote* on your behalf"[419] (emphasis added).

There are problems with the content of this epistle as well which disqualify it from being included in the New Testament. Clement appears to believe the mythological creature, the phoenix, was a real animal:

> "Let us consider that wonderful sign [of the resurrection] which takes place in eastern lands, that is, in Arabia and the countries round about. *There is a certain bird which is called a phœnix. This is the only one of its kind, and lives five hundred years.* And when the time of its dissolution draws near that it must die, *it builds itself a nest of frankincense, and myrrh, and other spices, into which, when the time is fulfilled, it enters and dies.* But as the flesh decays *a certain kind of worm is produced, which, being nourished by the juices of the dead bird, brings forth feathers.* Then, when it has acquired strength, it takes up that nest in which are the bones of its parent, and bearing these it passes from the land of Arabia into Egypt, to the city called Heliopolis. *And, in open day, flying in the sight of all men,* it places them on the altar of the sun, and having done this, hastens back to its former abode. The priests then inspect the registers of the dates, and find that it has returned exactly as the five hundredth year was completed."[420] (1 Clement 25, emphasis added).

Some have suggested Clement used this simply as an allegory, since in the very next chapter he references Job 19:25-26. It is believed Job also compared his own death to that of a phoenix (Job 29:18). However, the specific Hebrew word Job uses (*"chowl"*) is consistently translated "sand" throughout the Hebrew Bible, *all twenty-three times[421]*, as well as in every major Protestant English translation.[422] In addition, it is translated "palm

[418] Ibid.

[419] Ibid. Maier. *Eusebius: The Church History.* Book 4:23, pp.141-142.

[420] NewAdvent.org. *Letter to the Corinthians (Clement), Chapter 25. The Phœnix an Emblem of Our Resurrection.* Accessed from the Internet http://www.newadvent.org/fathers/1010.htm. Brackets in the original text.

[421] Blue Letter Bible. "Dictionary and Word Search for chowl (Strong's 2344)". Blue Letter Bible. 1996-2018. 13 Feb 2018. Accessed from the Internet http://www.blbclassic.org/lang/lexicon/lexicon.cfm?Strongs=H2344&t=NASB

[422] Blue Letter Bible. "The Trials of Job 29 - (NASB - New American Standard Bible)." Blue Letter Bible. 1996-2018. 13 Feb 2018. Accessed from the Internet http://www.blbclassic.org/Bible.cfm?b=Job&c=29&v=18&t=NASB#vrsn/18

tree" (but not "phoenix") in the New Catholic Version in Job 29:18, despite the New American Bible translating it "phoenix":

> "*Phoenix*: This meaning, originally intended in the Greek, later came to mean 'palm tree.' Some render the Hebrew as 'sand.'"[423] (footnote to Job 29:18 NAB)

The Greek word translated "Phoenix" (*"Phoinix"*) in the New Testament (Acts 27:12) refers to a harbor of Crete, which comes from the Greek root (*"phoinix/phoenix"*), which does mean "palm tree" (John 12:13; Revelation 7:9). Neither the New Testament nor the Old Testament (including the book of Job) understands this word, or its root, to refer to a real-life bird which lives for five-hundred years, dies, and then "resurrects" through a worm. Clement, no doubt, believed this mythological creature really existed, which explains why his epistle is not included in the New Testament, despite being written in the apostolic age, and who was (allegedly) a contemporary of the apostles.

THE DIDACHE

The *Didache* ("The Teachings of the Twelve Apostles") was a first century Christian manuscript which "was likely written between 70 and 120."[424] Like *1 Clement*, the *Didache* was most likely written during the apostolic age, but after the epistles of the apostle Paul. Some similarities between the *Didache* and the Pauline epistles include: *Didache* 5:1 and Romans 1:29-30; *Didache* 5:2 and Romans 12:9; *Didache* 10:6 and 1 Corinthians 16:22; *Didache* 13:1 and 1 Corinthians 9:13-14; 1 Timothy 5:17-18; *Didache* 16:4 and 2 Thessalonians 2:9; and *Didache* 16:6-7 and 1 Corinthians 15:22; 1 Thessalonians 4:16.[425] Considering 1 Timothy was one of the last non-Johannine Scriptures written in the New Testament around A.D. 62-64[426], the *Didache* most likely was written sometime after this, since it borrows so heavily from Paul and the gospel writers.

Despite its early dating, this piece of Christian literature is not Inspired Scripture and does not belong in the New Testament either. Eusebius refers to it as "the so-called Teachings of the Apostles [*Didache*]."[427] He includes it among the "spurious books" along with "the Shepherd [of Hermas], the

---

[423] Ibid. New American Bible, footnote to Job 29:18, p.591.

[424] Ibid. McDonald, Lee Martin. *The Biblical Canon*, p.261, footnote #54.

[425] Ibid, p.269, footnote #69.

[426] Ibid. The MacArthur Study Bible. *The First Epistle of Paul to Timothy, Author and Date*, p.1858.

[427] Ibid. Maier. *Eusebius: The Church History*. Book 3:25, p.101. Brackets in the original text.

Revelation of Peter, the alleged epistle of Barnabas.... In addition, some have included the Gospel of the Hebrews in the list."[428]

There are also doctrinal problems with the *Didache* which run counter to what the Inspired New Testament Scriptures teach. For example, in chapter seven concerning baptism, the *Didache* commands "before the baptism let the baptizer fast, and the baptized, and whatever others can; but you shall order the baptized to fast one or two days before."[429] In numerous passages in the book of Acts, the person being baptized was baptized *immediately on the same day* (or even that very hour) they were converted (Acts 2:41; 16:32-33; 19:4-5; 22:18). Likewise, the person doing the baptizing in these passages did not fast prior to baptizing the newly converted believer.

In the same chapter, if a body of water is not available to immerse a baptismal candidate into, the *Didache* instructs the baptizer to "pour out water *thrice* upon the head into the name of Father and Son and Holy Spirit" (emphasis added).[430] This baptismal formula of the Trinity is taken from passages, such as Matthew 28:19 (see also 2 Corinthians 13:14). Yet, when Jesus gave this command in Matthew's gospel, He said "in the *name* of the Father and the Son and the Holy Spirit" (emphasis added). The use of the *singular* "name," instead of the *plural* "names," is to emphasize a person is baptized into *one* "name" of God, despite being baptized into all three "Persons" of the Trinity. There is no instruction in any of twenty-seven New Testament Scriptures to immerse a person more than once during baptism.

Lastly, the *Didache* instructs during fasting, "But let not your fasts be with the hypocrites; Matthew 6:16 for *they fast on the second and fifth day of the week*; but fast on the fourth day and the Preparation (Friday)"[431] (emphasis added). Although Jesus commanded "Whenever you fast, do not put on a gloomy face like the hypocrites do" (Matthew 6:16), He never commanded what days to fast or to avoid fasting. Despite the hypocritical Pharisee stated "I fast twice a week" in Jesus' parable (Luke 18:12), Jesus did not disclose *which* days the Pharisees fasted, nor to refrain from fasting on the same days as the Pharisees. The disciples of John the Baptist were *fasting just like the Pharisees*, during the time Jesus and His disciples were not fasting (Matthew 9:14). Yet, Jesus did not command John's disciples not to fast on the same days as the Pharisees.

---

[428] Ibid. Brackets in the original text.

[429] NewAdvent.org. *The Didache, Chapter 7. Concerning Baptism.* Accessed from the Internet http://www.newadvent.org/fathers/0714.htm

[430] Ibid.

[431] Ibid. "Matthew 6:16" and "(Friday)" in parentheses included in the original text from NewAdvent.org.

THE SHEPHERD OF HERMAS

The second century *Shepherd of Hermas* does not qualify, because it was written far too late. The *Muratorian Fragment*, dated around A.D. 180-200[432], disclosed it was written around this time and not to be read publicly in the church for this reason:

> "(73) But Hermas wrote the *Shepherd* (74) very recently, in our times, in the city of Rome, (75) while bishop Pius, his brother, was occupying the [episcopal] chair (76) of the church of the city of Rome. (77) And therefore it ought indeed to be read; but (78) it cannot be read publicly to the people in church either among (79) the prophets, whose number is complete, or among the apostles, for it is after [their] time. (*Muratorian Fragment* lines 73-80, Metzger, *Canon of the Old Testament*, 307)."[433]

Eusebius even doubts the validity of its authorship as being that of the "Hermas" mentioned in Paul's epistle to the church of the Romans (Romans 16:14): "But since the same apostle in the salutations at the end of Romans refers to a Hermas, the reputed author of *The Shepherd*, that book has also been rejected by some and therefore should not be placed among the accepted books."[434] Furthermore, *The Shepherd* erroneously refers to a uninspired book as "Scripture," and even mistakenly uses the metonym "it is written" when quoting it:

> "...the *Shepherd of Hermas* called the ancient writing *Eldad and Modad* Scripture: 'The Lord is near those that turn to him, as it is written [*hōs gegraptai*] in the Book of Eldad and Modat, who prophesied to the people in the wilderness' (*Herm. Vis.* 2.3.4, LDL)."[435]

Despite early church fathers like Irenaeus, who "acknowledged the authority of the Shepherd of Hermas and 1 Clement,"[436] and Clement of Alexandria who "quotes from Barnabas, 1 Clement, Shepherd of Hermas...and the Didache,"[437] simply "acknowledging" or "quoting" from

---

432 Ibid. McDonald, Lee Martin. *The Biblical Canon*, p.369.

433 Ibid, p.369 footnote #19, and p.371. Citation of the Muratorian Fragment taken from Metzger and parentheses are in the original text. Quoted from Metzger, B.M. *Canon of the New Testament: Its Origin, Development, and Significance*. Oxford: Clarendon, 1987, 305-307.

434 Ibid. Maier. *Eusebius: The Church History*, Book 3:3, p.81.

435 Ibid. McDonald, Lee Martin. *The Biblical Canon*, p.404. Italics, brackets, and reference to the *Shepherd of Hermas*, Vision (*Herm. Vis.*) in parentheses are in the original text.

436 Ibid, p.301.

437 Ibid, p.302.

early Christian writings does not equate with them being Inspired Scripture. Neither does it qualify them to be included in the New Testament canon, due to either their late dating, questionable or false authorship, theological and/or historical errors, contradictions with previous Scriptures, or other characteristics which disqualify their canonicity.

THE EPISTLES OF IGNATIUS OF ANTIOCH

Ignatius of Antioch lived from the first into the second century A.D. NewAdvent.org states, "It is also believed, and with great probability, that, with his friend Polycarp, he was among the auditors of the Apostle St. John. If we include St. Peter, Ignatius was the third Bishop of Antioch and the immediate successor of Evodius (Eusebius, Church History II.3.22)."[438] He was also "a devoted disciple of Paul."[439] Ignatius wrote seven epistles to churches and individual Christians.[440] Although some approximate his death "between 98 and 117,"[441] more specifically, he "was arrested and martyred (probably c. 110) in Rome."[442]

This would put his epistles into the second century, over a decade after the completion of the New Testament (Jude v.3; Revelation 22:18-19) and the last apostle, John, died. Ignatius' writings were written too late to be included in the New Testament canon.

Even though Ignatius faithfully taught Christian and Biblical orthodoxy in his epistles, and "All the sterling qualities of [sic] ideal pastor and a true soldier of Christ were possessed by the Bishop of Antioch in a preeminent degree,"[443] Ignatius did make some errors in his epistles. In his epistle to the church of the Smyrnaeans, Ignatius misquoted Jesus from the gospel of Luke – *twice*:

> "For I know and believe that He was in the flesh even after the resurrection; and when He came to Peter and his company, He said to them, *Lay hold and handle me*, and see that I am not a *demon* without a body."[444] (emphasis added)

---

[438] NewAdvent.org. *St. Ignatius of Antioch*. Accessed from the Internet http://www.newadvent.org/cathen/07644a.htm. Parentheses in the original text

[439] Ibid. Litfin, *Getting to Know the Church Fathers*, p.36.

[440] Ibid. NewAdvent.org. *St. Ignatius of Antioch, Collections*.

[441] Ibid.

[442] Ibid. Maier. *Eusebius: The Church History*, p.117. Parentheses in the original text.

[443] Ibid. NewAdvent.org. *St. Ignatius of Antioch*.

[444] Ccel.org. *Apostolic Fathers, The Epistle of Ignatius to the Smyrnaeans, IgnaSmyrna.3*. Accessed from the Internet http://www.ccel.org/ccel/lightfoot/fathers.ii.viii.html?=ignatius,epistle,to,smyrnaeans

Not only does Luke 24:39 not mention any of the disciples "handling" Jesus after the resurrection, Jesus did not use the word "demon" in Luke's gospel. Some English translations of Ignatius' epistle interpret the word as "spirit."[445] The actual Greek word used by Ignatius was "demon" (*"daimonion"*)[446] which specifically refers to a fallen angel, which Luke uses elsewhere in his gospel (Luke 4:33; etc.), not "spirit" (*"pneuma"*) which refers more generally to a disembodied essence devoid of any matter (Luke 1:47; etc.)

Ignatius also deviated with the New Testament epistles, which defined the "pastor (shepherd)-elder-overseer (bishop)" as a *single* church office in a local church (Acts 20:17,28; 1 Peter 5:1-2):

> "Ignatius owns the distinction of being the first advocate of the *monepiscopacy*, in which a single bishop serves the entire Christian community in a city. The *episkopos* (= bishop or overseer) became the senior pastor of the whole urban area, assisted by elders called *presbyteroi*. This is a refinement of New Testament terminology, where *episkopos* could be substituted interchangeably with *presbyteros* to designate the elders of a congregation."[447]

This was a recent change from the New Testament model, since *1 Clement* wrote there was still a plurality of pastor-elder-bishops in the local church in the late first century, even in the church of Rome. Dr. Michael Kruger reveals:

> "A letter known as 1 Clement (c.96) also has much to say about early church governance.... The letter affirms the testimony of the book of Acts when it tells us that the apostles initially appointed 'bishops (ἐπισκόπους) and deacons' in the various churches they visited (42.4). After the time of the apostles, bishops were appointed 'by other reputable men with the entire church giving its approval' (44.3). This is an echo of the Didache which indicated that bishops were elected by the church."[448]

---

[445] NewAdvent.org. *The Epistle of Ignatius to the Smyrnaeans, Ch.3 Christ was possessed of a body after His resurrection.* Accessed from the Internet http://www.newadvent.org/fathers/0109.htm

[446] Ibid. Ccel.org. *Apostolic Fathers, The Epistle of Ignatius to the Smyrnaeans, IgnaSmyrna.3.*

[447] Ibid. Litfin, *Getting to Know the Church Fathers*, p.42. Parenthesis and italics in the original text.

[448] Kruger, Michael. Canon Fodder: "Exploring the origins of the New Testament canon and other biblical and theological issues." *Were Early Churches Ruled by Elders or a Single Bishop?* Posted July 13, 2015. Copyright © 2019 Michael J. Kruger. Accessed from the

Although these early Christian works had been written very early on, as early as the first two centuries, they are not Inspired Scriptures. They simply do not meet the godly criteria the twenty-seven-book New Testament canon does. Like these uninspired works, the Deuterocanonical books also contain numerous theological and historical errors and contradictions, which are not present in either the thirty-nine-book Hebrew Bible nor the twenty-seven-book New Testament (see Appendix B).

1 ENOCH AND THE EPISTLE OF JUDE

Although the Pseudoepigraphical book of *1 Enoch* is not part of either the Catholic nor the Protestant Old Testament, because the New Testament epistle of Jude quotes from it should be addressed. Does Jude quoting from it call into question the Inspiration of *his* epistle, since *1 Enoch* is not Inspired? If *1 Enoch* "is" Inspired Scripture, why is it not included in the Biblical canon, considering so many early Christian writings in the second century refer to it as "Scripture"?

Genesis 5:22 states Enoch "walked with God." In this setting, the Hebrew word for "walked" means more than just physical ambulation. It has a much deeper spiritual context which means "to live a manner of life." This phrase, "walked with God," is only used one other time in the entire Old Testament. It is used to describe Noah, which Moses wrote, "Noah was a righteous man, blameless in his time; Noah walked with God" (Genesis 6:9).

Scripture states "Enoch walked with God; and he was not, for God took him" (Genesis 5:24). The writer of Hebrews clarifies this means, "By faith Enoch was taken up so that he would not see death; AND HE WAS NOT FOUND BECAUSE GOD TOOK HIM UP; for he obtained the witness that before his being taken up he was pleasing to God" (Hebrews 11:5). Elijah was the only other person recorded in all of Scripture who was privileged to be ushered into heavenly glory without experience death (2 Kings 2:11). Jude's testimony of Enoch's "prophecy" recorded in *1 Enoch* needs to be dealt with in regard to the canon of Scripture.

McDonald points out, "The issue is not whether Jude cited 1 Enoch, of course, but how he cited it."[449] Although McDonald assumes "from the early church fathers, it appears that he cited it as Scripture,"[450] there are

Internet https://www.michaeljkruger.com/were-early-churches-ruled-by-elders-or-a-single-bishop/. Parenthesis in the original text.

[449] Ibid, McDonald. *The Biblical Canon*, p.107.

[450] Ibid.

compelling reasons from the text *itself* Jude did not consider the actual book of *1 Enoch* to be Inspired Scripture.

Jude records "Enoch, in the seventh generation from Adam, prophesied" (Jude v.14). Although this term "prophesied" is used in the New Testament to refer to prophecies recorded in the Old Testament Scriptures (e.g.: Matthew 15:8-9, cf. Isaiah 29:13), the term is also used to refer to *verbal "prophesy" by individuals* (Matthew 7:22). Matthew 2:23 states a prophecy of Jesus was "*spoken* through the prophets" (emphasis added). Although the gospel writer may have had passages like Psalm 22:6-8, Isaiah 49:7 and 53:3 in mind, there is no specific *written* Old Testament "prophecy" which records "He shall be called a Nazarene."

The apostle Paul also used this term in his first epistle to encourage the church of Corinth to *verbally* "prophesy" (1 Corinthians 14:1-5). Jude is simply saying Enoch, himself, "prophesied."

In William MacDonald's *Believer's Bible Commentary*, he quotes William Kelly's analysis that Jude did not actually take this "prophecy" from the actual book of *1 Enoch* itself:

"It [Enoch] has every mark of having been written subsequent to the destruction of Jerusalem [and therefore after Jude's Epistle was written], by a Jew who still buoyed himself up with the hope that God would stand by the Jews."[451]

MacDonald continues:

"While we do not know how Jude learned of this ancient prophecy, a simple and plausible explanation is that the Holy Spirit revealed the words to him just as He guided in all the rest of the Epistle."[452]

This view is in perfect harmony from the Biblical teaching "All Scripture is inspired by God" (2 Timothy 3:16) written by "men moved by the Holy Spirit spoke from God" (2 Peter 1:21). Even if Jude did take this prophecy from *1 Enoch*, as MacArthur points out:

"The source of this information was the Holy Spirit who inspired Jude. The fact that it was recorded in the nonbiblical and pseudoepigraphical Book of Enoch had no effect on its accuracy."[453]

---

[451] Ibid. MacDonald. *Believer's Bible Commentary, The Epistle of Jude, Commentary*, p.2343. Quoted from William Kelly, "Lectures on the Epistle of Jude," *The Serious Christian*, 1:123. Brackets in MacDonald's original text.

[452] Ibid, p.2344.

[453] Ibid. The MacArthur Study Bible, *The Epistle of Jude*, footnote on verse 14, p.1987.

"Since Jude was writing under the inspiration of the Holy Spirit (2 Tim. 3:16; 2 Peter 1:20,21), and included material that was accurate and true in its affirmatives, he did no differently than Paul (cf. Acts 17:28; 1 Cor. 15:33; Titus 1:12)."[454]

McDonald cites Beckwith who wrote, "Jude need not be doing the same as the Epistle of Barnabas, ... which calls 1 Enoch 'Scripture.'"[455] McDonald further asserts from Beckwith, "Jude merely 'borrows' from *1 Enoch*."[456] This would be consistent when Jude cites "Enoch's prophecy," he does not use one of the New Testament metonyms for the Old Testament listed in Chapter Nine and Appendix A, when he refers to "Enoch."

1 ENOCH 7 AND GENESIS 6

Even if one insists Jude referenced the "epistle" of *1 Enoch*, rather than the "man" Enoch, there are contradictions between *1 Enoch* and the Inspired Hebrew Bible. When *1 Enoch* referenced the pre-Flood inhabitants, it equated the offspring of the "sons of heaven" and the "daughters of men" with the "giants," or "Nephilim," from Genesis 6:4:

> "It happened after the sons of men had multiplied in those days, that daughters were born to them, elegant and beautiful. And when the angels, the sons of heaven, beheld them, they became enamoured of them, saying to each other, Come, let us select for ourselves wives from the progeny of men, and let us beget children.... Then they took wives, each choosing for himself; whom they began to approach, and with whom they cohabited; teaching them sorcery, incantations, and the dividing of roots and trees. *And the women conceiving brought forth giants.*" (1 Enoch 7:1-2,10-11, emphasis added)[457]

When we examine Genesis chapter six, Moses wrote the Nephilim ("giants" in the NKJV) *existed at the same time* on the earth <u>with</u> the offspring of "the sons of God" and "the daughters of men":

> "Now it came about, when men began to multiply on the face of the land, and daughters were born to them, that the sons of God saw that the daughters of men were beautiful; and they

---

[454] Ibid. *Interpretive Challenges*, p.1984.

[455] Ibid. McDonald. *The Biblical Canon*, p.231. Quoting Beckwith, R. T. *The Old Testament Canon of the New Testament Church and Its Background in Early Judaism*, p.402 Grand Rapids: Eerdmans, 1985.

[456] Ibid, p.231 (quoting Beckwith, *The Old Testament Canon*, p.403).

[457] *The Book of Enoch*, Translated from Ethiopic by Richard Laurence, London, 1883. Accessed from the Internet http://www.johnpratt.com/items/docs/enoch.html#Enoch_7

took wives for themselves, whomever they chose.... The Nephilim were on the earth in those days, and also afterward, *when the sons of God came in to the daughters of men*, and *they bore children to them. Those were the mighty men who were of old, men of renown.*" (Genesis 6:1-2,4, emphasis added)

In other words, the "mighty men who were of old, men of renown" were <u>not</u> the same as the "Nephilim" (aka: "giants"). These were *two different groups* of individuals who existed at the same time during the antediluvian era. The former were the offspring of "the sons of God" and "daughters of men," while the latter were not. While there is disagreement within Jewish and Christian circles to their identity, what is clear from *1 Enoch* is the "giants" and the "Nephilim" were believed to be different groups:

> "The Greek texts vary considerably from the Ethiopic text here. One Greek manuscript adds to this section, 'And they [the women] bore to them [the Watchers] three races–first, the great giants. The giants brought forth [some say "slew"] the Naphelim [sic], and the Naphelim brought forth [or "slew"] the Elioud. And they existed, increasing in power according to their greatness.' See the account in the Book of Jubilees." (1 Enoch 7:11, footnote #7, emphasis added)[458]

Not only does *1 Enoch* state "the women conceiving brought forth giants," but also these "giants" were *distinct* from the "Naphelim." Genesis 6:4, however, distinguishes between the "Nephilim [who] were on the earth in those days, *and also afterward*" and "the mighty men who were of old, men of renown" (emphasis added). It does not say "the mighty men who were of old, men of renown" *also* existed after the Flood, like the Nephilim did.

The Hebrew noun (*"nĕphiyl"*) to describe the Nephilim is derived from the Hebrew verb *"naphal,"* meaning "to fall, to cast down, or to overthrow."[459] It is used one other time in the Hebrew Bible after the Flood to describe the descendants of Anak in Canaan, when the Israeli spies reported back to Moses (Numbers 13:33). Although translations, like the NKJV, equate the "Nephilim" with the "giants," *1 Enoch* distinguishes between them. Likewise, Genesis 6:4 distinguishes between the "Nephilim" and "the mighty men who were of old, men of renown."

---

[458] Ibid. Brackets included in the original text.

[459] Blue Letter Bible. "Dictionary and Word Search for *naphal (Strong's 5307)*". Blue Letter Bible. 1996-2018. 21 Mar 2018. Accessed from the Internet < http://www.blbclassic.org/lang/lexicon/Lexicon.cfm?Strongs=H5307&t=NASB >

Jesus acknowledged the book of Genesis as Inspired Scripture (Matthew 19:4-5, cf. Genesis 1:27; 2:24). He even referenced the antediluvian events from Genesis 6:1-4 (Matthew 24:37-38), as did both of the Inspired epistles of the apostle Peter and Jude (2 Peter 2:4-5; Jude v.6). However, none of the New Testament writers, including Jude, acknowledged *1 Enoch* as an Inspired writing, which clearly contradicts the identities found in Genesis chapter six.

Whether Jude was referencing Enoch the *man* or the *epistle* allegedly attributed to him, Jude was not claiming this uninspired writing was Scripture. This confirms the *epistle of Barnabas* is not Inspired Scripture since it falsely referred to *1 Enoch* as "Scripture" (see above). Therefore, the Inspiration of Jude's own epistle, as well as its place in the New Testament canon, need not be put into question.

LUTHER AND THE NEW TESTAMENT EPISTLES

Although Luther questioned the Inspiration of some of the New Testament books, such as the epistle of James referring to it as "a letter of straw,"[460] over a millennia earlier Eusebius *also* classified it as a "disputed" book, along with "Jude, 2 Peter, and the so-named 2 and 3 John."[461] Likewise, "nor does he [Irenaeus] mention James, Jude, or 2 Peter,"[462] and Clement of Alexandria "makes no mention of James, 2 Peter, or 3 John."[463] Cardinals during the Reformation, such as Cardinal Cajetan "questioned the authority of certain NT [New Testament] books, especially Hebrews."[464] As discussed in Chapter Four, even the Council of Carthage of 397 originally omitted the book of Revelation.

Metaxas explains Luther's rationale for questioning some these New Testament writings, including James:

> "whereas he [Luther] considered the Word of God sacred, he nonetheless felt comfortable ranking things in accordance with how closely they hewed to this central message of the Gospel.... Common sense has always tacitly understood that not all things

---

[460] Catholic.com. *Epistle of Saint James, Letter attributed to saint commonly identified with the Lord's brother. Contents: 2 II. TRADITION AS TO CANONICITY.* Accessed from the Internet https://www.catholic.com/encyclopedia/epistle-of-saint-james#II._TRADITION_AS_TO_CANONICITY

[461] Ibid. Maier. *Eusebius: The Church History.* Book 3:25, p.101.

[462] Ibid. McDonald, Lee Martin. *The Biblical Canon,* p.301. Brackets inserted by me for clarity.

[463] Ibid, p.302.

[464] Ibid. Gallagher, Ed. *Our Beans: Biblical and Patristic Studies, especially dealing with the reception of the Hebrew Bible in Early Christianity,* "Cajetan on the OT Canon." Brackets inserted by me for clarity.

in the Bible are equal. For example, who would say that the famous verse from John 3:16... is equal to this verse from 2 Timothy 4:13, 'When you come, bring the cloak that I left with Carpus at Troas, and my scrolls, especially the parchments'? ... some verses are more important than others... This is all that Luther meant."[465]

Luther *did*, however, include <u>all</u> of these books, including James, in his German New Testament. He even placed them in a similar order towards the back of the New Testament, which you also find in Catholic New Testaments, including the New Catholic Version and New American Bible. Even though Luther has been criticized for placing some of the New Testament epistles in a "different order" than what was in the Latin Vulgate, the same could be said about Catholic Old Testaments with the Deuterocanon. For example, while the New Catholic Version places 1 and 2 Maccabees after Malachi[466], the New American Bible places them after Esther.[467]

Luther was going through the same objective discovery process numerous early church fathers did with the New Testament epistles. The only difference was Luther ended up keeping all of the twenty-seven New Testament writings in his German translation, unlike many of them.

Luther also included the Deuterocanonical books in his German translation. However, unlike the Hebrew Bible and the New Testament, Luther did not consider them to be Inspired Scripture. Although he did consider them to be worthy of reading (just as some of the early church fathers did), he placed them in a separate uninspired Addendum in-between the Old and New Testaments. Likewise, the 1611 King James Version of the Bible (KJV) originally included the Deuterocanon, and like Luther, the translators of the KJV rejected their Inspiration. To avoid confusion to its status, later Protestants removed them. Despite the Deuterocanon originally being in Luther's translation and the KJV, *neither* of their authors believed they were Inspired.

Although the Deuterocanon and other uninspired works are recorded in many lists of the early church fathers, including those of canonized saints, relying on their authority is not a dependable measure of what belongs in the Bible. This is another example of why relying on their authority for any Christian doctrine, including the canon of either the Old or the New Testaments, is problematic. They often disagree with each other on the

---

465 Ibid. Metaxas. *Martin Luther*, p.292-293. Brackets inserted by me for clarity.
466 Ibid. New Catholic Version, p.v.
467 Ibid. New American Bible, p. [7].

exact canon of Scripture, including Irenaeus a "Doctor of the Church,"[468] Clement of Alexandria, and others.

On the other hand, *all twenty-seven books* of the New Testament pass the godly criteria for Inspiration and canonicity. They *all* lack theological and historical errors and contradictions. They *all* were written in the apostolic era in the first century A.D. during an explosion of miraculous works to verify the authors' Inspired writings. Furthermore, they *all* eventually had a general consensus by the early church.

Even though the epistle to the Hebrews is anonymous, it possesses the same godly criteria as the books of the New Testament with named authors. Early Christian writers, like Origen, professed: "Traditions reaching us claim it was either Clement, Bishop of Rome, or Luke, who wrote the Gospel and the Acts,"[469] while Eusebius believed the author of Hebrews was the apostle Paul.[470] Regardless, it was either written by an apostle or a close associate of one.

THE INSPIRATION OF THE NEW TESTAMENT IN THE EARLY CHURCH

The Inspiration of the New Testament canon is evident in the testimony of the early church. Ryan Turner, from the *Christian Apologetics and Research Ministry* (CARM.org), indicates:

"These early Church Fathers wrote numerous books and letters in which they made over 38,000 quotations from the New Testament. From their writings alone we could reconstruct the entire New Testament minus about 11 verses."[471]

There is also strong evidence the original autographs of the New Testament were still in existence in the second century. Bible.org writes:

"Tertullian, writing in c. 180 CE, said, 'Come now, you who would indulge a better curiosity, if you would apply it to the business of your salvation, run over [to] *the apostolic churches, in which the very thrones of the apostles are still pre-eminent in their places, in which their own authentic writings are read,*

---

[468] ETWN.com. *St. Irenaeus of Lyons, DOCTOR OF THE CHURCH.* Accessed from the Internet https://www.ewtn.com/saintsholy/saints/l/stirenaeus.asp

[469] Ibid. Maier. *Eusebius: The Church History.* Book 6:25, p.207. Eusebius quoted from *Origen's Homilies on the Epistle to the Hebrews.*

[470] Ibid. Book 3:38, p.111.

[471] CARM.org. *Has the New Testament been corrupted? Go ahead, destroy the New Testament Manuscripts:* by Ryan Turner. Accessed from the Internet https://carm.org/new-testament-corrupted

uttering the voice and representing the face of each of them severally.'…. Tertullian goes on to discuss each of these 'authentic writings' *as being found in the very churches to which they were written.* He mentions Corinth, Philippi, Thessalonica, Ephesus, and Rome."[472] (emphasis added)

Another very early testimony for the Inspiration of the New Testament, particularly Paul's epistles, involves a letter written by Ignatius of Antioch around A.D. 110 to the bishop of Ephesus. This bishop was a man named Onesimus. In his book *Twelve Unlikely Heroes*, Pastor John MacArthur quotes the New Testament scholar F.F. Bruce, giving a defense "why" this might be the same "Onesimus" mentioned by the apostle Paul in Colossians 4:9 and Philemon v.10:

"…the part of Ignatius' letter to Ephesus where the language of Philemon is echoed is the part in which Bishop Onesimus is mentioned – the first six chapters. In these six chapters the bishop is mentioned fourteen times."[473]

MacArthur adds Bruce has "suggested that Onesimus was likely instrumental in collecting and preserving the letters of Paul. If so, he would have made sure to include this epistle [Philemon], which was written on his behalf by the honored apostle."[474] However, the epistles of Ignatius were most likely written *after* the completion of the New Testament – too late to qualify for their inclusion in it. They were written towards the end of his life, as late as the early second century.[475]

Litfin wrote concerning Irenaeus:

"Note that the term 'new covenant,' which translates the same Greek word as 'testament,' was already in use to speak about the new salvific arrangement ushered in by Jesus (Luke 22:20; 2 Cor. 3:6). But Irenaeus appears to be the first Christian to use the term *'New Testament' with reference to a collection of writings in sacred scripture.*"[476] (emphasis added)

---

[472] Bible.org. *Did the Original New Testament Manuscripts still exist in the Second Century?* Accessed from the Internet https://bible.org/article/did-original-new-testament-manuscripts-still-exist-second-century-0. Brackets in original text.

[473] MacArthur, John. *Twelve Unlikely Heroes: How God Commissioned Unexpected People in the Bible and What He Wants to do with You*, pp.208-209. Published by Thomas Nelson, Inc.: Nashville, Tennessee, 2012. [Section quoted by F.F. Bruce, *Paul: Apostle of the Heart Set Free* (Grand Rapids: Eerdmans, 2000), 402.]

[474] Ibid, p.209. Brackets inserted by me for clarity.

[475] EWTN.com. *St. Ignatius of Antioch, BISHOP, MARTYR.* Accessed from the Internet https://www.ewtn.com/saintsHoly/saints/I/stignatiusofantioch.asp

[476] Ibid. Litfin, *Getting to Know the Church Fathers*, p.276, footnote #23. See also pp. 90 and 109.

Even though Irenaeus did not espouse to the exact same New Testament canon Catholics, Protestants, and others do today (see Chapter Five), the concept of a "New Testament" canon – distinct from the Old Testament canon – was a very early belief as far back as the second century Christian Church, and even earlier (Jude v.3; Revelation 22:18-19).

These very early testimonies in the first and second century church strongly demonstrate the New Testament canon is just as Inspired as the Old Testament canon. They also demonstrate, along with the godly criteria found *only* in the New Testament canon, we can have confidence to trust in the sufficiency in the inerrant, Inspired New Testament Scriptures *alone*, which reveals to us the canon of the Old Testament Scriptures – the Hebrew Bible.

Before concluding this final chapter, I believe it is important to address where the authority of "the church of the living God, the pillar and support of the truth" (1 Timothy 3:15), fits in terms of the establishment of the Biblical canon.

THE CHURCH: THE PILLAR AND SUPPORT OF THE TRUTH

There is no question from the pages of the New Testament Jesus did not "build" a book. Rather, He "built" a church (Matthew 16:18). This church would be "the household of God, which is the church of the living God, the pillar and support of the *truth*" (1 Timothy 3:15, emphasis added).

Although Jesus "built" a church, Jesus sent "the Spirit of *truth*" (John 15:26, emphasis added) to "breathe" Scripture (2 Timothy 3:16) through "men moved by the Holy Spirit spoke from God" to write it down (2 Peter 1:20-21). For instance, Jesus and other heavenly beings commanded the apostle John to "*Write* in a book" to the seven churches of Asia (Minor) what He was about to reveal to him (Revelation 1:11; 2:1,8,12,18; 3:1,7,14; 14:13; 19:9; 21:5).

The Greek word translated "truth" (*"alētheia"*) to describe God's church in 1 Timothy 3:15 is the same word to describe the Holy Spirit in John 15:26. The apostle John used this same word in John 17:17 when Jesus was praying to the Father on behalf of His disciples: "Sanctify them in the truth; *Your word is truth*" (emphasis added).

This same Greek word reveals the "One *True* Church" is subordinate to the "truth" of God's Word "breathed" by the "true Spirit" of God, the Holy Spirit, Who "moved men" to write Scripture. When we continue reading past the passage of 1 Timothy 3:15 where Paul mentions the church being the "pillar and support of the truth," Paul goes on to explain the standards for this "church of truth":

> "But the Spirit explicitly says that in later times some will fall away from the faith, paying attention to deceitful spirits and doctrines of demons, by means of the hypocrisy of liars seared in their own conscience as with a branding iron, *men who forbid marriage* and *advocate abstaining from foods which God has created* to be gratefully shared in *by those who believe and know the truth*." (1 Timothy 4:1-3, emphasis added)

The apostle Paul uses the same Greek word for "truth" (*"alētheia"*) in verse three which he used in the previous chapter to describe "the church of the living God, the pillar and support of the *truth*" (1 Timothy 3:15). What Paul warns is those who are not of this "truth" will "forbid marriage" and "advocate abstaining from foods which God has created" (1 Timothy 4:3).

After God created the world, "The earth brought forth vegetation, plants yielding seed after their kind, and trees bearing fruit with seed in them, after their kind; and *God saw that it was good*" (Genesis 1:12, emphasis added). After God created Adam and Eve, He said "Behold, I have given you every plant yielding seed that is on the surface of all the earth, and every tree which has fruit yielding seed; *it shall be food for you*" (Genesis 1:29, emphasis added).

Everything God created for food, He told mankind that it was "*good food*" for them to eat. It would not be until after the Fall, once Adam and Eve disobeyed God and ate of the tree of the knowledge of good and evil (Genesis 2:16-17; 3:6), when God commanded mankind *not* to eat certain foods. Later in the Old Testament, God imposed certain dietary laws on *Israel*.

After Jesus atoned for the sins of the church (as well as the Old Testament saints), the *church* was not bound by those dietary laws imposed on *Israel*. When God spoke to the apostle Peter after the church was established, Luke wrote:

> "A voice came to him, 'Get up, Peter, kill and eat!' But Peter said, 'By no means, Lord, for I have never eaten anything unholy and unclean.' Again a voice came to him a second time, '*What God has cleansed, no longer consider unholy.*'" (Acts 10:13-15, emphasis added)

Later, at the Council of Jerusalem (~A.D. 50), when the topic of whether or not Gentiles should be circumcised, Peter spoke up to reiterate the Gentile Church under the *New* Covenant should not be bound by the same commands imposed by God on Israel under the *Old* Covenant: "why do you put God to the test by placing upon the neck of the disciples a yoke which neither our fathers nor we have been able to bear?" (Acts 15:10). According to the Code of Canon Law of the Catholic Church, Cann. 1250 and 1251 reads:

> "The penitential days and times in the universal Church are *every Friday of the whole year* and the season of Lent. *Abstinence from meat, or from some other food* as determined by the Episcopal Conference, is *to be observed on all Fridays*, unless a solemnity should fall on a Friday. *Abstinence and fasting are to be observed on Ash Wednesday and Good Friday.*"[477] (emphasis added)

Cann. 1252 specifies the age boundaries: "The law of abstinence binds those who have completed their fourteenth year. The law of fasting binds those who have attained their majority, until the beginning of their sixtieth year."[478]

The New Testament does not give any such command to the church about *mandatory* abstinence of food or fasting, including during specific times of the year or on certain days. Jesus' faithful Jewish disciples ate "meat," the Passover lamb, with Him on that first Good Friday, because God had commanded Israel to eat it on the Passover (Exodus 12:3-8). This was the same day Jesus was crucified (Matthew 26:17-19), because Jewish days were from "evening to morning" to the next evening (Exodus 27:21, cf. Genesis 1:5).

This command from the Code of Canon Law to abstain from eating meat on these days contradicts the command given by God to "Get up, kill and eat! What God has cleansed, no longer consider unholy" (Acts 10:15). The apostle Paul reinforced this freedom to eat, or not eat, regardless of what day or time of year it is:

> "One person regards one day above another, *another regards every day alike. Each person must be fully convinced in his own mind.* He who observes the day, observes it for the Lord, and *he who eats, does so for the Lord,* for he gives thanks to God; and he who eats not, for the Lord he does not eat, and gives thanks to God." (Romans 14:5-6, emphasis added)

---

[477] Vatican.va. *The Code of Canon Law, Book IV. Function of the Church (Cann. 834-848), Part III: Sacred Places and Times, Title II: Sacred Times (Cann. 1244-1258), Chapter II: Days of Penance. Can. 1250 to 1251.* Accessed from the Internet http://www.vatican.va/archive/ENG1104/_P4O.HTM

[478] Ibid. *Can. 1252*

"Therefore *no one is to act as your judge in regard to food or drink or in respect to a festival* or a new moon or a Sabbath day—things which are a mere shadow of what is to come; but the substance belongs to Christ." (Colossians 2:16-17, emphasis added)

It also conflicts with the warning given by the apostle Paul that the "true" church will <u>not</u> "advocate *abstaining from foods* which God has created" (emphasis added). Paul even rebukes the apostle Peter when he begins to side with the Judaizers regarding eating with the Gentiles:

> "But when Cephas [Peter] came to Antioch, I opposed him to his face, because he stood condemned. For prior to the coming of certain men from James, he used to eat with the Gentiles; but when they came, he began to withdraw and hold himself aloof, fearing the party of the circumcision. But when I saw that *they were not straightforward about the <u>truth</u> of <u>the gospel</u>*, I said to Cephas in the presence of all, 'If you, being a Jew, live like the Gentiles and not like the Jews, how is it that you compel the Gentiles to live like Jews?'" (Galatians 2:11-12,14, emphasis added)

The seriousness of Peter's rebuke by Paul was an issue pertaining to the "truth (*"alētheia"*) of the *gospel*" (v.14). In the previous chapter, Paul warned the churches in Galatia not to accept a "*different* gospel" (Galatians 1:6), including if it came from one of the apostles (including Paul, himself) or "an angel from heaven" (v.8) or "if *any* man is preaching to you a gospel contrary to what you received, he is to be accursed!" (v.9). Despite Peter being a writer of two Inspired epistles (1 Peter 1:1; 2 Peter 1:1), Paul rebuked him for listening to the Judaizers who were "not being straightforward about the <u>truth</u> of the <u>gospel</u>."

THE COUNCIL OF TRENT (1546) AND THE CANON

This same "accursed" warning from the apostle Paul was later used at the Ecumenical Council of Trent (1546). It forewarned *anyone* who rejected the "entirety" of the canon of Scripture defined at this council:

> "If anyone does not accept as sacred and canonical the aforesaid books in their entirety and with all their parts, as they have been accustomed to be read in the Catholic Church...let him be anathema [accursed]."[479]

---

479 Standebach, F. J. "The Old Testament Canon in the Roman Catholic Church." Pages 35-36 in *The Apocrypha in Ecumenical Perspective: The Place of Late Writings in the Old Testament among the Biblical Writings and Their Significance in the Eastern and Western Church Traditions.* Edited by S. Meurer. Translated by P. Ellingsworth. United Bible Societies

The Greek word for "accused" ("*anathema*") means "a person or thing doomed to destruction; devoted to the direst of woes; bind under a great curse; excommunicated; damned."[480] The footnote to Galatians 1:8 in the New Catholic Version defines "anathema" as "cursed, excluded from the kingdom of God."[481]

Refusal to believe in the gospel of Christ's shed blood on the cross for the sole Atonement of our sin for salvation (*solo Christo*) results in God's judgment of eternal condemnation (Mark 16:16; John 3:18). Paul's rebuke to Peter, who was listening to the Judaizers to not eat certain foods Gentiles ate, could lead to Peter teaching a false gospel, since the church is not under the dietary laws previously imposed on Israel.

This condemnation of being "accursed" was used at the Council of Trent to extend to the rejection of the canon of Scripture as well. In response to the Protestant Reformation, this modest assembly of approximately forty clergymen[482] (others insist fifty-three[483]) "excluded" anyone "from the kingdom of God," who rejected the so-called Deuterocanonical books.

Would this "excommunication" of being "doomed to destruction" include early church fathers and "Doctors" of the Church, such as Irenaeus, Athanasius, Cyril of Jerusalem, and even Jerome, who *also* did "not accept as sacred and canonical" some, or all, of these books? Would it extend to *everyone* at the fourth and fifth century church councils, like Augustine, since they did not include Baruch and the epistle of Jeremiah in their canons? Would popes like Damasus I, Siricius, Boniface I, Innocent I, and Gregory I be "bound under a great curse" since they too rejected the Deuterocanon, either "in their entirety" or they did not accept them "all in their parts"?

Would this apply to all those who convened at the Second Ecumenical Council of Nicaea of 787, whose canon differed from the later Ecumenical Councils of Florence and Trent, since Nicaea omitted the book of Baruch

---

Monograph Series 6. New York: United Bible Societies, 1991. Brackets inserted by me for clarity.

[480] Blue Letter Bible. "Dictionary and Word Search for anathema (Strong's 331)". Blue Letter Bible. 1996-2018. 28 Apr 2018. Accessed from the Internet < http://www.blbclassic.org/lang/lexicon/lexicon.cfm?Strongs=G331&apm;amp;t=NASB >

[481] Ibid. New Catholic Version, footnote to Galatians 1:8, p.243.

[482] The Gospel Coalition, U.S. Edition. Carter, Joe. "9 Things You Should Know About the Council of Trent." December 5, 2013. Accessed from the Internet https://www.thegospelcoalition.org/article/9-things-you-should-know-about-the-council-of-trent/

[483] *The Rambler: A Catholic Journal and Review of Home and Foreign Literature, Politics, Science, Music, and the Fine Arts – Volume Tenth*, p.49. London: Burns and Lambert, 1853. (Unknown author).

because it was not in the Vulgate yet? Jimmy Akin affirms this: "Catholic scholars have long recognized that when an ecumenical council applies this phrase to a doctrinal matter, then the matter is settled infallibly."[484]

Which ecumenical council was "settled infallibly" – the Second Ecumenical Council of Nicaea or the Ecumenical Council of Trent which "defined" the canon? The canon of the Old Testament is no doubt a "doctrinal matter." Due to the Council of Trent pronouncing "anathema" on anyone who would deny any of these writings, anathema would extend to *all* those at Nicaea. According to Trent, Nicaea rejected the canon "in their entirety and with all their parts," which extended to rejecting the gospel (Galatians 1:8-9). To further complicate the "defining" of the Deuterocanon at the Council of Trent, Gallagher reveals:

> "...the status of the deuterocanonical literature remained an open question.... Even then, there seems to have been substantial debate at the Council and the delegates apparently did not intend their pronouncement to settle the matter. It looks like what had been intended as a working position became established law."[485]

Although in his epistle to the Galatians, Paul's rebuke to Peter was Peter's plan to *perpetually* refuse to eat with the Gentiles, this is not the same kind of rebuke Paul gave in 1 Timothy 4:3 regarding "men who...advocate abstaining from foods." There is nothing in the context of this passage Paul is indicating his rebuke is *strictly* towards those who "advocate *perpetual* abstinence."

In context, Paul is simply saying men who command others to abstain from foods – even if it is a command of "temporary" abstinence – are not "those who believe and know the truth." The church is not Israel, which had been bound by dietary laws imposed on them through Moses, since "the Law was given through Moses" (John 1:17, cf. Deuteronomy 5:1-3), not the church which "*grace and truth* were realized through Jesus Christ" (emphasis added). *Any* kind of mandatory dietary abstinence (permanent or temporary) is a violation of this command by Paul, as well as from our Lord (Acts 10:13-15).

In addition to these unbiblical commands to abstain from eating meat on Fridays, and Ash Wednesday and Good Friday during Lent, according to Can. 1087 in the Canon Law on Vatican.va, the Catholic Church rebukes

---

[484] Catholic.com. Akin, Jimmy. "Anathema." Posted April 01, 2000. Accessed from the Internet https://www.catholic.com/magazine/print-edition/anathema

[485] Ibid. Gallagher, Ed. *Our Beans: Biblical and Patristic Studies, especially dealing with the reception of the Hebrew Bible in Early Christianity*, "The Old Testament Canon in the Early Sixteenth Century."

"Those in sacred orders [who] invalidly attempt marriage."[486] Catholic.com also affirms this unbiblical "blocking" of valid marriages:

"the Church has established impediments that block the validity of marriages attempted by those who have been ordained. Canon 1087 states: 'Persons who are in holy orders invalidly attempt marriage.'"[487]

The New Testament never gives a command to "forbid marriage" to *anyone* in the church, including the clergy. After God created Adam on the sixth day, He declared that "It is *not good* for the man to be alone; I will make him a helper suitable for him" (Genesis 2:18, emphasis added). After God created Eve on that same day, He created marriage (Genesis 2:22-24, cf. 1:27), and said "it was *very good*" along with the rest of His creation (Genesis 1:31, emphasis added).

Jesus Himself emphasized it was *GOD* Who ordained marriage: "Have you not read that He who created them from the beginning MADE THEM MALE AND FEMALE, and said, 'FOR THIS REASON A MAN SHALL LEAVE HIS FATHER AND MOTHER AND BE JOINED TO HIS WIFE, AND THE TWO SHALL BECOME ONE FLESH'? So they are no longer two, but one flesh. What therefore God has joined together, let no man separate" (Matthew 19:4-6, cf. Genesis 1:27; 2:24).

This command from the Canon Law to "forbid" marriage of male clergy in the Latin Rite also contradicts the warning of the apostle Paul "some will fall away from the faith...by means of the hypocrisy of liars...men who *forbid marriage*" (1 Timothy 4:1-3).

In a *USA Today* article, "Pope Francis said he is open to the possibility of permitting married men to become priests to address the serious shortage of Catholic priests in some countries."[488] The article also pointed out "The Vatican accepts married priests in certain circumstances, such as those in the Eastern Rite sects of the church, and married members of the Anglican or Episcopal churches who convert to Catholicism."[489]

---

[486] Vatican.va. *Code of Canon Law, Book IV. Title VII: Marriage (Cann. 1055-1165), Chapter III: SPECIFIC DIRIMENT IMPEDIMENTS, Cann. 1087*. Accessed from the Internet http://www.vatican.va/archive/ENG1104/__P3Y.HTM. Brackets inserted by me for clarity

[487] Catholic.com. "Why can't a priest ever marry?" Posted August 4, 2011. Accessed from the Internet https://www.catholic.com/qa/why-cant-a-priest-ever-marry

[488] USATODAY.com. *"Pope Francis open to allowing married priests in Catholic Church,"* by Doug Stanglin. Published 8:25 a.m. ET March 10, 2017 | Updated 1:35 p.m. ET March 10, 2017. Accessed from the Internet https://www.usatoday.com/story/news/2017/03/10/pope-open-allowing-married-priests/98998496/

[489] Ibid.

When it comes to single men who were born into Catholicism who are *already ordained*: "He ruled out the prospect of allowing single men who are already priests to marry but was open to the idea of allowing unmarried laymen or men already married to be ordained."[490] This means the only male clergy who are allowed to marry are those who converted to Catholicism who were *already married*, and (perhaps) married Catholic layman who desire to become priests, because they are "'tested men,' to be ordained in places with a scarcity of priests."[491] Yet, if a *single* Latin Rite Catholic priest desires to marry, he is "forbidden" to marry.

This is not supported by the New Testament either. Nowhere does it teach if a male clergy is single, then he is "forbidden" from marriage, regardless if he was single or married, before or after his conversion, or what Rite he belongs to. In Canon Law 1078, if the priest desires to leave the priesthood and desires to marry:

> "Only the supreme authority of the Church can add a nullifying clause to a prohibition. The local ordinary can dispense his own subjects residing anywhere and all actually present in his own territory from all impediments of ecclesiastical law except those whose dispensation is reserved to the Apostolic See. Impediments whose dispensation is reserved to the Apostolic See are: the impediment arising from sacred orders or from a public perpetual vow of chastity in a religious institute of pontifical right."[492]

The New Testament does not require nor command the only way a single male clergy can get married is to have the head of the church "nullify" his ordination. There are numerous examples of church leaders in Scripture and in the early church who were married. The apostle Peter was clearly married, since he had a mother-in-law (Matthew 8:14), as well as "the rest of the apostles and the brothers of the Lord" (1 Corinthians 9:5). None of them were commanded by Jesus or Paul to "nullify" their ordination in order to be married, nor were they "forbidden" from marriage if they were ordained.

In the Old Testament era, male priests were allowed to marry, right up to the New Testament era. For example, "there was a priest named Zacharias, of the division of Abijah; and he had a wife from the daughters of Aaron, and her name was Elizabeth" (Luke 1:5). He was both a priest *and* he was married.

---

[490] Ibid.

[491] Ibid.

[492] Ibid. Vatican.va. *The Code of Canon Law, Book IV, Title VII, Chapter II: DIRIMENT IMPEDIMENTS IN GENERAL, Can. 1077 §2 to Can. 1078 §1 and §2 1/*

Even in early Catholicism, priests and even popes were allowed to marry. In a letter from Jay Koch to Fr. Robert J. Levis on EWTN.com, Mr. Koch shared:

> "History reports that the first prohibition (in Canon xxxiii) against clerics marrying occurred between 295 and 302 via the Council of Elvira.... Even a cursory look at history shows that during the so-called 'Dark Ages', (circa 500 AD), the disciplines initiated in the 4th century were, in many instances abandoned, with some priests even keeping concubines.... In 1045, Pope Boniface IX resigned in order to marry, hence dispensing himself from celibacy.... Most scholars place the date of church law absolutely forbidding clergy to marry at the Second Lateran Council in 1139, becoming an official church discipline in 1563 at the Council of Trent."[493]

Mr. Koch also provided a link from NewAdvent.org which gives an "excellent synopsis of clerical celibacy in the Roman Catholic Church"[494] demonstrating "that celibacy was definitely NOT consistently a part of church law/discipline since the time of the apostles."[495] Fr. Levis admitted, "It is not a dogma that priests may not marry, but an accustomed way of life that evolved very early in the Church" and "it wasn't until the 7th century that we [Catholicism and Eastern Orthodoxy] have a parting in the ways."[496] This was centuries before "The Great Schism" occurred in the eleventh century (see Chapter Six). This demonstrates *any* clergy who married in the first several centuries of Catholicism remained in full communion with the papacy.

It was *GOD* Who commanded the purpose of marriage was to "Be fruitful and multiply, and fill the earth" (Genesis 1:28). Pastor John Piper quoted C. S. Lewis on the subject of God and His holy intent on the beauty of sex in marriage:

> "I know some muddle-headed Christians have talked as if Christianity thought that sex, or the body, or pleasure, were bad in themselves. But they were wrong....God Himself once took on a human body, and that some kind of body is going to be

---

[493] EWTN.com. *EWTN Catholic Q & A, History of Priestly Celibacy.* Question from Jay Koch on 06-21-2005. Accessed from the Internet http://www.ewtn.com/v/experts/showmessage_print.asp?number=441998&language=en Parenthesis included in original text.

[494] Ibid. This is the link Mr. Koch provides from NewAdvent.org: http://www.newadvent.org/cathen/03481a.htm

[495] Ibid, ETWN.com. *EWTN Catholic Q & A, History of Priestly Celibacy.*

[496] Ibid. Brackets inserted by me for clarity.

given to us even in Heaven and is going to be an essential part of our happiness, our beauty, and our energy."[497]

Thus, by the Catholic Church "forbidding" male priests in the Latin Rite from marrying, as well as commanding Catholics from "abstaining" from eating meat on Fridays, and Ash Wednesday and Good Friday during Lent, it cannot be the "the church of the living God, the pillar and support of the *truth*" (1 Timothy 3:15). Neither can it be the church Jesus "built" (Matthew 16:18). It does not have the authority to declare the "truth" of what the Biblical canon is, including the Old Testament. Since it is not the "true" church, and it does not have the "true" canon of Scripture, then it does not have the "true" gospel of salvation either (Galatians 2:14).

The New Testament canon *does*, however, have that authority since it *is* God-breathed Scripture, given by Inspiration by the "[Holy] Spirit of *truth*" (John 14:17; 15:26; 16:13; 1 John 4:6). What has been witnessed from this book – and more importantly from the Inspired New Testament – is the complete Christian Old Testament is the *Hebrew Bible*, which contains the exact same books found in the Protestant Old Testament...no less, but also no more.

---

[497] Piper, John. *The Pleasures of God: Meditations on God's Delight in Being God*, pp.64-65. Published by Multnomah Books: Colorado Springs, Colorado, 2012. Quote from C. S. Lewis taken from *Mere Christianity*, in *A Mind Awake: An Anthology of C. S. Lewis*, ed. Clyde Kilby (New York: Harcourt, Brace and World, 1968), 210-211.

CONCLUSION

"Abraham believed God, and it was credited to him as righteousness."
(Romans 4:3)

2004 was a particularly special year for me. Not only was it the twenty-year anniversary of when I was elected the Treasurer of the Knights of the Altar of my former parish, it was also the year I was saved. I accepted Jesus Christ not only as my Savior, but just as importantly, I submitted to Him as my *Lord*. This meant I was not a mere "servant" anymore, but rather His *slave*. His "God, [was] my God" (Ruth 1:16). His will was my will. His desires became my desires. This did not mean I no longer sinned...*hardly!* Scripture is clear we do: "for *all* have sinned and fall short of the glory of God" (Romans 3:23, emphasis added). The apostle Paul also warned us "the wages of sin is death" (Romans 6:23a), but the good news of salvation is "the free gift of God is eternal life in Christ Jesus our *Lord*" (Romans 6:23b, emphasis added).

The Greek word for "Repent" was mistranslated into Latin in the Vulgate as "do penance," which was then mistranslated later into English in the Douay-Rheims (see Chapters Three and Five). Several centuries later, it was correctly translated "Repent" in modern English translations such as the New Catholic Version and the New American Bible. This later correction mirrored Luther's earlier sixteenth century translation of "Repent" in his *95 Theses*, which sparked the Reformation. This demonstrates another example of the lack of consistency and validity of the *church's* sole authority (*sola ecclesia*) to translate doctrinal issues correctly, let alone their sole authority to define the Biblical canon.

WHY IS THIS IMPORTANT?

As I mentioned in Chapter Ten, this is important because this is a *gospel* issue, which means this is a *salvation* issue. The apostle Paul warned, having the wrong *gospel* means you do not have the *truth* (Galatians 2:14), and he equated preaching a "different gospel" to "another Jesus":

> "For if he who comes preaches *another Jesus whom we have not preached*, or if you receive a different spirit which you have not received, or a *different gospel* which you have not accepted—you may well put up with it!" (2 Corinthians 11:4 NKJV, emphasis added)

If a church does not have the "true" and complete canon of Scripture, they cannot be "the church of the living God, the pillar and support of the *truth*" Jesus built, because they are not teaching the *truth* of the *gospel*. They are either teaching a false doctrine of "doing penance" based on a bad translation of "repent," or they are teaching a false gospel based on their incomplete canon, because they have either "added to" or "taken away" Scripture. By doing this, they are teaching a false salvation plan which is not based on the complete canon of Scripture.

Another reason this is important: if Protestant Bibles are "missing" books, which belong in it, then they are omitting God-breathed Scripture which God originally intended to be included in it. However, if Catholic (and even "bigger") Bibles have "added" books believed to be Inspired, which are really man-made, then they are attributing these books to be God-breathed through the Holy Spirit when in reality they are not. Either way, believing in an incomplete Bible is an offense to the Holy Spirit. This is why <u>every</u> Christian *needs* to be assured of what books belong in the Bible...no less, but also no more. This book should be sufficient in providing that assurance.

When I spoke on the five-hundred-year anniversary of the Protestant Reformation, Pastor Daniel Bellavia described Martin Luther as an "Orthodox Innovator":

> "He's what I like to refer to as an 'Orthodox Innovator.' He goes backward to go forward. He looks to the Scripture in the past, but he projects it to the present. He's a translator, not just of German, but of the Scripture to modern and normal people."[498]

Yale professor of political science, Stephen Skowronek, defined an "Orthodox Innovator" by using past presidents as an example:

> "These presidents subscribe to the governing philosophy of a president who towers above all others historically, such as Abraham Lincoln, and then apply that philosophy from another time to new and different circumstances. So the orthodox innovator is the faithful son, charged finally to implement the agenda, to deliver the product, to secure the program to get the job done."[499]

---

[498] Bellavia, Daniel. First Baptist Church of Greater Toledo. Audio Files: Reformation Sunday – Part 2. Rev. Daniel W. Bellavia. October 29, 2017. Accessed from the Internet http://www.fbcogt.com/previous-sermons/index.html. For a video presentation of this sermon, go to the video on my YouTube channel: "Protestant Reformation 500 Year Anniversary - First Baptist Church (Pastor Dan)." Published Oct 31, 2017. Accessed from the Internet https://www.youtube.com/watch?v=FFrDSYK5aXA

[499] National Public Radio, Inc. (npr.org) *Professor: Bush Is an 'Orthodox Innovator.'* Published online November 28, 2005, 12:00 AM ET. Heard on Morning Edition. Host Renee Montagne talks with Yale professor of political science Stephen Skowronek about

In terms of the gospel and the canon of Scripture, Luther was indeed an "Orthodox Innovator" to the church in his time. Not only did Luther "apply" the gospel "from another time" (first century Israel) to "new and different circumstances" (sixteenth century Germany), he was also the "faithful son" who "secured" the true gospel of salvation by grace alone through faith alone. This was the same gospel Jesus and the first century church taught. Luther also "secured" the true Christian "Scripture in the past" and was a "translator of the Scripture to the modern and normal people" of Germany.

In 1505, Luther joined a very rigorous and theologically strict Order of the monastic life: the Observant Augustinian Order.[500] Like Augustine before him, Luther left his old secular life to become a monk. In fact, many of Luther's Reformed views were based on this strict Augustinian monasticism he belonged to. Contrary to popular belief, Luther's Reformation was not a "revolt" to introduce *new* and foreign doctrines into the church. Instead, it was a genuine desire and "innovation" to *return* to the "orthodoxy" of Christian theology based on the Scriptures, which Augustine had stressed over a millennium before Luther.

Luther did this by rediscovering the "true" Christian Old Testament by going "backward" to the Old Testament era, and then went "forward" to bring it to his own time. Today, we too can go "backward" not just to Luther, but further back to the New Testament, to rediscover for ourselves the complete Christian Old Testament – the Hebrew Bible – and bring it "forward" to the contemporary church. We too can be "Orthodox Innovators."

PURGATORY AND 2 MACCABEES

Does this mean if a person simply "uses" a Bible containing the Deuterocanon they are eternally damned? Not at all, because in addition to these uninspired writings, these Bibles have the exact same Inspired books found in the Hebrew Bible. Likewise, just because someone "uses" a Bible which omits the Deuterocanon, this does not automatically mean they are a genuine Christian either.

There are "Protestants" who espouse solely to the Hebrew Bible but are not true Christians, because they espouse to heretical theology. In like

---

President Bush's tendency to take his orthodoxy from predecessor Ronald Reagan. Copyright © 2005 NPR. All rights reserved. Accessed online
https://www.npr.org/templates/story/story.php?storyId=5028922

[500] Reeves, Ryan. "Martin Luther's Life as a Monk." (YouTube) Published on Jan 31, 2015. Accessed from the Internet https://www.youtube.com/watch?v=67QmuXeOB3U (Begins around 02:34 mark.)

manner, Jesus condemned the Pharisees for blaspheming the Holy Spirit for attributing Jesus' miraculous works to Satan (Matthew 12:24-32), despite the Pharisees "[having] Moses and the Prophets" (Luke 16:14,29). Nonetheless, by believing in some of the theological doctrines found in some of these uninspired books, it can lead a person to believe in a false gospel, such as the unbiblical doctrine of Purgatory.

Rather than our sins being atoned for (or reconciled to God) through Jesus' shed blood on the cross (2 Corinthians 5:18-19), the doctrine of Purgatory teaches our remaining sins are atoned for, or "purged," after death before we can advance to heavenly glory. NewAdvent.org defines this intermediate realm of atonement as:

> "Purgatory (Lat., "purgare", to make clean, to purify) in accordance with Catholic teaching is a place or condition of temporal punishment for those who, departing this life in God's grace, are, not entirely free from venial faults, or have not fully paid the satisfaction due to their transgressions."[501]

This means anyone who ends up in Purgatory will eventually attain Heaven once their remaining "temporal transgressions" have been "satisfactorily paid" in this transitional realm. This belief contradicts several examples from both the Old and New Testament where individuals went straight to Heaven into the presence of God without first being "purged."

As mentioned in Chapter Ten, both Enoch and Elijah went straight to Heaven into the presence of God in their earthly bodies without even experiencing death (Genesis 6:24, cf. Hebrews 11:5; 2 Kings 2:11). The apostle Paul was "caught up" to, and experienced, the "third heaven" (i.e.: Paradise) to hear "inexpressible words, which a man is not permitted to speak" (2 Corinthians 12:2-4). The apostle John was called to "Come up here" to Heaven to "show you what must take place after these things" (Revelation 4:1), where he was in the presence of God: "Immediately I was in the Spirit; and behold, a throne was standing in heaven, and One sitting on the throne" (v.2).

It was not because they were some sort of "super saints" who had amassed some sort of "treasury of merit." Their sins were "purged" *on the cross by Jesus* when He shouted out "It is finished!" (John 19:30). *Jesus* was the One Who "washed" (1 Corinthians 6:11; Titus 3:5) – or "purged" – us of our sins on the cross by shedding His own blood, because "*all things are cleansed with blood, and without shedding of blood there is no forgiveness*" (Hebrews 9:22, emphasis added).

---

[501] NewAdvent.org. *Purgatory, Catholic doctrine*. Accessed from the Internet http://www.newadvent.org/cathen/12575a.htm#V

The doctrine of Purgatory undermines the true gospel. It denies Jesus' "finished" Atonement which applied not just to our "sin" which separates us from God (John 1:29), but "*all* sin" (1 John 1:7 – emphasis added), "your iniquities" which "have made a separation between you and your God" (Isaiah 59:2). Purgatory is "a different gospel" (Galatians 1:6). As the apostle Peter commanded, genuine believers in Christ should always be "ready to make a defense to everyone who asks you to give an account for the hope that is in you, yet with gentleness and reverence" (1 Peter 3:15).

Some use verses in the Deuterocanonical book of 2 Maccabees 12:43-46 as evidence for the existence of Purgatory. There are a couple of problems with this. First, 2 Maccabees is not Inspired Scripture, neither from the authority of the New Testament nor from the testimony of early Jewish and Christian history. Second, even *if* 2 Maccabees could be used as an early historical Jewish source, the text is explicit the "sin" the slain Jewish men committed was them wearing "amulets sacred to idols of Jamnia, which the law forbids the Jews to wear" (2 Maccabees 12:40 NAB). After this, Judas Maccabeus and his army "prayed that the sinful *deed* might be fully blotted out" (v.42 NAB, emphasis added).

The "collection" they later gathered was for an "expiatory sacrifice" for the *act* the dead committed when they were alive (v.43 NAB). However, the initial "atonement" which was believed to take place to "purge" this sin, involved *prayer* (v.46 NCV). This text does not explicitly (nor implicitly) describe some sort of "intermediary spiritual realm" between earth and Heaven where a person's sins are "purged" after they die. It is simply talking about praying for the atonement of a person's sinful *acts* when they were alive, followed by taking up this collection, so the person's sin would not be counted against the nation of Israel. For all we know, the writer of 2 Maccabees believed the dead were *already in Heaven*, like Enoch and Elijah are. Nothing in the text even implies he believed this intermediary realm even exists.

Furthermore, this passage from 2 Maccabees does not actually teach the doctrine of Purgatory in the way the Catholic Church and others understand it. As Luke Wayne from CARM.org correctly points out:

> "Purgatory is only for those who have died in God's grace. If someone dies while guilty of a mortal sin for which they have made no absolution, they die outside of God's grace and under His wrath. They will not receive purification in purgatory. They will be justly punished in hell. Roman Catholic teaching regards willful idolatry committed in full knowledge of God's moral law to be a mortal sin. The passage is clear that these were not ignorant pagans. *They were Jews who knew that what they were doing was forbidden by God's law.* These men *died in*

unrepentant, willful idolatry and active devotion to false gods.
Therefore, on Roman Catholic teaching, they died outside of
God's grace."[502] (emphasis added)

Mr. Wayne goes on to cite from the verse where they were under
God's wrath and, therefore, were destined for Hell, not Purgatory: "The
noble Judas warned the soldiers to keep themselves free from sin, for *they
had seen with their own eyes what had happened because of the sin of
those who had fallen*" (2 Maccabees 12:42b NAB, emphasis added). So,
even 2 Maccabees cannot be used as evidence – Scriptural or Apocryphal –
for the existence of Purgatory.

Even *if* it could, this doctrine completely contradicts Scripture which
states it is through *the shedding of blood that atones for sin*, not prayer nor
financial sacrifices. This was the issue Luther had with the abuses of
indulgences the church in his time allowed, which included the "collection"
of money to "atone" for the sins of the faithful, rather than teaching *the
atonement of the cross*. Jesus, *Himself*, "made purification of ["purged"]
sins" (Hebrews 1:3).

As Martin Luther observed in his eighty-second "dispensation" of his
95 Theses: "Why does not the pope empty purgatory for the sake of holy
love and the dire need of the souls that are there if he redeems an infinite
number of souls for the sake of miserable money with which to build a
church?"[503]

Some may say "paying" for some kind of repentance, either in the
form of prayer or deeds is still required to decrease time in Purgatory and
advance to Heaven, not simply paying money to decrease time in
purgatory. Yet, that *is* what was happening in sixteenth century Catholicism
in Germany. The more money you or a loved-one paid, the less time you
spent in Purgatory. Luther's point was if the pope had the power to lessen
their time in Purgatory by accepting monetary indulgences (or by other
means), why not simply reduce their time without them?

If 2 Maccabees truly teaches the collection of monetary purging of sins,
then "why" was it swiftly abolished after Luther "protested" this abuse after
posting his *95 Theses*? Why are indulgences practiced today in the form of
prayers, reading Scripture, sacraments, pilgrimages, or by "follow[ing] these
same rites and devotional practices via television and radio or, always with
the proper devotion, through the new means of social communication"?[504]

---

[502] CARM.org. Wayne, Luke. *Purgatory and 2 Maccabees 12:39-45*. Accessed from the
Internet https://carm.org/purgatory-and-2-maccabees-12-39-45

[503] Ibid. Luther.de. *The 95 Theses*.

[504] Vatican.va. *Decree of the Apostolic Penitentiary according to which Special
Indulgences are granted to the faithful on occasion of the 28th World Youth Day [Rio de*

When was the last time, money was "collected" and taught it was for the purpose of "purging" the sins of souls to decrease their time in Purgatory?

As Pastor John Piper plainly and Scripturally wrote, "We are not capable of changing God. We cannot pay our own debt. 'Truly no man can ransom another, or give to God the price of his life' (Ps. 49:7) [ESV]."[505] This is another example of why the Deuterocanonical books, including 2 Maccabees, are not Inspired Scripture and do not belong in the Old Testament canon.

Just as Jimmy Akin from Catholic Answers affirmed *sola scriptura* by commenting on an apocryphal story, "It's not in the Bible so it's not reliable,"[506] as did his colleague Trent Horn during a debate with James White, "Our theology should come from the Bible, not the Bible from our theology,"[507] neither is the existence of Purgatory.

Lastly, according to the Catholic Church, a person can lose their salvation, despite Scripture teaching a genuine believer's salvation is eternally secure (John 3:16; 6:37-39; 10:27-29; Romans 8:1,38-39; 1 John 5:13, etc.) What if a deceased person, who you are praying for to "purge" their sins out of purgatory, is actually destined for Hell? There is simply no way of the one praying, let alone the Catholic Church, to know for certain *specifically* who is destined for Heaven versus who is destined for Hell after a person has died. This is yet another problem with the doctrine of Purgatory, why 2 Maccabees is not Inspired Scripture, and why we must rely on Scripture alone (*sola scriptura*) for our Inspired source of the assurance of our salvation, rather than "TEACHING AS DOCTRINES THE PRECEPTS OF MEN" (Matthew 15:9).

Janeiro, 22-29 July 2013]. Accessed from the Internet http://www.vatican.va/roman_curia/tribunals/apost_penit/documents/rc_trib_appen_doc_2 0130709_decreto-indulgenze-gmg_en.html

[505] Piper, John. *God is the Gospel: Meditations on God's Love as the Gift of Himself,* p. 43. Wheaton, IL: Crossway. Copyright 2005 by Desiring God Foundation. Quote from Psalm 49:7 is from the English Standard Version.

[506] Akin, Jimmy Akin. *Jimmy Akin & Karlo Broussard: Catholic Answers Live – 11/16/18.* "Catholic Answers." *How did the Old Testament canon develop?* Streamed live on YouTube, Nov 16, 2018. Accessed from the Internet https://www.youtube.com/watch?v=uPszmNaqwXM (Begins around the 21:34 mark.)

[507] Horn Trent. *Trent Horn vs. Dr. James R. White - Can a Christian Lose Their Salvation? (Full Debate)* "Catholic Answers." Published on YouTube, Jan 31, 2017. Accessed from the Internet https://www.youtube.com/watch?v=72TRODe8BdA (Begins around the 2:13:11 mark.)

IS AN INDULGENCE A "GET OUT OF HELL FREE" CARD?

Although the Catholic Church does not teach a person "gets out of Hell" by acquiring an indulgence ("the extra-sacramental remission of the temporal punishment due, in God's justice, to sin that has been forgiven"[508]), in effect, that is what happens. All those who end up in Purgatory *eventually* ends up in Heaven. NewAdvent.org affirms people cannot end up in Hell once they are "secured" in Purgatory, which occurs when the penitent is issued an indulgence:

> "When the Church, therefore, *by an indulgence, remits this penalty,* her action, according to the declaration of Christ, *is ratified in heaven.*"[509] (emphasis added)

> "If a man departs this life with lighter faults, he is condemned to fire which burns away the lighter materials, and *prepares the soul for the kingdom of God*, where nothing defiled may enter."[510] (emphasis added)

NewAdvent.org stresses an indulgence "is not a permission to commit sin, nor a pardon of future sin…it supposes that the sin has already been forgiven."[511] Yet, once an indulgence is issued there is nothing one can do to "lose their spot" reserved in Purgatory. This contradicts the Catholic belief that a person can "lose" their salvation. Theoretically, a person could even commit the "unforgiveable sin" – the blasphemy of the Holy Spirit (Mark 3:29) – and still end up in Purgatory, and ultimately Heaven, because they possess an indulgence. This occurs even quicker when a plenary indulgence is granted.

Unlike a partial indulgence which "commutes only a certain portion of the penalty,"[512] a plenary indulgence remits "the *entire temporal punishment* due to sin so that *no further expiation is required in Purgatory*"[513] (emphasis added). Once possessors of plenary indulgences die, they "bypass" Purgatory and are transported immediately to Heaven.

The Pope can give "authority to archbishops, cardinals and their dioceses, and bishops to grant partial indulgences,"[514] as well as "priests,

---

[508] NewAdvent.org. *Indulgences, What an indulgence is.* Accessed from the Internet http://www.newadvent.org/cathen/07783a.htm

[509] Ibid. *Indulgences, The Power to grant indulgences.*

[510] Ibid. NewAdvent.org. *Purgatory, Proofs, Tradition.*

[511] Ibid. NewAdvent.org. *Indulgences, What an indulgence is not.*

[512] Ibid. *Indulgences, Various kinds of indulgences.*

[513] Ibid.

[514] Ibid. *Indulgences, Who can grant indulgences.*

vicars general, abbots, and generals of religious orders" provided they are "specially authorized to do so" and even to a "cleric who is not a priest."[515]

An indulgence can also be granted to the individual without appealing to any of these intermediaries to the Pope. According to the New Catholic Version, the individual penitent can acquire "An indulgence of five years" by reciting "a prayer before the reading of any part of Holy Scripture,"[516] and even "A plenary indulgence under the usual conditions is granted if the prayer has been recited daily for a month."[517] The New American Bible grants a partial indulgence for reciting the "Prayer to the Holy Spirit,"[518] and a separate "partial indulgence is granted to the faithful who use Sacred Scripture for spiritual reading with veneration due the word of God."[519] "A plenary indulgence is granted if the reading continues for at least one half hour."[520] It is fairly easy for the individual Catholic to acquire partial, and even plenary, indulgences to secure one's position in Purgatory and eternity in Heaven without fear of "losing" one's salvation.

The Pope "alone can grant plenary indulgences,"[521] which "confession and Communion are usually required."[522] Although NewAdvent.org professes, "These indulgences are not applicable to the souls departed,"[523] elsewhere it states, "indulgences may be applied to the souls *in purgatory*"[524] (emphasis added). Pope Paul VI further stressed in the *Indulgentiarum Doctrina* of the Apostolic Constitution of Indulgences, "Partial *as well as plenary indulgences can always be applied to the dead* by way of suffrage"[525] (emphasis added).

Pope Paul VI continued: "*To acquire a plenary indulgence* it is necessary to *perform the work* to which the indulgence is attached and to fulfill three conditions: sacramental confession, Eucharistic Communion and

---

515 Ibid.

516 Ibid. New Catholic Version, p. ii. *A Prayer Before The Reading Of Any Part of Holy Scripture.* Imprimatur, Francis Cardinal Spellman, Archbishop of New York, August 28, 1961.

517 Ibid.

518 Ibid. New American Bible, p.[4]. Partial Indulgence. *Enchiridion Indulgenitarum,* 1968, no. 62.

519 Ibid. *Enchiridion Indulgenitarum,* 1968 edition, no. 50.

520 Ibid.

521 Ibid. NewAdvert.org. *Indulgences, Who can grant indulgences.*

522 Ibid. *Indulgences, Dispositions necessary to gain an indulgence.*

523 Ibid. *Indulgences, Who can grant indulgences.*

524 Ibid. NewAdvent.org. *Purgatory, Indulgences.*

525 NewAdvent.org. His Holiness Pope Paul VI. *Indulgentiarum Doctrina,* Apostolic Constitution on Indulgences. Chapter V, Norms, Norm 3. Promulgated on January 1, 1967. Accessed from the Internet http://www.newadvent.org/library/docs_pa06id.htm

prayer for the intentions of the Supreme Pontiff. It is further required that all attachment to sin, even to venial sin, be absent"[526] (emphasis added).

Provided all of "these three conditions are fulfilled" and "detachment from even venial sin" is met, the penitent can bypass Purgatory upon death, and/or they can apply the "work performed" on behalf of a deceased loved one in Purgatory, who can then be ushered instantly into Heaven. Even if they are not actually *in* Purgatory, the promise granted from the plenary indulgence "supposes that the sin has already been forgiven."

It was Pope Sixtus IV in 1476 who extended the offer of indulgences to apply to a person's loved ones who "were languishing in purgatory" in order "to alleviate the sufferings of their relatives in purgatory" – the "suffering dead" – because "these poor souls were suffering the torments of purgatory."[527] This included the issuance of both partial and plenary indulgences. Metaxas revealed in Luther's day:

> "...in Rome lay the fabled Crypt of Callixtus, which was said to hold the bones of forty popes and seventy-six thousand martyrs! If one journeyed through a certain one of these catacombs five times while Mass is celebrated, one earned an indulgence allowing a single soul to be freed from purgatory."[528]

"It was stipulated in Luther's time that the pilgrim ascending these stairs [the Scala Sancta (Holy Stairs)] must upon each step recite the *Pater Noster* (Our Father). Doing this would count toward decreasing the suffering of any deceased relatives in purgatory."[529]

Luther also learned at St. John Lateran "it had been stipulated that a priest saying Mass there could obtain his own mother's salvation."[530] As Metaxas correctly observed, "Still, who knew how this had all been calculated?"[531] How could any ecclesiastical institution know *exactly* how many temporal years could be "shaved off" in the non-temporal realm of the afterlife? Although time in this world is transitory, the hereafter is eternal (Matthew 25:46; 2 Corinthians 4:18).

Another problem dispensing a temporal penance to expunge time spent in the hereafter: what if the indulgence granted is *greater* than the actual time one is to "spend" in Purgatory? Would this function as a type

---

[526] Ibid. Norm 7.

[527] Ibid. Metaxas, Eric. *Martin Luther*, p.46.

[528] Ibid, p.60.

[529] Ibid, p.61. Parentheses and italics in the original text. Brackets inserted by me for clarity.

[530] Ibid.

[531] Ibid, p.60.

of plenary indulgence where the penitent bypasses Purgatory and proceeds directly to Heaven? Does the penitent's "indulgence credit" get "redeposited" in the so-called "treasury of merit"? Does he or she get canonized as a saint, whose "treasure" can be used again by someone else? How would anyone on earth know? Would this not be "double-dipping"? Metaxas referenced Roland Bainton (*"Here I Stand"*):

> "By 1520, there were 19,013 relics in Frederick's [the Wise, elector of Saxony's] collection, and it had been carefully calculated that those who visited these relics on the day appointed – and made whatever contributions were required – were able to shorten their own time in purgatory, or the time of a loved one, by nearly two million years. *The exact number tabulated was 1,902,202 years and 270 days.*"[532] (emphases added)

How does anyone come up with such an astronomical number? As Metaxas questioned, "who knew how this had all been calculated?" How does one amass nearly TWO MILLION YEARS worth of sins committed in such a short lifetime? Even Methuselah – the longest living person in the Bible – only lived "nine hundred and sixty-nine years" (Genesis 5:27)! What if the actual time in Purgatory was even half this? What happens with the extra million?

The unbiblical belief in the existence of Purgatory and the issuance of man-made indulgences grants the penitent a future license to sin, since they are guaranteed a reservation in Purgatory and ultimately Heaven. It is even quicker with the acquisition of a plenary indulgence. This authorization of iniquity is condemned by the apostle Paul, "What shall we say then? Are we to continue in sin so that grace may increase? May it never be! How shall we who died to sin still live in it?" (Romans 6:1-2). This is what can result from believing and practicing this unscriptural doctrine, which undermines the true gospel of salvation by "Christ <u>alone</u>" (*solo Christos*), and why Purgatory and indulgences are not found in the Protestant Bible.

Scripturally, when genuine believers in Christ die, they are *immediately* ushered into the presence of God where they are "absent from the body and to be at home with the Lord" (2 Corinthians 5:8). The apostle Paul recollected from his own personal experience when he was stoned in Lystra and left for dead (2 Corinthians 11:25, cf. Acts 14:19-20). He had undertaken his heavenly journey without any mention of having to wait for his own sins to be "purged" before arriving in heavenly glory:

---

[532] Ibid. p.76. Metaxas references Bainton, Roland. *Here I Stand*, 57. Nashville: Abingdon Press, 2013. Brackets inserted by me for clarity.

"I know a man in Christ who fourteen years ago—whether in the body I do not know, or out of the body I do not know, God knows—such a man was *caught up to the third heaven*. And I know how such a man—whether in the body or apart from the body I do not know, God knows—was *caught up into Paradise* and heard inexpressible words, which a man is not permitted to speak." (2 Corinthians 12:2-4).

ABRAHAM WAS CREDITED RIGHTEOUSNESS

One question often asked is: "If we are supposed to rely on the New Testament canon to reveal to us the boundaries of the Old Testament canon, as well as the gospel of salvation, how were Old Testament saints like Abraham able to know the way of salvation, since they did not have most (or any) of the Old Testament written down?" The apostle Paul answers this question, when he quoted Moses' account of Abraham in the book of Genesis:

"For what does the Scripture say? 'ABRAHAM BELIEVED GOD, AND IT WAS CREDITED TO HIM AS RIGHTEOUSNESS.'" (Romans 4:3, cf. Genesis 15:6)

In Genesis chapter twenty-two, God commanded Abraham to go to the land of Moriah and sacrifice his son Isaac as a burnt offering to test his faith (Genesis 22:2). After Abraham believed God, he demonstrated his faith in Him by binding Isaac to the wood to sacrifice him (v.9-10). What Abraham "believed" was God's promise to him that he would have a son "who will come forth from your own body, he shall be your heir" (Genesis 15:4). God promised Abraham if he could "count the stars.... So shall your descendants be" (v.5). God made it clear to Abraham His promise would not be through, Ishmael, the son of Sarah's maid, but through Isaac, whom Abraham had with his wife Sarah (Genesis 17:15-19,21; 21:12).

Abraham "believed God" would fulfill His promise through Isaac, his "only [legitimate] son" (Genesis 22:2; Hebrews 11:17) with Sarah even if Isaac died at Abraham's own hand (Hebrews 11:19). God was able to "see" Abraham's faith – not so much of what he was about to do – but because Abraham "*believed* God" (Romans 4:3, emphasis added, cf. Hebrews 11:8-12).

The apostle Paul explained Abraham was "credited" righteousness "just as [King] David also speaks of the blessing on the man to whom God credits righteousness *apart from works*" (Romans 4:6, emphasis added). Paul then asked "How then was it credited? While he [Abraham] was circumcised, or uncircumcised? Not while circumcised, but while uncircumcised" (v.10). Abraham was not circumcised until *after* God made this promise to him (Genesis 17:24).

Although not a single word of the Old Testament had been written yet in the days of Abraham, he "believed God" through "faith alone" (*sola fide*) "apart from works" (Romans 4:6): "Then he believed in the LORD; and He reckoned [credited] it to him as righteousness" (Genesis 15:5, cf. Galatians 3:6). God had *spoken* to Abraham the same faith he believed, which was later *written down* in Scripture so we may have, and hear, this same faith "taught, whether by word of mouth *or* by letter" (2 Thessalonian 2:15, emphasis added).

When Jesus spoke about the rich man and Lazarus who both died and went to Hades, Lazarus "was carried away by the angels to Abraham's bosom" (Luke 16:22) where he was "being comforted" (v.25). When sinners *truly* believe and *genuinely* repent, they too will be "with" Abraham in Heaven along with Lazarus when they die. They are also saved by "faith alone," which is "apart from works" (Romans 4:6).

JUSTIFIED BY WORKS AND *NOT* BY FAITH ALONE?

What about later when James wrote "a man is justified by works and *not* by faith alone" (James 2:23, emphasis added)? What James is referring to is if a person has genuine faith, it will be *demonstrated to other people*: "You have faith and I have works; *show me* your faith without your works, and I will *show you* my faith BY my works" (v.18, emphasis added).

Here, James is explaining it is not *God* who is the one he is "showing" his faith *to*. It is to the hypothetical person he is addressing in his epistle ("I will show *you* my faith *by* my works"). The evangelist Mark demonstrated Jesus' Deity by writing, "And Jesus *seeing their faith*" (Mark 2:5, emphasis added). This is something only God can do, which is why He was able to say "Son, your sins are forgiven" (v.5, cf. Psalm 103:3). Matthew wrote after hearing the Pharisees, Jesus was "knowing their *thoughts*" (Matthew 12:25), which only God can "see the *mind* and the heart" (Jeremiah 20:12).

Mankind cannot "see" faith in the way God can, which is invisible. The only way I can "*show you* my faith" is "*by* my works" (James 2:18). In terms of human beings, "actions speak louder than words." If I do not prove the genuineness of my faith by "showing" it to you "by" my works, then it is a phony or "dead" faith (v.17,26). Unlike the Omniscient God, this is the only way people can demonstrate their faith is genuine, or "alive," to another person and not "dead." A genuine believer will demonstrate their faith to other people *by* their works. However, works is the *result* of salvation, not the *means* of it. This was what Luther and the Reformers meant by "faith alone" (*sola fide*).

When James was addressing the story of Abraham and used the same phrase Paul used: "AND ABRAHAM BELIEVED GOD, AND IT WAS RECKONED TO HIM AS RIGHTEOUSNESS" (v.23), James was explaining Abraham demonstrated his genuine faith *to the men* who accompanied him and Isaac to Moriah when he "offered up Isaac his son on the altar" (v.21):

> "So Abraham rose early in the morning and saddled his donkey, and *took two of his young men with him* and Isaac his son.... Abraham said *to his young men*, 'Stay here with the donkey, and I and the lad will go over there; and we will worship and *return to you.*'" (Genesis 22:3,5, emphasis added)

After believing in God and then "showing" his faith to the two men "by" his works, Abraham returned with Isaac to the young men who were eyewitnesses of his faith (v.19). While Paul was explaining Abraham's *trust* in *God* by "faith alone," James was describing Abraham's *demonstration* of his faith to the *men* "by" his works.

We can be confident in this same faith Abraham had, without God audibly talking to us, because we have His *written* Word at our disposal, which we can trust for our salvation Timothy trusted in: "and that from childhood you have known *the sacred writings* which are able to give you the wisdom *that leads to salvation through faith* which is in Christ Jesus" (2 Timothy 3:15, emphasis added). As the apostle Peter wrote, "So we have the prophetic *word* made more sure" (2 Peter 1:19, emphasis added).

The apostle John also encouraged us to have this same confidence in Jesus' Atonement of our sins for our salvation, based on what he had *written*: "These things I have *written* to you who believe in the name of the Son of God, *so that you may know* that you have eternal life" (1 John 5:13, cf. John 20:31, emphasis added).

Unfortunately, not all Christians believe in this same "faith alone" in the Scriptures which Moses, Paul, Peter, James, John, the Protestant Reformers, and genuine believers have possessed throughout the millennia. As a result, in this lack of unity and sole authority in the Scriptures (*sola scriptura*), doubt in the exclusivity and sufficiency of the Christian faith has led many to doubt, and even abandon, it. In my book, *"Not Really 'Of' Us: Why Do Children of Christian Parents Abandon the Faith?"* I discovered this is one of the "Top Ten" reasons why children born into Christian families give for walking away from the faith:

> "...diversity among people who may share a common core belief (or disbelief) isn't evidence that something is not true. The fact that there are a wide variety of views about Christianity, as well as different and often conflicting interpretations of the Bible, only demonstrates that even Christians can be no different than

222

the secular world or other religions for accounting for 'why' things are, like why the universe exists.[533]

...it's because I believe in the <u>Truth</u>, which much of what we see in the world is supported *by* the claims of the Bible, while many of the beliefs of other Christians are not...which is either largely based on 'their' opinion or that of their particular church, rather than on 'accurately handling the word of truth' (2 Timothy 2:15), by allowing *Scripture* to explain *Scripture*, including using it 'for reproof, for correction' (2 Timothy 3:16)."[534]

Before Christendom can possess this "unity," it must first universally embrace the same canon of Scripture – both *New*, as well as *Old*, Testaments. It must also trust in both the sufficiency of Scripture, as well as Christ's Atonement, for the assurance and sufficiency of our salvation. This was evident in the "update" to the Nicene Creed at the Second Ecumenical Council of Constantinople in A.D. 381, when it highlighted the magnitude and dependence of the Scriptures which define the Christian faith:

"he was crucified for us under Pontius Pilate, and suffered, and was buried, and the third day he rose again, *according to the Scriptures*"[535] (emphasis added)

Centuries earlier, the apostle Paul stressed this same importance and reliance on the Scriptures in his first epistle to the church of Corinth, when he wrote: "For I delivered to you as of first importance what I also received, that Christ died for our sins *according to the Scriptures*, and that He was buried, and that He was raised on the third day *according to the Scriptures*" (1 Corinthians 15:3-4, emphasis added).

In the church's infancy, the importance and sufficiency of our salvation through Christ "according to the Scriptures" was emphasized by the writers of the New Testament, like Paul. It was also stressed in the early church in those first few centuries, including the fourth century Ecumenical Councils of Nicaea and Constantinople, which reflected this same sufficiency.

As a church, we need to get back to trusting in that same sufficiency of Scripture, rather than simply relying on a particular church body, which may or may not rely on this sufficiency. However, it must first begin with trusting in the same canon of Scripture – including the Old Testament canon Jesus, His disciples, and the early church embraced – the Hebrew Bible, which is supported by the canon of the New Testament.

---

[533] Ibid. Christie, Steve. *Not Really 'Of' Us*, pp.169.

[534] Ibid, p.170. Italics in the original text.

[535] Ccel.org. *The Nicene Creed*. Accessed from the Internet http://www.ccel.org/ccel/schaff/creeds1.iv.iii.html

THE BOOK OF ISAIAH: "THE LITTLE BIBLE"

Many have referred to the book of Isaiah as "the little Bible." The major themes of the book can be divided into two parts: the Law and Grace (or Redemption), just how the Old and New Testaments are divided. *The MacArthur Study Bible* states "Isaiah spoke much about the grace of God toward Israel, particularly in his last 27 chapters."[536]

Even Vatican.va refers to Isaiah chapters forty through sixty-six as "the *second part of the book of Isaiah* that is known as 'the book of consolation' (Isaiah 40-66)"[537] (emphasis added). NewAdvent.org mirrors this statement: "The canonical Book of Isaias is made up of two distinct collections of discourses... (chapters 40-66) styled by many modern critics the 'Deutero- (or Second) Isaias,'"[538] even though the prophet Isaiah was the author of the entire book.

Another striking correlation is the number of chapters of the book of Isaiah to the number of books in the Protestant Bible. In his book *"The Gospel According to God,"* MacArthur illustrates:

> "Isaiah is divided into two sections, the first containing thirty-nine chapters and the second twenty-seven chapters. The Bible also is divided into two sections: the thirty-nine books of the Old Testament and the twenty-seven books of the New."[539]

MacArthur goes on to explain the "second major division of Isaiah begins and ends exactly where the New Testament begins and ends,"[540] beginning with the ministry of John the Baptist and concluding with the new heavens and the new earth. The Life Application Study Bible (NASB) further correlates this "two-fold" division of Isaiah based on the number of chapters between the first and second halves of Isaiah. This mirrors the number of books in the Protestant Bible:

> "The 39 chapters in the first half of Isaiah generally carry the message of judgment for sin.... The 27 chapters in the second half

---

[536] Ibid. The MacArthur Study Bible, The Book of Isaiah, *Historical and Theological Themes*, p.953.

[537] Vatican.va. MISSA PRO ELIGENDO ROMANO PONTIFICE, HOMILY OF HIS EMINENCE CARD. ANGELO SODANO, DEAN OF THE COLLEGE OF CARDINALS, Vatican Basilica, Tuesday, 12 March 2013. *The Message of Love.* Accessed from the Internet http://www.vatican.va/sede_vacante/2013/homily-pro-eligendo-pontifice_2013_en.html

[538] NewAdvent.org. *Isaias, The Book of Isaias.* Accessed from the Internet http://www.newadvent.org/cathen/08179b.htm

[539] MacArthur, John. *The Gospel According to God: Rediscovering the Most Remarkable Chapter in the Old Testament*, p.16. Published by Crossway: Weaton, Illinois, 2018.

[540] Ibid.

of Isaiah generally bring a message of forgiveness, comfort, and hope."[541]

The Protestant Bible contains thirty-nine books in its Old Testament and twenty-seven books in its New Testament. The Catholic Old Testament contains *forty-six books* in its Old Testament – an additional seven books, plus "additions" to Esther, Daniel, and Jeremiah, as well as "subtractions" from Jeremiah in some Catholic versions. Despite "The canonical Book of Isaias is made up of two distinct collections of discourses" and "the second part of the book... Isaiah 40-66" is made up of twenty-seven chapters, the number of books in the Catholic Old Testament are not reflective of the thirty-nine chapters in the book of Isaiah.

Even though the number of books in the Catholic *New* Testament mirror the number of chapters in the "second half" of the book of Isaiah, the number of books in the Catholic *Old* Testament do not reflect the number of chapters in the "first half." The Protestant Old Testament does.

~~~~~~~~~~~~~~~~~~~~~~~~~~~~~~~~~~~~~

Dr. Michael Kruger, mentioned in the Introduction, stated during the 2018 G3 Conference: "I think there's room for a new evangelical, hopefully reformed, work on Old Testament canon. Maybe someone in this room will write it someday."[542]

So much more could be written to support the canonicity of the Hebrew Bible, from both the pages of the New Testament, as well as from early Jewish and Christian history. However, this book should more than suffice for anyone who has a genuine desire to know what the *true* canon of Scripture is, the consequences of a church which does not embrace it, and why Protestant Bibles are smaller.

I felt this book was important to write to reinforce to Protestants their Old Testament canon of Scripture is both complete and true, which is supported both Scripturally as well as historically. It was also written to encourage our Catholic, Eastern Orthodox, and other friends to see for themselves the thirty-nine-book Protestant canon really "is" the complete "God-breathed" Christian Old Testament.

This gives us *one-hundred percent assurance* the sixty-six-book Protestant Bible truly is the Inspired Word of God (John 20:31; 21:24; 1 John 5:13), and not the writings of the traditions of men (Matthew 15:3-

---

[541] Life Application Study Bible, New American Standard Bible-Updated Edition. *The Blueprint* to the book of Isaiah, p.1137. Published by Zondervan: Grand Rapids: Michigan, 2000.

[542] Ibid. *James White & Michael Kruger on the Biblical Canon.* (YouTube.com). "Alpha & Omega Ministries." (Begins around the 46:20 mark.)

9). It also gives complete confidence to the reader that the Protestant canon proves Jesus did indeed rise bodily from the dead to demonstrate His death on the cross was sufficient for the final payment of our sins (John 19:30). This was prophesied in the Old Testament (Psalm 16:10) and fulfilled in the New Testament (Acts 2:27, cf. 13:35) "according to the Scriptures" (1 Corinthians 15:3-4), since ALL Scripture (i.e.: the Protestant Scriptures) is undeniably God-breathed (2 Timothy 3:16).

I have purposely reserved the theological and historical errors and contradictions in the Deuterocanon for Appendix B, because I felt it was important to first establish "what" writings were Inspired and canonical *first*. This needed to be done for both the Old Testament, as well as the New Testament, in order to compare these errors and contradictions in the Deuterocanon *to* these inerrant, Inspired texts. Before I conclude this book, I wanted to reserve some space for my wife, Lucia, who came from a country, which is predominantly Eastern Orthodox, for her to share some of her thoughts. I also reserved space for my mother, Darlene, who was also brought up Catholic and who led me to Jesus.

"For whatever was written in earlier times was written for our instruction, so that through perseverance and the encouragement of the Scriptures we might have hope." (Romans 15:4)

THOUGHTS FROM THE AUTHOR'S WIFE

If you are like me and want to really know the truth about which books belong in the Bible, then you should consider learning about the history of the Bible. The historical accounts should be written by inspired authors within a window of the authors lifetime, not hundreds of years after they died.

My mother, Racheriu Victoria was born in Romania in 1931, into the orthodox religion-based family. She adored the orthodox priest as if he was next to God, and she strongly believed in traditionalism and superstition. As a child she understood a priest should be holy and never commit any sins. When she heard of his sins, she was 13 years old and decided to read the Bible on her own. This is how my mom learned about the truth and later on she converted to Protestantism. The priest's teaching was based mainly on traditions instead of the word of God. Afterward she realized that the Orthodox Church have more traditions and more books in their Bible than the Catholic Church.

"Read the Bible, Lucia," she would say to me. "It is very important."

When I was young my mom taught me the Bible and the true word of God. I was not interested about the history of the Bible or apologetics back then. I was too young, and I grew up trusting the Lord our Savior without questioning. I wished I knew more so I could teach my children Sabina and Iselin so that they would be prepared to defend their faith.

"Do not be deceived: God is not mocked, for whatever one sows, that will he also reap" (Galatians 6:7 ESV).

"and the devil who had deceived them was thrown into the lake of fire and sulfur where the beast and the false prophet were, and they will be tormented day and night forever and ever" (Revelation 20:10 ESV).

Because of the media our times have changed enormously. People who do not search diligently about the truth, can be easily deceived by some writers who are spreading false information about the Bible. These writers are trying to even change the history, not knowing that the time in which this false information was recorded is wrong.

My husband was raised Catholic, and I believe in the same way as my mother he was trusting the Catholic priest and never questioned the traditions. My husband was converted to Protestantism 15 years ago and he was very thirsty and very eager to know the Bible. I met my husband 3 years after his conversion, and it happened that I was in his Church visiting when he gave his testimony. I was impressed by his testimony because he already had a much-advanced knowledge of the Bible. Steve is very passionate about God's word. I can say the same thing about Steve, as Pastor Bellavia said... "he is weird."

Steve likes to study meticulously and that is why he reads more than one version of the Bible. He was very surprised by the multitude of errors and confusion created in some of the Bibles. If readers do not pay attention to the words and the order of history, they will be led astray.

After two years of research and debates, mostly on Catholic blogs, I encouraged my husband to write a book so he doesn't have to repeat himself to everyone who may have the same questions. Or if they want more information it would be available in one big resourceful compiled book.

I am amazed myself of the multitude of information available supporting these inspired books, and only these inspired books belong to the Protestant Bible.

I want to thank my husband for being faithful and trusting the Lord, and for taking the time to study and write this book. My hope is that all readers will be convinced about why certain books from the Catholic Bibles do not belong there.

May God be glorified through all this information. His word belongs to Him, One and Only GOD. Amen!

I love these following verses in which God is warning us that if anyone who knows and read the Bible should be afraid to add anything to it:

"Marturisesc oricui aude cuvintele proorociei din cartea aceasta ca, daca va adauga cineva ceva la ele, Dumnezeu ii va adauga urgiile scrise in cartea aceasta. Si daca scoate cineva ceva din cuvintele cartii acestei proorocii, ii va scoate Dumnezeu partea lui de la pomul vietii si din cetatea sfanta, scrise in cartea aceasta." (Apocalipsa 22:18-19 Versiunea D. Cornilescu)

"I warn everyone who hears the words of the prophecy of this book: if anyone adds to them, God will add to him the plagues described in this book, and if anyone takes away from the words of the book of this prophecy, God will take away his share in the tree of life and in the holy city, which are described in this book." (Revelation 22:18-19 English Standard Version)

- Lucia Christie

THOUGHTS FROM THE AUTHOR'S MOTHER

I was raised Catholic by a Polish mother and an Irish father in a middle-class family. My parents had me baptized at birth and later I received my First Communion and Confirmation. Attending parochial school taught me discipline, respect for elders (which included the nuns and priests). Every day we went to church and studied Catechism; however, the Bible was never in our curriculum. I remember seeing a Catholic Bible in a beautiful pine box in our home, but it was only opened to place holy cards and dried flowers from funerals inside of it.

I started thinking back to my youth before Vatican II when it was a mortal sin to eat meat on Fridays and not attending Mass on Sundays would doom you to hell. After Vatican II, these sins could be absolved by a priest. Additionally, there were some minor changes, i.e., the Mass was no longer in Latin, the priest began to face the congregation rather than towards the statue of Jesus, no one was allowed to touch the Eucharist, and later not only did everyone touch it but wine was also added to communion.

As I became an older adult, I thought back to that Bible and wondered what it was all about. I was invited to a Bible study and was in complete awe and wanted to learn more. I realized God is in control, all my good deeds would not get me into heaven, and there is only one way to Heaven and that is through Jesus.

After reading this book, I learned the Catholic Old Testament changed over the centuries and was different than the Protestant Old Testament. This book explains the different translations: Greek (the Septuagint), Latin (the Vulgate), early English (Douay-Rheims), as well as the fourth century church councils, which included most of the books found in Catholic Bibles which are not in Protestant Bibles. What I did not know was they were not all identical.

After I accepted Christ and repented of my sins, I was saved. A year later my son's eyes were opened, and he too was saved. He accepted Jesus Christ as his Lord and Savior and we were baptized together.

As a former devout Catholic, I would have found this book to be very helpful in knowing for certain what the complete Old Testament canon is. Had this book been available to me in my youth, I would have known what qualifies as Inspired Scripture. No literary work has ever come close to matching the qualifications of the Bible as being God-breathed, including the additional books found in Catholic Old Testaments. At last, this work is available to anyone who is willing to read it and wants to be certain.

    – Darlene Christie

APPENDIX A – Old Testament Metonyms Used in the New Testament

"And He [Jesus] said to them, 'It is written, "MY HOUSE SHALL BE CALLED A HOUSE OF PRAYER"; but you are making it a ROBBERS' DEN.'" (Matthew 21:13, cf. Isaiah 56:7; Jeremiah 7:11)

As mentioned in Chapter Nine, the New Testament uses several metonyms to define and classify Old Testament Scriptures. In this Appendix, I have created a nearly exhaustive list (approximately three-hundred New Testament passages) which show they only define books found *originally* in the Hebrew Bible, and none of them are used to describe any of the Deuterocanonical books *independent* of the Hebrew Bible.

Not *every* book from the Hebrew Bible has a New Testament metonym attributed to it. However, when a metonym is used to describe a division of the Old Testament, or even a subdivision, that entire division or subdivision of writings is classified as Inspired writings as well. Matthew 27:9 quoting "Jeremiah the prophet" is an example, even though the quote was from Zechariah (Zechariah 11:12-13). The twelve "minor prophets," which were originally placed in one book, and Zechariah classifying the "former prophets" together (Zechariah 1:4,7,12) are others.

Some of these metonyms listed in Chapter Nine include: "It is written"; "He has spoken"; "Have you not read?"; "Scripture(s)"; "the Law and the Prophets"; "Moses and the Prophets"; "(the Law of) Moses"; "written by the Prophets"; "the Prophet(s)"; "Psalm(s)"; and "the true Proverb." As discussed in Chapter One, the metonym "it is written" has always been understood in both the church, as well as in ancient Judaism in the Old Testament era, to be in reference to an eternal written truth and an unchanging continual authority from the Word of God (e.g.: Joshua 8:31, cf. Exodus 20:23-25).

Out of the thirty-nine books of the Hebrew Bible, the New Testament uses one of these metonyms for at least twenty-eight* of them. This does not even take into account the other books in the Hebrew Bible the New Testament quotes from without these metonyms.

I have listed the three-tiered division of the twenty-four-book canon of the Hebrew Bible, known since at least the second century A.D. as the *TaNaKh*: The Law ("Torah"), The Prophets ("Nevi'im"), and the Writings ("Ketuvim"). I also underscored and boldfaced each of the sections and subsections to demonstrate they are all represented by at least one New Testament metonym.

As MacArthur pointed out, "In the 22 book canon, Jeremiah and Lamentations were considered one, as were Judges and Ruth."[543] Even though the New Testament does not have a specific metonym for the book of Lamentations, it is still included since the book of Jeremiah did have some (e.g.: Matthew 21:13, cf. Jeremiah 7:11).

After the *TaNaKh* is a list of New Testament verses which contain one or more of these metonyms, followed by the verse or verses it is referring to in the Hebrew Bible. For example, Matthew 21:13 uses the metonym "It is written" and quotes both Isaiah 56:7 and Jeremiah 7:11. For simplicity, I will begin each section with a different metonym, followed by the New Testament verse where it is found, alongside the Old Testament verse or verses the metonym is referencing.

THE TANAKH

Torah ("Teaching" or "The Law" – Five Books of Moses)

- Genesis, Exodus, Leviticus, Numbers, Deuteronomy

Nevi'im ("The Prophets")

- The 'Major Prophets'

    o The 'Former Prophets' – Joshua, Judges, (I & II) Samuel, (I & II) Kings

    o The 'Latter Prophets' – Isaiah, Jeremiah, Ezekiel

- The 'Minor Prophets' (1 Book)

    o Hosea, Joel, Amos, Obadiah, Jonah, Micah, *Nahum?, Habakkuk, Zephaniah, Haggai, Zechariah, Malachi

Ketuvim ("The Writings")

- The 'Poetic Books' – Psalms, Proverbs, Job

- The 'Five Rolls' ('Megilloth') – Song of Solomon, Ruth, Lamentations, Ecclesiastes, Esther

- The 'Historical Books' – Daniel, Ezra-**Nehemiah?, (I & II) Chronicles

---

543 Ibid. The MacArthur Study Bible, *How We Got the Bible: Canonicity*, p. xv.

*Although Romans 10:15 is referencing Isaiah 52:7 with the metonym "it is written," it may also be echoing Nahum 1:15 as well. **When Matthew 23:31-35 and Luke 11:49-51 refer to "Zechariah," it is either referring to the last martyred "prophet" in Nehemiah 12:16 or in 2 Chronicles 24:20-21 (see Chapter Eight for a more in-depth explanation).

"IT IS WRITTEN"

Matthew 4:4; Deuteronomy 8:3
Matthew 4:6; Psalm 91:11-12

Matthew 4:7; Deuteronomy 6:16
Matthew 4:10; Deuteronomy 6:13-14

Matthew 11:10; Malachi 3:1
Matthew 21:13; Isaiah 56:7 & Jeremiah 7:11

Matthew 26:24; Psalm 22 & Daniel 9:26
Matthew 26:31; Zechariah 13:7

Mark 1:2; Malachi 3:1 & Isaiah 40:3
Mark 7:6; Isaiah 29:13

Mark 9:12-13; Malachi 3:1; 4:5 & 1 Kings 19:1-2
Mark 11:17; Isaiah 56:7 & Jeremiah 7:11

Mark 14:21; Psalm 22 & Isaiah 53
Mark 14:27; Zechariah 13:7

Luke 2:23-24; Exodus 13:12 & Leviticus 12:8
Luke 3:4-6; Isaiah 40:3-5

Luke 4:4; Deuteronomy 8:3
Luke 4:8; Deuteronomy 6:13

Luke 4:10-11; Psalm 91:11-12
Luke 4:12; Deuteronomy 6:16

Luke 7:27; Malachi 3:1
Luke 10:26-27; Deuteronomy 6:5 & Leviticus 19:18

Luke 19:46; Isaiah 56:7; Jeremiah 7:11
Luke 24:46; Psalm 22

John 6:31; Psalm 78:24
John 6:45; Isaiah 54:13

John 8:17; Deuteronomy 17:6 & 19:15
John 10:34-35; Psalm 82:6

John 12:14-15; Isaiah 40:9 & Zechariah 9:9
Acts 1:20; Psalm 69:25 & Psalm 109:8

Acts 7:42-43; Amos 5:25-27
Acts 15:15-17; Amos 9:11-12

Acts 23:5; Exodus 22:28
Acts 13:33; Psalm 2:7

Romans 1:17; Habakkuk 2:4
Romans 2:24; Isaiah 52:5

Romans 3:4; Psalm 51:4
Romans 3:10-12; Psalms 14:1-3 & 53:1-3

Romans 3:13; Psalms 5:9 & 140:3
Romans 3:14; Psalm 10:7

Romans 3:15-17; Isaiah 59:7-8
Romans 3:18; Psalm 36:1

Romans 4:17; Genesis 17:5
Romans 8:36; Psalm 44:22

Romans 9:12; Genesis 25:23
Romans 9:13; Malachi 1:2-3

Romans 9:33; Isaiah 9:33 & 28:16
Romans 10:15; Isaiah 52:7; (? Nahum 1:15)

Romans 11:8; Isaiah 29:10 & Deuteronomy 29:4
Romans 11:9-10; Psalm 69:22-23

Romans 11:26-27a; Isaiah 59:20-21
Romans 11:27b; Isaiah 27:9

Romans 12:19; Deuteronomy 32:35
Romans 12:20; Proverbs 25:21-22

Romans 14:11; Isaiah 45:23
Romans 15:3; Psalm 69:9

Romans 15:9; 2 Samuel 22:50 & Psalm 18:49
Romans 15:10; Deuteronomy 32:43

Romans 15:11; Psalm 117:1
Romans 15:12; Isaiah 11:10

Romans 15:21; Isaiah 52:151
1 Corinthians 1:19; Isaiah 29:14

1 Corinthians 1:31; Jeremiah 9:24
1 Corinthians 2:9; Isaiah 64:4; 65:17

1 Corinthians 3:19; Job 5:13
1 Corinthians 3:20; Psalm 94:11

1 Corinthians 9:9; Deuteronomy 25:4
1 Corinthians 10:7; Exodus 32:6

1 Corinthians 14:21; Isaiah 28:11-12
1 Corinthians 15:45; Genesis 2:7

1 Corinthians 15:54; Isaiah 25:8
1 Corinthians 15:55; Hosea 13:14

2 Corinthians 8:15; Exodus 16:18
2 Corinthians 9:9; Psalm 112:9

Galatians 3:10; Deuteronomy 27:26
Galatians 3:13; Deuteronomy 21:23

Galatians 4:22; Genesis 16:1-16 & 21:1-7
Galatians 4:27; Isaiah 54:1

Hebrews 10:5-7; Psalm 40:6-8
1 Peter 1:16; Leviticus 11:44-45

"HE HAS SPOKEN" / "IT IS (ONE WHO) SAID" / "IT IS ATTESTED (COMMAND)"

Luke 4:12; Deuteronomy 6:16
John 1:23; Isaiah 40:3

Acts 2:25-28; Psalm 16:8-11
Acts 2:34; Psalm 110:1

Acts 13:34; Isaiah 55:3
John 12:39-41; Isaiah 6:1,9-10

Romans 9:25-26; Hosea 1:9-10 & 2:23
Romans 9:27-28; Isaiah 10:22-23

Romans 9:29; Isaiah 1:9
Romans 10:16; Isaiah 53:1

Romans 11:9-10; Psalm 69:22-23
Galatians 3:16; Genesis 22:18

Ephesians 4:8; Psalm 68:18
Ephesians 5:14; Isaiah 60:1

Hebrews 3:15; Psalm 95:7-8
Hebrews 7:17; Psalm 110:4

Hebrews 7:21; Psalm 110:4
Hebrews 10:5-7; Psalm 40:6-8

Hebrews 12:20; Exodus 19:12-13
Hebrews 10:16-17; Jeremiah 31:31-34

James 2:11; Exodus 20:13-14
James 4:6; Proverbs 3:34

"HAVE YOU NOT READ (NEVER HEARD)?"

Matthew 12:3-4a; 1 Samuel 21:4-6
Matthew 12:4b; Leviticus 24:5-9

Matthew 12:5; Numbers 28:9-10
Matthew 19:4-5; Genesis 1:27 & 2:24

Matthew 22:31; Exodus 3:6
Mark 12:26; Exodus 3:6

Mark 12:10; Psalm 118:22-23
Luke 6:3-4a; 1 Samuel 21:4-6

Mark 6:4b; Leviticus 24:5-9
Romans 10:18; Psalm 19:4

"SCRIPTURE(S)"

Matthew 21:42; Psalm 118:22-23
Matthew 22:29; Exodus 3:6

Matthew 26:54; Isaiah 50:6 & 53:2-11
Matthew 26:56; Zechariah 13:7

Mark 12:10; Psalm 118:22-23
Mark 12:24; Exodus 3:6

Mark 14:49; Isaiah 53:7-9
Mark 15:28[544]; Isaiah 53:12

Luke 4:18-19,21; Isaiah 61:1-2
John 2:17,22; Psalm 69:9

---

[544] Although Mark 15:28 is not included in the earliest and most reliable copies of Mark's gospel, Luke 22:37 also cites Isaiah 53:12 with the Old Testament metonym "it is written."

John 5:39; Isaiah 34:16
John 7:38; Isaiah 44:3 & Jeremiah 17:13

John 7:42; Psalm 132:11; Jeremiah 23:5; Micah 5:2
John 10:34-35; Psalm 82:6

John 13:18; Psalm 41:9
John 17:12; Psalm 41:9 & 109:6-8

John 19:24; Psalm 22:18
John 19:28; Psalm 22:15

John 19:36; Exodus 12:46 & Numbers 9:12
John 19:37; Zechariah 12:10

John 20:9; Psalm 16:10
Acts 1:16,18; Zechariah 11:12-13

Acts 1:16,20; Psalm 69:25 & 109:8
Acts 8:32-33; Isaiah 53:7-8

Acts 8:35; Isaiah 53:7-8
Romans 1:2-3; 2 Samuel 7:12-14

Romans 4:3; Genesis 15:6
Romans 9:17; Exodus 9:11

Romans 10:11; Isaiah 28:16 & 49:23
Romans 10:13; Joel 2:32

Romans 11:2-4; 1 Kings 19:10 & 19:18
Romans 15:4; Psalm 119:81,115 & Jeremiah 14:8

Romans 16:26; Psalm 119:81,114

1 Corinthians 15:3-4; Psalm 16:8-11 & Ch.22; Isaiah 53
Galatians 3:8; Genesis 3:8

Galatians 3:22; 1 Kings 8:46 (cf. Psalm 143:2; Proverbs 20:9; Ecclesiastes 7:20; Isaiah 53:6)

Galatians 4:30; Genesis 21:10
1 Timothy 5:18; Deuteronomy 25:4

James 2:8; Leviticus 19:18
James 2:23; Genesis 15:6

James 4:5; Genesis 6:5 (cf. 8:21; Proverbs 11:10; Ecclesiastes 9:3; Jeremiah 17:9)

1 Peter 2:6; Isaiah 28:16
1 Peter 2:7; Psalm 118:22

1 Peter 2:8; Isaiah 8:14
2 Peter 1:20-21; Genesis 40:8

"THE LAW AND THE PROPHETS"

Matthew 7:12; Leviticus 19:18
Matthew 22:37,40; Deuteronomy 6:5

Matthew 22:39-40; Leviticus 19:18
Acts 24:14-15; Job 19:26-27 & Daniel 12:2

"MOSES AND THE PROPHETS"

Luke 16:29-31; Isaiah 8:19b-20 & 34:16
Luke 24:44; Psalm 119:17 & Isaiah 29:18

John 1:45; Deuteronomy 18:15-19 & Isaiah 4:2
Acts 26:22-23; Psalm 16:10 & Ch.22

"(THE LAW OF) MOSES"

Matthew 19:7; Deuteronomy 24:1-4
Matthew 22:24; Deuteronomy 25:5-10

Mark 1:44; Leviticus 14:1-32
Mark 7:10; Exodus 20:12 & 21:17

Mark 10:3-4; Deuteronomy 24:1-4
Mark 12:19; Deuteronomy 25:5-10

Mark 12:26; Exodus 3:6
Luke 2:22; Leviticus 12:2-5

Luke 5:14; Leviticus 13:1-46
Luke 20:28; Deuteronomy 25:5-10

Luke 20:37; Exodus 3:6
John 1:17; Deuteronomy 5:1-5

John 3:14; Numbers 25:5-9
John 5:45-47; Deuteronomy 18:15-19

John 6:32; Exodus 16:15
John 7:19; Deuteronomy 5:1-5

John 7:22; Genesis 17:10-12
John 7:23; Leviticus 12:1-3

John 8:5; Leviticus 20:10
John 9:29; Exodus 19:19-20

Acts 3:22-23; Deuteronomy 18:15,19
Acts 7:31-32; Exodus 3:6,15

Acts 7:31,33-34; Exodus 3:5,7-8
Acts 7:35; Exodus 2:14

Acts 7:37; Deuteronomy 18:15
Acts 7:44; Exodus 25:8-9,40

Acts 15:1,5; Genesis 17:10-12
Romans 5:14; Genesis 3:6-Exodus 2:2

Romans 9:15; Exodus 33:19
Romans 10:5-8; Deuteronomy 30:12-14

Romans 10:19; Deuteronomy 32:21
1 Corinthians 9:8-9; Deuteronomy 25:4

1 Corinthians 10:2; Exodus 13:21 & 14:26-31
2 Corinthians 3:15; Exodus 34:33-35

Hebrews 7:14; Genesis 49:8-10
Hebrews 8:5; Exodus 25:40

Hebrews 9:19-20; Exodus 24:3-8
Hebrews 10:28; Deuteronomy 17:2-7

Hebrews 12:21; Deuteronomy 9:19

Revelation 15:3; Exodus 15:1-21 & Deuteronomy 32:1-43

"THE LAW"

Matthew 22:36-39; Leviticus 19:18 & Deuteronomy 6:5
Matthew 23:23-24; Leviticus 11:4,23

Luke 2:27,39; Exodus 13:12 & Leviticus 12:8

Luke 10:26-28; Leviticus 18:5 & 19:18 & Deuteronomy 6:5

John 12:34; Psalm 89:35-37 & Isaiah 9:7 & Ezekiel 37:25

Acts 7:53; Deuteronomy 33:2
Acts 21:23-24; Numbers 6:1-21

Acts 23:3; Leviticus 19:33-35 & Ezekiel 13:10-16
Romans 2:23-24; Isaiah 52:5

Romans 3:19; Psalm 107:42
Romans 3:20; Psalm 143:2

Romans 7:7; Exodus 20:17 & Deuteronomy 5:21
Romans 7:10-12; Psalm 19:8

Romans 13:8-10; Exodus 20:13-17 & Leviticus 19:18
Galatians 3:11; Habakkuk 2:4

Galatians 3:12; Leviticus 18:5
Galatians 3:17; Exodus 12:40

Galatians 3:19; Genesis 22:18 & Deuteronomy 33:2
Philippians 3:5; Genesis 17:12

1 Timothy 1:8; Psalm 19:7
Hebrews 7:5; Numbers 18:21-24

Hebrews 9:22; Exodus 19:10 & Numbers 16:46
Hebrews 10:8-9; Psalm 40:6-8

James 1:25; Psalm 19:7
James 2:9; Leviticus 19:15

James 4:11; Exodus 23:1

"WRITTEN BY (THROUGH/IN) THE PROPHETS"

Matthew 2:5-6; 2 Samuel 5:2 & Micah 5:2
Matthew 2:15; Hosea 11:1

Luke 18:31-33; Psalm 22 & Isaiah 53 & Daniel 9:26
John 6:45; Isaiah 54:13

Acts 7:42-43; Amos 5:25-27
Acts 15:15-17; Amos 9:11-12

"THE PROPHET(S)"

Matthew 1:22-23; Isaiah 7:14 & 8:8,10

Matthew 2:17-18; Jeremiah 31:15

Matthew 2:23; Psalm 22:6-8 & Isaiah 49:7 & 53:3
Matthew 3:3; Isaiah 40:3-5

Matthew 4:14-16; Isaiah 9:1-2
Matthew 8:17; Isaiah 53:4

Matthew 12:17-21; Isaiah 42:1-4
Matthew 12:39-41; Jonah 1:17 & 3:5-10

Matthew 13:14-15; Isaiah 6:9-10

Matthew 13:35; Psalm 78:2 (cf. 1 Chronicles 15:17 & 2 Chronicles 29:30 – see Chapter Seven)

Matthew 21:4-5; Zechariah 9:9

Matthew 23:31-35; Genesis 4:8 & Zechariah 1:1 (cf. Nehemiah 12:16) vs. 2 Chronicles 24:20-21 (see Chapter Eight)

Matthew 23:37; Ruth 2:12 & Psalm 91:4
Matthew 24:15; Daniel 9:27 & 11:31 & 12:11

Matthew 27:9-10; Zechariah 11:12-13
Mark 1:2-3; Isaiah 40:3 & Malachi 40:3

Mark 6:15; Deuteronomy 18:15
Luke 3:4-6; Isaiah 61:1-2

Luke 4:17-19; Isaiah 61:1-2
Luke 4:25-26; 1 Kings 17:8-24

Luke 4:27; 2 Kings 5:1-14

Luke 11:49-51; Genesis 4:8 & Zechariah 1:1 (cf. Nehemiah 12:16) vs. 2 Chronicles 24:20-21 (see Chapter Eight)

Luke 13:34; Ruth 2:12 & Psalm 91:4
Luke 18:31; Psalm 22 & 69 & Isaiah 53

John 1:21,25; Deuteronomy 18:15,18
John 6:14; Deuteronomy 18:15,18

John 7:40; Deuteronomy 18:15,18
John 12:38; Isaiah 53:1

Acts 2:16-21; Joel 2:28-32
Acts 3:18; Psalm 22 & Isaiah 53

Acts 3:24; 1 Samuel 3:20
Acts 3:25; Genesis 22:18

Acts 7:48-50; Isaiah 66:1-2
Acts 8:28-34; Isaiah 53:7-8

Acts 13:20-21; 1 Samuel 9:2
Acts 13:20,22; 1 Samuel 13:14

Acts 13:40-41; Habakkuk 1:5
Acts 28:25-27; Isaiah 6:9-10

Romans 11:3; 1 Kings 19:10
James 5:10-11; Job 42

2 Peter 2:16; Numbers 22:21-35
2 Peter 3:2-7; Psalm 50:1-4; Malachi 4:1-2

Revelation 10:7; Amos 3:7

"THE PSALM(S)"

Luke 20:42-43; Psalm 110:1
Acts 1:20-21; Psalm 69:25 & 109:8

Acts 13:33; Psalm 2:7
Acts 13:35; Psalm 16:10

"THE TRUE PROVERB"

2 Peter 2:22; Proverbs 26:11

"THE WISDOM OF SOLOMON"

Matthew 12:42; 1 Kings 10:1-13
Luke 11:31; 1 Kings 10:1-13

"JEREMIAH"

Matthew 27:9; Zechariah 11:12-13

"DAVID"

Acts 4:25; Psalm 2:1-2
Hebrews 4:7; Psalm 95:7-8

APPENDIX B – Errors and Contradictions in the Deuterocanon

"In the third year of the reign of Jehoiakim king of Judah, Nebuchadnezzar king of Babylon came to Jerusalem and besieged it." (Daniel 1:1)

"Now Nebuchadnezzar, king of the Assyrians, sent messengers to all the inhabitants of Persia, and to all those who dwelt in the West." (Judith 1:7 NAB)

In Chapter Ten, one essential criterion for a writing to qualify as Inspired Scripture is the absence of any theological or historical errors or contradictions, including with already qualified Inspired Scriptures. Both the thirty-nine books of the Hebrew Bible and the twenty-seven books of the New Testament meet this qualifying criterion. When it comes to the Deuterocanon, they do not meet it, because they contradict either the Hebrew Bible, the New Testament, or both. Sometimes, the Deuterocanon also contradicts historical events and even *itself!*

Before I cite these contradictions, which disqualify all of the Deuterocanonical books as Inspired Scripture, I have to clarify what qualifies as an error or contradiction. Some would say Matthew 8:28 mentioning two demon-possessed men, while both Mark 5:2 and Luke 8:27 only mention one is an example of a contradiction. The omission of mentioning someone is not really an error, unless Mark and Luke stated there was *only* one demon-possessed man, which they do not. Mark and Luke electing to only mention one of them is not a contradiction.

"THE GREAT DEBATE IX" – WHITE VERSUS MICHUTA

Dr. James White posted a formal discussion on his YouTube channel he had with Mr. Gary Michuta in 2004 on the Old Testament canon. This came to be known as "The Great Debate IX." During the debate, Dr. White addressed obvious errors in the Deuterocanon including Judith 1:1,7 and 2:1,4 incorrectly describing Nebuchadnezzar as King of the Assyrians rather than King of Babylon. This is how the Hebrew Bible and even the Deuterocanonical book of Baruch correctly identify him. Rather than acknowledge this actual contradiction in the book of Judith, Mr. Michuta instead referred to this as an "apparent error."[545] When Dr. White pressed him asking if it was an error calling Nebuchadnezzar the King of the Assyrians, Mr. Michuta replied:

"Well, James, yes that is true, but reconciling what is said in that particular book to what we understand is to consider this to be an absolute error or not, or merely an apparent error. As you well know, there could be problems in textual transmission. There could also be difficulties in a literary device that could be used in different literary forms. But I'm not going to try to reconcile this, because as I said, it's really begging the question. You have already determined that this book is not Inspired, and that when you find an error in it, you're saying this is a real error, instead of an apparent error."[546]

Mr. Michuta's rejection of this "absolute error" in Judith (which Mr. Michuta admits it *is* an error) is based on the church not possessing the original Biblical text. Because we do not know what it originally said, Mr. Michuta argued we cannot say with certainty the book of Judith is really in error by calling Nebuchadnezzar, "King of the Assyrians." Although he attempted to use the same defense Protestants use to reconcile "apparent errors" in the Hebrew Bible and the New Testament, his rationale fails on two points.

First, the "apparent errors" found in the Hebrew Bible and the New Testament are easily reconcilable (e.g.: spelling variations, word choices and order, mistranscription of a word such as the "second Cainan" in Luke's gospel – see Chapter Five). Due to the benefit of textual criticism, which involves comparing thousands of ancient Biblical manuscripts, we can have confidence with nearly one-hundred percent certainty what the original Inspired, inerrant texts said.

Textual criticism cannot account for incorrectly naming the nation a king ruled over. A scribe copying the original text simply would not have made this kind of transcribed error unintentionally – four times in the same book – like he would with a simple misspelling of a word. In every ancient copy of Judith discovered, this same error is present. *None* say Nebuchadnezzar was King of Babylon.

Second, Mr. Michuta's fallacious reasoning leads to being uncertain anything in Scripture today is what the original texts said. This includes Jesus' death on the cross for the payment of our sins or the church being

---

[545] Ibid. White, James & Michuta Gary. *The Great Debate IX: Is The Apocrypha Scripture? (White vs Michuta).* (Mr. White's cross-examination of Mr. Michuta begins at about the 1:47:27 mark. Mr. Michuta's reply begins at about the 1:45:57 mark.)
[546] Ibid.

"the pillar and support of the truth" (1 Timothy 3:15), since we do not possess the original gospels nor this first epistle of Paul to Timothy. For all we know, Paul's original letter did not say this. Mr. Michuta's argument from silence does not help him defend either the inerrancy or the Inspiration of the Deuterocanon. Rather, it sheds doubt on the validity of the entire canon of Scripture, both Old and New Testaments, including the authority of the church itself.

These mental gymnastics performed by Mr. Michuta are not necessary for the Hebrew Bible and the New Testament like they are for the errors and contradictions in the Deuterocanon, as this second Appendix will demonstrate. When Dr. White asked Mr. Michuta to address the obvious errors in Judith and other Deuterocanonical books, this may explain Mr. Michuta's evasive response: "So, in answer to your question, James, I'm not going to answer your question."[547]

JUDITH

Judith 1:1 is a clear contradiction in the Deuterocanon which refers to "Nebuchadnezzar, king of the *Assyrians* in the great city of Ninevah" (NAB, emphasis added, see also Judith 1:7; 2:1,4), while Daniel 1:1 correctly identifies him as "Nebuchadnezzar king of *Babylon*" (emphasis added). The New Catholic Version attempts to explain this by saying Judith's Nebuchadnezzar was "Not the king of Babylon, who took and destroyed Jerusalem, but another of the same name, who reigned in Ninive [sic]."[548]

The books in the Hebrew Bible consistently and unanimously refer to Nebuchadnezzar as "the king of Babylon" (2 Kings 24:1; 2 Chronicles 36:6; Ezra 5:12; Nehemiah 7:6; Esther 2:6; Jeremiah 21:2; Ezekiel 26:7; Daniel 1:1). Chapter six of the Deuterocanonical book of Baruch (i.e.: the epistle of Jeremiah) and the "additions" to Esther *also* refer to him as "Nebuchadnezzar, king of the *Babylonians*" (Baruch 6:1 NAB; the "additions" to Esther A:3 NAB). Judith, Baruch, and the "additions" to Esther were all written during the Intertestamental Period between the Hebrew Bible and the New Testament eras.

There is no historical record of another "Nebuchadnezzar" who was king of Assyria during the Old Testament era.[549] The *only* place you find a

---

547 Ibid. (Begins around the 1:45:37 mark.)

548 Ibid. New Catholic Version, *The Book of Judith*, p.524, footnote on Judith 1:5.

549 Every "King Nebuchadnezzar" from either Biblical and/or secular history during the Old Testament era were all rulers over Babylon. None of them ruled over Assyria: *Nabuchodonosor* http://www.newadvent.org/cathen/10666c.htm. See also: *Nebuchadnezzar I* (1125-1104 B.C.) https://en.wikipedia.org/wiki/Nebuchadnezzar_I; *Nebuchadnezzar II* (605-562 B.C.); https://en.wikipedia.org/wiki/Nebuchadnezzar_II;

Nebuchadnezzar who was king of Assyria, either Scripturally or historically, is in the Deuterocanonical book of Judith. The book of Judith is undoubtedly in error.

The Introduction to the New Catholic Version attempts to rationalize this obvious contradiction by stating: "the book of Judith calls Nabuchodonosor [sic] 'King of the Assyrians who reigned in Ninive [sic]' (Jud.1:5) when the simple fact that *Judith is a piece of edifying fiction* written to teach *not history* but a moral, is known and acknowledged"[550] (emphasis added). In the Introduction to the book of Judith in the New American Bible, it states: "Any attempt to read the book directly against the backdrop of Jewish history in relation to the empires of the ancient world is bound to fail."[551] Yet, the New American Bible lists the book of Judith under the *Historical* Books under its Table of Contents.[552]

Below are verses from the other Deuterocanonical books, followed by verses from the Inspired Hebrew Bible, the Inspired New Testament, or both, which illustrate examples of how the Deuterocanon contradicts these previous and later Inspired texts. Intermingled are blatant theological, historical, and even scientific errors found in the Deuterocanon. Unless otherwise specified, the verses from the Hebrew Bible and the New Testament are taken from the New American Standard Bible. Verses from the Deuterocanonical books will either be from the New Catholic Version (NCV) or from the New American Bible (NAB).

SIRACH (ECCLESIATICUS)

"Children, hear the judgment of your father, and so do that you may be saved." (Sirach 3:2 NCV)

"He who honors his father atones for sins." (Sirach 3:3 NAB)

"Water quenches a flaming fire, and alms atone for sins." (Sirach 3:29 NAB)

"For the life of the flesh is in the blood, and I have given it to you on the altar to make atonement for your souls; for it is the blood by reason of the life that makes atonement." (Leviticus 17:11)

Nebuchadnezzar III (522 B.C.); https://en.wikipedia.org/wiki/Nebuchadnezzar_III; *Nebuchadnezzar IV* (fl. 520s B.C.) https://en.wikipedia.org/wiki/Nebuchadnezzar_IV.

[550] Ibid. New Catholic Version, *Introduction*, p.iii. Rev. J. Edgar Bruns, S.T.D., S.S.L. St. John's University Graduate School of Theology.

[551] Ibid. New American Bible, Introduction to *The Book of Judith*, p.485.

[552] Ibid. *Contents*, p. [7].

"Of Him all the prophets bear witness that through His name everyone who believes in Him receives forgiveness of sins." (Acts 10:34)

"For 'WHOEVER WILL CALL ON THE NAME OF THE LORD WILL BE SAVED.'" (Romans 10:13, cf. Joel 2:32)

"all things are cleansed with blood, and without shedding of blood there is no forgiveness." (Hebrews 9:22)

~~~~~~~~~~

"Do good to the just man and reward will be yours, if not from him, from the LORD. No good comes to him who gives comfort to the wicked, nor is it an act of mercy that he does. Give to the good man, refuse the sinner. With twofold evil you will meet for every good deed you do for him." (Sirach 12:2-4a,6 NAB)

"Do good to the humble, and give not to the ungodly; hold back thy bread, and give it not to him, lest thereby he overmaster thee. For thou shalt receive twice as much evil for all the good thou shalt have done for him." (Sirach 12:6-7a NCV)

"If your enemy is hungry, give him food to eat; And if he is thirsty, give him water to drink." (Proverbs 25:21, cf. Romans 12:20)

"For if you love those who love you, what reward do you have? Do not even the tax collectors do the same? If you greet only your brothers, what more are you doing than others? Do not even the Gentiles do the same?" (Matthew 5:46-47)

"But I say to you who hear, love your enemies, do good to those who hate you, bless those who curse you, pray for those who mistreat you. Whoever hits you on the cheek, offer him the other also; and whoever takes away your coat, do not withhold your shirt from him either. Give to everyone who asks of you, and whoever takes away what is yours, do not demand it back." (Luke 6:27-30)

TOBIT

"For alms deliver from all sin, and will not suffer the soul to go into darkness." (Tobit 4:11 NCV)

"For almsgiving saves one from death and expiates every sin / and the same is that which purgeth away sins, and maketh to find mercy and life everlasting." (Tobit 12:9a NCV / 12:9b NAB)

"the blood of Jesus His Son cleanses us from all sin. If we confess our sins, He is faithful and righteous to forgive us our sins and to cleanse us from all unrighteousness." (1 John 1:7,9) "how much more will the blood of Christ, who through the eternal Spirit offered Himself without blemish to God, cleanse your conscience from dead works to serve the living God?" (Hebrews 9:14)

~~~~~~~~~~

"And Tobias said to him: I pray thee, tell me, of what family, or what tribe art thou?" (Tobit 5:16 NCV)

"Pray, then, in this way: *'Our Father* who is in heaven, Hallowed be Your name." (Matthew 6:9, emphasis added)

When Tobias asked the angel Raphael from what family he was from (Tobit 5:16 NCV), he lied about his true identity: "Raphael answered, 'I am Azariah, son of Hananiah the elder, one of your own kinsmen'" (Tobit 5:13 NAB). Holy angels, in both the Old and New Testament, never lie about their true identity when directly asked, and even reveal they are angels in Scripture (e.g.: Luke 1:19,26; Jude v.9; Revelation 12:7). Raphael also gave some false, and almost witchcraft-like, medicinal advice and bizarre instructions on exorcism, to Tobit's son Tobiah:

> "The angel then told him: 'Cut the fish open and take out its gall, heart, and liver, and keep them with you; but throw away the entrails. Its gall, heart, and liver make useful medicines....' 'Brother Azariah, what medicinal value is there in the fish's heart, liver, and gall?' He answered: 'As regards the fish's heart and liver, if you burn them so that the smoke surrounds a man or a woman who is afflicted by a demon or evil spirit, the affliction will leave him completely, and no demons will ever return to him again. And as for the gall, if you rub it on the eyes of a man who has cataracts, blowing into his eyes right on the cataracts, his sight will be restored." (Tobit 6:5,7b-9 NAB).

~~~~~~~~~~

"I, Tobit...my kinsmen and my people who had been deported with me to Nineveh, in Assyria. When I lived as a young man in my own country, Israel, the entire tribe of my forefather Naphtali had broken away from the house of David and from Jerusalem.... All my kinsmen, like the rest of my forefather Naphtali, used to offer sacrifice on all the mountains of Galilee as well as to the young bull which Jeroboam, king of Israel, had made in Dan.... Tobit died peacefully at the age of a hundred and twelve." (Tobit 1:3-5; 14:1 NAB)

Tobit claims to have been alive when Jeroboam revolted (Tobit 1:4-5 NAB, cf. 1 Kings 11:26) (931 B.C.) and also when Shalmaneser king of Assyria conquered the northern kingdom of Israel (Tobit 1:2 NAB, cf. 2 Kings 17:3,5) (722 B.C.), which spans *two-hundred and nine years.* Later,

248

though, the book of Tobit claims he only lived for *one-hundred and twelve years* (Tobit 14:1 NAB). This is an error of at least ninety-seven years. (The NCV states he only lived *one-hundred and two years* – Tobit 14:2 NCV, which contradicts the NAB in chapter one by one-hundred and seven years and in chapter fourteen by ten years, respectfully.)

Tobit records when "Shalmaneser died and his son Sennacherib succeeded him as king" of Assyria (Tobit 1:15 NAB), even though Sargon king of Assyria (Isaiah 20:1) succeeded King Shalmaneser (2 Kings 17:3-6, cf. 18:9). King Sennacherib then succeeded *Sargon* (2 Kings 18:13, cf. Isaiah 20:1; 36:1). This may explain why the footnotes of Tobit 1:15 state: "Inconsistencies such as this point to the fact that the book of Tobit is a *religious novel.*"[553] The Introduction to the book of Tobit confesses "The *seemingly historical data* – names of kings, cities, etc. – are used merely as vivid details to create interest and charm"[554] (emphasis added), even though the NAB lists Tobit under the *Historical* Books,[555] as it does Judith.

WISDOM

Although the NAB notes the author of the Deuterocanonical book of Wisdom: "At times he speaks in the person of Solomon,"[556] the NCV discloses "it is uncertain who was the writer."[557] This may explain why both the Council of Rome in A.D. 382 and Augustine of Hippo rejected the book of Wisdom as being that of Solomon (see Chapter Four). Like other Deuterocanonical books, the book of Wisdom also contains errors and contradictions with Inspired Scripture.

~~~~~~~~~~

"For not without mean was your almighty hand, that had fashioned the universe from formless matter." (Wisdom 11:17 NAB)

"In the beginning God created the heavens and the earth." (Genesis 1:1)
"By faith we understand that the worlds were prepared by the word of God, so that what is seen was not made out of things which are visible." (Hebrews 11:3)

When Moses wrote "God created the heavens and the earth," this meant God did not create them "from formless matter" and "not made out

---

553 Ibid. Footnote to Tobit 1:15, p.471
554 Ibid. Introduction to *The Book of Tobit*, p.470.
555 Ibid. *Contents*, p. [7].
556 Ibid. Introduction to *The Book of Wisdom*, p.750.
557 Ibid. New Catholic Version, Introduction to *The Book of Wisdom*, p.696

249

of things which are visible." God created the universe "out of nothing" (Latin: *ex nihilio*) spoken through His "word."

~~~~~~~~~~

"And I was a witty child and had received a good soul. And whereas I was more good, I came by a body undefiled." (Wisdom 8:19-20 NCV)

"Behold, I was brought forth in iniquity, And in sin my mother conceived me." (Psalm 51:5)

"So then as through one transgression there resulted condemnation to all men, even so through one act of righteousness there resulted justification of life to all men. For as through the one man's disobedience the many were made sinners, even so through the obedience of the One the many will be made righteous." (Romans 5:18-19)

~~~~~~~~~~

"For by wisdom they were healed." (Wisdom 9:19 NCV)

"who Himself bore our sins in His own body on the tree, that we, having died to sins, might live for righteousness—by whose stripes you were healed." (1 Peter 2:24 NKJV)

~~~~~~~~~~

"For she [Wisdom] is the brightness of eternal light, and the unspotted mirror of God's majesty, and the image of his goodness." (Wisdom 7:26 NCV)

"He who is the blessed and only Sovereign, the King of kings and Lord of lords, who alone possesses immortality and dwells in unapproachable light, whom no man has seen or can see. To Him be honor and eternal dominion! Amen." (1 Timothy 6:15b-16)

"And He is the radiance of His glory and the exact representation of His nature, and upholds all things by the word of His power. When He had made purification of sins, He sat down at the right hand of the Majesty on high." (Hebrews 1:3)

Although "Wisdom" is personified in the first person in the Hebrew Bible as "she" and "her" (i.e.: Proverbs 1:20; 3:14-18; 8:1-22; 9:1-12), "Wisdom" is used *by God* so we may know the origin from where that "Wisdom" came *from* "Him" (cf. Proverbs 3:19; 8:22-36; 1 Kings 3:28; 1 Corinthians 1:21,24; Ephesians 3:10), instead of "Wisdom" being a personification of God *Himself* (Wisdom 7:26 NCV).

This is why Jesus referred to God the Father as "Him" or "He" (Matthew 6:8; 23:9), rather than "She" or "Her." Likewise, Jesus is referred to as the "Bridegroom" and the church as His "bride" (John 3:29; Revelation 18:23), who He "marries" (Revelation 19:7). This is reflective of God in the Old Testament being referred to as the "Husband" (Isaiah 54:5) and "Bridegroom" to Israel (Isaiah 62:5), who He was "married" to (Jeremiah 3:14 NKJV).

Jesus illustrated the "wisdom *of God*" (Luke 11:49, emphasis added) as coming *from Him*, which McDonald indicates "This may be an allusion or simply common language circulating among Jews in the first century and earlier."[558] GotQuestions.org illustrates the context of the Hebrew word for "wisdom":

> "The Hebrew word is *chokmoth*, and it is grammatically feminine. In Hebrew, it would have been natural to speak of wisdom as a 'she.' In other words, since the word *wisdom* is feminine (in Hebrew grammar), Wisdom personified becomes a 'she' to satisfy the demands of diction—not to add information to its object."[559]

This may be another reason why the Council of Rome and early church fathers, like Augustine, failed to attribute the book of Wisdom as being from Solomon. Oddly enough, the second century A.D. Muratorian Fragment[560] "includes the Wisdom of Solomon...in a *New Testament* collection,"[561] despite it being written before the New Testament era. In *Eusebius: The Church History* where Irenaeus quotes both the *Shepherd of Hermas* and calls it "Scripture," along with "quoting loosely, too, from the Wisdom of Solomon,"[562] McDonald uses Eusebius' citation for these two books being in Irenaeus' *New* Testament list. McDonald also cites from the Muratorian Fragment regarding the book of Wisdom as being "written by the friends of Solomon in his honour,"[563] as opposed to being attributed to Solomon himself.

---

[558] Ibid. McDonald. *The Biblical Canon*, p.98, footnote #67.

[559] GotQuestions.org. *"Why is wisdom referred to as a she in Proverbs?"* Accessed from the Internet https://www.gotquestions.org/wisdom-she-Proverbs.html. Italics are in the original text.

[560] Ibid, McDonald. *The Biblical Canon*, p.371.

[561] Ibid, p.374. Italics in original text (see also *Appendix C: Lists and Catalogues of New Testament Collections, Table C-2*, p.449). McDonald also includes the book of Wisdom as part of the *New* Testament list of Irenaeus in Appendix C, Table C-1, p.445, which he based on Eusebius (Ibid. *Eusebius: The Church History*, Book 5:8, p.165).

[562] Ibid. Maier. *Eusebius: The Church History*. Book 5:8, p.165.

[563] Ibid. McDonald. *The Biblical Canon*, p.371. In footnote #19 (p.369), McDonald cites the Muratorian Fragment from the work of B. M. Metzger, *The Canon of the New Testament: Its Origin, Development, and Significance*. Oxford: Clarendon, 1987.

In the Old Testament canon of Bishop Epiphanius of Salamis (ca. A.D. 315-403),[564] "His list also parallels the current Protestant OT [Old Testament] canon, and it depends on the twenty-two-letter Hebrew alphabet ('so twenty-two books are completed according to the number of the twenty-two letters of the Hebrews')."[565] (See Appendix A for the difference between the arrangement of the twenty-two-book canon of the Hebrew Bible versus the Protestant Old Testament, while preserving the exact same writings.)

Concerning the Deuterocanonical books of Wisdom and Sirach, McDonald further cites Epiphanius who called them "helpful and useful but are not included in the number of the recognized (*Pan.* 8.6.1)."[566] Like Irenaeus and the Muratorian Fragment, Epiphanius included the book of Wisdom in his *New* Testament list, as well as the book of Sirach.[567]

Not only did Epiphanius have an Old Testament canon similar to Athanasius' which excluded most of the Deuterocanonical books (see Chapter Five), "Athanasius and Epiphanius…had a greater influence on the church than many lesser-known figures."[568] Regarding Epiphanius, NewAdvent.org comments "His zeal for the monastic life, ecclesiastical learning, and orthodoxy gave him extraordinary authority."[569]

FIRST AND SECOND MACCABEES

First and 2 Maccabees provide some invaluable, historical accounts: the reign and death of Alexander the Great (1 Maccabees 1:1-8 NAB); the origination of Hanukkah (1 Maccabees 4:52-59; 2 Maccabees 1:18; 2:19; 10:1-8 NAB), which the apostle John records as the "feast of Dedication" (Hebrew: *"chanukkah"*) (John 10:22); and the tyrannical reign of Antiochus Epiphanes over Israel (1 Maccabees 1:10,43-53 NAB), including "erecting the horrible abomination upon the altar of holocausts" (v.54 NAB). Both the prophet Daniel and Jesus referred to this as "the abomination of desolation" (Daniel 11:31; Matthew 24:15).

Despite these historical accuracies, these books also contain historical and theological errors and contradictions not only between them and the

---

[564] Ibid, p.159.

[565] Ibid, p.204. Brackets inserted by me for clarity.

[566] Ibid. McDonald quotes Epiphanius, *Refutation of All Heresies* from S. Z. Leiman's work, *The Canonization of the Hebrew Scriptures: The Talmudic an Midrashic Evidence*, pp.44-45. Hamden, Conn: Archon, 1976.

[567] Ibid, *Appendix C, Table C-2*, p.447.

[568] Ibid, p.414.

[569] Ibid. NewAdvent.org. *Epiphanius of Salamis*. Accessed from the Internet http://www.newadvent.org/cathen/13393b.htm

Hebrew Bible and the New Testament, but also between themselves. Even the NAB acknowledges the author of 2 Maccabees "effects his purpose by...giving exaggerated figures for the size of armies and the number killed in battle."[570]

Although 2 Maccabees "is not a sequel to 1 Maccabees"[571] the footnotes to 2 Maccabees 1:14-17 willfully acknowledges "A different account of Antiochus IV is given in 2 Mc [sic] 9, 1-20, and *another variant account* in 1 Mc [sic] 6, 1-16. The writer of this letter had probably heard a *distorted rumor* of the king's death"[572] (emphasis added).

Like Tobit and Judith, the Table of Contents in the NAB list them both as *Historical* Books.[573] This may be why "The Books of Maccabees [had] been accepted by the Catholic Church as inspired, on the basis of apostolic *tradition*"[574] (emphasis added). The NCV confesses 1 Maccabees was "chose rather to be directed by *tradition*...than by that of the scribes and Pharisees"[575] (emphasis added). This explains why the apostle Paul did not accept it, since he was a Pharisee (Acts 23:6; 26:5; Philippians 3:5).

First Maccabees records Antiochus Epiphanes IV died "in Persia" (1 Maccabees 6:5,16 NAB), where "he took to *his bed*" (v.8 NAB) "*dying in bitter grief* in a foreign land" (v.13 NAB, emphasis added) "in the year one-hundred forty-nine" (v.16 NAB). Before his death, the Israelites had "pulled down the Abomination which he had built upon the altar in Jerusalem" (vv.6-7 NAB).

Second Maccabees likewise records Antiochus Epiphanes IV died after he "arrived in Persia" (2 Maccabees 1:13-16 NAB). However, it states he *died at the hands of* "the priests of the Nanaeon" when "they opened a hidden trapdoor in the ceiling, hurled stones at the leader and his companions and struck them down. They dismembered the bodies, cut off their heads and tossed them to the people outside" (vv.15-16 NAB, emphasis added). Later, 2 Maccabees 9:1 recorded "Antiochus retreated in disgrace *from the region of Persia*" (emphasis added), who wrote a letter "On returning *from the regions of Persia*, I fell victim to a *troublesome*

---

[570] Ibid. New American Bible, Introduction to *The Second Book of Maccabees*, p.546.

[571] Ibid. See also the New Catholic Version, Introduction to The Second Book of Machabees [sic], p.1061.

[572] Ibid. New American Bible, footnote to 1 Maccabees 1:14-17, p.547.

[573] Ibid, *Contents*, p. [7].

[574] Ibid. Introduction to *The First Book of Maccabees*, p.513. Brackets inserted by me for clarity.

[575] Ibid. New Catholic Version, Introduction to the *First Book of Machabees* [sic], p.1026.

illness" (v.21 NAB, emphasis added), and then "*died a miserable death* in the mountains of a foreign land" (v.28).

Not only does 1 Maccabees and 2 Maccabees record *different locations* where Antiochus died ("in Persia" versus "returning from Persia"), they also record *different methods* of his death ("dying in his bed in bitter grief" versus "dismemberment and beheading" versus "falling victim to a troublesome illness"). These are clear contradictions between, and within, these two books.

First Maccabees also records three years before the death of Antiochus Epiphanes, "On the fifteenth day of the month of Chislev, *in the year one hundred and forty-five*, the king erected the horrible abomination upon the altar of holocausts, and in the surrounding cities of Judah they built pagan altars" (1 Maccabees 1:54 NAB, emphasis added). However, in 1 Maccabees 4:52-54 the author writes, "Early in the morning on the twenty-fifth day of the ninth month, that is, the month of Chislev, *in the year one hundred and forty-eight*, they arose and offered sacrifice according to the law on the new altar of holocausts that they had made. On the anniversary of the day on which the Gentiles defiled it, on that very day it was reconstructed with songs, harps, flutes, and cymbals" (emphasis added). Between the year one-hundred and forty-five and the year one-hundred and forty-eight is *three years*.

In contrast, 2 Maccabees 10:1-5 records after the Israelites "recovered the temple and the city" and "destroyed the altars erected by the Gentiles...they offered sacrifice for the first time in *two years*" (NAB, emphasis added), "On the anniversary of the day on which the temple had been profaned by the Gentiles, that is the twenty-fifth of the same month of Chislev" (NAB).

First Maccabees records the time difference between the "abomination upon the altar of holocausts" and the "offering of sacrifice on the new altar of holocausts" as being *three years*, while 2 Maccabees records the difference as being *two years*. This is a clear contradiction between these two books. Antiochus appears to die at least *twice*, even though Inspired Scripture records "it is appointed for men to die *once* and after this comes judgment" (Hebrews 9:27, emphasis added).

There are people in Inspired Scripture who did die more than once, such as Zarephath's son (1 Kings 17:17-23), the Shunamite's son (2 Kings 4:18-37), and Lazarus (John 11:43-44). However, this was because they had died and were miraculously risen from the dead. Hebrews 9:27 explains what *normally* happens when one dies. Neither 1 Maccabees nor 2 Maccabees state anything about Antiochus Epiphanes rising from the dead and then dying again. By 1 Maccabees and 2 Maccabees recording the death of Antiochus Epiphanes "twice," not only do they contradict each other, they also contradict the writer of Hebrews.

~~~~~~~~~~~

"And making a gathering, he sent twelve thousand drachms of silver to Jerusalem for sacrifice to be offered for the sins of the dead." (2 Maccabees 12:43 NCV)

"But Peter said, 'I do not possess silver and gold, but what I do have I give to you: In the name of Jesus Christ the Nazarene—walk!' And seizing him by the right hand, he raised him up; and immediately his feet and his ankles were strengthened." (Acts 3:7)

"Now when Simon saw that the Spirit was bestowed through the laying on of the apostles' hands, he offered them money, saying, 'Give this authority to me as well, so that everyone on whom I lay my hands may receive the Holy Spirit.' But Peter said to him, 'May your silver perish with you, because you thought you could obtain the gift of God with money! You have no part or portion in this matter, for your heart is not right before God.'" (Acts 8:18-21)

~~~~~~~~~~~

"And because he considered that they who had fallen asleep with godliness, had great grace laid up for them. It is a therefore a holy and wholesome thought to pray for the dead, that they may be loosed from sins." (2 Maccabees 12:45-46 NCV)

"As for the person who turns to mediums and to spiritists, to play the harlot after them, I will also set My face against that person and will cut him off from among his people." (Leviticus 20:6)

"There shall not be found among you anyone...who casts a spell, or a medium, or a spiritist, or one who calls up the dead." (Deuteronomy 18:10a,11)

"And Jesus said to him, 'Blessed are you, Simon Barjona, because flesh and blood did not reveal this to you, but My Father who is in heaven.... Whatever you bind on earth shall have been bound in heaven, and whatever you loose on earth shall have been loosed in heaven.'" (Matthew 16:17,19, cf. 18:18)

~~~~~~~~~~~

"Then in the same way another man appeared, distinguished by his white hair and dignity, and with an air about him of extraordinary, majestic authority. Onias then said of him, 'This is God's prophet Jeremiah, who

255

loves his brethren and fervently prays for his people and their holy city.'"
(2 Maccabees 15:13-14 NAB)

"Then Saul said to his servants, 'Seek for me a woman who is a medium, that I may go to her and inquire of her.' And his servants said to him, 'Behold, there is a woman who is a medium at En-dor.' Then the woman said, 'Whom shall I bring up for you?' And he said, 'Bring up Samuel for me.' He said to her, 'What is his form?' And she said, 'An old man is coming up, and he is wrapped with a robe.' And Saul knew that it was Samuel.... Then Samuel said to Saul, 'Why have you disturbed me by bringing me up?'" (1 Samuel 28:7,11,14a,15a)

~~~~~~~~~~~

"There had not been such a great distress in Israel since the time prophets ceased to appear among the people." (1 Maccabees 9:27 NAB) / "And there was a great tribulation in Israel, such as was not since the day, that there was no prophet seen in Israel." (1 Maccabees 9:27 NCV)

"Do not think that I came to abolish the Law or the Prophets; I did not come to abolish but to fulfill." (Matthew 5:17)

Pharisees, like the apostle Paul, would have understood this Old Testament metonym "the Law and the Prophets" to be limited to the boundaries of the canon of the Hebrew Bible (Romans 3:21, see also Chapter One). The author of 1 Maccabees confesses there was "no prophet seen in Israel" (NCV) / "since the time prophets ceased to appear among the people" (NAB). From these two Catholic versions it was not merely a matter that there *were* prophets in Israel during this time who simply chose not to appear. Rather, they had "*ceased* to appear," since there was no prophet "seen *in*" Israel, because there were "none *in*" Israel during the time of the Maccabees.

As the grandson of the author of Sirach in the Foreword of that book willfully admits, as well as the footnote to the Foreword in the NAB (see section above on the book of Sirach), this metonym ("the Law and the Prophets") refers to the books contained in the boundaries of the Hebrew Bible (cf. Matthew 23:35; Luke 11:49-51; 24:27,44-45). Even 2 Maccabees 15:9 refers to it as "the law and the prophets" (NAB).

Second Maccabees ends with an "Author's Apology" in its Epilogue. The author suggests the real possibility "my own story" may have been "poorly done and mediocre" (2 Maccabees 15:37-39 NAB), despite allegedly being "Scripture [which] is inspired by God" (2 Timothy 3:16)! It is no wonder Jerome declared the church in his time did not consider the books of Maccabees part of the canonical Scriptures (see Chapter Three).

BARUCH AND THE EPISTLE OF JEREMIAH

The Deuterocanonical book of Baruch correctly identifies Nebuchadnezzar as being the King of Babylon (Baruch 6:1 NAB). While it agrees with the Hebrew Bible (Daniel 1:1), it contradicts the Deuterocanonical book of Judith (Judith 1:7). However, the book of Baruch also includes errors and contradictions with the Hebrew Bible.

~~~~~~~~~~

"Now these are the words of the scroll which Baruch, son of Neriah...wrote in Babylon." (Baruch 1:1 NAB)

"with Jeremiah the prophet and Baruch the son of Neriah— and they entered the land of Egypt" (Jeremiah 43:6-7)

Although Baruch, along with Jeremiah, were among the four-thousand six-hundred Jews who Nebuchadnezzar had "carried into exile" from Judah to Babylon (Jeremiah 52:28-30, cf. 32:15), Baruch *never* wrote any Inspired Scripture *in* Babylon. Rather, they were carried away into the land of Egypt (Jeremiah 43:6-7). Baruch wrote while he and Jeremiah were still in Judah, when Jehoiakim was king prior to the Babylonian exile (Jeremiah 45:1-4; 2 Kings 23:36). The Deuterocanonical book of Baruch is in error claiming Baruch "*wrote* in Babylon."

~~~~~~~~~~

"[Baruch] wrote in Babylon, in the fifth year [on the seventh day of the month, at the time when the Chaldeans took Jerusalem and burnt it with fire]." (Baruch 1:1b-2 NAB)

"Then they captured the king and brought him to the king of Babylon at Riblah, and he passed sentence on him.... Now on the seventh day of the fifth month, which was the nineteenth year of King Nebuchadnezzar, king of Babylon, Nebuzaradan the captain of the guard, a servant of the king of Babylon, came to Jerusalem. He burned the house of the LORD, the king's house, and all the houses of Jerusalem; even every great house he burned with fire." (2 Kings 25:6,8-9)

"Now on the tenth day of the fifth month, which was the nineteenth year of King Nebuchadnezzar, king of Babylon, Nebuzaradan the captain of the bodyguard, who was in the service of the king of Babylon, came to Jerusalem. He burned the house of the LORD, the king's house and all the houses of Jerusalem; even every large house he burned with fire." (Jeremiah 52:12-13)

The Deuterocanonical book of Baruch claims it was written in the *fifth* year of the reign of King Nebuchadnezzar, when the Chaldeans took control of Jerusalem and burned it, even though both 2 Kings and the book of Jeremiah state this event occurred in the *nineteenth year* of his reign. Even the footnotes of the NAB declare: "Jerusalem fell on the seventh day of the fifth month; cf 2 Kgs 25, 8; Jer 52, 12"[576] (emphasis added), not the *fifth* year. The footnote in the NAB goes on to claim, "Either the text was originally 'the fifth month,' or it refers to the observance of an anniversary of the fall of Jerusalem in 587 B.C."[577]

The problem with the "anniversary observance" assumption is Baruch claims to be *writing in the fifth year* of King Nebuchadnezzar's reign (Baruch 1:1-2 NAB), which would be fourteen years before the actual event recorded in the Inspired books of 2 Kings and Jeremiah. The footnote acknowledges this translation "might" be in error by saying "fifth *year*" ("the text read originally "the fifth *month*" – emphasis added). The NCV also writes "fifth *year*" (Baruch 1:2 NCV), as does the Douay-Rheims,[578] the Vulgate,[579] and the Septuagint.[580] In contrast, every major Protestant translation of the book of 2 Kings states the event occurred in the "fifth *month*, which was the nineteenth *year*,"[581] as does every major Protestant translation of the book of Jeremiah.[582]

Although 2 Kings 25:8 records these events occurred on the "*seventh* day of the fifth month," while Jeremiah 52:12 records they occurred on the "*tenth* day of the fifth month" (emphasis added), these dates are easily reconciled, which MacArthur clarifies:

> "The parallel phrase in 2 Kin. 25:8 reads 'seventh day.' Nebuzaradan (v.12), 'captain of the guard,' started from Riblah on the seventh day and arrived in Jerusalem on the tenth day."[583]

There is no contradiction between the Inspired books of 2 Kings and Jeremiah. However, no reconciliation is possible between them and the

---

576 Ibid. New American Bible, footnote to Baruch 1:2, p.964. Italics added by me for emphasis.

577 Ibid.

578 Ibid. DRBO.ORG. *Prophecy Of Baruch Chapter 1.* Accessed from the Internet http://drbo.org/chapter/30001.htm

579 LatinVulgate.com. *THE PROPHECY OF BARUCH: Chapter 1.* Accessed from the Internet http://www.latinvulgate.com/lv/verse.aspx?t=0&b=30

580 BibleStudyTools.com. Septuagint Bible w/ Apocrypha LXX. *Baruch 1 LXX.* Accessed from the Internet https://www.biblestudytools.com/lxx/baruch/1.html

581 BlueLetterBible.org. Accessed from the Internet: Blue Letter Bible. "Book of 2 Kings 25 - (NASB - New American Standard Bible)." Blue Letter Bible. 1996-2018. 12 Apr 2018. http://www.blbclassic.org/Bible.cfm?b=2Ki&c=25&t=NASB

582 BlueLetterBible.org. Accessed from the Internet: Blue Letter Bible. "The Major Prophet Jeremiah 52 - (NASB - New American Standard Bible)." Blue Letter Bible. 1996-2018. 12 Apr 2018. http://www.blbclassic.org/Bible.cfm?b=Jer&c=52&t=NASB

583 Ibid. The MacArthur Study Bible, footnote to Jeremiah 52:12, p.1137.

Deuterocanonical book of Baruch, which is in clear contradiction with them.

~~~~~~~~~~

"When you reach Babylon you will be there many years, a period of seven generations long" (the epistle of Jeremiah, i.e.: Baruch 6:2 NAB)

"For thus says the LORD, 'When seventy years have been completed for Babylon, I will visit you and fulfill My good word to you, to bring you back to this place.'" (Jeremiah 29:10)

While the NAB footnote acknowledges the error of the writer of Baruch 6:2: "He has multiplied the *seventy years* of Jer, 10 by three of four,"[584] the footnote in the NCV defends Baruch 6:2 is being literal: "*Seven generations. That is seventy years.*"[585] So, how long is a Biblical "generation"?

The specific Hebrew word for "generation" used in both the book of Jeremiah and Lamentations ("*dowr*") simply means "those living during a period of time."[586] Out of the one-hundred and sixty-four times it is used in the Hebrew Bible, it is never used even once to describe a ten-year period of time, which is how Baruch 6:2 uses it ("*Seven generations. That is seventy years.*")

In the New Testament, the Greek translation of *"dowr"* (*"genea"*) is defined as "the successive members of a genealogy; an age (i.e. the time ordinarily occupied by each successive generation), a space of 30 - 33 years."[587] Dictionary.com also gives a similar definition for "generation" as: "the term of years, roughly 30 among human beings, accepted as the average period between the birth of parents and the birth of their offspring."[588]

The gospel of Matthew describes the "generations" (*"genea"*) of Jesus "from Abraham to David are fourteen generations; from David to the deportation to Babylon, fourteen generations; and from the deportation

---

584 Ibid. New American Bible, footnote to Baruch 6:2, p.970. Italics in original text.

585 Ibid. New Catholic Version, footnote to Baruch 6:2, p.889. Italics in original text.

586 BlueLetterBible.org. Accessed from the Internet: Blue Letter Bible. "Dictionary and Word Search for dowr (Strong's 1755)". Blue Letter Bible. 1996-2018. 12 Apr 2018. < http://www.blbclassic.org/lang/lexicon/Lexicon.cfm?strongs=H1755&amp;t=NASB&page=5 >

587 BlueLetterBible.org. Accessed from the Internet Blue Letter Bible. "Dictionary and Word Search for *genea (Strong's 1074)*". Blue Letter Bible. 1996-2018. 12 Apr 2018. < http://www.blbclassic.org/lang/lexicon/lexicon.cfm?strongs=G1074&t=NASB&page=1 >

588 Dictionary.com. *Generation.* Accessed from the Internet http://www.dictionary.com/browse/generation?s=t

to Babylon to the Messiah, fourteen generations" (Matthew 1:17). Clearly, a Biblical generation is far more than ten years, since Matthew includes the "generation" in Babylon, which was seventy years (cf. 2 Chronicles 36:21; Jeremiah 25:11-12; 29:10; Daniel 9:2). Therefore, the epistle of Jeremiah (i.e.: Baruch chapter six) is also in error here.

Interestingly, in Jimmy Akin's "list" although the book of Baruch is included as being alluded to in the New Testament, the epistle of Jeremiah is not.[589] The relevance is his argument for including the Deuterocanon (which would include the epistle of Jeremiah) is their allusions in the New Testament. This argument, however, would exclude the epistle of Jeremiah, since it was a *separate writing* from the book of Baruch (see Chapter Two) and not in his "list."

Despite some early church fathers "attaching" the Deuterocanonical book of Baruch and the epistle of Jeremiah to the Inspired *book* of Jeremiah, the errors and contradictions between them and the Hebrew Bible and the New Testament disqualify them as being Inspired Scripture. The late dating of Baruch and the epistle of Jeremiah, which were written during the Intertestamental Period (see Chapter Four), also eliminates any possibility of them being authored by Jeremiah's scribe, Baruch (Jeremiah 36:26), who had been dead for centuries.

THE ADDITIONS TO ESTHER AND DANIEL

Before I conclude the second Appendix of this book, I must address the passages which were "added" later to the original Inspired Old Testament books of Esther and Daniel. Although Catholic apologists, like Jimmy Akin, prefer to describe these sections as the "*parts* of Esther and Daniel,"[590] the dating between the texts found in the Hebrew Bible versus these later "additions" are far too long of a period of time for them to have been part of the originals. Like the other Deuterocanonical books, the "additions" to Esther and Daniel were written during the Intertestamental Period between the completion of the Hebrew Bible (around 400 B.C.) and the New Testament era.

The author of the book of Daniel from the Hebrew Bible is clearly Daniel, since he identifies himself frequently as the author with the salutation: "I, Daniel" (Daniel 8:15,27; 9:2; 10:7; 12:5). The book of Daniel was written sometime during his lifetime "before ca. 530 B.C."[591] However, the Deuterocanonical "additions" to the book of Daniel were written "later

---

[589] Ibid. JimmyAkin.com. *Deuterocanonical References in the New Testament.*

[590] Ibid. Akin, Jimmy. *How did the Old Testament canon develop?* "Catholic Answers." YouTube.com. (Begins around the 1:52 mark.)

[591] Ibid. The MacArthur Study Bible, *The Book of Daniel, Author and Date,* p.1225.

than 164 B.C."[592] More specifically: "The Story of Susanna" (early first century B.C.)[593]; "The Song of the Three Children" (164 B.C.)[594]; and "The Story of Bel and the Dragon" (100 B.C.)[595] were written centuries after Daniel died, who wrote the book bearing his name.

McDonald observed, "The practice of writing under an assumed name was common during the intertestamental period, when writers frequently made use of well-known names from the OT [Old Testament] (Solomon, Enoch, Moses, etc.)."[596] McDonald referenced D.E. Aune ("*Prophecy in Early Christianity*") that one of the motivations during this time "for the practice of writing pseudonymously: 1) it arose at a time when *the biblical canon was already closed* and well-known names were used to secure acceptance"[597] (emphasis added).

The apostle Paul was aware of this ancient form of literary "identity theft." To assure his readers, he authenticated his own Inspired epistles by writing "in my own hand" (1 Corinthians 16:21; Galatians 6:11; Colossians 4:18; 2 Thessalonians 3:17; Philemon v.19). Later false gospels, like *The Gospel of Thomas*, were written during the church age attempting to attribute apostolic authorship in order to gain acceptance. The later Greek "additions" to Esther and Daniel (as well as the book of Baruch and the epistle of Jeremiah) used these four "well-known names" from the Old Testament to gain acceptance as being part of these earlier Hebrew and Aramaic original Inspired writings.

These much later writings were clearly "additions" to Daniel and not part of the original Inspired text. Even the Introduction to the book of Daniel in the NAB refers to them as "The *added* episodes of Susanna, Bel, and the Dragon"[598] (emphasis added) and refers to them collectively as the "Appendix."[599] MacArthur explains how the much earlier dating of the book of Esther makes it impossible for the much later Deuterocanonical "additions" to have been originally a part of it:

> "The account in Esther ends in 473 B.C. before Ahasuerus died by assassination (ca. 465 B.C.). Esther 10:2 speaks as though Ahasuerus' reign has been completed, so the earliest possible

---

[592] Ibid. Goodspeed, & Hadas. *The Apocrypha: an American translation*, p. xxi.

[593] Ibid, p.347.

[594] Ibid, p.355.

[595] Ibid, p.365.

[596] Ibid. McDonald. *The Biblical Canon*, p.344. Brackets inserted by me for clarity.

[597] Ibid. McDonald, p.345. McDonald references Anne, D. E. *Prophecy in Early Christianity*. Grand Rapids: Eerdmans, 1983, p.109.

[598] Ibid. New American Bible, Introduction to *The Book of Daniel*, p.1021.

[599] Ibid, p.1039.

261

writing date would be after his reign around mid-fifth century B.C."[600]

Even the NCV grants, "Some of the sources probably go back to Persia, perhaps Mardochai [sic] as may be gathered from chap. 9 ver. 20,"[601] which states, "Then Mordecai recorded these events" (Esther 9:20).

The dating for the "additions" to Esther, however, is much later around the first century B.C.,[602] or possibly as early as 114 B.C.[603] Like the "additions" to Daniel and the rest of the Deuterocanonical books, the "additions" to Esther were written centuries later towards the end of the Intertestamental Period – far too late to be part of the original Inspired text of Esther. This may explain why the Introduction to the book of Esther in the NAB describes the *entire* book as "a free composition – *not a historical document*"[604] (emphasis added) – even though its Table of Contents list Esther with the *Historical* Books, along with Tobit, Judith, 1 Maccabees, and 2 Maccabees.[605]

"GODDING UP" ESTHER

One of the most obvious – and oddest – parts of the "additions" to Esther are the chapter "insertions." The NCV appears to follow the Douay-Rheims in regards to chapter order, beginning with the first chapter found in the Hebrew Bible.[606] Then, it follows the order of the Hebrew Bible up through Esther 10:3.[607] The "additions" begin after Esther 10:3 and continue through chapter sixteen in both the NCV and the Douay-Rheims.[608]

In contrast, the "additions" in the NAB are more blatant and neither follow the NCV nor the Douay-Rheims. In-between its chapter *numbers*, which are from the Hebrew Bible, the NAB "inserts" chapter *letters* from "A to F."[609]

The NAB "moves" verses thirteen through seventeen from chapter eight of the Hebrew Bible to a spot in-between "chapter E" and chapter

---

[600] Ibid. The MacArthur Study Bible, *The Book of Esther, Author and Date*, p.681.

[601] Ibid. New Catholic Version, Introduction to *The Book of Esther*, p.538.

[602] Ibid. Goodspeed, & Hadas. *The Apocrypha: an American translation*, p. xxi.

[603] Ibid, p.165.

[604] Ibid. New American Bible, Introduction to *The Book of Esther*, p.500.

[605] Ibid. *Contents*, p. [7].

[606] Ibid. DRBO.ORG. *Book Of Esther Chapter 1*. Accessed from the Internet http://drbo.org/chapter/19001.htm

[607] Ibid. *Book Of Esther Chapter 10*. Accessed from the Internet http://drbo.org/chapter/19010.htm

[608] Ibid.

[609] Ibid. New American Bible, pp.501-512.

nine,[610] which makes comparing Bible translations – even between other Catholic versions – very difficult to do! Like the "additions" to Daniel, the NAB also declares they were "additions" and not part of the original text of Esther: "the portions preceded by the letters A through F indicate the underlying Greek *additions* referred to above"[611] (emphasis added).

Within these "additions" of these "chapter letters" of Esther "contain 107 additional verses, inserted at appropriate places within the Hebrew form of the text"[612] (emphasis added). Unlike the book of Esther from the Hebrew Bible which does not mention God even <u>once</u> within its ten Inspired chapters, the "additions" to Esther explicitly mention Him – either as "God," "Lord," "King," "Maker," "Ruler," or "Savior" – at least *forty-two times within these one-hundred seven verses!*

Apparently, the writers of the "additions" to Esther felt the need to mention God so frequently to "make-up" for His omission in the actual book of Esther. Because all Scripture is God-breathed (2 Timothy 3:16), which includes Esther, it was not necessary for Esther to mention God specifically. It is obvious the God of Esther is the same as the God of the rest of the Old Testament, despite the book of Esther not mentioning Him by name or by title. The "additions" to Esther contain contradictions with the Hebrew Bible – *including with the book of Esther…and even within the "additions" to Esther itself!*

~~~~~~~~~~

"Mordecai lodged at the court with Bagathan and Thares, two eunuchs of the king who were court guards. He overheard them plotting, investigated their plans, and discovered that they were preparing to lay hands on King Ahasuerus. So he informed the king about them." ("additions" to Esther A:12-13 NAB)

"while Mordecai was sitting at the king's gate, Bigthan and Teresh, two of the king's officials from those who guarded the door, became angry and sought to lay hands on King Ahasuerus. But the plot became known to Mordecai and he told Queen Esther, and Esther informed the king in Mordecai's name." (Esther 2:21-22)

~~~~~~~~~~

"The king also appointed Mordecai to serve at the court, and rewarded him for his actions." ("additions" to Esther A:16 NAB)

---

610 Ibid, p.510.
611 Ibid, Introduction to *The Book of Esther*, p.501.
612 Ibid.

"It was found written what Mordecai had reported concerning Bigthana and Teresh, two of the king's eunuchs who were doorkeepers, that they had sought to lay hands on King Ahasuerus. The king said, 'What honor or dignity has been bestowed on Mordecai for this?' Then the king's servants who attended him said, 'Nothing has been done for him.'" (Esther 6:2-3)

Unlike the "additions" to Esther which states Mordecai was rewarded *immediately*, the book of Esther reveals his reward was *delayed* (Esther 6:4-11).

~~~~~~~~~~

"Haman, however, son of Hamedatha the Agagite, who was in high honor with the king, sought to harm Mordecai and his people because of the two eunuchs of the king." ("additions" to Esther A:17 NAB)

"When Haman saw that Mordecai neither bowed down nor paid homage to him, Haman was filled with rage. But he disdained to lay hands on Mordecai alone, for they had told him who the people of Mordecai were; therefore Haman sought to destroy all the Jews, the people of Mordecai, who were throughout the whole kingdom of Ahasuerus." (Esther 3:5-6)

~~~~~~~~~~

"we hereby decree that all those who are indicated to you in the letters of Haman...shall, together with their wives and children, be utterly destroyed by the swords of their enemies...on the fourteenth day of the twelfth month, Adar, of the current year." ("additions" to Esther B:6 NAB)

"Letters were sent by couriers to all the king's provinces to destroy, to kill and to annihilate all the Jews, both young and old, women and children, in one day, the thirteenth day of the twelfth month, which is the month Adar, and to seize their possessions as plunder." (Esther 3:13)

~~~~~~~~~~

"For instance, Haman, son of Hamedatha, a Macedonian" ("additions" to Esther E:10 NAB)

"But Haman the son of Amadathi the Bugite" ("additions" to Esther 12:6 NCV)

"Haman, however, a son of Hamedatha the Agagite" ("additions" to Esther A:17 NAB)

"After these events King Ahasuerus promoted Haman, the son of Hammedatha the Agagite." (Esther 3:1, cf. 3:10; 8:3,5; 9:24)

Not only do the "additions" to Esther contradict the book of Esther, which only states Haman was an Agagite, it also contradicts *itself* (a Macedonian versus a Bugite versus an Agagite). "Chapter A:17" of the NAB parallels the "additions" to Esther 12:6 in the NCV, even though the former identifies Haman as an "Agagite," while the latter identifies him as a "Bugite." The NCV follows the Douay-Rheims which also identifies him as a "Bugite,"[613] and contradicts both the NAB as well as with every major Protestant translation of Esther.[614]

These blatant errors and contradictions in the "additions" to Esther explain why the Introduction to the book of Esther in the NAB led to commenting on these "insertions" to Esther: "the difficulties of the book is to be found in its literary presentation rather than in a forced attempt to square detailed data of the narrative with facts.... The Greek text with the abovementioned additions is probably a later literary paraphrase in which the author seeks to have the reader share his sentiments."[615]

~~~~~~~~~~

"For this purpose he arranged two lots: one for the people of God, the second for all the other nations." ("additions" to Esther F:7 NAB)

"Haman sought to destroy all the Jews, the people of Mordecai, who were throughout the whole kingdom of Ahasuerus. In the first month, which is the month Nisan, in the twelfth year of King Ahasuerus, Pur, that is the lot, was cast before Haman from day to day and from month to month, until the twelfth month, that is the month Adar." (Esther 3:6b-7, cf. 9:24-26)

Just as Jimmy Akin's "list" does not contain the epistle of Jeremiah as being cited in the New Testament, as evidence of it being Inspired Scripture, his "list" also does not include the "additions" to Esther either.[616]

DANIEL AND THE LIONS' DEN...ONCE OR TWICE?

One of the most familiar stories found in the book of Daniel is when Daniel was thrown into the lions' den for violating the decree of King Darius of the Medo-Persian Empire and surviving it (Daniel 6:7-23).

---

[613] Ibid. DRBO.ORG. *Book Of Esther Chapter 12*. Accessed from the Internet http://drbo.org/chapter/19012.htm

[614] BlueLetterBible.org. Accessed from the Internet Blue Letter Bible. "The Story of Esther 3 - (NASB - New American Standard Bible)." Blue Letter Bible. 1996-2018. 12 Apr 2018. http://www.blbclassic.org/Bible.cfm?b=Est&c=3&t=NASB

[615] Ibid. New American Bible, Introduction to *The Book of Esther*, pp.500-501.

[616] Ibid. JimmyAkin.com. *Deuterocanonical References in the New Testament*.

However, in the "additions" to the book of Daniel, which the NAB labels as "the Appendix,"[617] Daniel experiences the lions' den a *second* time:

"When he saw himself threatened with violence, the king was forced to hand Daniel over to them. They threw Daniel into a lions' den, where he remained six days." ("additions" to Daniel 14:30-31 NAB)

The "additions" to Daniel identify this king as "Cyrus the Persian" (14:1 NAB), where "Daniel was the king's favorite and was held in higher esteem than any of the friends of the king" (v.2 NAB). This is how Cyrus is described in the book of Daniel (Daniel 10:1). However, this same "Cyrus" is likely King "Darius the Mede" (Daniel 5:31), which MacArthur explains:

"Possibly Darius is not a name, but an honorary title for Cyrus, who with his army entered Babylon Oct. 29, 539 B.C. It is used in inscriptions for at least 5 Persian rulers. History mentions no specific man named Darius the Mede. In 6:28 it is possible to translate, 'Darius even...Cyrus.'"[618]

The footnotes to the NAB suggest: "The Median kingdom had already been conquered by Cyrus the Persian, and it was Cyrus who captured Babylon."[619] The book of Daniel explicitly states: "That same night Belshazzar the Chaldean king was slain. So, Darius the Mede received the kingdom at about the age of sixty-two" (Daniel 5:30-31) indicating Darius and Cyrus were the same person.

The book of Daniel records "this Daniel enjoyed success in the reign of Darius and in the reign of Cyrus the Persian" (Daniel 6:28). Daniel also records "In the first year of Darius the Mede, I arose to be an encouragement and a protection for him" (Daniel 11:1), similar to the way Daniel is described in his relationship to "Cyrus the Persian" in the "additions" to Daniel.

"King Darius/Cyrus" had already thrown Daniel once into the lions' den for violating his decree. Why would he throw him into the lions' dead a *second* time, considering no harm came to him the *first* time? Some Catholic commentaries have suggested this was the same event mentioned in chapter six of the book of Daniel.

The footnote to the "additions" to Daniel 14:31 in the 2011 Revised Edition of the New American Bible states: "this story provides a *different account from chapter six* as to why Daniel was associated with the lions'

---

617 Ibid, the "additions" to Daniel in the New American Bible begin at chapter thirteen with the title "III. Appendix," p.1039.

618 Ibid. The MacArthur Study Bible, footnote to Daniel 5:31, p.1236.

619 Ibid. New American Bible, footnote to Daniel 6:1, p.1030.

den" (NAB-2011, emphasis added).[620] However, the NCV correctly points out this was a separate event:

"Daniel was *twice cast into the den of lions, once* under Darius *because he had transgressed the king's edict*, by praying three times a day; and *another time* under Evilmerodach *by a sedition of the people*. This time he remained *six days* in the lions' den; the other only *one night*."[621] (emphasis added)

Which Catholic commentary authorized by the Confraternity of Christian Doctrine is correct? Was it the same event or a different one? Even if these were two different events, the same question could be asked: "What would be the point of throwing Daniel in the lions' den *again*, knowing God had protected him once before?" This suggests the latter six-night event never really happened, and Daniel only entered the lions' den *once*. It is no wonder why the 2011 Revised Edition of the New American Bible acknowledges the story of Susanna, the story of Bel and the Dragon, and this story from chapters thirteen and fourteen from the "additions" to Daniel were not part of the original text:

"The short stories in these two chapters exist now only in Greek and other translations.... They were *never part of the Hebrew-Aramaic Book of Daniel, or of the Hebrew Bible*."[622] (NAB-2011, emphasis added)

BEL AND THE DRAGON AND SUSANNA

Chapter fourteen of the "additions" to the book of Daniel begins with the story of Bel and the Dragon. Like the rest of the "additions," the 2011 Revised Edition of the New American Bible questions much of the historical authenticity of its contents:

"This story preserves the *fiction* of a successive Median and Persian rule of Babylon."[623] (NAB-2011, emphasis added)

"In chapter fourteen, readings in the Septuagint differ markedly from those in Theodotion, which is followed here...the translation is that of Collins, *Daniel, pp.405ff*, with brackets

---

[620] New American Bible, Revised Edition, 2011, St. Joseph Medium Size Edition, Confraternity of Christian Doctrine, Inc.: Washington, DC, Copyright 2010, 1991, 1986, 1970. All rights reserved, footnote to the "additions" to Daniel 14:21, p.1085.

[621] Ibid. New Catholic Version, footnote to the "additions" to Daniel 14:30, p.972.

[622] Ibid. New American Bible, Revised Edition, 2011, footnote to the "additions" to Daniel 13:1-14:42, p.1082.

[623] Ibid, footnote to the "additions" to Daniel 14:1-3a NAB-2011, p.1084.

indicating additions to the Septuagint according to Collins."[624] (NAB-2011)

"*Dragon*: or 'serpent.' Sacred snakes are well attested in the ancient world...though evidence for their veneration in Babylon is doubtful."[625] (NAB-2011)

These self-incriminating "fictional" historical events and contradictions with the original Hebrew text of Daniel are not merely limited to the story of Bel and the Dragon, but also Susanna from the "additions" to Daniel, as well as other Deuterocanonical books, like the "additions" to Esther:

"Its *fictional* character [Esther]..."[626] (NAB-2011, emphasis added)

"It [the book of Esther and the "additions" to Esther] has come down to us in two versions: an older Hebrew version, and *a Greek version* based on a text similar to Hebrew, but *with additions and alterations* as described below."[627] (NAB-2011, emphasis added)

"...there are only a *few contradictions* between these Greek additions and the older Hebrew text"[628] (NAB-2011, emphasis added)

"The Greek version of the book dates back from ca. 116-48."[629] (NAB-2011)

The second to third century early church father, Julius Africanus, in "A letter that he wrote to Origen is extant in which he suggests that the story of Susanna in the book Daniel is spurious."[630] Africanus also went on to comment regarding the story of Susanna from the "additions" to Daniel: "it is elegantly written, is plainly a more modern forgery."[631] The NCV concedes even Jerome centuries later "detached it from hence; because he

---

[624] Ibid, footnote to the "additions" to Daniel 14:1-22 NAB-2011, p.1084. Italics in original text. See Chapter Two regarding more on Theodotian and the Septuagint.

[625] Ibid, footnote to the "additions" to Daniel 14:23 NAB-2011, p.1085. Italics in original text.

[626] Ibid, Introduction to the "additions" to Esther NAB-2011, p.527. Brackets added by me for clarity.

[627] Ibid. Brackets added by me for clarity.

[628] Ibid.

[629] Ibid, p.528.

[630] Ibid. Maier. *Eusebius: The Church History*, Book 6:31, p.209.

[631] Ibid. CARM.org. Accessed from the Internet https://carm.org/early-church-fathers-apocrypha. Taken from *Julius Africanus, A Letter to Origen from Africanus About the History of Susanna*.

did not find it in the Hebrew: which is also the case of the history of Bel and the Dragon."[632]

Fictional? Alterations? Contradictions? Modern forgery? Like the Deuterocanonical book of Judith, which the NCV described earlier was a "piece of edifying fiction," how can God-breathed Scripture be fiction? Even other characters from the "Poetic Books," as well as others from the Old Testament, were regarded as real people by both the Hebrew Bible and the New Testament, like Job, Daniel, and Noah (Ezekiel 14:14,20; James 5:11), including Lot's wife (Luke 17:32).

Unlike parables which are simply extended stories to teach an eternal truth, when people are mentioned *by name* in Inspired books, they are understood to be *real people* involved in *real historical events.* Jesus mentioned Lazarus and Abraham *by name*, who were in the "good" part of Hades (Luke 16:23-25). They were not "fictional" characters in the Old Testament era. They were *real people.* By saying the characters of Judith and Esther were "fictional" demonstrates the commentators of the NCV and NAB are professing they were not real historical people, even though both books are listed under the *Historical* Books in the Table of Contents of the NAB.[633]

The Deuterocanonical "additions" to Esther and Daniel are clearly fictional, due to their numerous theological and historical errors and contradictions with the Hebrew Bible and the New Testament. Therefore, they are not Inspired Scripture. However, the actual books of Esther and Daniel from the Hebrew Bible describe *real* people, who lived during *real* historical events. Hence, they are Inspired Scripture, due to their authenticity and lack of theological error with other Inspired Scripture, and therefore belong in the Old Testament.

THE PRAYER OF AZARIAH AND THE SONG OF THE THREE CHILDREN

Like the rest of the "additions" to Daniel, these twenty-seven verses were not originally in the book of Daniel in the Hebrew Bible. They were inscribed centuries later around 164 B.C.[634] during the Intertestamental Period when the rest of the Deuterocanonical books were written.

In the book of Daniel from the Hebrew Bible, Daniel and his friends had their names changed by "the commander of the officials [who] assigned

---

[632] Ibid. New Catholic Version, footnote to the "additions" to Daniel chapter thirteen, p.969.

[633] Ibid. New American Bible, *Contents*, p. [7].

[634] Ibid. Goodspeed, & Hadas. The Apocrypha: an American translation, p.355.

new names to them; and to Daniel he assigned the name Belteshazzar, to Hananiah Shadrach, to Mishael Meshach and to Azariah Abed-nego" (Daniel 1:7). Daniel's friends refused to serve King Nebuchadnezzar's gods and worship the golden image he set up (3:12-18). As a consequence, the king ordered them to be tied up and they "were cast into the midst of the furnace of blazing fire" (v.21).

The Aramaic word for "midst" used in the book of Daniel means "in the middle, or within." It means to touch or have direct contact with something. Daniel's three friends were literally in physical contact in "the midst of the furnace of blazing fire" (v.23). The Prayer of Azariah begins by saying "They walked about *in the flames*" ("additions" to Daniel 3:24 NAB, emphasis added). It goes on to say the angel of the Lord "drove the fiery flames *out of the furnace*, and made the inside of the furnace as though as dew-laden breeze were blowing through it. *The fire in no way touched them* or caused them pain or harm" (3:49-50 NAB, emphasis added). Yet, in the book of Daniel, King Nebuchadnezzar states "Was it not three men we cast bound *into the midst of the fire?*" (Daniel 3:24, emphasis added). He goes on to emphasize they were "walking about *in the midst of the fire*" (v.25, emphasis added). Even though the fire did not *harm* them, it clearly *touched* them.

When Daniel's three friends were singing, they also said "He has *freed us from the raging flame* and delivered us *from the fire*" ("additions" to Daniel 3:88 NAB, emphasis added). These "additions" to Daniel which states the fire did *not* touch them clearly contradicts the book of Daniel stating that it did.

While they were "in the midst of the fire," Azariah prayed to God "We have in our day no prince, *no prophet*...to find favor with you" ("additions to Daniel 3:38 NAB). However, Jesus referred to Daniel as "the prophet" (Matthew 24:15). These "additions" to Daniel conflict with Jesus and the New Testament as well.

Lastly, when they are first cast in the fire "singing to God and blessing the Lord" ("additions" to Daniel 3:24 NAB), the writer refers to Abed-nego by his Hebrew name "Azariah" (v.25 NAB). Although Daniel refers to Azariah by his Hebrew name in the first two chapters of his book (Daniel 1:6,7,11,19; 2:17), after this he *only* refers to him as "Abed-nego" (2:49; 3:12,13,14,16,19,20,22,23,26,28,29,30). Daniel *never* again refers to him as "Azariah" in the Hebrew Bible. Although the Song of the Three Children refer to him as "Azariah" ("additions" to Daniel 3:88), these "additions" were clearly written much later by someone other than the author of the Inspired book of Daniel.

270

Not only were these much later written "additions" to Esther and Daniel not part of the original texts, they are also not God-breathed, no more than the rest of the Deuterocanon. Therefore, they do not belong in the Christian Old Testament.

THE PRAYER OF MANASSEH

Although the *Prayer of Manasseh* is not included in modern day English Catholic Old Testaments, as mentioned in Chapters Two and Three it was originally in the Septuagint and the Vulgate. So, it is worth mentioning at the end of this Appendix. Not only was it included in these two early Catholic translations of the Old Testament, but it was also written during the same time period as the Deuterocanonical books in the "Intertestamental Period" around 100 B.C.[635] Because it was not part of the "Protocanon" ("first canon") of the Hebrew Bible, one could argue it too is part of the "Deuterocanon" ("second canon") based on the time period it was written.

The *Prayer of Manasseh* is also found in early Christian literature as early as the third century A.D. McDonald cites R. M. Grant (*"The Formation of the New Testament"*): "The Prayer of Manasseh is found in the Syriac *Didascalia* (third century C.E.), in *Apostolic Constitution* 2.22.12-14 (second half of the fourth century C.E. in Syria), and in the Codex Alexandrinus (fifth century C.E.)."[636] Yet, it did not make it into any of the church councils of the fourth and fifth centuries, despite its inclusion in an early Catholic Bible from the same era.

What this demonstrates is the early church "removed" this uninspired book from its Old Testament for the same reason later Protestants "removed" the Deuterocanon: they were not part of the *original* Old Testament which predated the Septuagint and the Vulgate. They were written far too late after the conclusion of the Old Testament, which ended with the completion of the Hebrew Bible around 400 B.C.

...and it further explains why Protestant Bibles are smaller.

---

[635] Ibid, p.369.

[636] Ibid, McDonald. *The Biblical Canon*, p.198 citing Grant, R. M. *The Formation of the New Testament*, p.44. New York: Harper & Row, 1965.

Printed in Great Britain
by Amazon

78790763R10154